**196**

# 1960

When Art and Literature
Confronted the Memory
of World War II and
Remade the Modern

—

## AL FILREIS

Columbia University Press

*New York*

Columbia University Press
*Publishers Since 1893*
New York   Chichester, West Sussex
cup.columbia.edu
Copyright © 2021 Columbia University Press
All rights reserved

Library of Congress Cataloging-in-Publication Data

Names: Filreis, Alan, 1956– author.
Title: 1960 : when art and literature confronted the memory of
World War II and remade the modern / Al Filreis.
Description: New York : Columbia University Press, [2021] |
Includes bibliographical references and index.
Identifiers: LCCN 2021011166 (print) | LCCN 2021011167 (ebook) |
ISBN 9780231201841 (hardback) | ISBN 9780231201858 (trade paperback) |
ISBN 9780231554299 (ebook)
Subjects: LCSH: Literature and history—History—20th century. |
Avant-garde (Aesthetics)—History—20th century. | Nineteen sixty, A.D. |
War Word II 1939–1945—Influence. | Literature, Experimental—20th
century—History and criticism. | LCGFT: Literary criticism.
Classification: LCC PN50 .F55 2021 (print) | LCC PN50 (ebook) |
DDC 809/.93358—dc23
LC record available at https://lccn.loc.gov/2021011166
LC ebook record available at https://lccn.loc.gov/2021011167

Cover design: Lisa Hamm
Cover image: Jean Tinguely, *Homage to New York,*
installation, MoMA, 1960. AP Photo.

Everything forgets. But not a language.

—GEORGE STEINER, "THE HOLLOW MIRACLE,"
FEBRUARY 18, 1960

# Contents

# Preface

This is a book about how in the year 1960 artists turned back to the war of 1939–45 and, in a way that was new, to the horror and mass killings of that period. In one sense it is a study of deferred retrospection, of the complex and compelling reasons for that belatedness. It is also an inquiry into the start of the sixties, a reradicalization marking the end of the supposed end of ideology in the fifties. (And yes, I do think what we call "the sixties" began in the year 1960.) As such this work of interpretation continues the literary-historical analysis I set out in *Counter-Revolution of the Word: The Conservative Attack on Modern Poetry, 1945–1960*, except that here poetry, although a major focus, is only part of the story, especially in chapters 4 through 10. The avant-garde explored here is more generational than generic, and is broadly defined. Many of the artists encountered in these pages were a few years too young to have experienced the left-right arguments waged in the 1930s, too junior in the 1940s to feel responsible for the war's tragedies. They create their projects to turn away from deradicalization in many genres in addition to poetry: fiction, theater, film, memoir, sculpture (especially assemblage), teleplays, painting, sci-fi/fantasy, musical theater, and (in the end) jazz.

The book is meant through its organization—and at times nonhierarchical exposition—to emphasize the crossing and interrelation implied by such a generic range, and to feature a patient elaboration or refrain of themes across otherwise heterogeneous works dealing with trauma, exile, exophony, disaster, racist hatred, and testimony. To make my argument the materials, projects, and artists it features recur throughout chapters. James Baldwin appears and reappears, and then returns in the final section of chapter 10 on John Coltrane as supposedly an "angry young tenor." Baldwin, in the book's opening pages, faces the same assumption of anger that Coltrane encounters in the end, at the "beginning of beyond" heading into the 1960s. Appearances of Paul Celan, Hannah Arendt, Jerome Rothenberg, Frantz Fanon, Ingeborg Bachmann, Amiri Baraka, and others function similarly. Few of the chapters present discrete material; the analysis is typically additive, conjoined, and complementary. Chapter 5 is a relatively focused approach to the Zero group and affiliated artists—the closest this integrative narrative comes to a stand-alone survey—yet their counterintuitive ideas about postwar hope extend the lesson in absurdism to be learned from the Kafka resurgence as told in chapter 4, which in turn further elaborates the special connotation of triumph described in chapters 1 through 3, typified by this assertion of Jerome Rothenberg's (which becomes anthemic for the book): "In a nation that buries the past from its children, the pain of their song is a triumph."[1]

*1960: When Art and Literature Confronted the Memory of World War II and Remade the Modern* is a study of the future of memory as reckoned at a moment in time. What does it mean for an avant-garde (nominally a trailblazing group, ahead of its epoch) to be looking not ahead but—at least initially—backward to the past? In this context I refer variously to forms of modernism: modernist antifascism, the modernist poetics of witness, anti-anticommunist modernism, antimodernism, etc. Then, too, there was the renewed embrace of modernism as a counter to the brutal fascist equation of modernism and Jewishness that had supported Nazi efforts to eliminate both supposed degeneracies through one aggression—as *both together*, modernist and Jew, created "infernal, bolshevistic attempts to destroy the inner balance."[2] Such various senses of the modern and of complex postwar motives for reaffirming it—its nontransparency, nonnarrativity, metatextuality (qualities all deemed "degenerate" by the antimodernist extreme right during the nightmare years)—will be delineated in context throughout this telling. But insofar as an overall prefatory definition of these related plural modernisms can be helpful as a guide, it is especially because postwar detractors of modern art continued to attack all its connotations, and because the artists presented in this book looked back and embraced prewar experimental groups and movements in order indeed to defy fascist destructions but also to resist the deradicalizing efforts of those Cold War–era detractors. Thus modernism here is certainly a historical category the defining of which encouraged a positive retrospective on the part of radicals of 1960: the revolt against representational transparency that came to stand for the previous era and its artistic movements prior to fascism's suppressions. My book *Counter-Revolution of the Word* details the postwar deradicalization against which the artists in this new book respond. At times modernism for them is an art whose most heretical processes can be restored with a hopefulness best explained by its readiness to confront the war experience. The chapter on the Zero artists is again one of the places in this book where the case for counterintuitive (and doubly negative) hope is made explicitly. They "oppose[d] the anti-everything" in a manner that helps describe many otherwise quite different artists whose work is explored thenceforth in chapters 6 through 10—artists and works not typically associated with such an ultimately positive view, such as Primo Levi of *The Truce*, Roberto Rossellini returning in *It Was a Night in Rome* to the liminality of that beloved city under fascist occupation, Louis Zukofsky in a new installment of his epic poem *"A"* as he wanders past the site of the traumatic Triangle Shirtwaist Factory fire, Coltrane venturing an unironic reckoning of favorite things, Sari Dienes doing buoyant rubbings of sewer grates, Bob Kaufman writing Afro-Beat verse in jail after brutalization at the hands of the police, Rod Serling in otherwise depressing early *Twilight Zone* scripts, Jean Tinguely insisting that "Homage to New York" (a sculpture at MoMA created to be destroyed) symbolized the *opposite* of suicide.

I quickly discovered in the process of writing this book that the self-imposed compositional constraint of referring only (or almost entirely) to works of 1960 was exhilarating as a scholarly and writerly practice. Such a constraint makes breadth a practice yet depth ever more a requirement. I begin acknowledgments, then, by thanking my capable research assistants for their dauntless library sleuthing: Kristen Martin, Dawn Androphy, Jesse Schwartz, Emily Harnett, George Gordon, Kate Herzlin, Julie Levitan, Rumela Mitra, Andie Davidson, Ben Wiebracht, Amaris Cuchanski, Anna Zalokostas, and Sophia DuRose.

I am also grateful to Stuart Kaufer (for Russian translation from Rossellini and advice on Russian folk revival), Nili Gold (for working closely with me on Appelfeld's "Smoke"), Ariel Resnikoff and Rivka Weinstock (for their translation from the difficult Hebrew of "Smoke"), Selena Dyer (for her translation of Bachmann's "Das schreibende Ich"), Max McKenna (for his translation of Alain Bosquet's introduction), Michael Nardone (for his transcription of my public interview with Rothenberg), and generally to Pierre Joris for his extraordinary efforts over the years as critic, editor, and translator of Paul Celan.

Many people provided guidance, indulged me for interviews and extended conversation, responded to my frequent emails—too many to name all. I do want to acknowledge Jerome Rothenberg (several interviews, many emails); William J. Harris and Aldon Nielsen (on Baraka in Cuba); the late Jackson Mac Low; Daniel Dornhofer (of the Institut für England- & Amerikastudien at Geothe-Universität Frankfurt in Frankfurt am Main, on the dating of Bachmann's lecture); William C. Taubman (for his help sorting through Khrushchev's shoe-banging incident), Marjorie Perloff (informal discussions over the years on the European politics of modernism and the rise of fascism); Xaviera Flores (of the Chicano Studies Research Center, UCLA, for her help in my use of the Raphael Montañez Ortiz papers); Mattie Taormina and Tim Noakes at Stanford University's Special Collections (Robert Creeley papers); Barbara Pollitt and the Sari Dienes Foundation; Mattijs Visser (on Nul/Zero artist Henk Peeters); Steve Coy of the Mandeville Special Collections Library at the University of California, San Diego (Mac Low collection); Dan Meyer and Christine Colburn of the Regenstein Library at the University of Chicago (Mac Low–Henry Rago and Robert Duncan letters in the *Poetry* archive); Heather Cole and James Capobianco of the Houghton Library, Harvard University (Robert Lowell letters and manuscripts); Siegfried Reich and Peter Kramml of the research division of the Municipality of Salzburg, Austria; Clive Howard of Tate Images at Tate Modern Museum, London; Stephanie Tallering of Artists Rights Society; Bob Arnold, Anne Tardos, and Jeffrey Twitchell-Waas, executors, respectively, of Cid Corman's, Jackson Mac Low's, and Louis Zukofsky's literary estates; and Nick Okrent, always available even during a pandemic, of the reference department at Penn's library. I am grateful to David Wyatt, once my teacher and always a sane mentor, for modeling this project in his own work and for including an essay consisting of versions of passages from chapters 7 and 8 in a book he edited, *American Literature in Transition, 1960–1970* (Cambridge, 2018). I wish to thank J. Gordon Faylor and my fellow editors at *Jacket2* for publishing an early version of fifteen pages of chapter 10 as "The Unprepared Future of an Exophonic Refugee" in 2012. My essay "The End of the End of Poetic Ideology, 1960," was included in *The Oxford Handbook of Modern and Contemporary American Poetry* (2012), edited by Cary Nelson; as it happens, no more than a few sentences of the material from that essay have found their way into this book, but the commission presented me a first opportunity to test my ideas and refine the underlying literary history.

Many generous friends and colleagues at the Kelly Writers House, Center for Programs in Contemporary Writing, PennSound, ModPo, PoemTalk, RealArts, and *Jacket2* have helped me, too many to mention all here. They share my concept of a free and open collaborative (and often crowdsourced) pedagogy, and I love the projects we undertake together daily. Charles Bernstein, whose incessant anti-anti-intellectualism derives from the radical modernism of (Jewish) Europe, has been an overall inspiration for this book even before knowing its details; he is one person I feel confident can find something to enjoy on every page! Let me add that I cherish the work Charles and I have done together on PennSound, which has informed ideas about orality, cultural dissemination and movement, and sound recording here. Jamie-Lee Josselyn has shared with me the years-long development of our ideas about genocide and inherited trauma, and I have learned a great deal from her insistence that loss can be ultimately compensating. My appointments at Penn include Kelly Family Professor and Faculty Director of the Kelly Writers House, so let me say how honored I am that the late and much-missed Paul Kelly (who was a sophomore at Penn during the year I describe) opted twenty-five years ago to support me and my ventures with his true generosity and his deep concern about the future of the writing arts. My open-minded and supportive editor at Columbia University Press, Philip Leventhal, has been unfailingly responsive; I feel immensely lucky to have worked with him.

I dedicate this book to my mother, Lois Filreis; to my children, Hannah Filreis Albertine and Ben Filreis; and to my beloved wife Jane Treuhaft, who makes books as a profession and has heard too much about this one not to be credited as the most patient and loyal person I know.

I hope this work at least indirectly helps me honor the memory of my father, Sam Filreis (1926–2016)—a World War II Navy vet whose family had all lived in Warsaw and could not abide anything German; nearly every Filreis and Handscher was murdered by gassing at Treblinka—for persuading me to study German language and literature in school. Study *German*? It was definitely not a thing the liberal-left children of new Depression/wartime-generation Jewish suburbanites in the United States did in the 1960s. And in that intense classroom of teacher and five students, the intrepid Karl Dötzel showed me (because he knew I am Jewish?) an untranslated poem by Paul Celan written in what didn't quite seem to me to be German. That was it. I was completely hooked—not so much on that language, at which I persisted although alas didn't learn well, but on writing that deliberately presented all of its difficulties, for linguistic but also for traumatic historical reasons. By reaching back a few years earlier to 1960 for the focus of research for this book, I believe that I have been exploring the immediate antecedent of that psychohistory. And of course *that* history, in turn, utterly depends upon bad memories of 1939–45. This perspectival chronology is my book in sum. Someone who came of age in the 1960s looks back at 1960 as it took a last look back at the war before moving forward.

There follows thus one final note on my own educational psychohistory, which brings me to my fondest hope for this volume—that it is insightful enough to honor also the memory of my late teacher Terrence Des Pres, whose book *The Survivor* I have taught in my course "Representations of the Holocaust" for thirty-seven years (at last count). I did not intend to let my teaching of the holocaust find its way into my writing for publication. I imprecisely deemed the topic semisacred, belonging only to my protected classroom. I told everyone, for decades (and they have often asked), that I would not write about genocide. Now, more or less, I have done so. It comes from teaching *The Survivor* so often that the wisdom of Terrence's words have finally rung through in print, a grateful return of the unrepressed: "All things human take time."

# 1960

# Part 1

---

## Emerging from the Night of the Word

# 1

# An Introduction to the Survivor

## New Contexts for Genocide

*Isn't there, I must now ask . . . [a] calling-into-question that all poetry today must come back to, if it wants to go on questioning?*

—PAUL CELAN IN A TALK HE GAVE IN DARMSTADT, WEST GERMANY, OCTOBER 22, 1960

*The world in which we live has to be named all over again.*

—JAMES BALDWIN, DURING THE Q AND A SESSION AFTER A TALK HE GAVE IN SAN FRANCISCO, UNITED STATES, OCTOBER 22, 1960

I suspect that these two writers, Celan and Baldwin, have not been much compared, if ever. Yes, they both gave an important speech—an urgent *ars poetica* in each case—on the evening of October 22, 1960. The talks, Celan's "The Meridian" and Baldwin's "Notes for a Hypothetical Novel," call on the contemporary writer to provide a new experimental version of historical perspective. The arguments of the talks follow a particular retelling of twentieth-century history, even as they offer oblique (and thus perhaps easily missed) references to the recent murderous, traumatic past. From Baldwin and Celan—and soon in this first chapter we will add Jerome Rothenberg—we can discern examples of the special convergence of modernism and radicalism as a belated response to World War II that is the topic, one way or another, of each of this book's ten chapters, in the work of artists as variously situated as Yves Klein, Rod Serling, Grigori Chukhrai, Muriel Rukeyser, Frantz Fanon, Barbara Guest, Raphael Montañez Ortiz, Larry Eigner, Primo Levi, Ingeborg Bachmann, Parker Tyler, Bob Kaufman, Nelly Sachs, Chinua Achebe, Louis Zukofsky, Aharon Appelfeld, Roberto Rossellini, Oscar Hammerstein, Sari Dienes, Charles Reznikoff, Marceline Loridan-Ivens, Jackson Mac Low, John Coltrane, and others. Why did these people feel the need, at this moment, to construe the story of the century specifically as a postdisaster representation? I begin by reflecting on a statement made by Baldwin on the same day as Celan's speech, augmented by Rothenberg's perhaps surprisingly similar (and synchronous) heretical project; these events exemplify the many efforts in 1960 against deradicalization.

We open in San Francisco, a Saturday evening, October 22. *Esquire* has been hosting a symposium titled "Writing in America Today," and this is the third evening of presentations. On the twentieth, John Cheever gave a talk at UC Berkeley decrying the "abrasive and faulty surface of the United States" in recent years and succinctly generalized about the current situation: "The United States in 1960 is hell." He continued by adding that the "only possible position for a writer now is negation." The next night at Stanford University the featured speaker was Philip Roth. During the Q and A session after Cheever's talk Roth insisted that "There is no reason for optimism." Then in his own keynote Roth outlined the total "alienation of the writer in America," chided the "unwarranted optimism and affirmation" of several other novelists,[1] chastised the Beats for their dopey bewailing, affirmed another writer's judgment that "It's the age of the slob," and in the end set the bar of hopefulness no higher than mere survival. "Certainly to have come through a holocaust in one piece, to have survived, is nothing to be made light of," Roth said. "*However*, when survival itself becomes one's *raison d'être* . . . we then, I think, do not have much reason to be cheery."[2] On the third night the three writers and their host, editor Arnold Gingrich of *Esquire*, decamped a final time at the San Francisco State University Poetry Center, where a new communitarian generation of poets had recently gotten into the habit of making audio recordings of readings. A 115-minute recording of the gathering on October 22 preserves Baldwin's "Notes for a Hypothetical Novel" in its first telling; it was published in 1961 in *Nobody Knows My Name* after slight revisions. The tape includes a long, never-published discussion that followed the talk, among Cheever, Roth, Baldwin, Gingrich, and members of the audience.

Listening to the Q and A six decades later, one gets the sense that no one much noticed—or anyway felt ready or able to comment upon—the visionary democracy called for in Baldwin's conclusion, which stood vividly in contrast to the nihilism of Roth and Cheever. "A country is only as strong as the people who make it up and the country turns into what the people want it to become," Baldwin said. "Now, this country is going to be transformed. . . . I don't believe any longer that we can afford to say that it is entirely out of our hands. We made the world we're living in and we have to make it over."[3] He was in search of a new language. The idiosyncratic brilliance of this talk was that it was composed of words and sentences that theorized and constantly indicated their very inadequacy. Especially when heard aloud, the speech sounds both unyieldingly definitive and improvisationally tentative. Yes, "the world in which we live has to be named all over again," and this very talk, aptly dubbed hypothetical, could not itself entail such newness. That incapacity was the source of its productive distress.

The novelist began with an outline of "an unwritten and probably unwritable novel." He longed to compose this work but could not do so until he was able to comprehend a particular but still mysterious history that had formed him, and had produced the radicalizing "something"—a term repeated without antecedent—that was always Baldwin's topic. Where then would the new language come from? He provides a special history—more about that history in a moment—but he also describes a disposition that would not bring about the new words. The hypothesized innovation would not describe, or even merely complain about, the "Cadillacs, refrigerators or all the paraphernalia of American life," because as Baldwin "suspect[s], . . . there is something much more important and much more real which produces the Cadillac, refrigerator, atom bomb, and what produces it, after all, is something which we don't want to look at."[4] To discern contemporaneous versions of this seemingly unsayable thing, a cipher X inhibiting utterance, that called-into-question *something*—realized variously at the start of the 1960s by Baldwin and by a number of other venturesome artists of his generation—is the ambition of this book.

The tone of the Q and A after Baldwin's talk notwithstanding—a conversation that was harmonious and included repeated pious assertions by all parties that they were in agreement—Baldwin's "Notes" took a gnostic stance against Cheever's well-reasoned "negation" and opposed Roth's smart, world-weary critique of "unwarranted optimism." Baldwin's speculative position followed from his understanding of the previous few decades. Just one person, posing the penultimate audience question, sought further comment on that history. It was Harvey Swados, the novelist and essayist known for fierce independence and resistance to intellectual fads (whose book *A Radical's America* was then underway),[5] a writer whose experiences in the U.S. Merchant Marines off the coasts of five continents during World War II shaped his ideas about labor and antifascism.[6] Swados directed his question from the floor to Baldwin, and the *Esquire* editor-host, taking it to be a request apt for the entire panel, called on Cheever and Roth to offer responses too. Swados was struck by Baldwin's conclusion and asked him to elaborate on its politics. The current situation was not beyond "managing" the agony—thus Swados characterized Baldwin's "Notes," although "managing" was not Baldwin's word. People were capable of transcending tragic conditions caused by initial "self-deception." In response, the writer as citizen had an obligation to explore the will postwar people possessed to improve things rather than lament powerlessness and fate. But since 1945 self-deception could lead to mass annihilation; the writer's situation in this period would seem to be new and thus would require experimentation of a new sort.

Interpreting Swados's use of the word "annihilation" as referring to nuclear destruction, Cheever conceded that the burden on the writer was "heavier than it's ever been," yet declined to agree that the situation of post–World War II writing was historically unprecedented, and, deferring to the great tradition of fictional narrative, gave the example of Russian literature prior to the czar's demise. Roth for his part said he agreed with "John and Jimmy," but then took Cheever's view: the writer's duty "seems the same as it has ever been." Insofar as the burden was perhaps more complicated in 1960 than previously, Roth added, it is only because one "feels more dutiful *but not more powerful*," thus negating Baldwin's final visionary point that the coming transformation would and could be willed by the people, that it was "not out of our hands."

Baldwin's own response to Swados's question: "Frankly, yes." He did in fact believe the situation was unprecedented. He then summarized, extended, and stood by the talk's conclusion about the unwritable fiction:

> What the American writer has to do I can't quite imagine because it hasn't been done. I have to be a blind optimist to imagine that it *can* be done. But it does mean that the world in which we live has to be named all over again and things have to go . . . to be . . . I don't know. . . . It's very difficult to talk about revolutions that have not occurred. But it is absolutely certain that the American writer has to re-create society, to create the people, and the terms he has to use to do this have never been used in the world before.[7]

Swados was right it seems to ask Baldwin about self-delusion in response to the historical situation framed by mass death. That history was in Baldwin's talk:

he began by pondering the eras of his generation's and Harlem neighbors' coming of age, imagining a novel to be written about (and also somehow collaboratively written *by*) "these people"—elsewhere he refers to them as "my people," as "a group of lives," as "incoherent people in an incoherent country"[8]—and he had then described what his imagined novel would *not* be. It would not be sentimental, or one of those "long, warm, toasty novels." "We don't need another version of *A Tree Grows in Brooklyn* and we can do without another version of *The Heart Is a Lonely Hunter*."[9] The *something* was "something *more implacable*" toward which his hypothetical novel would aim. The two American works he identified were wartime novels (published in 1943 and 1940, respectively) and each is about the 1920s and 1930s. What, then, might have been the perspective of the 1940s on the 1930s? Baldwin was speculating on the development of the novel since the Second World War. Now the question was: What should be the view from 1960 of that wartime view of the previous "incoherent" moment? This *something* would have to account for, as Betty Smith and Carson McCullers could have but did not, "that unseen prisoner in Germany," a figure who is "going to have an effect on the lives of these people," meaning his Harlem generation—people for, of, and *through* whom he longed to write. The "unseen prisoner" was the incipient Adolf Hitler. Although Hitler is referred to twice in Baldwin's talk, he is not named. Yet the not-naming is more than just a nod to sickening familiarity even fifteen years later. Baldwin's point is that fascist racism and its effects "can't be left out of the novel without falsifying" the experience of those Americans who will survive to become narrators.

Earlier in the talk, Baldwin referred to Hitler as "a peculiar man in Germany who was plotting and writing." That mention followed a quick summary of modernist Black culture from the Negro Renaissance of the twenties to the "militant or the new Negro" of the thirties. The turbulence that had accompanied these shifts left much self-destruction, only to be followed by global war. Baldwin soon tired of capsule history and capitulated for the moment: "I will not really insist upon continuing this roster." But to that point, he added, "I have not known many survivors. I know mainly about disaster."[10]

Survival was a central point for Baldwin throughout his career as a writer (even as his political views shifted), and he would repeat it not long after giving this talk, in "Letter from a Region in My Mind" (1962), published in *The Fire Next Time*: "Just before and then during the Second World War, many of my friends fled into the service, all to be changed there, and rarely for the better, many to be ruined, many to die."[11] His idea was that European fascism would have to be somehow made present in an ideal novel if it would truly represent the people of Baldwin's Harlem, and he openly conceded that this might seem a "ridiculous" notion to his audience: *"Because no matter how ridiculous this may sound,"* he had said, "that unseen prisoner in Germany is going to have an effect on the lives of these people." The connection was becoming something of an obsession, a fundamental problem pertaining to race he knew he had to work through in order to progress as a novelist. It was the effort to know what survival of racist hatred constitutes, and how it must effect a nonreductive, nontransparent renaming of all things—the beginnings of a demand for the right to opacity (as Édouard Glissant later framed it) in representations of the survivor.[12] In another essay of 1960, "Fifth Avenue, Uptown," published in *Esquire* in July, Baldwin's descriptive survey of the long blocks of Harlem opened with an observation of absence. Starting with what cannot be seen, and with lost people who cannot serve as witnesses, was an unusual strategy for a glossy magazine article meant in part as a tour of uptown culture. "All along the block, for anyone who knows it, are immense human gaps, like craters. These gaps are not created merely by those who have moved away, inevitably into some other ghetto." There were others, including "those who, by whatever means—War II [*sic*], the Korean War, a policeman's gun or billy— . . . are dead." He went on to stipulate that in this piece "I am talking about those who are left; and I am talking principally about the young."[13]

The "human gaps" inspire intentional, creative, lyrical blurring. Such a choice of style in Baldwin's prose programmatically masks a detailed knowledge of the issues. He knew in quite precise terms the troubling prewar and wartime history he was summoning. His beloved middle school teacher-mentor, Orilla "Bill" Miller, had early conveyed to him "the economics of racism" from the point of view of a Depression-era (WPA-employed) white leftist, showing him how to reinterpret canonical stories, taking him to see the film version of *A Tale of Two Cities* (1935), for instance, as indicative of the "inevitable human ferment" that "explodes into . . . revolution."[14] At DeWitt Clinton High School he befriended the children of Jewish European proletarians who lived in the nearby cooperative housing built for the left-wing Amalgamated Clothing Workers; a number of these classmates had literary ambitions and were already political activists.[15] As Hilton Als has summarized this period, "Baldwin was introduced to leftist politics, and in short order the nineteen-year-old writer was a card-carrying Trotskyist" (although, to be sure, "he didn't remain one long").[16] He was invited by his close friend Stan Weir to join the (Leninist) Workers Party in 1942;[17] he heard the intense arguments raging among factions of the intellectual left over the virtues and difficulties of a united front against fascism and about the consequences of U.S. intervention in Europe.[18] Baldwin was surrounded by the conversation about the spreading effects of fascist prejudice abroad and its connection to domestic anti-Blackness. He was taught in a fiction writing workshop by a communist revered in New York for her loyal support of young writers of color, Mary Elting, who was later viciously redbaited by congressional committees.[19] By 1948 Baldwin was looking back on his brief but formative experience with American radicalism, recalling his arguing against the anti-Semitism of a Black leftist colleague. "It did no good to point out, as I did, that the exploitation of which she accused the Jews was American, not Jewish."[20]

Baldwin's antifascist views provide the background for his talk in San Francisco fifteen years after the war. By 1960, he knew himself as one of "those who are left"—he meant survival but it was also a pun on progressive partisanship—and he was knowledgeable about the forces that caused his community's absences. If, as Hilton Als keenly observes, "Baldwin used his blackness as a kind of surrogate Jewishness"— he felt that "the Jewish intellectuals who knew persecution at first hand could understand racism as persecution of a different hue"[21]—then this is a way of following Baldwin's conscious (and, relative to others, early) adaptation of survivor language ("witness," "testimony," "survivor") and his reflections on the mass killings of the war. He criticized American writers whose writing failed to serve as "testimony" to (for instance) their origins as immigrants or refugees, and reserved his highest praise for writers whose essential role was that of "witness," a term he often chose to describe his own aim of representing the American experience as it had been structured by cruel mistreatment and survival.[22]

The connection between fascism and racism Baldwin was improvisationally exploring in the talk on October 22 concluded with a description of himself as a "blind optimist" about prospects for a new mode of representing a people's suffering and absences. Baldwin's approach went against the cynical literary grain, as evidenced by the dour arguments put forward by Cheever and Roth, and obviously did not strike him as the least bit "ridiculous." His sense of how to redress the experience of the 1930s and 1940s in the contemporary American novel, and his sense that he had personally "know[n] mainly about disaster" rather than survival, led him in "Notes" to make references to several chimerical figures from his youth. The characters in his prospective Harlem novel would be almost entirely Black. Why? "Because, remember that we're projecting a novel, and Harlem is in the course of changing all the time, very soon there won't be any white people there, and this is also going to have some effect on the people in my story." He recalled that "in the beginning I only knew Negroes except for one Jewish boy, the only white boy in an all-Negro elementary school, a kind of survivor of another day in Harlem." This boy did not return in the telling of "Notes." Baldwin's hearers and then readers—especially those puzzling over his references to European fascism and its effects on American survival—might well have wondered. Had this young person become one of those Harlem absences by way of flight to the postwar suburbs? Or had he, like others Baldwin knew from boyhood, gone off to fight that war against fascism and not returned? The latter path would be a keener tragedy, surely, but not ultimately an outcome of a separate origin.[23]

In "Letter from a Region in My Mind" we do learn more in ways that deepen Baldwin's concepts of disaster, witnessing, and survival begun in "Notes." The boy eventually returns in a key, traumatic anti-anti-Semitic scene. The Jewish boys Baldwin knew at DeWitt Clinton in the Bronx "were troubling because I could find no point of connection between them and the Jewish pawnbrokers and landlords and grocery-store owners in Harlem."[24] They troubled a stereotype young Baldwin had learned from his church elders and his father. These Jewish children were a long way from Egyptian "incarcerat[ion]" and "far from the fiery furnace" described in the Old Testament. "Fiery furnace" was a phrase Baldwin would repeat, used previously in "The Harlem Ghetto" (1948): "The Negro identifies himself almost wholly with the Jew. The more devout Negro considers that he is a Jew, in bondage to a hard taskmaster and waiting for a Moses to lead him out of Egypt. The hymns, the texts, and the most favored legends of the devout Negro are all Old Testament and therefore Jewish in origin: the flight from Egypt, the Hebrew children in the fiery furnace."[25] Emile Capouya, a close friend from DeWitt Clinton, noticed that young Baldwin tended "to see everything in biblical terms," and further: "It often annoyed him that his friends, several of them skeptical Jewish intellectuals, were not as impressed with his biblical [Old Testament] references as he was."[26] Baldwin then recalls his best friend, who was white—a Jewish boy, quite possibly Capouya. The friend visited Baldwin's house, whereupon his stepfather, David Baldwin, asked if the friend was Christian. Was he saved? Possibly from innocence or possibly from "venom," Baldwin answers: "No. He's Jewish." "My father slammed me across the face with his great palm, and in that moment everything flooded back—all the hatred and all the fear, and the depth of a merciless resolve to kill my father rather than allow my father to kill me."[27] This is deep memory: in the retelling of the event, it becomes traumatic again, triggering a rush of cotemporality, the painful seconding of an old wound. A fantasy of defensive patricide leads to a personal contemplation of the cause of genocide. The prose recollecting the blow flows with nonsemantic conjunctions, the "and" that helps to smooth over what survivor-psychiatrist Dori Laub has called the jarring, fragmenting dread of the return.[28] The father's physical and emotional abuse, in the name of Christian zeal, the writer of these sentences "suddenly" associates with the holocaust. The anti-anti-Semitism of this Harlem story about the father and the best friend becomes the special version of antifascist poetics outlined in the San Francisco speech, as Baldwin mapped out what sort of modern writing would guide him to accept the responsibility of "renaming the world" with a counterintuitive "blind optimis[m]" that Cheever and even Roth, himself obsessed with Jewish postwar fate, could afford to eschew.[29] Baldwin hated his father because his father's hatred of his friend would soon abet racist mass murder. Baldwin felt he was "expected to be glad that a friend of mine, or anyone, was to be tormented forever in Hell, and I also thought, suddenly, of the Jews in another Christian nation, Germany. They were not so far from the fiery furnace after all, and my best friend might have been one of them."[30] Baldwin collected himself and then said to David Baldwin, "He's a better Christian than you are," whereupon the son turned heel and left the father's house—in effect permanently, feeling guilty but also relieved and free.

In the second half of the long essay "Letter," Baldwin narrates his difficult meeting with Elijah Muhammad in Chicago. Given that famous encounter, one could say that after leaving one father he would have to face another plausible Black paternalism, and that the first well (albeit complexly) prepared him for the second. He readies himself to enter the Nation of Islam enclave. Despite being skeptical about proposals for a separate Black economy, he realizes he is largely persuaded on another point—that Christianity is to blame for this striking truth: that Black people in the United States were *not* surprised by the mass murder of European Jews. "White people were, and are, astounded by the holocaust in Germany. They did not know that they could act that way." Although "authoritatively assured that what happened to the Jews in Germany could not happen to the Negros in America," he recalls historical knowledge that Europe's Jews "had probably believed similar counsellors."[31] At the start of the 1960s, was this lucid but perhaps obvious summary of the enormous historical irony of the holocaust unnecessary? To the contrary, what Baldwin wrote about in "Letter" and conveyed in "Notes" (passingly, although at least Swados perceived it and invited him to elaborate) was at the time new as a mode of expressing a particular contemporary problem of representation. In the next chapter we will see how writers such as William Shirer (in *The Rise and Fall of the Third Reich*, another work of 1960) continued the confident premodern tradition of capably putting into words this unthinkable history; Shirer is a writer who competently *explained as a problem of content* rather than skeptically *explored as a problem of language* the consequential not-saying of (to take a ghoulish example) the Wannsee Conference of 1942: that people who manage to survive deportation, then outlast slave labor, finally after that (in the circumlocutious Nazi phraseology Shirer quotes) "must be treated *accordingly.*"[32] For the most part, this book is about artists who learn on the contrary to face the greater "troubling . . . *something* more implacable" that Baldwin cannot quite write but will repeatedly attempt, the belated postwar poetics of the unimaginable. Baldwin's central concern—Jerome Rothenberg's and George Steiner's, too, as we will see shortly—was how and why "a death so calculated, so hideous, and so prolonged" could and should *not* be confidently explained. A decade and a half after the war, Baldwin provided the following analysis, and in the context of fascist racism it was new:

> The terms "civilized" and "Christian" begin to have a very strange ring, particularly in the ears of those who have been judged to be neither civilized nor Christian, when a Christian nation surrenders to a foul and violent orgy, as Germany did during the Third Reich. For the crime of their ancestry, millions of people in the middle of the twentieth century, and in the heart of Europe—God's citadel—were sent to a death so calculated, so hideous, and so prolonged *that no age before this enlightened one had been able to imagine it, must less achieve and record it.* . . . The fact of the Third Reich alone makes obsolete forever any question of Christian superiority, except in technological terms.[33]

Anti-anti-Semitism, as a form of an always-experimental mode of antiracism, directed Baldwin toward an idea about writing that augured a revised version of postwar modernism. This idea has two aspects. One entails the desire to create decentered points of view, narrative social intersubjectivity, and multivocality. The second entails the tolerance, indeed the embrace, of incoherence as both a principle and a form of writing, a stubborn reversal of its negative connotation. "Notes" approaches both ideas provocatively. Baldwin's hypothetical novel, as has been noted, would feature the Harlem figures from his youth, and he wants them *all* somehow to narrate this prospective fiction. He does not yet know how but this aim leads him to tell a collective generational story and directs him to contemplate multiple effects of fascist racism "on the lives of these people,"[34] a democracy of voices that by its very aesthetic form would stand against authoritarianism. Through an experimental narrative ethnography he wants to "follow a group of lives." Baldwin writes: "I want to impose myself on these people as little as possible. That means that I do not want to tell them or the reader what principle their lives illustrate, or what principle is activating their lives, but by examining their lives I hope to be able to make them convey to me and to the reader what their lives mean." This anti-authoritarianism is "not altogether possible" but moves toward a new kind of postwar "point of view," goes beyond Smith and McCullers, beyond the 1930s-style populist naturalism of James T. Farrell and the communist naturalism of Richard Wright. In its very method of composition Baldwin's approach resists the effect "the unseen prisoner in Germany" will have on the lives of its characters. This idea about art's representation of surviving lives aligns with the postfascist modernism of writers such as Jerome Rothenberg, among others—Ingeborg Bachmann, Amiri Baraka, George Steiner, Bob Kaufman, Louis Zukofsky, for example—whose experiments in this vein we encounter in these pages.

## Doing Unheard-of Things

Now what of "incoherence"? How does it pertain to the history Baldwin explores? Unlike Roth and Cheever, and nearly everyone associated with the *Esquire* symposia, smugly condemning the incoherent American, Baldwin is gripped by this terrifying quality and sees that it beckons him toward innovative writing. "To try to deal with this enormous incoherence . . . this shapeless thing, to try and make an American well listen to them, and try to put that on a page. . . . To try to find out what Americans mean is almost impossible because there are so many things they do not want to face." "The Negro thing" is "simply the most obvious . . . example" but this—not "the Negro thing" per se, but the "something [still] *more* implacable"—postwar people cannot face yet must: it will be his subject matter, but also, as important, his poetics. Incoherence, although it "says *something* very terrifying about this country," is Baldwin's new postwar term for alienation.[35] Less ideologically freighted than alienation, far less politically determined than Wright's naturalism, but just as productive. Baldwin's reaching across through memory and geopolitics to the experience of Jews in Europe led him to a realization of racist America as "your alien homeland," the phrase Paul Celan uses in "Shibboleth," a poem about the racialized self as othered by language. In his own talk given that Saturday in October in Germany, Celan described the postwar antifascist writer as someone who "moves with the oblivious self into the uncanny and strange to free itself."[36] This is the counterintuitive, hopeful stance on American incoherence Baldwin took the same night in the United States. He shared with Celan a feeling of alienation from his own national language, always from within that troubled vocabulary ready to risk words as shibboleths, potentially to be misunderstood even by the disaffected, directly addressed other.[37] "My quarrel with the English language," Baldwin wrote in "Why I Stopped Hating Shakespeare" (1964), "has been that the language reflected none of my experience; but . . . perhaps the language was not my own because I never attempted to use it, and only learned to imitate it. If this were so, it might be made to bear the burden of my experience if I could find the stamina to challenge it, and me, to such a test."[38] In "The African Writer and the English Language," Chinua Achebe, the Nigerian novelist discussed in the next chapter, faces this challenge along with the antihero Obi Okonkwo in his second novel, *No Longer at Ease* (1960), to reflect on his own struggles with English, and was gratified to discover Baldwin's reckoning with Shakespeare. Achebe quoted the passage from Baldwin just cited, and added this warning: "Let no one be fooled by the fact that we may write in English, for we intend to do unheard of things with it."[39]

*Unheard-of things.* Celan, aspiring to the make such unrecognizable noises with his German, was almost entirely unknown in the English-speaking world when Jerome Rothenberg, himself searching for a poetics of the alien homeland—and hoping, too, to make unheard-of things out of American English—decided to bring Celan's opaque language to readers outside Germany and Austria. Rothenberg's first volume, *New Young German Poets*, published by City Lights Books in "The Pocket Poets Series" in 1959, introduced readers in the United States to an antifascist avant-garde, recommended and selected by a writer beginning to perfect his own merge of prewar high modernism and postwar mourning. Rothenberg perceived his problem in a way similar to what Baldwin outlined in San Francisco: as an artist he must try to enact a language-based "revolution" (per Baldwin), a new "revolution of the word" (per Rothenberg), by imagining what could not be imagined. Rothenberg saw that this was indeed not the typical historical situation of the writer, contrary to the approaches of Cheever and Roth. It was the special situation *now*—postwar but belatedly so.

On most topics covered during the *Esquire* panel, Baldwin had an ally in Roth, Swados, and others in the audience (the applause was loud and sustained). But listening now to the recording of "Notes" and the Q and A, one has the dismal sense that notwithstanding his radical optimism he was feeling rather alone, at least literarily, in arguing the way he did for an experiment in "nam[ing] all over again." Baldwin's essays on his mutually supportive relationship with Norman Mailer and his complicated connection to the novelistic legacy of Wright—both pieces written in 1960, his second attempt at assessing Wright—can similarly suggest intellectual individuation. Rothenberg, despite new compatriots among U.S. poets (his "Deep Image" colleagues and some of the "New American" poets gathered in Donald Allen's anthology of 1960), created his anthology of *German* poets primarily in order to locate allies in his own quest to rename the world after global war. Rothenberg chose, among others, Celan and Ingeborg Bachmann. In the inexpensive pocket-sized book these two were being introduced to English-speaking readers for the first time. Rothenberg translated Celan's "Night of the Word"—its traumatic postwar "beat" rendered pointedly as "howl" (*schlagen nun an*, or: starting to howl),[40] not a rebuke of Allen Ginsberg's *Howl* (translated into German in 1959 as "Das Geheul") but an implicit call for political contextualizing currents in experimental writing in the United States[41]—and Bachmann's poem "Psalm," with its hard-to-translate postfascist take on Catholic "extreme unction" ("the butchers / stifle the stripped body's breathing"): these poems and others offer themselves to us now, more than a half century later, as influences on Rothenberg's own first published book of poems, the Hawk's Well Press *White Sun Black Sun* (1960). That volume engaged ideas and modes of European modernist writing of the 1910s and 1920s—its title owing at least something, by way of Rothenberg's Hawk's Well Press, to Harry and Caresse Crosby's intrepid, avant-garde Black Sun Press[42]—but did not avoid, forget, or bypass the disaster that befell modernists in the 1930s and 1940s.

So it was not only Bachmann's "Psalm" as Rothenberg presented her poem under the auspices of City Lights but also his own early verse that were inscribed "In the afterbirth of our terror" (in her words as he rendered them).[43] "Seeing Leni Riefenstahl's Triumph of the Will, San Francisco 1959," a *White Sun Black Sun* poem, figures the speaker as the young poet's very first "Burning Babe" (one of many instances of this recurring trope he would deploy over the decades): "I am the child in the furnace." In "Leni Riefenstahl" the young artist has gone west to San Francisco, arguably ground zero of a new American experimental writing from a bottom-up perspective, where anything demotic and low could freely be realized as the subject matter of poetry. But simultaneously the speaker faces a murderous ultra-authoritarian aesthetic, the totalizing Olympian field of vision that had done as much rhetorically as any representation in the 1930s or early 1940s to authorize the "Final" plan enacted at Wannsee for rationalized annihilation. To Rothenberg, the Bay Area was exactly where he needed to be to face such reminders of fascist antimodernism.

Was the San Francisco screening of Riefenstahl's aesthetic only a historical irony? Hardly. "We are tired we have lived with war and hunger for twenty years / and *never known* what they were."[44] "Twenty years": from 1939 to the poem's present, 1959; thus the speaker's retrospective is marked not from the release of the film in 1935 but from the commencement of war, the invasion of the Rothenberg family's Poland. The tone of this first book is never outwardly presumptuous, but the San Francisco/fascism poem contends, as these works of 1960 do generally, that such never-knowing, induced first by war and hunger, has a direct effect on how well a writer will learn to hear the sounds of ghosts bespeaking an unreasonable, but productive, alternative to the logically prescriptive, murderous master language. From his reading of Gershom Scholem's wartime study *Major Trends in Jewish Mysticism* (1941) and now *Jewish Gnosticism* (1960)—we will return in subsequent chapters to the impetus for this encounter with mysticism—Rothenberg learned that the much-derided option of nontraditional Jewish epistemology provided a scholarly and rational basis for a poetics of intuition and the flight from reason, what Yves Klein was just then calling a "leap into the void."

This was the moment when Rothenberg began the long journey toward *Khurbn*, a much later book of poems that would finally fully confront the holocaust as a personal, aesthetic, and political influence and reckon with the ghostly presences whose voices he had heard while visiting Treblinka. *Khurbn* records his confrontation with the death camp where members of his family were exterminated; upon hearing such news his uncle, a member of the doomed partisans, "drank himself blind in a deserted cellar & blew his brains out." That work deploys its spectral writing in verses freer rather than stricter in form because in them the victims of crimes against humanity "practice your scream" in unruly modes—performing "poetry as the language of the dead." As Harlem was for Baldwin in "Fifth Avenue, Uptown" strewn with absences and a few incoherent survivors, the prompt for his own elliptical writing, so this haunted scene was for Rothenberg: writing made in "the *absence* of the living [that] create[d] a vacuum in which the dead . . . were free to speak"—sending "the clearest message I have ever gotten about why I write poetry."[45]

Rothenberg's first mature writings were too recent—his *Poems from the Floating World* project (volume 2 was published on January 1, 1960) and nascent Deep Image approach (emerging in the late 1950s but deployed as a term and "school" in 1960) had arrived on the scene just too late[46]—to earn inclusion in Donald Allen's big alt-canonical constellation, *The New American Poetry* (1960), even assuming Allen would have been open to it.[47] In any event, we miss in Allen's definitive-seeming collection one of several political contexts for the end of the supposed end of ideology. Rothenberg's and others' was fittingly a "New *American*" avant-garde mainly to the extent that readers could follow its specific postholocaust *European* context, its remnant derivation from a modernism that had had its language stolen, its mother tongue cut off in its mouth, drawn from a Celanesque night of the word, 1945 to 1960. What dawned after that long night was an idea of American experimentalism that it too must show "the scar of time / open[ed] up"—to quote Rothenberg's Celan in *New Young German Poets* in a direct anticipation of what I take to be the gist of Rothenberg's own curatorial contribution. This curation was narrower than Allen's, to be sure, but arguably more pertinent to what Baldwin was proposing: that in unsuccessful societies, it becomes impossible for language to change commensurately, whereupon a common language breaks down, and people no longer understand each other, and the "impossibility of telling" (to use Dori Laub's phrase about survivor testimony) should itself become the subject matter, and *that* move signifies a surprising turn back toward life.[48] "This breakdown," Rothenberg summarized, "is first articulated by a poet," by "the poet see[ing] the breakdown in communication as a condition of health, as an opening-up of a closed world." Or as Rothenberg's version of Austrian sound and concrete poet Ernst Jandl is given to lament in *Vienna Blood*, a later work by Rothenberg about European fascism and artists:

—KA KA—
the only music left us.[49]

This, then, is the moment to consider: Why would a young, reformist poet so openly embrace the particularities of modernism in 1960? Not primarily because "supreme Yiddish surrealist vaudeville"[50] would become in the 1960s and early 1970s one of the efficacious heretical counterstyles—although certainly in Rothenberg's book about the linguistic culture lost in the Holocaust, *Poland/1931* (1974), such a mode helped carry the message—but because experimental art after 1945 becomes a way of reckoning specifically with "the anti-modernism of the Nazi genocide of European intellectuals" and so, as Rothenberg quotes Dennis Tedlock, "To tell these words is to happen the beginning again." The origin story of the ethnopoetics movement of the 1960s and 1970s, seeking what in *Revolution of the Word* Rothenberg identified as a modernist "mediumistic language" discernible in archaic song,[51] emerges from efforts to use dadaist and surrealist tactics to reverse genocidal antimodernism. Here the response to the "anti-modernism of the Nazi genocide of European intellectuals" shifts from a negative analysis of the war's effects to a positive, even hopeful, avant-gardism—to a postfascist revival of radical modernism, to enact real "reversals in the history of language."[52] This is the gist of Baldwin's surprising hopefulness, too, and we will encounter a version of the turn back toward life in each chapter of this book. In Rothenberg's "The Holy Words of Tristan Tzara" we read that "logic is a complication! / logic is always wrong!" but then at the same time we are reminded of the nonparadoxical question posed by armed yet overwhelmed minoritarian resistance during the war, "like Yiddish dada in the street":[53] How does a moral person continue to live in an immoral world? This in essence posed the dilemma in which immorality is described in a language widely accepted as having made common sense in the twentieth century. We come to know through the work of artists like Rothenberg, who sought synthesis of modernism and antifascism rather than their 1950s-style separation, that such is a question asked not only by the likes of Ernst Jandl or Kurt Schwitters, or members of the largely German Zero movement, but also by the doomed resistance fighter Mordecai Anielewicz feeling the *duende* of nonrationally imagining reversals of fortune during the final hours of the besieged Warsaw Ghetto (he, a barely postadolescent Burning Babe). Rothenberg has written that Treblinka (to which killing field Anielewicz was bound had he not resisted and been immolated in the ghetto) is "an enormity that had robbed language . . . of the power to meaningfully respond, had thus created a crisis of expression (no, of meaning, of reality), for which a poetics must be devised if we were to rise, again, beyond the level of the scream or of a silence more terrible than any scream."[54]

Two tendencies now converged: first, Rothenberg's initial impulse toward archaic materials, manifested in *White Sun Black Sun* and *New Young German Poets* as, after total destruction, "telling words as a way of happening the beginning again"—first, a Burning Babe's nonsense words ("DA DA" = "KA KA"), uttered after the scream; and, second, the uncanny gesture toward a supreme Yiddish surrealist vaudeville as a methodology of Oral Torah, through which it is realized that the "stabilization of the text would hinder and destroy the infinitely moving, unfolding element within it."[55] Putting these two trends together, we grasp a convergence of formally disruptive art and radicalism, of postfascist Euro-modernism and American heretical politics doubtful about the Cold War, a confabulation that occurs when the art and politics of the avant-garde in (and around) 1960 synthesize as a delayed response to fascist war. "The Real Revolution Is Tragic," the title of a poem in *White Sun Black Sun* contends—but it is not a negative proposition. On the night of that poem, the forlorn young poet "face[s] . . . my secret America," asking: "Why are the eyes of it burning?" Here was the New American writer calling, as Baldwin did, for "the real revolution" of the word notwithstanding "the days without hope, in the years that are falling."

## Inheriting the Dead World

Rothenberg lived in Germany, in the destroyed city of Mainz, from 1953 through 1955. In 1953 he had received a master's degree from the University of Michigan, where his "most impressive teacher" had been Austin Warren,[56] the self-described "old New Critic" in whose seminar on Dickinson and Whitman Rothenberg enrolled.[57] Warren permitted the young poet to write a series of Dickinsonian poems, which the former student retains to this day. "But then Whitman was a problem for him. He knew he was dealing with a big writer, but a big writer who did not observe the meters." The eminent Warren pored through *Leaves of Grass* to find a few poems in which Whitman writes metrically. Rothenberg eventually wrote "a paper salvaging Whitman" from the New Critical paralysis, an effort at least to begin reviving the poet's protomodernist heterodoxy. But on the whole it had "seemed like such a ridiculous thing for an intelligent man like that to trip up on." Rothenberg recalls understanding then that a "critical ideology" stressing what Warren with René Wellek famously in *Theory of Literature* named "the 'intrinsic' approach" and "the intrinsic study of literature"[58] had blocked a "brilliant teacher" from extending his apprehension of Dickinson, notwithstanding her wild disjunctions, to the long-lined visionary free verse of Whitman. But the special usefulness of this uncapacious sense of modern writing wouldn't be realized until the end of the decade. It was his first witnessing of the miserable "migration of modernism into the desert of the 'New Critics,'" and while at the time there seemed little connection between leaving Warren's classroom and the next step, being stationed in the postwar wasteland of Mainz, certainly the German context provided a crucial view and circumstance of a possible emergent "Counter-Poetics" ("their first eruption in 1914 [and] their second in the 1950s"): a politico-aesthetic context that made increasingly coherent what was at stake, during Cold War, in the new "re-explor[ation] of the idea of an avant-garde" just now.[59] Because his spouse Diane Rothenberg had joined him in Germany when he was stationed in Mainz, the U.S. Army permitted them to live off base and in the middle of the unreconstructed city. He perfected his

German, began hearing of the new language being invented by the generation born between the early 1920s and early 1930s, gleaning the first inkling
"that there was something new happening in the post-Nazi situation there."[60]
That "over the ruins of Hitler's psychotic Reich" might "emerg[e] . . . a new avant-
garde" was "a miracle."

In the preface to *New Young German Poets* the new young Jewish American
poet used the term "miracle" with full political irony. He intended a contrast
between the emergence of a renewed avant-garde and the touted Wirtschaftswunder (the Economic Miracle—of U.S.-sponsored rehabilitation). That contrast
became an important topic for George Steiner in 1960, as we will see shortly.
For Rothenberg after his experience in Mainz, the real wonder was that more
than a decade following the war a radical idea of language was being commended
and shared by local artists living with daily privations yet developing an internationalist sensibility. He and Diane happened to reside in "a totally bombed-out
city,"[61] for Mainz was in the French zone; the French, irritated by the quickness
of U.S. financial if not also psychological forgiveness, deliberately slowed the
pace of German rebuilding. The pair of young scholar-artists frequented a tavern perfectly named Der Heiliger Geist and peered through its cracked windows out at rubble and misery, gaining a strong view that the effect of the war
was still a present tense, notwithstanding the sheer luck (and irony) felt inside
The Holy Ghost that *it* at least had miraculously escaped ruination. And interestingly, the persistence of ruins into the 1950s was, in a sense, French-made.[62]

After leaving the army, Rothenberg returned to the United States, where his
translations of seven poems by German prewar and wartime pacifist Erich Kästner in the *Hudson Review* caught the attention of Lawrence Ferlinghetti,[63] who
had followed Kästner's anti-Nazi literary cabaret and now contracted Rothenberg
to put together the small anthology. Ferlinghetti was impressed by Rothenberg's
generous rendering of the questions Kästner's verse negations raised—for instance,
what should a postwar Jewish translator do with a German's ironic regular
rhyme? Ferlinghetti sought more such translations. Rothenberg set out to edu-
cate himself about the work of Klaus Bremer, Ernest Dreyer, Heinz Piontek, and
other German poets whose work was hard to find in the United States and of
course was yet to be translated (except for Clement Greenberg's one attempt
in 1955 to render Celan's "Death Fugue").[64] The project didn't merely augur a
bit of royalties. Rothenberg discovered the thrill of working at the edge of an
art. "It was an open field," he recalled.[65] The project, moreover, presented a special
challenge of literary politics. It is difficult now to convey the problems of audience that could easily befall a book called *New Young German Poets* fifteen years

after the end of the global war. There was ongoing suspicion of those boosting German culture, a sense that the rebuilt German nation, including some of its intellectuals, flaunted an inability to mourn—factors surely complicated by the presence of a brash young Jewish writer, at a time of fervent Americanism, claiming that *this* is the writing that could "oppos[e] the inherited dead world."[66] What good could come of beginning one's career by publishing books that relocated a suppressed literary radicalism? "I think in some ways," Rothenberg has said, "it was better at that point [the end of the 1950s] to look toward European modernism . . . which had had limited impact on the U.S., but [these German writers] were equally there to look at and to learn from."[67]

Thus as an alternative to Austin Warren's aesthetic limitations and the prevailing literary-political Cold War scene of the 1950s, Rothenberg engaged with modern European art as a strategy for circumventing the deradicalization of modernism in the United States. Through this anti-deradicalization—the new engagement entailed in "taking the old experimental modernism, particularly through movements like Dadaism and Surrealism, as being political—radical—in nature"—Rothenberg realized "from 1960 on," as he has put it, how "connected" he was to other so-called New American movements, especially the Beats and "the [Robert] Duncan side" of Black Mountain poetics. He was learning a crucial lesson about experimental writing from the young Germans: that "there never was just a change of form but also a change of mind" and that "that was what it was to be avant-garde." Was there a connection, too, between one's sense of the enormous disaster wrought by World War II and a young artist's perception of the import of this reemergent sense of heretical style? "Yes, the holocaust," Rothenberg has said in response to this question, "was always in the foreground. The holocaust and Hiroshima and the capacity to destroy on that level. The war. The destruction of whole populations."[68] "I think I began to write poetry under the impact of that, . . . of the Second World War, the Holocaust, the great, very intense, brief period of destruction," he observed in an earlier interview. "I was still living under [it], as were others of my generation. I don't think I can define very clearly what I mean, but I understood then that, for the first time, I was willing to say that something of what had happened there was what brought me into poetry in the first place."[69]

From the perspective of 1960, then, the "miracle" Rothenberg refers to is not to be identified from signs of financial recovery (such signs were persistent in newspaper coverage throughout the year),[70] or from hyper-reconstruction that had a tendency to build directly atop ruins without linguistically or ethnographically sifting through them. No, the miraculous would be discerned in the way paroxysm and torment are inscribed in the representations of the survivor who dared to experiment with the "dead world [of] language" rather than to avoid it. Survivors' semantic meaning (*content*—their themes, their doleful descriptions) taken alone would not seem to justify such celebration of renewal. The psycholinguistic link between historical repression and the geopolitical victory to be read and heard in incongruous "Talk / broken under boots" (Ernst Jurgen Dreyer's phrase found in *New Young German Poets*) is tenuous and fragile and required a kind of close reading that was not at all about "resolving tension," as the New Criticism trained postwar Americans to do,[71] but rather about disjunctively replicating that tension, conveying in that way "something of what had happened there," in Rothenberg's phrase.

The anthology implies its fundamental question about writing such replication. Overall it asks: What if the discordance between the broken language and the new fiscal wholeness was to be left unresolved? Vocabularies of economics and poetics had been pried and then kept apart from 1945 through the 1950s, the prior intrepid merging of them (by modernists and leftists) deemed by conservatives and centrists to have been one cause, in the 1930s, of the crisis that ensued. Conservatives in particular, such as those appearing in the pages of the traditionalist, anti-interventionist magazine *Modern Age*, had trouble accepting what Henry Cord Meyer in a book titled *Five Images of Germany* (1960) described as persisting American "uneasiness" with "modern Germans" as postwar people whose "spectacular economic successes" could not be kept separate from the way memories of "SS-men and death camps" were to be now written and discussed.[72] Hannah Arendt, giving talks in Cologne and Frankfurt in December 1959 and January 1960, spoke with people who were "profoundly unhappy despite the wildest prosperity," who actually felt "malicious" toward Germany's recovery, "secretly hoping that everything will fall apart . . . full of resentment against everybody and everything. . . . The atmosphere it creates is dreadful."[73] For an essay published in a February 1960 issue of *The Reporter*, titled "The Hollow Miracle"—the title also referred satirically to the U.S.-aided Wirtschaftswunder—George Steiner delivered this fragment (rare in his critical prose): "A language being used to run hell, getting the habits of hell into its syntax."[74] Many of the poems Rothenberg selected feature the reversal Steiner describes (we will return to it) as unironic expressions of traumatic residue at the level of the line and phrase. It emerges in Celan's verse through moments of surrealism, certainly, as when that survivor's annual seasonal fall returns (in poems memorializing the autumnal disappearance of his mother, in a single leaf that perennially drops onto or from the poet-son's hand), reverses the a priori logic of nightmare and waking, implying a homonymic rhyme between dream (*traum*) and traumatic vision (*trauma*): "in dreams people sleep, / the mouth tells the truth" ("im Traum wird geschlafen, / der Mund redet wahr").[75]

In Celan's "Night of the Word," chosen for *New Young German Poets*, we begin journeying into light's absence, following Celan's typically insecure steps but unaided even by the diviner's rod. Where are we going? Will this poem guide us? Can one find one's way in the darkness of the poem itself? As is often the case with Celan at his most linguistically intense, "Night of the Word" gives instructions for its own reading as the reader forays forward. That is to say, it warns of the difficult implied analogy of footfall and "word-fall" with each word-by-word step. A shadow darkens every pace and cannot be purged. Finally a moon rises and we feel some traditional heavenly navigation is possible before the lyric ends, not so we can find a way by mapping the destroyed terrestrial landscape but through a poem that, if it honors tradition, looks to the sky, seeking a universal celestial context. Of course even this fixity is "helpless to save you." The last surreal image is a memory of a piece of fruit "your teeth closed around / years before." Is "Night of the Word" presenting an unconscious remnant lunar symbol, a reference to bygone creative fecundity, the outmoded traditional imaginative source? The formulation of the mouth to form the right night-words—the words on the page, as one reads—yet lost in the mouth?[76] The *something* meant by the word is implacable, in Baldwin's sense. If the word cannot get out, and if *that* needs to be the subject matter of art, as George Steiner was suggesting, such work will engage the modern to give new definition to reconstruction.

Ingeborg Bachmann's poem "Curriculum Vitae" makes a similar point, although the conceit suggests the progress of supposed personal maturation and postwar professionalization rather than navigation through tough terrain. The time of darkness is the same: "Long is the night," the poem begins. Bachmann's upbringing in Austria involved a mother who held to the "dream of the future of [her] men" and a silent gloomy father, a Nazi army officer who presumably at the time of the Anschluss in 1938 and through the war years never "thought past tomorrow" and whom Bachmann at the end of the war felt she needed to forget. ("We don't talk about Daddy any more," she wrote in a diary in June of 1945.)[77] The speaker's impressive postwar CV has only to offer the experience of what the previous generation did not offer. For what sort of occupation is Bachmann's speaker now suited? In this night of the word a lunar appearance too is listed as a credential, but the "goddamn long / . . . night" is endured "under the sputum / of a jaundiced moon, whose light / stunk gall." How this stubborn young Austrian skeptic, daughter of the Nazi soldier, was educated and then retrained herself we will save for the next chapter, when we look at her short fiction of 1960, but here in "Curriculum Vitae," chosen by Rothenberg, as if to warn his American readers against employing her mode of life-writing ("My hair won't turn white, / for I crept from a womb of machines"),[78] she recalls the perhaps normal ecstasies of schoolgirl lessons—"those towering nights with their square- / root dilemmas"—in the context of becoming one of those young postwar Austrians who had been nursed on "wolf's milk." Thus the poem conjures the inhuman origin of the most ostentatious imperial botch prior to the Third Reich. Bachmann's final stanza begins:

> O if I had no fear of death!
> If I had the word
> (nor knew its loss)

Because having "the word" is deployed in a subjunctive mood, an employable credential only prospectively, it is difficult to transpose into plainer language the apparently continuing negative ("nor . . .") of the next line. *Were I not afraid of dying and had I possessed the language to describe the "goddamn long / . . . night" and put words to "the powerless cries / of my friends," and at the same time remained unaware of the death of my own language. . . .* The catalogue of *ifs* continues, from this wordlessness to an encounter, ambiguously unwanted ("Let the earth not *lead me on*, / but lay me long") and apparently sexual,[79] with a horrifying animal embodiment of the night of the word.

The title of Bachmann's poem refers of course to a genre of writing that presents the speaker's credentials for new work, testifies to her readiness for gainful forward progress and, in historical context, for participation in the recovery miracle. It creates a contrast with the psychological state of being unaware of the loss of language. In a time of ubiquitous utterances of officially optimistic catchphrases, "cold war," "economic miracle," "clean bomb," "collectivism," "thousand flowers" (these are in a list Rothenberg adduces to introduce *New Young German Poets*), Celan's and Bachmann's long nights of the word bear out the young American poet's promise that in his volume of poets one will encounter people "quick to sense the darkness behind the current slogans."[80] Celan was never quite this angry in public, but in a recently published notebook of 1960 he expresses acute frustration with the "humanistic phrasemongers, posthumous caretakers of Jew.[ish] thought inheritance," and adds: "I do not say this to have my words be part of some present or future judgment—but: time is running out. And so I say it: so that <u>they</u> . . . should tremble and turn back."[81]

For both Rothenberg and George Steiner the hollowness of reconstruction's miracle was linguistic, just as the key to the critique of the Wirtschaftswunder was artists' learning to live aesthetically inside the night of the word. And rather than being a cause for bleak assessment, "the thing that has gone dead" (Steiner's striking circumlocution for the German language) offers the opportunity to look back on aesthetic ideas that had created such vibrant newness before the war. Make It New again. The memory of and return to spontaneity was essential. "Actions of the mind," Steiner wrote for *The Reporter* in his essay "The Hollow Miracle," that were once spontaneous "bec[a]me mechanical, frozen habits (dead metaphors, stock similes, slogans)."[82] And when exactly had German "leapt to life"?[83] Steiner's answer is the same as Rothenberg's: it had happened when the modernist avant-garde held sway, a "glorious" time when "German literature and art shared in that great surge of western imagination which encompassed Faulkner . . . Joyce, Eliot, Proust . . . Picasso, Schonberg, and Stravinsky."[84] Rothenberg's choice of Celan and Bachmann in particular implied his sense that they were participating in a renewal of that surge on their own terms, by examining and rejecting the frozen habits of fascist antimodernism.

## Thinking What We Are Doing, a Postdisaster Poethics

George Steiner had just completed a Fulbright professorship in Innsbruck, Austria, for the academic year 1958–59, a linguistic encounter of the sort sensitively described in Bachmann's fiction of just this time. Although a polyglot, his cultural linguistic background in German was more Austrian than German per se. The generalizations of "The Hollow Miracle" are certainly pertinent—that "the German language was not innocent of the horrors of Nazism," among other overviews. But dense idiomatic details—for example, Steiner's reading of the alleged recent lengthening of German words—express as much the point of view of an expatriate Jewish Austrian dealing linguistically with what Celan calls "your alien homeland" as they indicate a sociolinguistic *reportage* from almost inside the dead language. Born in Paris in 1929 to Jewish Viennese parents, Steiner was one of only two people from his school grade to survive the war. By 1960 genocide was as much in the "foreground" of his work as it was for Rothenberg.

During his time teaching at Cambridge, Steiner faced a typical form of academic anti-Semitism for that era—directed not so much at suspicions of the Jewish personality, the "firebrand with a foreign accent," as through expressions of doubt about the relevance of the holocaust he wouldn't stop mentioning in his lectures.[85] Be it obsession, an intellectual working-through, the flaunted hubris of the academic outsider, or some other postwar complex—the insistent implication of the relevance of bearing witness to the topics of subsequent lectures and essays "on difficulty,"[86] on language's theoretical relation to silence,[87] on the central importance of learning to read "covert meanings,"[88] etc., arises from how the holocaust taught avatars of modernism to read "opaque" writing "resistant to immediacy and comprehension" and also to understand that style as part of the "language-act most charged with the intent of communication, of reaching out to touch the listener or reader in his inmost."[89] The writer in this situation "must literally create new words and syntactic modes." And Steiner reminded his readers on February 18, 1960, in "The Hollow Miracle" that modern art had already taught all this before the disaster of the 1940s, for "this was the argument and practice of the first Dada, of Surrealists, of the Russian 'Futuro-Cubist' Khlebnikov." "The Hollow Miracle," although focused specifically on refuting the empty language of American claims to full rehabilitation of German social order, is more importantly a preamble to his and others' embrace of aesthetic difficulty as reinvestment in the radical tradition. It was time not so much to make it new as to revive the original experimental revitalization. The "radical" writer "will not forge a new tongue but will attempt to revitalize, to cleanse 'the words of the tribe' "—will "reanimate lexical and grammatical resources that have fallen out of use."[90]

In response to words having "lost their original meaning and acquired nightmarish definitions," Steiner, Celan, Baldwin, and Rothenberg were urging people to learn to hear in dislocated postwar voices how "habits of hell [gotten] into its syntax" will not imply that such language is "being used to run hell." Steiner notes that in Gestapo cellars stenographers took careful notes toward a bizarre project of recording the expressions of "fear and agony wrenched, burned, or beaten out of the human voice,"[91] every scream, every severance of agonized articulation, every word trapped halfway in the mouth. Fifteen years of keeping almost complete ethical distance from such "experiments"—for in the hands of the Nazi doctors, as psychiatrist Robert Jay Lifton has shown, these had been deemed intellectually valid, academically constructive innovations, nominally "experimental"[92]—the very notion of *experimentation* needed to be reclaimed. Hannah Arendt's *The Human Condition* (1958) began to undertake precisely such reclamation. W. H. Auden, living in the United States, responded favorably to Arendt's ideas about alienated language, quoting Nazi scientist-turned-ally Wernher von Braun: "Basic research is when I am doing what I don't know what I'm doing," and Auden observes in a piece he called "Thinking What We Are Doing" that "the historical consequence of these deeds has been the alienation of man, not from himself, but from his world." This was the particular passage in Arendt to which Auden responded: "What men now have in common is not the world but the structure of their minds, and this they cannot have in common, strictly speaking. . . . The reason why it may be wise to distrust the political judgment of scientists qua scientists is that they move in a world where speech has lost its power."[93] After the war Arendt felt that the line between the comprehensible and the incomprehensible had been crossed in the final stages of totalitarianism, at the moment when Nazi anti-Semitism evolved into a mechanized "scientific" program for extermination. For Arendt "incomprehensibility" should suggest a leap into the void not as a counterresponse—but rather, remarkably, as a *strategy*.[94] Yet "we have no tools to hand," she confided to the psychiatrist-philosopher Karl Jaspers in December 1960 about the upcoming trial of Adolf Eichmann, "except legal ones with which we have to judge and pass sentence on *something that cannot be adequately represented.*"[95]

Auden's reading of Arendt led to his essay of November 1959 on Shakespeare's *Henry IV* and Falstaff, in which he defined forgiveness as impossible to convey in language (unless it is asked for), to which Arendt responded in a long letter dated February 14, 1960, about judicial pardon and the Nuremberg Trials—a letter, to which we will return in chapter 4, that predates Eichmann's capture by just eleven weeks. For an ethical modernist like Celan, the troubling similarities between the attitude evinced by Wernher von Braun toward scientific truth and that of artists claiming detachment from their own processes—artists such as Jackson Pollock, whose abstract expressionism had led him to claim that "When I am in my painting, I'm not aware of what I'm doing"[96]—created a special dilemma for those whose creativity responded to mass destruction by dwelling as, at best, an "I-latency" or, at worst, a "You-distance" (in Celan's terms) inside the survivor's art of fragmentation.[97] As we will see in chapter 5, the avant-garde artists associated with the Zero movement felt a similar distrust of Art Informel (the term given to European equivalents of Abstract Expressionism). In January 1960, a member of the Zero group observed that "Pollock no longer us[ed] art as inquiry—but as an object of anger."[98]

The survivor's art of the fragment was reckoned as a strategy for inquiry. If for George Steiner what was wrenched from victims of Nazi "scientific" torture was duly recorded as difficult fragments about which the critic and theorist should feel obliged to inquire, then one could initiate separation from the torturous motive and yet in one's own writing affirm the language of the severed fragment. This affirmation formed a postdisaster ethical poetics, or "poethics," as Joan Retallack, following John Cage's *Silence* (1961), has put it in *The Poethical Wager*.[99] To be sure, the fragment carries with it a sense of distance, separation, and estrangement, but it does not imply a claim of unknowingness. It is incomplete but not unconscious, not disengaged from ethics. "Fragments," wrote Maurice Blanchot in *The Writing of the Disaster*, "are written as unfinished separations."[100] Writing disaster entails constructive "remembrance as absence," observed Celan, "'as on the houses of the Jews . . . something always has to be left unfinished.'"[101] From this exilic sense of fragmentation "the poem estranges."[102] "You = who is absent," Celan jotted in his notebook of 1960, "you help build the shape of the poem: from its distance."[103] "Art," he wrote in a draft of the speech he gave on October 22, "makes for distance from the I" and yet: "I am *not* looking for a way out."[104] In a poem called "Praise of Distance," Celan seems further agonized by his own apostasy—using the language that killed his parents and set him psychically adrift; he is incapable of presenting a scene of swearing as a tortured voicing or unheard-of sound. That voice is, rather, "the *glare* of an oath"—synaesthetically "den Glanz eines Schwures," in which *Glanz* is a glance having the connotation of gloss or luster, something truly to be seen. The bright yet indistinct lambency of sound forms the key paradox near the end of this text: "embracing we sever."[105]

Embrace entails severance for James Baldwin also, and that paradox powers the hypothetical novel he outlined for his own audience on October 22, the talk in which he began to work out his relationship to the lost people of his world. The "blind optimist" "I" stood alone in the same special glare Celan faced straight on but would seek narratively to find a way of giving the role of subjectivity over to others. "I am not looking for a way out" is an emotionally potent revelation, and helps articulate Baldwin's plan for somehow involving multiple narrative voices, his gnosis of poethical inclusion. The contrast with John Cheever on the same stage is instructive here. His biographer, summarizing Cheever's perspective on the *Esquire* symposium, writes: "It was not a miscalculation to invite a Wasp, a Jew, and a Negro, two of whom were . . . reputedly angry about things."[106] "Angry"? In the final pages of this book I will compare Baldwin's and John Coltrane's simultaneous speculative expressions in 1960 of hope, in the face of others' racist assumptions of their anger, but for now, here in this introduction to the idea of the survivor in 1960, it suffices to sever "a Jew, and a Negro" on the one hand from the "Wasp" Cheever, on the other, who argued that "the only possible position for a writer now is negation." Cheever's symposium talk outlined a strategy opposed to Baldwin's, which included the displaced, spectral, marginal, and murdered people inside the renewed language of the hypothetical novel. Cheever's talk, on the contrary, was called "Some People, Places, and Things That Will Not Appear in My Next Novel," a witty list of everything and everyone he "wished to eliminate."[107] It was a clever and ironic purging, and of course he was only talking about the people and places he felt it was best for aesthetic purposes to *write out* of his writing—not nullification in any material sense. But Baldwin's radical democracy of voices was a promise the younger writer was making to *write in* the threatened other as a counter to the materializing effects the "unseen prisoner in Germany" was still having "on the lives of these people,"[108] those whose lives he knew now his work would embrace and include.

# 2

# Pain-Laden Rhymes

## Challenges to Narrative and the Radical "Writing I"

Leaving the economic miracle aside—whether really miraculous or not, it was by now an established, unalterable priority—George Steiner contemplated the project of the language of survival and insisted, as Baldwin, Rothenberg, and Celan did each in their way, that the writers and speakers of that post-traumatic language "must literally create new words and syntactic modes." These words and modes would need to be deployed within a greater idea of postwar narration finally aware of itself as commensurately discontinuous, doubtful, and still bereft, its very "I" an ongoing problem. Here we explore instances of that revitalized self-consciousness and also, comparatively, a striking contemporaneous lack of it.

## Then Came My Tears

Severance from family and from language, at once, constituted Celan's experience. Pierre Joris, a poet himself and the leading contemporary translator of Celan, has written: "Celan's language, though German on the surface, is a foreign language. . . . Celan's German is an eerie, nearly ghostly language; it is both mother tongue, and thus firmly anchored in the realm of the dead, and a language the writer has to make up, to re-create, to re-invent, to bring back to life."[1] During three years after his parents were picked up in an overnight raid in June 1942 and force-marched across the

Dniester and Bug Rivers, Celan endured forced labor in several Romanian camps run by Nazi proxies. In fragments and across months he received news of the deaths of both parents. In 1944 friends secured him a job in a psychiatric hospital, but he remained "a raw orphan," as John Felstiner has put it, "with literally nothing left but his mother tongue."[2]

His mother had "inculcat[ed] her love of the German language and culture"— and High German was spoken at home, notwithstanding the dialectical German with "its Austrian informality and Slavic breadth" mixed with Yiddishisms all around them in Czernowitz, the capital of Bukovina, a Habsburg province that had fallen to Romania in 1920.[3] Celan's decision after the war to continue writing verse in German, which he referred to as the language of the culture that had murdered his parents, itself forms one of the consistent themes of the writing. Owing to that focus, the majority of Celan poems are metapoetic; they are about the predicament of the very language they use. If "the Nazi tone survives the Nazi vocabulary," he wrote in 1960, the problem of semanticism might diminish but the dilemma then became what tenor and diction the survivor could use to compose counterwords.[4]

In some poems each chosen German term seems to carry iterative remembrances of traumatic severance. In "Winter," the speaker stands in a spot called "here" and imagines his mother freezing elsewhere, in the Ukrainian snows. A *here* of the postwar life wrings memories from remnant language. It is a postwar *after here* displaced from the German-speaking place, contrasted with a *during there*, fixing a scene of murderous criminality in the distant East. *There* is the origin of seasonal weather, which *here* somehow drifts back toward the bereft, change-repressing speaker. The presumed therapeutic effect of bearing witness to the severance from Mother is nil. Words of the poem do not wash away the image of a forced march across the river. "Here all my tears reach out to you in vain." The word Celan selected was *Tränen*—crying with an emphasis on watering, implying that the speaker seeks through tearfulness to be part of the fateful pilgrims' river-crossing into the Ukraine and under the precipitation. The weather is here and now. "Es fällt *nun*, Mutter"—*now*. Felstiner renders: "It's falling, Mother, snow in the Ukraine," with "now" implied in weather reports' typical present tense.[5] That which falls in chilly autumn and winter are impossible "black flakes." In the poem of that title, as in "Winter," weather no longer occurs in its natural cycle, which precipitates the ashes of bodies burned in open graves. The fog of this atrocious war is both usual and artificial. Smoke arising from genocidal incineration "obeys physical laws like any other: the particles come together and disperse according to the wind," as André Schwarz-Bart observed in *The Last of the Just* (French, 1959; English, 1960)—his parents, torn from him too, had been deported to Auschwitz—and yet "the only pilgrimage . . . would be to look with sadness at a stormy sky now and then."[6]

The Mother of Celan's "Winter," whose words are delivered, as by the post, like an autumn leaf "from Ukrainian slopes," returns to the scene of her surviving child a maternal message that overtakes his writing. Her words as conveyed by him occupy twelve lines of the nineteen-line poem. The world will never turn green again, the Mother's missive observes. "Now you're learning to weep": to suggest not that he knows finally how to grieve in such a way as to live a life without her, getting beyond the killings, but that the poems, conveyed in her cherished German, flow painfully forth. "Winter" ends, as many of Celan's poems do, with a sound—or, rather, a reference to the way words make sounds—to which the speaker strives in vain to be attuned. The wintry weather of "Winter" strokes across the "torn / strings of a strident and discordant harp," an Aeolian instrument enabling the Mother-muse to play her song through the poet as receptacle, a medium of lyric voice. It is a "discordant" instrument, but every so often in verse written otherwise "in vain" and "at times" "a rose-filled hour is tuned"—and only *then* does the Mother die, waking to the fact that the son too "sank in snows of the Ukraine." Inside such words-about-sound they are briefly reunited.[7]

"Nearness of Graves" somewhat clarifies the language problem. The disappeared Mother is again addressed. Are the waters of the Bug River, navigating the fraught Poland-Ukraine border, able to report blows that struck her? The question is asked in a rhymed couplet, ending "Bug" / "schlug." Four further couplets pose rhymed versions of the question about Mother's fate. The final query refers to the son's choice of language for overall asking. "And can you bear, Mother, as once on a time, / the gentle, the German, the pain-laden rhyme?" Felstiner's choice "pain-laden" for *schmerzlichen*, rather than "painful," maintains the regularity of the meter. The final line is nearly a waltz. The seeming ease of reading the poem, with competently deployed sounds, both rhythm and rhyme, and its neat parallel couplets (one each on river, field, trees, god, and language), creates contrast with linguistic self-loathing. The speaker expresses guilt that the Mother taught him such a language of deep historical and familial resonance, a way of maintaining class and ethnic differences from others in Czernowitz, those who had gone more culturally local—there at the eastern edge of the Germanic world. After her death at the hands of German ideology, she must endure her own son's perfecting of its "gentle" usage. The graves are so near, indeed, that they reside at the end of every crafted couplet.[8] All poetry after the

Nazis' Einsatzgruppen—mass murderers of families in these forests and steppes—should perhaps be barbaric, as Theodor Adorno would have it in 1949, but in fact this is *not*, and it *rhymes*, and *that*, not the absence of poetry but its presence in an ongoing prosodic language (and it can even waltz like any self-respecting Austrian), was the tragedy.

In 1960 three crucial elements of Paul Celan's life and work converged: (1) his intellectual and amorous extramarital relationship with Ingeborg Bachmann was intensified by cross-purposed, sometimes misinterpreted messages and letters and by several extended meetings; (2) the awarding of a major prize and with it the opportunity to give the October 22 speech, which he used to formulate his most important statement about poetics, and arguably one of the most difficult and influential expressions of why experimental art is vital in a world in which mass killing had become imaginable; and (3) the clarification of his "ambivalence to embody his whole truth" about his Mother's murder, in a struggle with a poem that was virtually his only direct expression in verse. This last factor entailed a poetic effort intensifying his anger over accusations of hermeticism. As for the speech, it asserted, in a counterversion of what has become known as the survivor's belief in the will to bear witness, that "the poem today . . . *clearly* shows a strong tendency towards silence" and yet the "tendency" is a way, a means, a path toward a poetic situation never arrived at, as it resists and counters silence, and thus, in a complex theorization of indirectness, such a poetics "has only *indirectly* to do with the difficulties of vocabulary, the faster flow of syntax or a more awakened sense of ellipsis."[9] As for the rare non-opaque poem and the lover: the lover interpreted that poem as accusing *her* of murder, even though it is addressed to the mother, and puts its own troubling spin on witnessing and silence: "Mother, no one interrupts when the murderers talk."[10]

"Wolfsbohne" ("Wolf's Bean") is the title of the atypical poem. Celan was working on it in 1959; a copy of the typescript thus dated reached translator Michael Hamburger, who eventually published it with the permission of Celan's son Eric after the poet's suicide. As Celan gathered work for the collection titled *Niemandsrose* ("The No One's-Rose" according to Felstiner; "The Noonesrose" per Joris)[11] a series indicating the "semantic explosion" of poems written from 1960 to 1962,[12] he pondered whether to include "Wolfsbohne." As late as just a few months before *Niemandsrose* was published, that poem was included in the contents. In the end he excised it from the book and "suppressed" it thereafter, although, as Hamburger notes, he "took care to preserve it."[13] The poem's ingenuous candor—it is almost stylistically aligned with the kind of writing celebrated as "confessional" by Robert Lowell in 1959 (*Life Studies*) and 1960 ("For the Union Dead")—leads Hamburger to conclude that it bears a relation to Celan's struggle against the critics' equation of, on one hand, his strategy of "resorting to extreme, insoluble polysemy" and, on the other, his inability or unwillingness "to embody his whole truth"—in other words, the facile therapeutic assumption that the maintenance of an intense Shoah Complex depended on linguistic isolation and exacerbated hermeticism. What better a way of avoiding reintegration and "adjustment" to postwar Germany, to the hollow miracle, than relentless opaque neologism? He affirmed this alienation not just by residing in Paris, but by doing occasional reality checks when on forays into Germany, during one of which he wrote in a letter to his wife, Gisèle Celan-Lestrange: "The German with which I construct my poems has nothing to do with the one that is spoken here."[14] (This is not the same as saying, "What was said in German under Nazism is a death," a point made by Jacques Derrida when asked about Celan's writing and "crime[s] against the German language.")[15]

In October 1959 Celan found and read a review of his *Sprachgitter* in a Berlin daily newspaper and then mailed it to Bachmann, asking her for her response. "He is less inhibited [than other poets writing in German] and burdened by the communicational character of the language," the reviewer, Günter Blöcker, wrote. "Admittedly, however, this is precisely what often induces him to speak into a vacuum. It seems to us that his most convincing poems are those in which he does not abandon all connections to the reality located outside the combinatorial fervour of his intellect."[16] Hamburger has recommended reading "Wolfsbohne" as a challenge to such a sense of abandonment: had Celan "been able to bring himself to include the 1959 version in his book, every responsive and responsible critic would have had to think twice before describing Celan as a 'hermetic' poet." (Inside the translator's personal copy of *Niemandsrose* Celan inscribed the words "ganz und gar nicht hermetisch"—absolutely not hermetic.)[17] Whereas earlier poems had shifted from address to the Mother to other subjectivities in all manner of verbal displacement, including the logic, grammar, and vocabulary of address itself—bearing out the concept of difficulty "aris[ing] from the obvious plurality and individuation which characterize world and word," as George Steiner put it in "On Difficulty"[18]—here "Mutter" was directly addressed in nearly all of the poem's lines. "Mother, / Mother, whose / hand did I clasp / when with your / words I went to / Germany?" And:

> Mother, I
> am lost.
> Mother, we

are lost.
Mother, my child who resembles you.)

Push the bolt to: There
are roses in the house.[19]

These lines suggest that Celan was attempting to conceive of this poem as indeed befitting the new book he was assembling. If there are "roses in the house," one can bar the door—a definitive version of "Niemandsrose," the rose of no one. It's as if a psychoanalytic reading of the titular theorizing was being made too readily available. That atrocious dreamwork runs something like this: *The son decides to stay out overnight in a hiding spot with friends, returning to the family house in daylight to find it sealed off by the local fascists, and from that moment, terrifyingly abrupt loss of Home and Mother, a scene is repeated in every manner of posttraumatic poetic stress; yet now imagine a ready-at-hand symbol (of love and domesticity and of poetry), and place it inside the house, and then seal off intimate nonworldliness from inside, and one needn't ever have imagined separation from the Mother—a* heimlich *fantasy of prelapsarian unindividuation offering a total counterfactual history, no linguistic alienation from German, no doubled lostness, no son of the son who too comes from the Mother (though not the wife).* The poem perhaps did after all belong in the unpublished notebooks (as in a diary) rather than in a published collection. Doubtless it was too much; it would seem Celan was right to excise a poem that can be read as merely confessional in such a way as to inhibit rather than augment the connection language makes with the world. Such "plurality and individuation which characterize world and word" in an effort like "Black Flakes" are achieved because the Mother's dead letter from beyond the river gives her voice but is framed, and as one reads one begins to believe that the poet-speaker is "learning to weep" because of the "anguish" of "*this world* that will never return green, my child, for your child." It is not a nature poem (rather, indeed, its opposite) and similarly it is not a poem about the state of the poet's mind in which words emerge as mere recombinatory effects of painful solipsism. The poet's own child (a toddler at the time "Black Flakes" was composed) offers evidence of a regeneration despite the Mother's dire prediction. She is wrong about her prospective grandson but she is right about the world. She can issue the warning of the victim of genocide even as the poem mourning her acknowledges the poet's child's difference from her. Only "*Then* came my tears" for Celan as poet. Insofar as the emotional import of this writing is brought through a distortive screen, or speech-grille

(*Sprachgitter*), it connects "aslant" ("schräg") what is otherwise personal neuro-sis with a greater social state of loss,[20] where "We are lost" refers not to Mother and son but to "this world" of "Black Flakes."[21] The politics of style present a paradox not especially difficult, and can lead to the conclusion that is precisely the opposite of that drawn by Blöcker, who purportedly sought Celan's "most convincing poems . . . in which he does not abandon all connections to the real-ity located outside the combinatorial fervor of his intellect." Ironically it's in the emotionally direct speech of "Wolfsbohne," a work the critic might otherwise have better liked aesthetically for its directness, that Blöcker's doubts are most borne out, with its wish to bar the door against anything other than Mother— indeed, "abandoning all connections to the reality located outside." To be sure, however, Blöcker was complaining about just the opposite sort of poem.

Celan was certain that Blöcker's review was anti-Semitic.[22] For a time, Inge-borg Bachmann agreed. But soon she shifted her concern toward Celan's hyper-sensitivity to criticism. "I often worry that you do not see at all how much your poems are admired." His "fame" meant that "people will keep trying to detract from it in any way they can, finally culminating in *attacks with no motive*—as if something unusual were so unbearable and intolerable to them." Celan's sub-sequent responses suggest there is reason to believe that Bachmann's move from affirming Blöcker's anti-Semitic reaction to the poems to her sense of Celan's own depression struck him as *itself* a kind of anti-Semitism (or, more exactly: an insufficient anti-anti-Semitism—the kind that sees "attacks with no motive" as less real than felt by the sensitive Jewish friend about whom one confesses worry).[23] He must have shown Bachmann the typescript of this poem in 1960. He had broken things off in a letter of November 12, 1959 ("I must now ask you not to write to me, not to call me, not to send me any books"), responding to her comment about fame. "You expect me to be content with my fame"—to accept the anti-Semitic response of German critics as motiveless jealousy of an emi-nence. But he turned quickly to the obvious personal reasons why their affair seemed destructive: "I have to think of my mother. I have to think of Gisele and the child."[24] The relationship resumed, and indeed intensified, in early 1960. On February 1, Bachmann violated his request that she not send her writing, and mailed him a copy of her new story "Alles" ("Everything"), which as we will see further into this chapter can be read both as an expression of postfascist mod-ernism and as a response to Celan's particular precarious situation. In late November the lovers met for parts of three days in Zurich at the Hôtel du Louvre, at which liaison she made him a birthday gift of a German translation of

Gertrude Stein's *Three Lives*. Then, or at another point during 1960, Celan showed Bachmann a version of the confessional "Wolfsbohne."[25]

Bachmann wrote Celan a 1,017-word letter she never sent. In this she spectacularly interpreted the poem as accusing *her* of poetically murdering his mother. The letters' editors believe that these are the relevant lines: "Yesterday / one of them came and / killed you / a further time in / my poem"—but note that " 'one of them' is undoubtedly Günter Blöcker." So Bachmann first internalized Blöcker's anti-Semitism, then read it back to Celan as motiveless and nonideological, and then projected herself into that position. She cannot forgive herself for not hating him. "Has someone you love ever accused you of murder, when you are innocent?" Thus the thesis of the long, frank letter is that Celan "want[s] to be the victim." She insists that she *can* understand "the many injustices and injuries" they have endured—leaving open whether this is or is not a specific reference to post-Nazi life—although "the ones you inflicted have always been the worst." She does not "think the world can change, but we can." "We" being the two of them, or perhaps Nazis' victims overall. Then, reproducing the circumlocution Celan sometimes used to refer to the genocide in which his parents were caught, she refers to "the awful things that come from outside" as part of a project to persuade him that "the greater misfortune lies *within* you" and "may poison your life, but you can get through it, you have to get through it."[26]

## The "I" Without a Guarantee

At the beginning of the next chapter we will return to Celan's "Shibboleth," a poem about what happens when an experimental writer sets up a kind of language test that others cannot pass—words themselves as among "the awful things that come from outside." "Shibboleth" is at the same time, as we will see, an expression of Jewish antifascism. Note for now that its inclusion by Rothenberg in *New Young German Poets* presents an opportunity to outline a rough but, I hope, suggestive ratio: Celan accused of irrelevance and hyperopacity is to Bachmann, his equivocal reader-addressee whom he associates with expressions of homeland alienation, as the Rothenberg of the City Lights *New Young German Poets* is to the ambivalent climate of that project's reception in the United States. There was first the problem of association with Ferlinghetti, City Lights Books, and City Lights Press, thus the impression that Celan, Bachmann, Karl Krolow, and the others were somehow meant to align with the Beat aesthetic, which official literary culture in the United States had begun barely to tolerate and somewhat to imitate yet repeatedly assumed was typified by pointless immature whining against American cultural failures, complaints assumed in Roth's *Esquire* symposium speech ("the Beats," he quipped, "the whole thing is a kind of joke. America, ha-ha")[27] and in Paul O'Neill's major *Life* magazine feature, published on November 30, 1959, subtitled "THE SHABBY BEATS BUNGLE THE JOB IN ARGUING, SULKING AND BAD POETRY."[28] O'Neill's coverage was a target hard to resist for the Beat avant-garde, whose work was devoted to extending the dadaism and surrealism the reporter had ignored or misunderstood, whereupon William S. Burroughs and Brion Gysin, taking aleatory revenge, applied the cut-up method to their copy of *Life* itself and produced a poem scrambling O'Neill's words for their book *Minutes to Go* (1960). The cut-up poem was called "Open Letter to Life Magazine":

> *and plunged aint-dancers wit unfortunate malfunct Molotov last seen wait on Varso-message-knives-costume in hort 22. Sample a drug called heavy commitments.*[29]

The point, of course, was that a random dadaist sampling made as much sense about disjunctive postwar life as the *Life* reporter had made. *They* weren't the "aint-dancers"; the square journalist was—strung out on his own heavy realist commitments. *Poetry* magazine, hardly *Life* but capable of publishing condescending pieces about the Beats even as late as 1960, assigned *New Young German Poets* to Theodore Holmes. Holmes was a poet favored then by editor Henry Rago at *Poetry*,[30] *lauded* by R. P. Blackmur as "*free* of experimentation" and someone who was said to "out-Wordsworth Wordsworth," writing a language so transparent and self-evident as to be "impervious to the annotation" (itself a swipe at the cyclonic historical modernist mode of Pound and contemporary Poundians—Charles Olson, Louis Zukofsky—among the New American poets).[31] Holmes's October 1960 review engaged in the habit of assigning guilt by beatnik association. Rothenberg's anthology, Holmes opined in *Poetry*, "has the shortcoming that marks *many of the things put out by this publisher.*" And what was that problematic quality? "The *bitterness* of these poems either cuts them off from their understanding or serves as a compensation for the lack of it."[32] Yet as we have seen, Rothenberg had made it clear—and I am arguing that the poems themselves do also—that a "new *avant garde* . . . is a miracle" and again that "in a nation that buries the past from its children, the pain of their song is a triumph."[33]

By placing a small selection of Celan's poems in the context of work by other German-language survivors, by no means only Jewish writers (they included Ingeborg Bachmann, of course), Rothenberg was asserting an early version of the point Derrida made later when asked about Celan's relationship to language: "the poet is someone who is permanently involved with a language that is dying and which he resurrects, not by giving it back some triumphant aspect but by making it turn sometimes, like a specter or a ghost. . . . *One has to be as close as possible to its remains.*"[34] As we have seen, Rothenberg's own writing about Treblinka derives whatever is triumphant in it from proximity to ghosts. That this kind of intermittently exultant gnostic verse is "Full of strange, meaningless words," to quote Karl Krolow's "The Final Night" from the anthology,[35] constitutes neither "bitterness" nor mere compensatory linguistic surface. Rothenberg had learned from his experience with this work the importance—to the potential development of a new avant-garde among U.S. artists—of what he described for Robert Duncan in a letter of September 27, 1960, as "word-magic," language that would convey the new flight from settled reason, and this is closely connected to his response to the specter of European disaster.

Bachmann was no dadaist or Deep Image poet when she began writing the stories that would be collected in *The Thirtieth Year* (1961). But she chose now to devote herself to the ghastly theory that "a nation that buries the past from its children" can produce songs both painful and triumphant. The plot, such as it is, of the story "Everything" entails a young German-speaking father burying his son and yet in the process excruciatingly instructing himself in the importance of language's mystical relation to mourning, and "learn[ing] the language of shadows!" This was a story she drafted in 1959, shared at a meeting of the Group 47 writers, apparently finished in early 1960, and then mailed to Celan on February 1, 1960, at the cessation of an off phase in their on-again-off-again affair that year.[36]

At least four of the stories published together in Bachmann's *The Thirtieth Year*—"Youth in an Austrian Town," "The Thirtieth Year," "Everything," and "Among Murderers and Madmen"—are about (and are themselves instances of) the languaging of the alien homeland. The narrators' dilemma is conveyed summarily by a question posed to himself, in reference to the next generation, by the young father of "Everything": "Should I not leave the world to him, blank and without meaning?"[37] This is not meant as a rhetorical question. The father abandons the son, yet grim as this sounds the story's theory of language expresses a special hope for the future. Hope is of course what a parent in normal times is supposed to feel about the prospects of a child, but this optimism is different. Are these not yet normal times? As in all the stories of 1959–60 it is easy to misread in "Everything" the parent's overtheorized indifference as disengagement and torpor, as a classic instance of postwar apoliticism. But its refusal of linguistic socialization is idealistic and its theoretical conception of "leav[ing] the world to him [as] blank and without meaning" is exactly as extreme as the story's plotless capaciousness (for it is indeed about *everything*).

Kristen Krick-Aigner, studying Bachmann's fictive strategies, is right I think to describe the young writer as "a child of World War II"[38] when mentioning her spectacular debut at a meeting of Group 47 in 1952. She won the Group's literary prize the very next year and seemed perfectly aligned with this network of postwar German-language experimentalists seeking to liberate writer and reader by making a complete split from the sociolinguistic history of Nazism. By 1960, after not so much abandoning poetry as moving from it to a kind of fiction writing that engaged the narratively disjunctive methods attempted in the verse, she fully developed an intersectional antifascism, concatenating themes (and formal aesthetic implications) of social oppression, war, gendered relations, mental illness, genocide, and linguistic xenophobia. The Nazi occupation of her Austrian hometown, Klagenfurt, beginning in the spring of 1938 had been an unforgettable agony. The effects of the Anschluss, as Krick-Aigner describes it, inspired in verse and playwriting and prose "her lifelong struggle against Austro-Fascism" and created in the mature synthesizing of the stories of *The Thirtieth Year* an integration of "gender issues and historical events of the Holocaust as a means of coming to terms with her experiences during the Third Reich."[39] The persistent reenactment—narration and characterization—achieved by writing through the "child of World War II" is strangely expressed in these stories by the (typically) thirty-year-old male narrator, for instance, the father by now in "Everything" who had been a teen then, and suggests a psychological reading of the narrator's own child as projected from the Bachmannian subject position. The focalizer is the child-victim, *not* the peer of the adult male first-person protagonist but his progenitor. So the linguistic socialization that the parent acting on strange principle refuses for the child is being done too to the *author* of these very words, distinct conceptually but not linguistically from the narrator as a character. Another plausible reading of "Everything" has it that the narrator-father is Bachmann's representation of Paul Celan: the story's autobiographical aspect is her aesthetically and politically (though perhaps not emotionally) sympathetic retelling of Celan's dilemma in relation to his own son, either in mourning for the child of Celan and Gisèle LeStrange who had died, or in response to the fears of disengagement from the surviving son, Eric—and thus a fictive rejoinder to Celan's reasons for withdrawal from her (that is, from Bachmann; "I have to think of my mother. I have to think of Gisèle and the child."). "Everything" might be a version of the long, blunter prose of the letter she never sent. Neither reading is necessary for full appreciation of the story's response to the notion of productive postfascist disaffection, since it is preceded by the story "Youth in an Austrian Town" and the dazzling Beckettian title story "The Thirtieth Year," a sequence of fictions that creates a context for the affirmation of "the language of shadows" with which we as readers of "Everything" must reckon.[40]

In "Youth in an Austrian Town," the distorted lives of the child's converged prewar *before*, wartime *during*, and postwar *after* are described by an unmoored, unnamed first-person narrator who sees the children as a single third-person plural entity, until the ending, which coincides with the end of the war, the new *after*, at which crisis point the narrator is suddenly revealed as an experienced "I" ("*I* was among [those] children") and declared to be a "witness" to *during*. In the perfectly vague penultimate paragraph of this story, readers learn what the children (now "we") "learned," despite the war's disruption of their academic socialization. During the war "we" learned that "everything was as it was, that everything is as it is, and you abandon the attempt to find a reason for everything." The emphatic statement is followed by an incantatory catalogue of seven poetic negatives. The "everything" that is not reasonable despite its being wholly familiar ("everything was as it was") sets up the contemporary narrator-father of "Everything," with his own horrific, unnamable *during*, he who realizes only *after* that he must "beg[i]n to look at *everything* in relation to the child" of the child of the war.[41]

In these stories Bachmann thematizes traditional socialization through schooling. "Youth in an Austrian Town" introduces the concept, by narrating a quick history of rote Ten Commandments–style learnings, followed by a stripping of denotation—by a kind of supercessive overwriting (they "take off old words and put on new ones"); by learning through erasure; by then realizing that words no longer "picture the world"; by unspelling words; by thus feeling deprived of dictionaries and thus left "wishing . . . to look up all the words they don't understand"; and, in the final phase, by falling "in love" but lacking knowledge of any object that might receive such love (or a state of anxiety, anxiety being desire severed from its object). Ultimately, there is the seemingly permanent end-of-war phase of fighting "over a counter-word that doesn't exist." Can one imagine a more compelling, or at any rate more succinct, retelling of the war's seven years—from March 1938, the time of the Anschluss, until VE Day in May 1945, the common Austrian circumlocution was "sieben Jahren"—as an analogue history of dislocated language acquisition? "It's outrageous what they're doing to us," Bachmann wrote in a recently discovered diary in late 1944 or early 1945, and "they" here were not Nazi bombers and strafers but *her own teachers*. "These grown-ups, these high-and-mighty 'educators,' who want to let us get killed." And: "No one in the whole flock of sheep had any idea of the arrogance of these teachers, our supposed role models." While at work in a field, supervised by those teachers, she and other children hid from planes' strafing in huts and a bombed-out market garden, while "a few of the older leaders from the Hitler Youth had come to check the trenches and they shouted 'Carry on [digging].' Despite that I left." The conclusion drawn in the diary: "No, there's no point in talking to grown-ups any more." Insofar as the words of one's teachers need to be unspelled or erased, she sees it as a kind of filicide.[42]

At one point the children in "Youth in an Austrian Town" are permitted to "forget their Latin" and instead of such canonical education they "learn to distinguish between the sounds of the engines in the sky." Thus they experienced for themselves the actual supercession of traditional Hapsburg pedagogy in favor of a new futurist language with its myriad terms for aural aerial destruction.[43] (The discovered diary confirms the lesson in modern discernment. The children knew the fine art of dodging "the low-flying planes [that] strafed," while a teacher nearby crawled around "like a startled weasel." They also knew that the instruction to hide in a cellar when hearing certain sounds from the air was "ridiculous" since "our little house . . . wouldn't stand up to a little bomb, never mind a 100 kg bomb." Here she added: "I'm not afraid any more, only a physical feeling when the bomb drops.")[44] Fifteen years later, the alienated father of "Everything," once himself one of these exhausted, resentful children—born in 1930, fourteen in 1944, thirty in 1960—acts in a sense out of a resistant, alternative instruction constructed of counterwords. "Did I not have it in my power, for example, to refrain from telling him [the son] the names of things, from teaching him the use of objects?" Just as the children in the first story end by reciting their enumerated negatives in (non)relation to the trees, ponds, and gardens because "very little is left to reveal things to us," so the father of "Everything" has a revelation about an antiacademic linguistic education of *after*: "And when the trees cast shadows I thought I heard a voice: 'Teach him the language of shadows!'" So father and son go for long walks "through the Vienna woods," whereupon terrestrial voices—was it a Johann Strauss waltz spookily updated?—continue to create guidelines for the new pedagogy ("Teach him the language of stones!" etc.). However, the parent of *during* cannot go with the child of *after* into this new linguistic realm, and that, in short, is the cause of the father's disaffection and the son's demise. "I knew and found no word of such language, had only my own language and could not pass beyond its frontiers."[45]

"Everything" is of course a fiction, an allegory of language socialization in this mode-changing transition, and that particular transition—expressed as narrative mode—is in sum the topic of this second chapter. Readers are at risk of misinterpreting the story if they feel compelled to condemn the narrator who enables his son's self-destruction because he prefers the most extreme refusal of Nazi-style denotation and seeks imprecise, mystical shadows as the *only* alternative he can enact. The key to "Everything"—to the story and, following Bachmann's double *entendre*, to all things associated with her teachers' corrupt command to "carry on"—is the realization that a new language must belatedly emerge and that the method of achieving such a state of writing is for elders to "leave the world . . . blank and without meaning." The vacant narrator of "Everything" constructs what Bachmann in a lecture, delivered exactly then, "The Narrator as Author," called a "dreamt-of identity." Such narrative as counterfactual wish necessitates the almost total sacrifice of realism. The new language would make use of the children's nondidactic capacity for vocabularistic and syntactical distinctions between and among the new myriad types of destruction: "I suddenly knew," says the father of "Everything,"

> it is all a question of language and not merely of this one language of ours that was created with others in Babel to confuse the world. For underneath it there smoulders another language that extends to gestures and looks, the unwinding of thoughts and the passage of feelings, and in it is all our misfortune. It was all a question of whether I could preserve the child from our language until he had established a new one and could introduce a new era.[46]

Insofar as Bachmann's linguistic subject position is distinct from the thirty-year-old male narrator who in 1960 sets out story and theme—is that of the "*child of World War II*" who through writing enables herself to become part of the new era mysteriously augured in "Everything"—she then becomes indeed the kind of writer who "could introduce" the great shift. In working out this complex distinction, Bachmann developed a major experimental prose writing, in which she (as Krick-Aigner puts it) "stays hidden behind insufficient words" upon seeing which others felt they were themselves bearing "witness."[47] Such a mode of witnessing Bachmann later called "Todesarten." This is not so much a *way of dying* as *death styles* or *forms of dying*, where *Arten* doesn't directly relate to the English *art* except through the connotations of *type* and *form*. Todesarten would become the basis for Bachmann's unfinished novel cycle and indeed its title. In narratological terms, all this, as a version of the distinction just outlined between writer and narrator (as implicitly between child witness and teacher/parent/adult bystander), was described in the lecture "The Narrator as Author."

The talk was given on December 9, 1959, at the University of Frankfurt am Main,[48] titled "Das schreibende Ich," sometimes rendered as "The Narrator as Author" as noted, but a literal translation, "The Writing I," better conveys its point, which is enacted in the experimental narration of *The Thirtieth Year*. The point of the lecture is that, although sadly "derided" and "mishear[d]" ("as if no one were speaking"),[49] the experimental " 'I' searches for, finds, and orients itself by nothingness." The "I" then "only comprehends its tragedy . . . as doom," and just "when no one believes him, . . . one *must* believe him . . . as it [the unconfi-dent ' "I" without a guarantee'] starts, as it gets a chance to speak, as it frees itself from the uniformity of the chorus, from the silenced congregation." Finally the "I" thus "will have its triumph" and will be "brought forward again and again in literature."[50] Working against the hugely popular related narrative genres of historical nonfiction and the "eyewitness" diary, Bachmann advocates for imag-inative art permitting the ethically generative confusion of several narrators and several versions of the single narrator inscribed into one text. That braiding causes a positive proliferation of "I-problems," the acceptance by the writer her-self of the "sentence coming from an 'I' without a guarantee" ("ich ohne Gewähr"), and the unidentifiable figure speaking out of words that "behaves itself quietly, trusting its own comprehension."

Bachmann at the Frankfurt podium expressed her frustration. This problem-atic subjectivity, no less difficult sometimes than the horrific, unsayable content she felt an obligation to convey, must be rendered in a lonely state. Such isola-tion, Bachmann contended, is a particular postwar phenomenon. "The 'I' is not a problem for us," she bitterly observed, "when a historical figure, such as a poli-tician, statesman, or an army officer, steps into a memoir with their 'I.' " Read-ers expect and applaud the stable "I" of "reports" penned by the likes of Charles de Gaulle and Winston Churchill. They read that first-person pronoun as "iden-tical to the author," even when it is obviously performative and only "conveys their opinions." But it is far from the " 'I' without a guarantee" necessary for bringing real change in representation. "The Writing I" proposed avant-garde narration as postwar poethics. The initial step was to object conscientiously against "this confident, unbroken 'I'" flowing "naturally in the famous memoirs," and to dissuade "the zombie-like [verblödet], disoriented readers [who] devour the leftover scum of memoir literature, allowing themselves to be impressed by the 'I' of SS Generals."[51] I doubt one can come closer than that strong assertion for an antifascist narratology.

## New World, New Language

In "The Writing I" there is no mention of Chaim Kaplan or Anne Frank, or of Elie Wiesel's Night (French, 1958; English, 1960), and in any case it was not Ingeborg Bachmann's intention to devalue the diary of traumatic witness. Yet she did want to explore how—in genres less well recognized as offering therapeutic value to the writer whose unsayable X urgently needed saying—there was an even greater historical responsibility because of the admission and inclusion of narrative I-problems. Krick-Aigner summarizes the concept of Bachmann's speech this way: "History is thereby reflected in the telling of the personal, historical-cultural narrative, and not in the history represented and assumed to be factual in traditional historical works."[52] It is not the historian or memoirist but rather the imaginative artist, affectively embracing the "derided" and marginal creative schreibende Ich, who will "fulfill the obligations of the 'I' coming out of his mouth, if he can handle it."[53]

It can now be noted that such thinking as described earlier about the relationship between the postholocaust will to bear witness and the complex problems of narration would not become an accepted aspect of the discussion, academic or otherwise, for another fifteen years. Acceptance came with the shift from genocide as largely the purview of diplomatic and regime historians, political scientists, and a few social psychologists in the academy, and political journalists outside it, to that of literary theorists, literary critics, experimental documentarists, conceptual artists, postmodern anthropologists, and theorists of historiography prepared to make this particular linguistic turn. The focus on survivor testimony, the "I-problem" of witness as narrator and of those who would engage self-consciously in interpretive literary devices (such as Primo Levi resorting to Dante's Inferno at the turning point in Survival in Auschwitz, a pivotal memory after of literary remembering during), was unusual in 1960— avant-garde in still another sense. A rare contemporary exception, along with

Levi, was the writer-psychiatrist Frantz Fanon, whose use of the serial first-person case study—more shortly on this mode—permitted witnesses traumatized by the experience of murderous authoritarian force to narrate their own mental illnesses. Bachmann's shift from relationships of subject-to-object to those of subject-and-subject—in her hyperempathetic connection with survivor-poet Nelly Sachs in poems such as "Dialects" (written in this period and published in *Poems 1957–1961*) and in "Das schreibende Ich"—encouraged a turn toward a focus on *content* that was itself language-oriented, otherwise lacking in discussions of the continuing effects of fascism.

Bachmann was right to observe in her Frankfurt talk that it was an era dominated by historians' methodological assumptions. It was a time when references to "the telling of the personal, historical-cultural narrative, and not . . . the history represented and assumed to be factual" would be "derided" as fictional, irresponsible, and worse. The best-selling narrative tome *The Rise and Fall of the Third Reich* by William L. Shirer was published in October 1960, a "monumental chronicle" based on access to German archives and on Shirer's notes and memories of his experiences in Germany as a journalist,[54] and I have found no comment even passingly mentioning the degree of certitude—"this confident, unbroken 'I,' " per Bachmann—expressed through the *form* of descriptive language Shirer used. "Lucidity and reliability" were the stalwart qualities of the *content*, aspects of it that were "compelling" rather than indications of a selective, affective writing method.[55] Nor was the point that the writer had let "the facts speak for themselves" meant as historiographical assessment,[56] or as a recognition of the potential trouble created by any whole synthesis of perpetrator history.[57] Yet the facts of psychological effects on subjugated people of racist theories put into active practice as state policy—Frantz Fanon's area of focus—most certainly do not "speak for themselves." They can at best be conveyed in the representation itself as a commensurate aspect. Shirer's was just the sort of journalistic narration of which Bachmann in "Das schreibende Ich," Fanon in *The Wretched of the Earth*, and Amiri Baraka in "Cuba Libre" bitterly complained. The writer's "historical role enforces the naïve announcement of his 'I,' " as Bachmann put it, and that naïvete unfortunately is "not based on [the historian's] authorial *talents*," or on methodological self-awareness of narrative problems associated with "the obligation [*Verbindlichkeit*] of the 'I' " reporting such traumatic history,[58] or on the historian's transference or readiness to serve as a secondary witness. Hugh Trevor-Roper's prominent review of Shirer's book went so far as to say that now "it is *easy to describe* Hitler's method in retrospect," and by that he did not mean anything but praise. Gordon Craig in the *Herald*

*Tribune* called Shirer's book "severely objective."[59] Even those who sensed affect motivating Shirer's project referred to it as "angry *description*."[60] Reviewers focused on asserting the ongoing primacy of historians. Whereas the Nazis represented their revolution as inexorable, it was the job of the writer, in contrast to any ideologist, right or left, to show plainly if ploddingly how "in fact nothing is inevitable in history" and that everything must be described and indeed can be.[61] No language of shadows here.

Shirer hewed to the "Luther to Hitler" line of German history and this led him to his method. If German fascism was "but a logical continuation of German history," in Shirer's phrasing,[62] then the writing of that tellable story would be traceably linear and, moreover, it would not ultimately alter anything if the sourcework was itself German—as if Hans Frank, Nuremberg defendant, hadn't said, "Isn't it funny how the German mania for making complete records of everything works out."[63] Fact-checked totalizing was no irony. "Here for the first time," the Simon and Schuster dust jacket announced, "is the complete story."[64] After Eichmann was captured in Buenos Aires on May 11, 1960, the animated discussion that ensued seemed naturally about what he had ordered to be done and which people or state had the right to describe it—not whether it *could* be adequately described from a certain perspective, or what mode of ascertainment could avoid misconveying the weird remoteness of this person's murderous zeal. The Mossad and government prosecutors were reluctant at first to bring Eichmann to trial on the basis of any witness testimony, for fear of establishing a future of war crimes trials "more vulnerable to a variety of justice system breakdowns."[65] That distinction made necessary nine months of interrogation and extrawitness fact-finding, and during the interval the problems of representation in this special situation, the vicissitudes of testimony—the I-problems we encounter in every child and parent in *The Thirtieth Year*—were largely absent from the discussion. Such self-consciousness would come with Hannah Arendt's decision to focus on the language of genocide in her reporting for *The New Yorker*, and even then the very idea of such a putatively secondary focus was controversial.

Notwithstanding the superficiality of analyses of the role of witnesses, the holocaust as a topic was back. The reasons cannot be wholly accounted, and in any case are not necessary for our understanding of the writings just then of the major figures of the three chapters in this book's first part, people whose motives as survivors and/or witnesses had never in the least diminished. But for most of the artists encountered in the second part, its latter seven chapters, the new awareness—and their counterresponse to its retrenched, normalizing manifestations—is crucial to their work as the 1960s began. Some elements of the fifteen-year delay owed to the unavoidable slowness of behind-the-scenes evidence-gathering for trials and also to inhibiting and distortive factors of Cold War politics, and to the increased willingness of not just traumatized witnesses but guilty bystanders to be involved in a collective retelling of stories of atrocities. For a few, suppression of trauma diminished over time after adamant calls, throughout the 1950s, for adjustment and socioeconomic normalcy. Then at a catalyzing moment—the resurfacing of Eichmann triggered it—there was a global, collective return of the repressed. To be sure, so much more was going on than Eichmann's capture. Fanon in Tunis felt he needed to remind those

2.1 Yasushi Nagao's photograph of Japanese politician Inejiro Asanuma being stabbed by Otoya Yamaguchi, October 12, 1960. The photo won the 1960 World Press Photo of the Year and the 1961 Pulitzer Prize. Originally published in *Mainichi Shimbun*. World Press Photo. Mainichi Photobank.

enrolled in his "Social Psychopathology" course in 1959–60 of the major pro-Nazi movements in wartime Iran and Iraq and of the many Algerians who had enlisted in the German army.[66] Albert Camus's *Resistance, Rebellion, and Death* (1960) was published, and finally for the first time his *Letters to a German Friend* became widely available; those bitter messages had been published clandestinely during the Nazi occupation but their warnings now read ominously as postwar predictions: "You will not be ashamed of your former victory," Camus had written to his German friend in 1943. "Rather, you will longingly remember it."[67] A decade and a half of once-intense denazification seemed on unfirm ground. Arendt, visiting Frankfurt during the winter of 1959–60, spoke with a woman who had lived through prewar and wartime, and said: "It's as if we were walking on swampland again."[68] Then there was the tense superpower confrontation over Berlin, causing anxiety among expatriate and refugee Europeans such as Arendt, and those remaining there on both sides of the separation; a plan for Dwight Eisenhower and Nikita Khrushchev to meet in Paris in May was scrapped because of the crisis following the downing of Gary Powers's U-2 spy plane on May 1. Between 1959 and 1961 forms of Nazism were resurgent in West Germany; neofascism became a partisan political and electoral issue in a way that in many regions had been held off since 1945. A wave of neo-Nazi, anti-Semitic, and racist vandalism swept Europe, and inspired copycat incidents globally. Emboldened police in South Africa, during the mass killing on March 21, 1960, known soon as the Sharpeville Massacre, engaged in "a degree of deliberation in the decision to open fire" and murdered fifty antiapartheid protestors (not, in other words, merely "frightened police officers losing their nerve").[69] The next day this atrocity was featured in a front-page *New York Times* story,[70] and by April 15 the Mississippi House of Representatives voted a resolution commending the South African government "for its steadfast policy of segregation . . . in the face of external agitation."[71] A member of the right-wing *uyoku dantai* group, Otoya Yamaguchi, cried out for the return of Imperial Japan as he murdered the head of the Socialist Party during a public debate. The debate in essence was reassessing Japan's relationship with the victors of World War II, the first time in fifteen years the U.S.-Japan security alliance was seriously in doubt. A photograph taken at the very moment Yamaguchi withdrew his sword from the body of Inejiro Asanuma (figure 2.1) won the 1960 World Press Photo award and, for Barbie Zelizer, not only significantly shaped global news just then of fascism's reprise but has permanently influenced how "news images move the public."[72] Meanwhile in Rome the neofascist Tambroni Cabinet ran the Italian government from March through July—Fernando Tambroni had been with the paramilitary blackshirts during the war[73]—and in Cologne swastikas were being painted on the synagogue.[74]

While researching the West German response to Shirer's popular historicizing, Gavriel Rosenfeld discovered numerous "thinly cloaked references in the German press to American Jews as responsible for rising anti-German sentiment in the U.S." A *Der Spiegel* article suggested that "Jewish predominance as shapers of public opinion" was what prevented Americans from forgetting "the last war as quickly or as thoroughly as the citizens of the Federal Republic." To blame was "that narrow communications-clique . . . that forms public opinion" located "on the east coast and New York City."[75] Alongside such magical thinking about forgetting, charges were renewed in January and again in April against former Nazis in high government positions in Bonn, for example, Theodor Oberländer, who had once advocated the cleansing of the European East of Poles and Jews and was now the minister for refugees (of all regrettable posts).[76] On May 21 the *New York Times* reported that 950 Germans accused of involvement in crimes against humanity at Auschwitz would face charges issued by the chief prosecutor of Frankfurt.[77] The investigations into the mass gassings by SS at Treblinka also took a significant turn in 1960, when August Wilhelm Miete, nicknamed "the Angel of Death," who was involved in many if not most of the killings while stationed at the "Undressing Yard," was arrested and imprisoned in Düsseldorf on May 27.[78] On June 23 Franz Albert Rum, an assistant of Kurt Franz at Sobibor and Treblinka, was seized; Rum had brutalized prisoners with a whip and aided in one hundred thousand murders.[79] Richard Baer, the last commandant of Auschwitz, was found working as a woodcutter in a German village,[80] while the English translation of the autobiography of Rudolf Höss, Baer's predecessor, was published after fourteen years of inaccessibility.[81] Whereas Shirer's idea for a big definitive book about the Third Reich had made no headway with editors and publishers in 1954 and 1955, by 1960—as enormous sales and widespread reviews indicate—the reading public seemed ready.[82] Niklós Nyiszli, "the prisoner pathologist,"[83] published the blockbuster book *Auschwitz: A Doctor's Eyewitness Account* during the summer.[84] In late July the "In and Out of Books" column of the *New York Times* casually noted ("Speaking of trials . . ."!) that there were already "at the moment" five books about Eichmann "either just out or coming out."[85] Six weeks later the same column, announcing the advent of a new English translation of Hitler's *Mein Kampf,* was illustrated by a sketch of a proper lady in a bookstore, searching for gardening books but consternated by shelves overflowing with tomes about Nazis (figure 2.2).[86]

**2.2** Sketch embedded in the "In and Out of Books" column, *New York Times Book Review*, September 18, 1960. Illustrator unknown.

The clamor was rising fast but the mode of representations was narrowly defined. That "Nazi Criminals [Are] Still a Problem" (to quote the headline given a piece of news analysis published back on January 10) was the inadequacy of jurisprudential scope, the earlier prosecutorial limitation of the Nuremberg Trials—not relevant to the narrative difficulties of *das schreibende Ich* expressed through the convergence in language (rather than the separation) of "the beater and the beaten / the persecutor and the persecuted," as Bachmann phrased it in the poem "Dialects." Even Bruno Bettelheim, who had been pondering literary genre (fairy tales) and psychoanalysis in relation to survivor testimony—in his preface to Nyiszli's account of "medical" work done on behalf of Josef Mengele in the pseudoscientific "lab" operated from a "passion for Auschwitz research" and motivated by conventional "academic ambition"[87]—did not when writing about these matters raise the issue of *how* a person experiencing subjugation creates a narration of the kind that Bachmann, Baldwin, Celan, Sachs, Steiner, Fanon, Baraka (then LeRoi Jones) after visiting Cuba in July 1960, and Achebe in his new novel *No Longer at Ease* (1960) now argued was urgently needed if the goal was to explore the complex interior life of racist hatred. Was the prisoner-doctor narrator in Dr. Nyiszli's writing stripped of the will that had been inculcated in him through rigorous medical training as a forensic pathologist in Germany? Did his explicit preference later for a purely analytical approach to memoir and his repression of transference (the tendency to become affectively implicated in the witnessing) as a writer of such a history,[88] telling his story "not as a reporter but as a doctor," have anything to do with the "exact clinical methods" he used on living prisoners just prior to the dissection he was forced to conduct after their murders?[89] Was his selfhood under duress *during* (at the death camp) and *after* (in the postwar writing)? Might his own suffering—leaving aside that of his prisoner patients—be sociogenic? Can maladies the doctor observed in his slave laborer "patients" be observed of himself as a writer inside the written witnessing? Yes; yes; yes; yes; and unfortunately no—are probably the right answers. A quarter century later another humanistic psychiatrist, Robert Jay Lifton in *Nazi Doctors: Medical Killing and the Psychology of Genocide* (1986), caught up with these questions, but we do well to observe how Frantz Fanon, himself a survivor of harrowing war experiences and of global war's bitter ideological compromising, was just then dealing with them.

## Fanon, a Repositioning of Values

A key moment in the chapter titled "On Violence" in *The Wretched of the Earth* (1961) begins with the metaphor of the forced march, and with the appalling fact that the mass killing of forty-five thousand[90] people at and near Sétif on May 8, 1945, "could go unnoticed."[91] Sétif was a French Algerian market town, and May 8 was, of all days, Victory in Europe (VE) Day. A parade of five thousand Muslim Algerians celebrated the victory. Local French gendarmerie tried to seize paraders' banners critical of colonial rule, whereupon clashes ensued and spread to other gatherings. The very day the French were finally fully liberated, colonial authorities and European settlers committed atrocities against civilians of the sort Free French forces had so long decried and had provided a motivation to rout fascism. And why did the VE Day shootings "go unnoticed" by the press? An explanation pertains, Fanon reflects fifteen years later, to the journalistic ideology of objectivity. "For the colonized subject, objectivity is always directed against him." Photographs illustrating the sympathetic journalist's article covering the brutal colonial situation are intended to "provide proof that he knows what he is talking about and was actually there."[92] Getting the right expository photo is one thing, seeking to comprehend the victim's trauma quite another. The behavior and rhetoric of leaders of new African nations—that year *eighteen* declared independence; 1960 (already then) was named "The Year of Africa"[93]— were described in story after story as "impolite." Yet when the Sixth or Seventh U.S. Fleet was belligerently "heading toward some coast or another" or when Khrushchev ranted about Soviet interests in Cuba, the ex-colonized of Africa "get the impression *they* are being forced . . . into a frantic march."[94] This connection—when Americans and Russians bang away at the *Cuba* question, pain is felt by *Africans*—becomes crucial to an understanding of Baraka's "Cuba Libre" (1960) as a text of "the U.S. Third World Left" situated at the confluence of rising domestic dissent and international revolution,[95] of New Left and global civil rights. Fanon uses the figure of the forced march to associate (1) the imposition of faux objectivity in conventional writing about colonial subjectivity, (2) the distortive priorities of coarse superpower maneuvering, and (3) recent oft-used phraseology for World War II–era atrocity. He describes this, in ironic distinction from a priori assumptions by white people of postcolonial "impoliteness," as "a diplomacy . . . in rage, which contrasts strangely with the petrified, motionless world of colonization." Then he presents an unfunny scene: "When Mr. Khrushchev brandishes his shoe at the United Nations and hammers the table with it, no colonized individual, no representative of the underdeveloped countries laughs."[96] The infamous shoe-banging incident occurred on October 12, 1960, in response to a reasoned, critical speech given by a member of the Philippine delegation whose expertise was public accountability. No photo evidently needed to comprehend *this* racist impoliteness. None seems to have survived, anyway (see figure 2.3), although photographic documentation was likely faked.[97]

As Fanon writes "On Violence" here, the narrator is choosing to report genocidal fury destroying thousands of human lives on the day World War II *concluded* in Europe through an exploration of the sociogenic components of racism. I know of no passage in Fanon's writing better conveying why he trained to become a psychiatrist to support his effort to make sense of the vast inner contours of postwar anti-Blackness. His own experiences during the war and his wartime encounters with fascism and racism as a unified deadly force informed the topics he took up fifteen years later in the lecture titled "The Meeting Between Society and Psychiatry," given in his "Social Psychopathology" course during the academic year 1959–60, and in *The Wretched of the Earth* some months later.

When in 1943 Martinique was being run by people installed by the Vichy regime, young Fanon had fled to Dominica to meet up with resisters affiliated

**2.3** Photographs of Nikita Khrushchev at the United Nations, taken on September 23, 1960, and later used to represent the shoe-banging incident that took place on October 12. AP Archives, *Time*.

with the Free French. He returned home enthusiastically soon after Martinique's connection to the Nazis was abrogated, and planned to join de Gaulle's campaign in Europe. He disagreed for now with the Martinican eminence Aimé Césaire, who denounced the conflict as "a white man's war."[98] Fanon's beloved former teacher Joseph Henri also doubted this antifascist enthusiasm, but hearing Fanon's firm view that "freedom is indivisible," offered this warning: "When you hear people speaking ill of the Jews, keep your ears pricked; they're talking about you."[99] A friend later recalled Fanon's stance as he prepared to enlist: "Whenever human dignity and freedom are at stake, it involves us, whether we be black, white, or yellow. And whenever these are threatened in any corner of the earth, I will fight them to the end."[100] He did enlist, and was shipped to Oran. He witnessed Algerians rallying to Pétain, less in sympathy with German military plans than with Vichy's anti-Semitic Statut des Juifs, which deprived the substantial Algerian Jewish population (110,000 people) of their rights as citizens. Operation Torch, which liberated Algiers from conservative French colonial control and made the Allied arrival from the United States and West Indies (with Fanon aboard) possible, had been organized by an Algerian resistance group numbering 377, of which 315 were Jewish.[101] From there Fanon was ferried across the Mediterranean to join Operation Anvil, the Allied landing at Provence in August 1944. By November while under German attack he served an eighty-one-millimeter mortar (with its frenetic, ear-splitting thirty rounds per minute) and was hit by shrapnel from an incoming mortar round and badly wounded. Evacuated and hospitalized, he recovered—and then returned to the front to serve with a relatively "rested" (but constantly frozen) regiment that conducted nightly patrols along the Rhine. He was awarded the Croix de Guerre with a bronze star, the medal pinned on him by Charles de Gaulle in person.

After the war Fanon did not like to speak about these terrifying and disheartening experiences. When asked about his military travails, he preferred to cite a critical point made by Césaire in *Discourse on Colonialism* (1951): that there is a Hitler latent within the "Christian bourgeois of the twentieth century" and that this is the white Christian who condemns fascism because it "applied to Europe the colonial practices that had previously been applied only to the Arabs of Algeria, the coolies of India and the negroes of Africa."[102] Fanon returned again to this position in his 1959–60 Tunis lectures: "If Europeans are anti-Hitler, it is because Hitler tried to do to them what they did to the peoples that they had colonized."[103] Just as devastating was the point he made as a setup to that clincher: "There is a repositioning of values; when independence is acquired, no longer is there any glory for the former combatant."[104] A year later the concept was revised a final time for *The Wretched of the Earth* as follows: "When they have used violence to achieve national liberation, the masses allow nobody to come forward as 'liberator.'"[105] Here was Fanon's definition of the survivor's predicament.

The survivor, having survived the worst, becomes, somehow still worse, a victim of the triumph of the therapeutic. Fanon's attack on the definition of neurosis is founded on observations of this second-level violence. In his Tunis lectures he said, "The mad person is one who is 'foreign' to society. And society decides to rid itself of this anarchic element. Internment [not in concentration camps, of course, but in insane asylums] is the rejection. . . . The psychiatrist is [thus] the auxiliary of the police." This is the special deradicalizing "repositioning of values" that occurs after victory and putative liberation. The survivor, according to Terrence Des Pres and Lawrence Langer, tends to refuse the vocabulary of liberation. Resistance to closure "confirms the need to understand the unorthodox implications of the narrative."[106] The situation is, at best, as Primo Levi points out in *La tregua* (1961), a temporary cessation or truce. "The 'world' to which survivors speak is very much a part of their condition as witnesses," Des Pres writes. "The desire to hear his truth is countered by the need to ignore him . . . and [we] undermine the survivor's authority by pointing to his guilt." Guilt is thus "transfer[red] from spectator to victim."[107] This is Fanon on the tendency to blame the psychotic victim: "Since the patient has effectively lost the sense of the social, he must be resocialized." Referring in the Tunis lectures to life in Harlem (he was commenting on the novels of Black expatriate novelist Chester Himes), Fanon observes "a sort of introjection" by which others' "condemnation is adopted" and "the black individual 'assumes' his own condemnation" and in response to this situation we need to accept "the importance of feelings of guilt with the black as with the Jew."[108]

Fanon was moving from a counter-political psychiatry to a literary form of testimony as sociodiagnostic—a "departure," as Sylvia Wynter has put it, "from the 'particularity of the point of view' of the subjectively experiencing subject," and, as a result of this significant turn, "able to postulate a 'common reality' outside the terms of that point of view."[109] If his psychiatric practice is based on the radical idea that "the doctor has to *introduce himself with innovative principles, so madness is permitted*" (Fanon's emphasis),[110] then the problem of writing he confronted while composing *The Wretched of the Earth* was how to permit a recuperated madness its own way into a self-conscious form of telling that would not be merely confessional. This narrative innovation culminates in the book's long final section, "Colonial War and Mental Disorders," organized around case histories. It includes extended quotes in which those suffering psychiatric disability triggered by violent colonial degradation narrate their stories. Fanon knows this presents a major problem for expected modes of analytical, scientific writing but he is adamant about pursuing the aesthetic strategy. "Perhaps the reader will find these notes on psychiatry out of place or untimely in a book like this. There is absolutely nothing we can do about that." As a writer he felt he had no choice but to innovate. If form aligned with content conveyed by the traumatized, he was now writing out the consequences of well established knowledge from "a host of publications on the mental pathology of soldiers . . . after two major world wars . . . engaged in action as well as the civilian refugees and bombing victims."[111]

## Baraka in Cuba

Fanon of course was already proximate to a revolutionary situation. The contexts of rebellion and of sociogeny as an idea led to formal experimentation, not vice versa. Conversely, Amiri Baraka ventured into such a scene as a political tourist during the summer of 1960 in part because he "felt the need to break out of the type of form" that was constraining him, and because the generative idea of "The Negro as Non-American," to be further developed in *Blues People* (1963), was emerging. His renewed longing for "freedom" had been preliminarily described in "How You Sound??," written in 1959 for *The New American Poetry* anthology of 1960. As writing can be improvised making, its form invented for whatever it needs to convey, so can the poetic "I" be reconstructed. "MY POETRY is whatever I think I am. . . . *I* CAN BE ANYTHING I CAN." Still, at this point, "*I* can be completely free" meant *in the writing*, the only site where such a declaration of independence can be initiated.[112] And otherwise? From "How You Sound??" and prior to the Cuba trip, this Beat-identified statement of the form-content problem highlighted the frustration. "I guess," he told an interviewer later about the transitional moment, "this was not only because of the form itself but because of the content which was not my politics."[113] But now Baraka would discover, as Fred Moten has put it when writing about Fanon's psychopathological study of dispossession and repossession, "how program and informality, organization and spontaneity, go together." "Something emerges" in a revolutionary consciousness, such as Baraka would keenly feel in the summer of 1960, and this "something" is (says Moten of Fanon) "mistaken first as the splitting then as loss" but can then emerge as "affirmative refusal."[114]

"Cuba Libre," published in the *Evergreen Review* in its November-December 1960 number,[115] would lead to affirmative refusal but begins with a Fanonian analysis of the big lie inciting mass social delusion and leading to putatively individual psychosis. "If we all live our lives under lies," Baraka begins, "it becomes difficult to see *anything* if it does not have anything to do with these lies. . . . There are things, elements in the world, that continue to exist, for whatever time, completely liberated from our delusion. . . . That perhaps it is just this miserable subjection to the fantastic . . . that makes your/our worlds so hellish, is . . . presumption bordering on insanity." The essay then considers conventional journalistic "reports," for instance, those published in the *New York Times*, written "by middle-class Americans suffering from that uniquely American sickness called 'identification,'" which aids the spread of a "disease" causing the American

language to use the first-person plural possessive for instances of expropriation—
as in "'They're taking *our* oil.'"[116] Read as a document of its particular moment—
alongside the psychoses explored in "Everything" and *The Wretched of the
Earth*, and the guilty bystanding of "The Hollow Miracle," "The Meridian," and
Achebe's *No Longer at Ease*—the essay "Cuba Libre" is ultimately a critique of
postwar reason. Intellectuals in the United States have been ridiculed by political
leaders as "bumblers," but, worse, "the horrible residue of these paid liars is left
in our heads," such that Americans cannot imagine any view other than that
there is "the free world" (the United States its home base) and that, for instance,
the newly independent Democratic Republic of the Congo, led by Patrice Lumumba
from June until September, was deemed not just unfree but *unreasonable* in
demanding such a state of being. Likewise it was supposed to make sense that
there were some postwar Germans "freer" than other postwar Germans despite
arbitrarily having been split into halves (based on where World War II armies
had ended their forward advances fifteen years earlier). We tend to "reject the
blatant, less dangerous lie," Baraka observes, "in favor of the subtle subliminal
lie." This reflects Fanon's critique of noncoverage of the VE Day Sétif massacre.
Subjects are reduced to objects by assumed journalistic objectivity. "Cuba Libre"
gives over pages to an affective description of an hours-long rally attended by
hundreds of thousands of self-celebratory Cubans gathering at a remote site—
for Baraka, a hope-inspiring experience—only to conclude, in the essay's three-
sentence coda, with a disheartening glimpse of a *Herald* headline in Miami,
seen upon the writer's rearrival on the mainland: "CUBAN CELEBRATION
RAINED OUT."[117] It was a lie. Rained on, yes, but not rained out. The idiom is
political.

So "Cuba Libre" is offered as a counterheadline. If reason deems "the idea of
'a revolution'" to be "foreign," "'romantic,'" and "hopeless," then Baraka's
account must be begin to permit an antithetical state of writing's being, to explore
an emergent right to opacity in a Caribbean rather than a North American bohe-
mian space. Unreasonable, then, in what form? No longer—as this artist makes
the turn from Black Mountain or New York Beat aesthetics to something else—
would the unreason of "rebels . . . who grow beards" and engage in "Drugs, juvenile
delinquency, complete isolation from the vapid mores of the country" be sufficient. It was one thing for American rationalization to create a false sense of
voting in elections as bearing "the gravity of actual moral engagement," with
Republicans and Democrats—Richard M. Nixon and John F. Kennedy then cam-
paigning for the presidency—nearly identical on foreign policy. Quite another
to be deluded into thinking that the survival of international antifascism or

anti-authoritarianism on one hand and the end of ideology or countercultural withdrawal from politics on the other could coexist. Insofar as this ubiquitous "reason" is what "permits a young intellectual to believe he has said something profound when he says"—Baraka was citing his many pacifist colleagues, including dear friends—" 'I don't trust men in uniforms,' " then we must acknowledge the complete demise of the constructive social and aesthetic energies that had been required to intervene against state-led racist hatreds in the early 1940s. For Baraka visiting Cuba, sanity by dint of socialization—our having "been taught since public school to hold [heterodox solutions to dire problems] up to the cold light of 'reason' "—has led to the "rotting of the [American] mind which had enabled us to think about Hiroshima as if someone else had done it." Baraka felt lucky to have experienced this epistemic break, to discover that "we" (by which he meant even the youngest generation of American intellectuals and artists) "were an *old* people already," and that Cubans "and the other *new* peoples (in Asia, Africa, South America) didn't need us."[118] When Cynthia Young sought to define Baraka's work in her essay "Havana up in Harlem" as befitting the "U.S. Third World Left," in a chronicle of the Baraka-Harold Cruse debates that featured early radical-left contexts for Baraka, she knew to provide a detailed ideological interpretation of the visit to Cuba, seeing it as deriving its analysis from the experience of "*new* peoples" during the Year of Africa, notwithstanding its Caribbean focus. In a work of prose largely aware, at least in its final paragraphs, of its status as a document of the Black Atlantic, Baraka was witnessing the formation in 1960 of that emergent U.S. Third World Left writing its way toward possible fusions of countercultural modernity and Black Arts, domestic rebellion and international independence movements, emergent New Left and worldwide civil rights.[119] That fusion would return as a feature of an essay of 1961, "The Jazz Avant-Garde," in a Black modernism being theorized that is not foreign to Black reality—"we are, all of us, *moderns*, whether we like it or not"— shaping European art as much as drawing upon it. "Ideas are things that must drench everyone."[120]

In Werner Sollers's book-length argument for Baraka's "populist modernism," the chapter on "Cuba Libre" began by identifying 1960 as the "crucial turning point," not just for Baraka but generally for an American generation. Sollors cited Staughton Lynd on the rise of the New Left: "The beat writings . . . helped young people take the first groping steps toward a psychological freedom from convention which, in 1960, suddenly found political expression." As Lynd had noted, the year 1960 was "crowded so thickly with events that any summary seems arbitrary."[121] Arbitrary, perhaps, but nonetheless instructive. Consider just New Left emergences. As the year began, Students for a Democratic Society (SDS) was formed in Ann Arbor. On February 1 lunch sit-ins at lunch counters began in Greensboro, and quickly spread. The Student Non-Violent Coordinating Committee (SNCC) was founded in April. That month the Fair Play for Cuba Committee (FPCC) was established in New York. Baraka, for his part, was active in FPCC's activities almost from the start.

Much of what we know about Baraka and FPCC—dates, meetings, projects, leadership roles—owes to detail-obsessed dispatches in his FBI file. At least one complicit informant (likely more) fed specifics. His FBI minders knew (but it was no secret) that his Cuba trip was sponsored by FPCC. They knew that "Cuba Libre" was reprinted as a pamphlet published by FPCC with the "permission of 'Evergreen Review,'" by the Beats—those dupes of the communists—there. Various federal agents summarizing for the Baraka file read "Cuba Libre" closely, or at least often. A "Succinct Resume" inaccurately concludes that the suspect poet "considers Cuba to be a paradise." When he "reached New York" after Cuba ("it seems my life was sucked away. The ground was not real") Baraka mailed a letter to Rubi Betancourt, the Yucatán-based revolutionary he had met in Havana, noting he was "fired from my job the first day" and "had to see the FBI."[122] During the interrogation he was questioned about his earlier involvement with projects seeking to persuade Americans "to show a little more tolerance," in his phrase (as transcribed), and the file reports that he told them one club "was composed mostly of Jewish and Negro students," and in passing used the phrase "both minorities." The phrase was a red flag. "Q: When you say both minorities, what do you mean?" "A: Jews and Negroes." The file takes special suspicious interest in *Yugen*, the journal bringing together Black Mountain, New York School, and Beat artists—a generative convergence with the avant-garde anti-anticommunist left whose contents are flattened by FBI summarizers as "poems written by the 'Beatnik' poets." An FBI informant ventured into the Eighth Street Book Shop, and "inquired" about *Yugen*; the file notes that "HETTIE COHEN" (not the less ethnic "Mrs. Jones," per normal FBI stylebook) was coeditor. Thus proving, of course, that "both" suspect minorities were implicated.[123]

In his letter to Rubi Betancourt, Baraka confesses that "so far" after Cuba "it has been impossible for me to write poetry" and that "something was beaten out of me by that visit." He had in fact written a poem during the trip, or at least drafted it on July 30 in Havana. "Betancourt" is revolutionary pastoral. Although not indicative of the turn toward the experimental form and synthesizing topicality about to come, it asks "What are influences?" and mentions "El hombre," an allusion to two influencers: Fidel Castro, the hombre of the hour, and William

Carlos Williams, who in the mid-1930s, the preceding moment of avant-garde poets' antifascist radicalization, had written his own series of experimental revolutionary pastorals, the leafy, greenery-filled proletarian portraits of *An Early Martyr and Other Poems*. "El hombre" in "Betancourt" seeks guidance from the "strange courage" Williams had previously sought in his famous modernist poem titled "El hombre."[124] The new poem was a "turning away," but *toward* what? Toward what new narrative form of witness to ecstatic antiracist responsiveness? For now there was, at best, a metapoetic take on that new direction. "As even / *this, now*"—the writing itself—

> a turning away. (I mean I think
> I know now what a poem
> is (A
> turning away . . .
> from what
> it was.

The closest "Betancourt" comes to that which "from what / it was / had moved us" is fleeting reference to "A / madness."[125] Such particular "madness" seems more about the state of mind of the aesthetically and ideologically confused North American witness, via "Cuba Libre," than that of the victim of colonial coercion misconstrued through big lies inscribed into descriptivist norms and promulgated by those in "miserable subjection to the fantastic" such that it "makes your / our worlds so hellish," and *thus* "border[s] on insanity." This disorder approaches the madness permitted by the narrative structure of Fanon's *Wretched*.

"The Cuban trip," Baraka recalled in his autobiography, "was a turning point in my life," although neither "Betancourt" nor "The Disguise," another poem responding to the visit, embodies in its form the integrations commensurate with having been "turned completely around"[126] and "shaken more deeply than even I [yet] realized."[127] That would await the writing of *The System of Dante's Hell*, a short experimental novel in which the narrator rages against the dissolutions and degradations of racism, especially in scenes where the narrator, stationed in the Air Force, is living in the American South. *System* is writing that is itself at times dissolute and knowingly degraded, as if to contend that such a modern art, which "scrambled and roamed" among "jagged staccato fragments," could be commensurate with the four developments Baraka felt now as productive if difficult instigations: (1) the "freedom" of "How You Sound??" now meant "shak[ing] off the stylistic shackles of the gang I'd hung around with and style myself after"; (2) insofar as seeing Cuba in 1960 had "shaken him more deeply," the new art must itself be made to shake, to the extreme point in composing *System* that "I didn't even want the words to 'make sense,'" because so much racism directed against rebellion from the North had purportedly made common sense; (3) a union of "Joycean stream-of-consciousness" and Free Jazz "modulation" that would put modernist originality to use in his effort to enact post-Cuba radicalism, moving past the unresisting "'ready-mades' that imitating Creeley or Olson provided"; and thus, (4) the adoption of a radical method for *System*, which he called "association complexes." Association complexes would enable him to connect fragments of witnessed racist experiences to both themes and forms of the "fast narrative" that writers across the Black Atlantic such as Aimé Césaire—whose *Return to My Native Land* was a model for Baraka as he wrote the prose *System*—were using to "break away from the heavy influence" of white Symbolist poetry for the era of global madness and unreason, turning the Beat questionings of "How You Sound??" into the "unheard-of sounds" that Chinua Achebe argued must be uttered from English-speaking mouths contorted by extremity. Baraka's model was to do to American English in *System* what Césaire did beginning in 1936 when he made a "profound new poetry" in prose that "show[ed] how even the French language could be transformed by the Afro-Caribbean rhythms and perception."[128] Putting the innovations of the essay "Cuba Libre" and the novel *System* together, we have: "new peoples" → "new poetry." *The System of Dante's Hell*, published in 1965, would seem to be a half-decade-belated response to the Cuba visit, which in turn had inspired a belated response to the formative experiences of infernal oppression—to growing up in "the torture of being the unseen object"; to being young and Black in the "social dichtomy" of Newark and then serving as a gunner in the U.S. Air Force along with "black m[e]n unfocused on blackness"; to being part of the postwar generation of color coming of age after the war. But as a matter of fact, Baraka wrote much or most of *System* in the months immediately after Cuba, precisely in that stop-making-sense moment described at large in this book.[129] And, as much as the novel looks forward (in Aldon Nielsen's words) toward "smash[ing] the Eurocentric hold on Western art by 'colorizing' the canon, by putting the Western tone scale of art through the signifying changes of African-American expressive transformation" in the 1960s,[130] it also looks back to the previous era, recalling the establishment of the big American lie of postwar reason that made the Cuba trip suddenly revelatory.

The *System* narrator, unfixed in age and often in location, splits into two for the chapter-length, one-act Air Force Base drama titled "The Eighth Ditch (Is Drama," "46" being the younger interlocutor, apparently a poet, while "64" encourages his bunkmate to "talk like where we are." Just when we think 46 is a version of LeRoi Jones, authorially positioning 64 as the wise but antiquated Black generational other, the "Narrator" breaks in and sounds just like the *older* figure, taking his side. 64's authorized reverie in this passage is located temporally in *1947* and presents us with the immediate postwar view:

> Narrator—The mind is strange. Everything *must* make sense, must *mean* something some way. Whatever lie we fashion. Whatever sense we finally erect . . . no matter how far from what exists. Some link is made. Some blank gesture toward light.
>     This is 1947.[131]

The narrator's and 64's shared skepticism of the Cold War injunction to make sense, of the existential lie we fashion "something some way," dated at the whiplash turning from wartime antifascist internationalism to postwar anticommunist reassertions of Jim Crow exclusions and xenophobia, mirrors Baraka's critique of imperial reason in "Cuba Libre" at the start of a new dissenting era. What Nielsen writes of the hellish *System* applies perfectly to the prose report from scorching yet refreshing summertime Havana, a site from which he is finally able to discern "that uniquely American sickness called 'identification.' "[132] "Baraka's inferno is lodged in the gap into which Reason collapsed in the modern era," concludes Nielsen in a chapter-length reading of *System* as Black intertext. "Baraka's knowledge of the gap and of its inhabitants is firsthand [Newark, Harlem, and Louisiana in *System*; Havana in 'Cuba Libre']; he knows that this is where he lives."[133]

## Achebe, the End of Eliotic Ease

So different, it would seem, from Baraka's *System*, the intentionally "flat unemotional style" of narration in Achebe's *No Longer at Ease* (1960),[134] a novel set in 1956–57 and published just as Nigeria on October 1 achieved independence from British colonial rule, enacts a number of similar agonizing psychological reversals—novelistic versions, like those of Baraka's topsy-turvy Dantesque

*System* after revolutionary Cuba and of Fanon's postsurvival Algerian "repositioning of values." Another reversal is conveyed through Obi Okonkwo's status as Nigerian colonial antihero, an ethically ambivalent character "feeling ashamed of studying English" in England yet proud of his having been nicknamed "Dictionary" at his Umuofia school because of a far-reaching English vocabulary; his story, told in Obi's own "been-to" English,[135] mixing in Ibo (Igbo) folkloric terms and conversational Lagos Pidgin, is given by an omniscient third-person narrator. Another rather stunning repositioning has to do with the nuanced political signifying of Obi's decision to write an admiring letter to Adolf Hitler during the war—a striking bit of protagonist's background Achebe observes twice in the novel, and to which we will shortly return. A third reversal occurs as Obi comes to understand the repugnant William Green, an Englishman directing the imperial government office in Lagos where Obi has attained his first job, "a European post," after four years of university in London. In conversation with a friendly white European coworker, who has conveyed to Obi the contents of a tea-time chat in which Green had uttered "the most outrageous things about educated Africans," Obi contends that this colonial overlord "will make a very interesting case for a psychologist." It's a joke to share with his white friend, but then again "Africa played him [Green] false." So Obi historicizes. Green's imperial type, once, back in 1900, was a respected missionary, but by 1935 would have had to make do "with slapping [Nigerian] headmasters in the presence of their pupils," and now at the end of the 1950s, angrier yet diminished, "could only curse and swear." Obi suddenly remembers "his Conrad"—he had studied English literature at university, not a discipline practical or remunerative in the colony as was law or engineering—and "with a flash of insight" decides ominously that his supervisor, Mr. Green, is Mr. Kurtz "before the heart of darkness got him." Obi's "flash" is tonally written to be subject to Achebe's readers' sarcasm, but the "insight" is unironic as a detailed Fanonian analysis of socio-psychopathology, for the deserved fate of Kurtz, at the time of Joseph Conrad's writing, was that he would "succumb . . . to the darkness," whereas Green now was edging toward mental illness in response "to the incipient dawn" (the impending brightening prospect of Nigerian independence).[136] "No Longer at Ease," a phrase taken from Obi's beloved T. S. Eliot ("The Journey of the Magi"), is darkly comic as a citation, yet—happily, even for the ambitious Obi—befits Kurtz/Green's dangerous psychic state. No sooner does Obi finish this analysis of Joseph Conrad's relevance to the situation in Lagos in 1957–58—a moment of serious postcolonial rereading inscribed into this skeptical text[137]—than he reverts to form and concludes that *he* "must write a novel on the tragedy of the Greens of this century."[138] This plan is of course doubly ironic: first, because it is an absurd aspiration as a matter of literary categories and of literary politics in the Year of Africa ("tragedy" is yet another doubtful word Achebe gives to confused Obi to say); and second, because Obi is *already* the main character in a novel, the sequel to *Things Fall Apart* (1958), written by a novelist seeking to make just such "a very interesting case for a psychologist" relevant to analyses, parallel to Fanon's, of the whole mutually destructive psychiatric situation.

Obi Okonkwo "knows book." He received his education on a grant awarded by his hardscrabble Ibo village, and in his Lagos apartment reaches for his volumes of T. S. Eliot or A. E. Housman whenever he needs poetry to make him feel a bit better. Taking Housman off the shelf once, he rediscovered, slipped into its pages, a manuscript of his own poem, titled "Nigeria," which he had written in London in 1955. Consisting of two six-line English stanzas, and regularly though awkwardly constructed (rhyming words are "purity," "jollity," and "unity"), it argues that "To win their freedom fight" Nigerians will want to "walk in unity" even while "Forgetting region, tribe or speech" and somehow still "caring always each for each." Yet Obi's relationship with English does not stand so foolishly against indigeneity as the novice's poem of uplift suggests. In London "he spoke Ibo whenever he had the least opportunity" and fully realized that it "was humiliating to have to speak to one's own countryman in a foreign language." These regrets, introduced early, stress Achebe's point about the situation of narrative language—about the exophonic quality of this book in which all its English readers are presented with the special psycholinguistic problems attending a grandson of the flawed precolonial Ogbuefi Okonkwo of *Things Fall Apart*. Although Obi at university spoke freely in his mother tongue with any Ibo-speaking Nigerian he met on a bus, when using English with a fellow Nigerian university student from another region and having little choice but to use English as a common language he "lowered his voice" so that "proud owners" of British English among Londoners nearby would not overhear and "naturally assume that one had no language of one's own."[139] Obi's choice of studying British literature was at that point a visceral rather than intellectual form of resistance and even of self-annihilation, a version of Bachmann's *Todesarten*. The choice was a rejoinder to the scholarship-awarding Umuofians back home who were "angry" when they heard of the young man's impractical decision to study the art of writing, and at the same time a bitter, instinctive response to white Europeans around him in London whose concept of a single colonial state, despite the merging, mixing, and crossing of many tribal cultures and languages, forced Nigerians into a foreign shared language in a way that served the purposes of chauvinistic "proud owners[hip]." And if the Ibo villager reading English at university could be credited as creating resistance from his opting for verse, then so must be his (and the narrator's) postcolonial interpretation of the looming end of Eliotic ease. This was the transposition Achebe meant when responding in 1964 to those who doubted his fateful choice of writing his fictions in English: "I feel that the English language will be able to carry the weight of my African experience. But it will have to be a new English, still in full communion with its ancestral home but altered to suit its new African surroundings."[140] The expiring "old dispensation" of T. S. Eliot's narrow messianic Magi would *not* entail the erasure of "an alien people clutching their gods"[141] but a reversal of that presumption of alienation. Weren't the *Magi* the aliens? One way for Achebe to guarantee that readers would not miss this deft turnaround was to make language itself a major theme of a novel,[142] and to experiment with that *thematized* narrative writing, by using—as Ben Mkapa (recent English major from a Ugandan college and later the president of Tanzania) observed in a contemporary review in *Transition*—"imagery ranging from Ibo folklore to static electricity," by rejecting novelistic realism through "characters [that] are representational rather than real," by writing overall a "novel [that] is inclusive," in which "one is even at a loss to know whether or not one ought to judge Obi," and *thus* by inscribing in the very writing "the genuineness of the transition" to independence.[143]

Obi's wartime letter to Hitler, a schoolboy's missive sent more than a dozen years before the novel's action, would seem only to serve the plot by shoring up readers' sense, early in the book, of the protagonist's annoying and absurd conservatism, his status as Achebe's antihero in a moment—the time of the novel's publication, that is—of antiauthoritarian feeling. The narrator reports that Obi's letter had "brought shame to the school." The headmaster, "almost in tears" at the thought of a Nazi sympathizer among his young charges, warned Obi that had he been a little older he would have been sent to jail "for the rest of his miserable life." Instead of prison, he got a half-dozen strokes of the cane on his buttocks. When reminded of this youthful escapade Obi is sometimes unable to interpret the point of a superheretical act, "wonder[ing] what came over me." "What was Hitler to me or I to Hitler?" But Achebe is up to something complexly antiauthoritarian in this apparent affirmation of looming fascist dominion. After all, among Nigerians, who almost unanimously accepted England's invitation to join the war, were Nigerian political leaders who had been critics of British colonial rule but reversed position and appealed to all Nigerians to support the war effort. Their role was militarily and economically to defend the British Empire in Africa (only later did Nigerians also join offensive units sent to eastern parts of the empire to combat the Japanese). If Obi's headmaster, as the child was caned, "pointed out . . . that he was a disgrace to the British Empire," our protagonist's eventual confusions might need to be forgiven. The main contradictory effects of Obi's situation—he "knows book" literally and thus won't attain lucrative work in the city, he can't return to parochial Umuofia after he's experienced modern London, he earns a low salary but maintains high social hopes and suffers precarity (spiraling debt) in spite of elitism—lead him to tell aspirational social lies, to engage in schemes triangulating lenders, and ultimately to commit bribery and suffer legal downfall. The Nigerian boy who became this man of ambivalence toward colonial life knew just enough of the conscription of every Nigerian English subject to have felt bitterly toward expectations directed by teachers toward the children. "I didn't like going into the bush every day to pick palm-kernels as our 'Win the War Effort.' "[144] Achebe was recalling the (at first) secret schemes of the British government to retain favorable foreign exchange and ensure the supply of commodities necessary for homefront sustenance in London and the feeding of British troops across the empire. This meant more than usual exploitative resource extraction in Nigeria and the experience of acute food scarcity (and severe rationing that lasted as late as 1948 in some parts of the country), even shortages of those very palm-kernels, the seed of the oil palm fruit, harvested by Obi and his classmates as unpaid laborers (and symbolic in this novel of the "heart of whiteness").[145] The seeds were used possibly as much as a lubricant for machinery as for cooking, the wartime export of which, in any case, was of intense concern to imperial officials.[146] Years later, on the verge of independence at the end of the 1950s, during a friendly argument with his old friend Joseph over their memories of Obi's insanely impolitic letter to Hitler, Obi enjoys the joke for a time, fondly recalling his precocious word choices and his moniker "Dictionary." But he suddenly becomes "serious," and says: "When you come to think of it, it was quite immoral of the headmaster to tell little children every morning that every palm-kernel they picked they were buying a nail for Hitler's coffin." Those stinging strokes of the cane, the experience of being branded as having "brought shame to the school," are searing memories that help create Obi the unlikeable adult colonial protagonist who, with all his flaws as an Okonkwo descendant, nonetheless has a talent for discerning in Green "a very interesting case for a psychologist."[147]

To prepare to write about Achebe's antiheroic exophonic narration, Baraka's choice after radicalization to finish a novel in which he "didn't want the words to make sense," Fanon's arrangement of microstories told by postcolonial psychiatric patients, and Bachmann's strange fictions promulgated by her PTSD-suffering thirty-year-old narrators, I first completed a project of reading eight novels about World War II—generically, "war novels"—published during 1960. Joseph Heller's *Catch-22* (composed through much of the 1950s and not published actually until 1961) finds its own exceptional way to connect psychotic "deadly unconscious logics" induced by the vicious absurdities of wartime victory with miscommunication,[148] parapraxis, lethal bureaucratic euphemisms (for instance, officers acting only "with *greatest reluctance*"),[149] and the overall structure of narrative dysfunction. But otherwise in conducting my survey of fiction just then returning to the war, to be sure, I have been struck by a stark divide. Not so much high vs. low in genre or commercial intent, or seriousness of writerly ambition, as awareness evident in the text itself of the need to connect total war and ideological racist hatred on one hand to the problem of narration on the other. William Golding's novel *Free Fall* explores the betrayal of an inmate fearing torture by the Gestapo in a Nazi camp; the "brutal honesty" of that book—per a review of February 14—does not at all extend to the narrator's sense of his own representation. Perhaps not an unexpected turn for the writer who had created the crisis of self-governance in *Lord of the Flies*,[150] a nonextreme form of writing about extremity, but the same can be said of Peter Matthiessen's *Raditzer*, Robert Shaw's *The Hiding Place*, and Glen Sire's plain mission saga *The Death-Makers* (despite its form-busting claim to "make . . . *From Here to Eternity* sound like a Mother Goose story"). "Our job is to destroy the enemy," says a typically literalistic Allied ranking officer in Sire's *The Death-Makers*. "Any thinking beyond that is pointless. . . . [We are] isolated, meaningless, unrelated as to cause and cure." And this officer's existential predicament? Well, never mind: "No one studies it."[151] "Let the world fall," proposes Sammy Mountjoy in Golding's *Free Fall*, "There was no peace for the wicked but war with its waste and lust and irresponsibility is a very good substitute. I made poor use of destruction."[152] As I examined the thousands of sentences comprising these and other otherwise compellingly plotted works, I had to keep reminding myself that Bachmann's stories and Baraka's experimental bildungsroman belong also to the genre of fiction at the same moment, and that Frantz Fanon and Glen Sire had somehow served in the same war. Bachmann's revelation that "I suddenly knew, it is all a question of language" (to quote the haunting volta of "Everything") occurred because thinking about global war's effects in this manner is hardly pointless or unrelated. Confronting irresponsibility straight on, it was antithetical to a "poor use of destruction." And what of a *good* use of destruction? "No new world without a new language," declares Bachmann in *The Thirtieth Year*.[153]

# Shibboleth

So now it can be asked: What is it about their investments in particular *forms* of testimony, for Celan, Bachmann, Fanon, Baraka, and Achebe—otherwise very different writers working with divergent material, even as they all engage with pivotal personal experiences of global conflict—that enables and indeed necessitates the strong connection between "new world" and "new language" (and crucially, as Baraka put it, "new peoples")? If a distinction between Bachmann's and William Golding's fictions composed at the same historical juncture, or between Achebe's and Peter Matthiesen's—such comparisons seem otherwise absurd and critically useless—must yet be accounted, it is in narrative functions of witness, that is to say, in narration taking form as an act of "secondary witness" rather than witnessing achieved through a strategic artful choice of narrative strategy and the acceptance of transference as the "extremely charged or 'cathected' implication of the historian in the process he or she studies" (as defined by Dominick LaCapra).[154] In these comparisons the effect of heterogeneity can be stretched perhaps to a limit. If so, consider then the tensions operating within the work of any one writer-witness. What, for instance, would it take to perceive a narrative antithesis between, on one hand, the Auschwitz prisoner-doctor Niklós Nyiszli, a pathologist who was himself victimized by Mengele's deathly "medical" command—and whose book-length testimony, *Auschwitz: A Doctor's Eyewitness Account* (1960), might be read as a bearing of witness akin to that of Levi, Celan, and Nelly Sachs (which is certainly how Lifton presents it)[155]—and, on the other hand, the Dr. Nyiszli who was exposed to what Lifton in *Nazi Doctors* identifies as the fascist delusion of scientific hyperprofessionalization?[156] By investing in counterintuitive hope for new uses of language to emerge from the night of the word, typified by Baldwin's certitude in "Notes for a Hypothetical Novel" that "all of us" can "*transform*" a racist nation only after it has been "named all over again,"[157] by Achebe's contention that if English is to "be able to carry the weight" of the experience of colonial racism "it will have to be a new English,"[158] and by the results Fanon was beginning to see (just prior to his early death in 1961) from an antiracist medical practice built upon avant-garde "ethnopsychiatric considerations,"[159] the texts I consider in these pages, describing a year of shift, turmoil, and turning, collectively propose in effect that one must learn to hear such a nuanced distinction, word for word, inside the writer's affective obligation to language about pain. That is the modern artist's postwar shibboleth—the linguistic turn in testimony arising directly first from extreme experience and second from contemplating matters of historiography—doing its radical including by way of the process set up for exclusion. It introduces itself by innovatively tolerating transference and by permitting madness, exactly in Fanon's sense, *before* any attempt to relieve pain would gain credence. Then it teaches readers how to listen for the dissonance of what Nelly Sachs in a poem about survivors calls "their mutilated music,"[160] paradoxically in "dialects that don't relinquish their native sound," as Bachmann put it.[161]

Consider the matter of dialect in relation to such atrocity. In "Dialects" Bachmann acknowledges her friendship with Sachs, and triangulates the Sachs-Celan-Bachmann relationship in a further complication of the Celan-Bachmann connection described in the first part of this chapter. Celan and Sachs, Jewish writers of supposedly difficult poems about survival, were close personally and aesthetically. They shared an interest in gnosticism as in part an apt rejoinder to genocidal super-Reason, and they each experienced a paranoia that is generally understood to have been exacerbated by their relationship.[162] "Dialects / for Nelly Sachs" begins by stipulating a "them" who can be recognized "by their dialects." "Mundart" is the word used to mean *dialect*, but in other contexts it is *idiom* and *vernacular* and, more literally, *mouth-forms*.

> One can recognize them by their dialects,
> the beater and the beaten,
> the persecutor and the persecuted,
> also the fools and the wise ones,
> dialects that don't relinquish their native sound.[163]

The progression of opposed pairings in lines 2 through 4 of this five-line poem—beater and beaten, persecutors and persecuted, foolish and wise—is neither of antonyms nor of equivalences. It's not that their language makes it impossible for "One" (is that the speaker? or any reader?) to distinguish them, in which case beaters, persecutors, and fools might linguistically camouflage themselves among the survivors. The poem suggests something Bachmann was learning from Sachs, and indirectly at the same time from Celan: that "dialects don't relinquish their native sound [*heimatlichen Klang*]"; that they cannot and should not ultimately be extracted from what Rothenberg calls "the darkness behind the current [postwar] slogans"—and also that the ability to hear the dissonances of the victims' localized yet displaced or exilic words, to move language consciousness to the center of the postwar investigation of guilt and forgiveness, is or should be the remedial starting point. The relevant concept of transference, LaCapra has observed in *Representing the Holocaust: History, Theory, Trauma*, is not "of itself explanatory; it does not solve problems but indicates their presence" in writing "working through" the extreme experience.[164] A shibboleth, its root in Hebrew, is an ultimately distinguishable vernacular custom or habit, an aural awareness of the presence of problems, a *heimatlichen Klang* (a recognizable sonority) that was not quite *heimatlich* (homey; at home), implying connotation and value judgment. A shibboleth has sometimes been used as encoded test to tell foe from friend—persecutor from persecuted. This discernment, a form of working through, requires close knowledge of Mundart as an art made phonemically in the mouth. The actuality of the posttraumatic languaged self is what Celan would begin to call "breathturn" ("Atemwende"), a concept animating "The Meridian" of October 22, his mature *ars poetica*. Breathturn provides a pressing, inexorable motive for that languaged self to emerge in a form that is commensurate with its radical dissolution, and in this sense one can read a breathturn in Fanon's *Wretched*, its "notes on psychiatry" seeming to the proponents of Shirer's sort of descriptive, nontransferential approach to be "out of place or untimely," just as Celan's collaged, non sequitur account of survival in "The Meridian" must have caused head-scratching among some in his audience. Celan might have said to them, as adamantly as Fanon to doubtful readers of *Wretched*: "There is absolutely nothing we can do about that."[165]

# 3

# Openings of the Field

## Deep Memory and Its Counterwords

### The Outermost Hard

The young editor included "Shibboleth" in his anthology, I think, because more than any of the poems Rothenberg curated it spoke to the challenge of conveying how to reconstitute a way forward that bypassed the worn paths of communism (and, of course, of anticommunism) yet entailed a radical project. A distressing encounter with Robert Duncan, as we will see, underscored that challenge. Was all this too great a burden for a poem to carry? Perhaps, but this was strategic anthologizing. And Celan's "Shibboleth" does seem perfectly situated as a sort of test of the unrepressed ideas—in other words, is itself shibbolethic. Its words point toward a revival of directly political antifascist writing of the 1930s (with its descriptions and its sometimes obvious symbols) that was somehow at the same time "a new avant garde" whose esotericism necessarily arose from precarity and thus, as the editor put it, stood as "oppos[ition to] the inherited dead world with a *modern* visionary language." He was learning to signal through such a coded European art the reunification of radicalism and modernism after its long wartime and Cold War separation. The modern enigma would compound the old political referent.

Cued from the title to be sensitive to that which is not discernible, readers of "Shibboleth" encounter these mysterious lines:

dark
and twin redness,
Madrid and Vienna

"Madrid"? An anthemic word for many, doubtless here it calls back to the Spanish Civil War (1936–39), such redness the blood in the streets, the murderous effect of mechanized strafing Nazi Junkers—likely a slant nod at Pablo Neruda's legendary poem of 1936 "Explico algunas cosas" ("I Explain a Few Things"), in which "Bandidos with planes . . . / com[e] down from the sky to kill children, / and in the streets the blood of the children" and through which Neruda's partisan speaker, we realize, need *not* explain such things.[1] For a twin of this redness we can see the signifying color of the revolutionary left. And so is the annexation of "Vienna" during the Anschluss of March 1938—its intellectual and artistic life immediately imperiled, its reputation in recent decades as a haven for socialists (the city's nickname from 1918 to 1934 was "Red Vienna") accelerating fascist motives—meant to be merged with the preceding (and ideologically *causal*) signal failure of the early antifascist fight? What aspect of shibboleth itself needs discernment here? The situation is difficult. The apprehensive speaker is "hauled" "into the dust of a market," compelled to salute a half-mast flag "to which I never had sworn." The fourth stanza of this six-stanza poem seems to bring the speaker's reverie to a point of sudden retrospect, triggered by what Lawrence Langer in his research on testimony names "deep memory."[2] Deep memory twins the experience of the round-up and a later, bitterly unallegiant witnessing:

Memory,
set up your flag at half-mast.
At half-mast
today and forever.

The fifth stanza of this poem then addresses itself to "Heart," as if "Memory" had to meet the test of enunciation distinctly from emotions. Heart is urged to return to that market and to "Thunder your shibboleth here in your alien homeland." (John Felstiner's translation has "Cry out the shibboleth / into your homeland strangeness"[3] and Joris has "your homeland's alienness."[4]) This is followed by a colon: readers know that what comes next should be the expected test. And here comes the shibboleth: *Febrero. No pasaran.* The latter phrase,

"They shall not pass," served during the long Siege of Madrid as a quick check of loyalty, a slogan used among allied brigades from many nations supporting the Spanish Republic, uttered in many foreign accents, the favored vocal shorthand for ideological solidarity. By 1960 that byword had come generally to mean any ennobled defense and resistance to resurrections of authoritarianism as they presented themselves even in the guise of anticommunism, that antonymic response to centrist adjustment and even resignation: "This too shall pass." For the German-language survivor to use so ideologically overdetermined a leftist slogan might seem facile, but then again the phrase had been unlocal and ecumenical almost from the start.

"Shibboleth" called paradoxically for a standard of breathturning that is inherently *comprehensible* inside the alienating homeland, be it postwar Czernowitz (where a tiny remnant of Jews now lived and where effectively all traces of Yiddish and Hebrew language and culture had been annihilated), or Celan's adopted Paris, or (for Rothenberg) postwar Jewish Brooklyn, or—the final place name given in the poem—"Estremadura." The reference might seem to come from nowhere: "let me lead you away / toward the voices / of Estremadura."[5] The far-western province of Spain was the historical extreme edge of Christendom and a symbol generally of any linguistic outpost, a site that has come to signify, from its Latin root, the "outermost hard," the limit of secure border in an occupied territory. The final lines of "Shibboleth," although they seem to point lyrically toward romantic Xanadu, an escapist's place attractive to the traumatized as mythic oblivion, contain at the same time a particular geopolitical reference, the western version of the writer's native "most easterly" Bukovina, once-proud Jewish edge of "Greater Germany" (as the poet described it in 1960).[6] Thus encoded in this versified shibboleth is a west-to-east memory of fascist empire at the ominous point of "oriental"[7] emergence.

Why such encoding? It must be said that Celan is certainly *not* a nonreferential poet. His interest in absurdist and nonrealist sources, and what Shira Wolosky has called "linguistic mysticism,"[8] never entailed eschewing specificity. As is the case with Duncan or Gertrude Stein, both of whose supposedly difficult phrasings can also seem to come from nowhere, reading Celan with attention to historical and political reference, especially in poems in which he worked out associations with terrifying absences, is not merely plausible but productive. The editorial efforts of Bernhard Böschenstein, Heino Schmull, and translator Joris to sort through the proliferated layering of drafts and notes Celan generated to prepare for "The Meridian" prove this again and again. What culminated

in the lecture as a condensed fragmentation of associative thought had been rear-
ranged repeatedly in the prewriting.

So what of the shibbolethic phrases in "Shibboleth"? "*Febrero. No pasaran.*"
We have looked at the latter—its usage dramatically peaked in 1939–40,[9] thenceforth a veritable shorthand for antecedents of World War II—but let us turn
now to "Febrero." Rothenberg apparently believed this to be a *pair* of references
to Spanish antifascism. Although Celan offered "*No pasaran*" in Spanish, he
wrote "*Februar*" in German. Felstiner has decided to translate the word into
English while retaining "No pasaran" in Spanish in the English. Joris further
stresses the bilingual original by properly accenting (although not italicizing)
"No pasarán" *after* translation.[10] Dates require thought about translation no less.
Dates correlating to the war, and especially with the impending and then actual
destruction wrought by Axis hatreds, are integral to this writer's terminologi-
cal dreamwork. Although apparently no draft of this poem is extant, nor is the
use of "Februar" glossed in correspondence, we can be fairly certain I think that
it serves as shorthand for "27 Februar"—the portentous day in 1939 when the
governments of England and France officially recognized the Franco regime,
with its implications for German power. It marked a key capitulation hailed as
progress. What those who rued the events of February 27 said on that day
expressed the overall position against "hypocritical pretense of non-intervention,"
a stance that sought to stem the spread of fascism.[11] If the central European
annexations of 1938, the Anschluss of Austria chief among them, migrated some
of the woes of Madrid to metropoles such as Vienna, February 1939 meant that
the full balance of the terror was inexorably coming. Celan's disjunctive shorthand evinces a contemplation of the beginning of the end. In a sense, Auden's
famous dated poem "September 1, 1939" would come too late in the effort to prevent such a calendar. Writing in time is a responsibility. Celan affirms it
implicitly—and in "The Meridian" somewhat more explicitly—as an important
form of making history, a subjective historiography for the new era. He asks rhetorically: "Don't we all write *ourselves* from such dates?"

When in a notebook of drafts for that speech he wrote of "The absurdity
of the whole beginning: woven in the poem," Celan used "absurdity" as a term of
linguistic mysticism. He was planning a kind of writing that concerns "the
strangest matter"—"the absurd [as] route into the other existence."[12] The expression of *after* derives from a deep memory of *during* as it followed from the
groundwork of *before*. "Febrero" is one way to historicize an end of a beginning.
Its condensation, although creating interpretive difficulty, was commensurate

with the degree to which this history should never again be easily represented, in spite of Trevor-Roper's recommendation of William Shirer's magnum opus as signaling the end of the indescribability of Nazi ascension. At the same moment, Celan commended the opposite. Another date had a similar extreme resonance for Celan as he prepared "The Meridian" through the spring of 1960— the date and the phrase, *January 20th*, compulsively returned to him and generated his keenest idea about what to say on October 22, 1960, about the "strangeness and distance"[13] inscribed in his writing.

As Celan was reworking drafts in Paris, Rothenberg in New York received his copies of *New Young German Poets*. Robert Duncan happened to be visiting. During Rothenberg's trip to San Francisco in 1959—it had been the occasion of his watching *Triumph of the Will* and of his poem about Jewish disaster in which "the eye of some Jew my mother's brother and son" has a tragic obscene vision of how "we . . . die in dark rooms"[14]—he had met up with Duncan at City Lights Books in North Beach, where they had been joined by Ferlinghetti and Philip Lamantia (figure 3.1). Now visiting the younger writer in New York, Duncan perused his gift copy of the City Lights anthology. He found Celan's "Shibboleth" and got stuck on the phrase "*No pasaran.*" "Duncan's reaction was rather odd," Rothenberg later recalled. In this moment his intense investment in the idea of an avant-garde revived from the European experience ran headlong into the old political arguments. A dozen years older, Duncan well knew the ideological import of the antifascist slogan and read the poem as communist. "Robert felt that Celan was a commie," as Rothenberg puts it. "I thought it [this reading] was ridiculous. Robert was of the left but was feeling that the communists had betrayed all that, so [in regard to this poem] there was an anticommunist feeling. That one phrase struck him and he jumped to a conclusion about it."[15] Like some artists for whom 1960 was a turning point—Baldwin, Bob Kaufman, Jackson Mac Low, Rod Serling, Sari Dienes, Alexander Kluge—Rothenberg was emerging as an anti-anticommunist modernist. This complex but actually readily identifiable position can be comprehended through Duncan's view of Spain via Celan's "Shibboleth" via the noncommunist left, along these lines: after World War II, the Francoist stance, which the left despised, developed as a dominant idea in Western Europe and the United States, as Cold War ideologies supplanted the notion that the Spanish Civil War had ever been an antifascist war.[16]

*The Opening of the Field* was also published in 1960, momentously. It was and is generally deemed "a creative turning point for Duncan."[17] He had already been a major figure among innovative poets. The book and his significant presence (with eight poems and a statement on poetics) in Allen's *New American Poetry*

**3.1** From left: Philip Lamantia, Jerome Rothenberg, Lawrence Ferlinghetti, and Robert Duncan, at City Lights Books, San Francisco, summer 1959. This was the moment Rothenberg first met Duncan. Photograph by Harry Riedel. Jerome Rothenberg.

put him near the center of the conversation, although his poetry and poetics were eccentric and did not easily align with other New American movements and groups. Rothenberg discovered in New York that *New Young German Poets* was Duncan's "only context then for Celan," that his contact with the postwar European situation was limited even fifteen years after cessation. An exchange was now going to happen between an elder postwar generation and the younger one coming of age at the start of the sixties, and Duncan was unaware of the way in which the European experience of genocide was recasting ideological language such that established political positions in the United States were unprepared to accommodate. To be sure, the convergence of Duncan and Rothenberg entailed a productive mutual transaction. Rothenberg would teach Duncan Celan ("I really had to give him Celan at that point. And he took to Celan with great enthusiasm") and as Duncan began quickly to follow Celan's method he perceived mysticism as its basis, and so "in the exchange" Duncan gave Rothenberg Gershom Scholem, of whose groundbreaking work on Jewish mysticism and kabbalah Rothenberg was then unaware.[18] A poetic gnosis made sense to Duncan because of the persistent failures of historicism, of naive transparency, of conventional rational political action and cause-and-effect history[19]—because of the "tongue of reason," as Louis Zukofsky put it as he was then investigating the problem for his Kabbalah-inspired alphabetic assemblage of quotations in *Bottom: On Shakespeare* (completed in 1960; see chapter 9). In encountering Rothenberg at this moment, Duncan was able to add, by way of Celan, a strong sense that Jewish nonrationalism in response to genocide eschewed neither rigorous logic nor referentiality. Scholem could teach these and other writers that an analytical *discipline* was necessary in the study of linguistic *ecstasy*—of, for instance, the "half-magical, half-mystical practice of 'putting on the Name'" or the kabbalist's "immers[ion] . . . in various combinations of letters and names," which caused the combinist to empty the mind of semantic sense and thus to focus wholly on the art of words.[20]

Rothenberg had already read Martin Buber's translations of Hasidic tales. The first Hawk's Well Press book published was a translation of Buber's *Tales of Angels Spirits & Demons* made by Rothenberg and his collaborator David Antin. Through Scholem's efforts mystical and gnostic texts and interpretive processes emerged in a way methodologically legitimate, and it was Duncan's awareness that Scholem would be right for him that led Rothenberg, he believes, to the work that would culminate in *Technicians of the Sacred* (1969), but only when he "was ready to declare myself as a willing participant in 'a world of Jewish mystics, thieves & madmen.'"[21]

One of the books Duncan recommended, which Rothenberg then closely read, was Scholem's *Jewish Gnosticism, Merkabah Mysticism, and Talmudic Tradition* (1960). It is a scholarly revolt against the premodern German Jewish rationalism that produced "the Science of Judaism" ("Wissenschaft des Judentums"), which submitted Jewish history and thought to the rigors of academic disciplines such as philology, hermeneutics, and literary criticism. Scholem did not intend to undo scholarly scientism as a method but rather to reverse the marginalization of mysticism forced by the rationalist mainstream. The argument for serious study of the neglected field coincided with the years immediately following the genocide, and with it a sense of the failure and possibly even the betrayal of conformist qualities of Jewish German liberal historicism. So Scholem's contention that mysticism was a bona fide aspect of Judaic thought—"not some strange flower," as he put it, "but an indigenous growth"[22]—was attractive to young artists who saw in esotericism the prospect of a new radicalism. In writing *Jewish Gnosticism* Scholem refuted the "historical criticism against the pretensions of Kabbalistic and mystical pseudoepigraphy" by redoing what historical method could entail. In the 1960 work Rothenberg now encountered, Scholem admitted that his earlier *Major Trends in Jewish Mysticism* "was not radical enough"—that there was a true "*continuity* of Gnosticism within the body of Judaism."[23] The doomed politics of intellectual culture—the story of German Jewish assimilation into mainstream interpretive methods then marginalizing and suppressing the embarrassingly nonrational origins of Eastern and Central European beliefs, only to have the latter survive the disaster in a way that seemed daring, new, and verifiably historical—found itself now being worked out among the U.S. avant-garde.

It might be said that mystical pseudepigraphy is one of Duncan's radical aims in *The Opening of the Field*, especially in openly esoteric poems like "The Maiden," which creates a strict but wholly invented (*made*, to use the key term in the book) symbolic mythic lineage. In a letter to Denise Levertov, Duncan had noted that the term "fiction" is the same for him as "field." The open-field writing he was attempting here, and the audacious opening of the field culminating in *The Opening of the Field* upon its publication, created a sense of the realm of poetics as much greater than versification. The proem to the book, "Often I Am Permitted to Return to a Meadow," outlines such a space. "The poem as composed by field. (Feel?)," he wrote Levertov in 1958, had as its source "the field that Abraham bought for the cave of Machpelah." In 1959, as he finished work on the book, he described for Henry Rago at *Poetry* magazine Abraham's "cleard [*sic*] field" as "our little holding chaos."[24] An earlier version of the opening poem included a telling variation: "Often I am permitted to return to a *poem.*"[25] This focus on the poem itself has led Ekbert Faas in *Portrait of the Poet as Homosexual in Society* to interpret Duncan's recurrent dream (the one that inspired "Often I Am Permitted") as marked by a "dialectic of self-creation," a "scene made up by the mind" to which the poet is permitted to return in poems. The "made place" is gendered not just because of its connection later in the book to "The Maiden" but through—as Dan Featherston has pointed out—the romanticism of the maiden (a place "maid of words").[26] Featherston reads *The Opening of the Field* as a "matrix of creation and destruction, history and prophecy,"[27] a written place where the dead are buried out of sight yet fecundly generative as a kind of counterhistorical unconscious past.

From the long letter Rothenberg wrote to Duncan on September 27, 1960, we know that the younger poet was not persuaded by this mystical mythic method. Rothenberg politely expressed "initial disbelief / skepticism" and noted that he was incapable of utilizing the kinds of materials Duncan can use and thus felt "overwhelm[ed]" by Duncan's new book. Because Rothenberg enters such poetry "without any of the old certainties"—implying again the generational difference—when he is faced with Duncan's eccentric yet rigorous traditional poeticisms he finds, at least "for a while," "much of your writing in the Field, etc., was closed to me, largely for the 'intrusion' of the tradition you prize so highly." This is nonetheless not a letter in which the young avant-gardist rejects an elder. He affirmed Duncan's interest in "self-abandonment to that which is not known," that Celanesque ethical pataphysics. Rothenberg was not depressed by but indeed inspired by Duncan's reference to "'rootlessness,'" and did not take it "as a liability." He wanted to be certain that Duncan understood that the poet who recently showed Duncan the poems of Celan did not see in exodus, diaspora, and statelessness any "lack of precedents" but a—presumably he means Jewish—"history . . . full of the uprooted." It is this tradition, the dislocation about which in *Moby-Dick* Herman Melville said "in landlessness alone resides highest truth," that augers "the great adventure of spirit in our time" and "the burden of the American poet" that must entail both responsibility and forgiveness as modern art had already taught us to converge them. "Where the destruction of the old certainties has gone further & strange cultures oppress consciousness with their conflicting demands"[28] can come an experimental art emerging from the destruction that somehow still pays "homage to the majesty of the absurd."

## The Still-Here

"Homage to the majesty of the absurd": the phrase comes at a moment of political confusion in Celan's "The Meridian." It is particularly disorienting in the final text of the "nuanced, layered, elaborately qualified, covertly and overtly allusive"[29] speech as Celan delivered it on October 22 because of the need he felt to integrate Georg Büchner's drama into his own modern art, the occasion of receiving the Büchner Prize being construed as requiring some engagement with this revered figure of the German literary tradition. If "the absurd" would not seem to follow from the tension between royalist conservatism and bloody revolutionary zeal depicted in Büchner's *Danton's Death*, or from Celan's thesis about the appropriateness now of the "'obscurity' of poetry," at least he attempts to clarify the ideological confusions and to apologize openly for "sound[ing] at first like allegiance to the 'ancien regime.'" But because "The Meridian" is the result of fierce condensation of ideas, sources, and histories as drafted and reworked obsessively in notebooks throughout the months leading up to the October event, it is possible from the archival and editorial work of Böschenstein, Schmull, and Joris (in *The Meridian: Final Version—Drafts—Materials*) to see how Celan associated, on one hand, the royalists' brave statements as constituting a radical new language in response to terror, "a word against the grain, the word which cuts the 'string,'"[30] and, on the other hand, his own commitment to the particular experimental lineage of art that sees "the <u>absurd</u> [as a]— route into the other existence"[31] and "moves with the oblivious self into the uncanny and strange to free itself." Celan is fearless about ideological mixing. A "word which cuts the 'string'" of terror is a "counter-word" and the writing he wants to create and to defend in this grand theory of art is made from that linguistic opposition. It is of course "not homage to any monarchy" yet it is "no less essentially radical" because it "does not bow to the 'bystanders and old warhorses of history.'" "It is an act of freedom" yet "It is a step."[32]

"Bystanders": Celan means those who reject the responsibility of serving as witnesses to terror, who refuse to face the necessary language of testimony—in other words, *guilty* bystanders. By the "old warhorses of history" he intends, through Büchner, to assert formally the point already implicit in his poems: traditional historiographical language, with its cause-and-effect narration and its adherence to settled terms for mass death and leaderly succession, will no longer do. It is in "strange" language that one "does not bow" to these modes. In one draft he reworked the royalist declamation "Long live the king," then repeated his apology (he "renders homage not to the monarchy"), and then added witnessing to the mystical linguistic alternative—"to the <u>majesty of the absurd</u> that witnesses for the creature." Facile talk about art, which throughout "The Meridian" Celan rebukes, is the language such bystanders speak.[33] Guilty witnessing occurs on left and right. Yet Celan's stance is never postideological. Progressive postwar politics do not inherently evince lessons of language. The postwar left is not free from riding the "old warhorses of history." The stepwise progression of strange writing is a main trope of "The Meridian." Progress is defined variously: "a certain direction"; not an accommodationist "way out" but "pushing the question farther in the same direction"; "for the sake of liberation, for the sake of the step"; "a step" as "an act of freedom"; the taking of a "direction, breath"; "a turning of our breath" as "poetry goes its way . . . for the sake of just such a turn."[34] "The ghosts right and left," as Celan jotted in a draft, indicate the masses of dead as the effect of total political failure. Here guilty bystanders include "the 'this way-that way' intellectuals." In another draft note he wrote of the art he wants to affirm: "The poem listens as little to the 'giddyap this way' of the politically engaged, as to the 'giddyap that way' of the aesthete."[35]

Celan's bold brief for avant-garde art as an apt response to the disaster enabled by many prewar and wartime intellectuals tends to align him with, as Rothenberg wrote to Duncan at exactly this time, modern "mystics [and] figures cut off from the mainstream of dogma." The burden of this particular minoritarian vision would seem to have augmented Celan's tendency already to devote himself to "the strangest matter: in You-distance" or "in the You-darkness." "The poem," he wrote in a draft of "The Meridian," "has, I am afraid, entered the phase of the total You-darkness—it speaks in the strangest matter."[36] He hopes he is advocating for "the poem [that] holds its ground on its own margin," writings of the neglected survivor who bespeaks the "still-here." But he knows that the language of witness "clearly shows a tendency towards silence."[37] His attraction, like Rothenberg's, to those "isolated mystics" and to others forced away from the mainstream led Celan's writing now to "Mysticism as wordlessness."[38] On October 4, just eighteen days before he was to deliver the final version, he dwelled on his notebook of drafts, trying to work through this dilemma.

On that day he wrote and rewrote several fragmented versions of "matters of the strange" and constructed the phrase "This 'who knows'" to describe the unsayable self-estrangement of the kind of marginalized writer whose poetics he must defend at all costs. This ferocity derived from what he elsewhere in drafts of the speech calls "the presencing of a person as language":[39] how "I speak, as I do in fact write poems; speak of the poem . . . in this matter as in its most own, toward a most strange." It was a version of the invention of You-distance / You-darkness and in turn caused him to connect such writing back to the temporal ("it hurries thought") and to date it from a particular moment. Breathturn, he again claims, is a progressive turning toward stepwise movement, but now it has a durational dimension: "Nobody can tell," he writes, "*how long* the breath pause" (emphasis added). This notion of dating provides a breakthrough, as Celan was connecting three elements of his art: (1) the estrangement of the speaking I, concurrent with Bachmann's *schreibende Ich*, (2) dislocation as the refugee's landlessness, and (3) an emergent specific avant-garde historicist (documentary) poetics. If poems are "everything that estranges us, which separates it from that unknown (through all that densely settled human un-land something uncommonly impatient impatiently restless)—not: impetuous—is (despite all restraint) with the poem, as with us all: we lie beneath the ruins of the scales, on which we could have been weighed"[40]—then from when, and from what, do such poems date? The answer is scrawled atop this draft passage like a banner:

*20th January → Poems—*

In the final version of "The Meridian" the mostly unexplained reference to "20th of January" occurs twice, and just one passing contextual clue is given,[41] for the meaning of the date. These passages run as follows:

> Perhaps we can say that every poem is marked by its own "20th of January"? Perhaps the newness of poems written today is that they try most plainly to be mindful of this kind of date?
> But do we not all write from and toward some such date? What else could we claim as our origin?

And near the end:

> Both times. I had written from a "20th of January," from my "20th of January."
> I had . . . encountered myself.[42]

I am able to count twenty-four efforts in the drafts and notebooks in which Celan thinks through "my '20th of January.'" The date, verging on mantra, becomes the means of unifying the disparate, incomprehensible points in the speech, and in the end justifies, I think, a reading of "The Meridian" as a survivor's modernist poetics of witness. Here is a sampling of those notes:

> Again and again we write the 20 January, "our" 20 January.
> We write (reservedly, i.e. with all clarity) always still the 20th January, this 20th January; we write ourselves from it . . . whereby a (particular typogenic) language structure dictated only by stanza- and rhyme-constraints is in no ways to be understood—,
> Under such dates do we write, from such dates we write ourselves today—* perhaps most clearly in the poem. Most clearly: that means with all the clarity we owe—or believe we owe—to what we have experienced both on the outside and the inside, and thus to what still needs to be reckoned with . . .
> Where does the poem stand today, how does it relate to ~~the~~ its time, to the problems of lyric poetry? . . . I must pick up the thread from here. Again and

again we write the 20th of January . . . in the poem as the result of word-creations, word-concretions, word-destructions. . . .

From such dates and moments we write ourselves, the poem writes itself.* These dates and moments, they are not readable (cannot be read) off calendars and horologes. The "old war-horses and by-standers of history" have (blinkers) no eyes for it, only the victims of what, under <the> perspective of those bystanders, appears as history.

What is new in the German poem . . . is arguably that this is the clearest attempt to remain mindful of such dates.[43]

One could say that "The Meridian" calls for reparations. Celan is thinking about what is owed by facile historical bystanders who fail to keep January 20 clearly in mind. But there's an even greater sense of responsible exactitude. "The clarity we owe" does not indicate easy, comprehensible talk of art. The debt is not paid by transparent representation, or through a simplifying of the disjointed "encounter" with an experience that could potentially "remain unsaid because perhaps unsayable," a traumatizing X lost in deep memory to which one's words cannot return but which are nonetheless used. Through this illogic the writer is willing to embrace "an artless poetry." Supposed artlessness is a cogent counterresponse. The survivor's problem is to avoid easy speech, but the opposite is "*not* speechlessness." "[T]he poem shows—*not* a tendency to speechlessness" but "in the highest sense to language itself." The "self-encounter" must be historical. The "linguistically possible I-forms" date specifically. The "You-latency, you-lessness / I-latency" had a moment of birth. The encounter with "my 20th of January" is specific: "uniqueness of the encounter: by inclusion of the absent parallel world [*Mit-welt*]."[44]

This was the day in 1942 when exclusion of the *Mitwelt* officially became a language, in a house in a leafy suburb of Berlin, at a meeting at which every word was minuted and transcribed. It was the so-called "Wannsee Conference," where the Final Solution, as carefully described there, could proceed from a set of language rules—the genocidal idiom, grammar, and syntax that Hannah Arendt, attending the Eichmann trial the next year, came to observe as a primary need of the defendant. "He [who had been in attendance at Wannsee and took careful notes] was quite capable of sending millions of people to their death," she observed, "but he was not capable of talking about it in the appropriate manner without being given his 'language rule.'"[45] The capture and extradition of Eichmann in May immediately made available general information about his importance at Wannsee and about its centrality to the cases of both the prosecution and the defense as each prepared for the war crimes trial.[46] As Celan worked through the Wannsee date repeatedly in his notebook he troubled it, rendered it disjunct—broke subject-object patterns, reversed agency, and violated logics of time, and suppressed normal assumptions of authorship. In one draft version of the statement, Celan says that "the poem writes—always still the 20th January." At its simplest, the argument against the effect of the Wannsee protocols on German-language writing after the deterritorializing and annihilation of modern art and modernists as "degenerate" (un-German, Jewish, communist, mentally ill, nomadic or itinerant, queer) subsequently reinforced among the remnant the tradition of art as "a puppet-like, iambic, five-footed thing"[47]—a totalitarian aesthetic with "a (particular typogenic) language structure dictated only by stanza- and rhyme-constraints."[48] Blaming the persistence of rhymed and regularly metrical poetry on Wannsee is facile criticism, to be sure, but perhaps was in this instance personally warranted: January 20, 1942, marked the true birth of Celan's motherlessness and thus of his pain-laden rhyme. Iambic pentameter might as well be to blame. Less obviously, though, and crucially, the origin point in the language of the new poetry, "the poem today,"[49] is at first unseen—just as some hearers of the speech in Darmstadt on October 22 and many readers of the text of the speech over the years have experienced the date as skimmable cryptic reference, some code known best to historicist insiders. But there seems little doubt of the importance of observing the mention, for the speech insists that new writing writes itself from this date "toward the horizons which become visible <u>from there</u>." Furthermore, it writes itself "in no way toward the imaginary."[50] Here is a strong refusal of fiction about the holocaust—of "imaginative writing" engaged to describe what followed from the invention of language at Wannsee. It is as radical in its rejection of the imagination—which is after all central to the whole history of poetry as truth—as Claude Lanzmann's later harsh statements against fiction or his advocacy of an extreme "fiction of the real," directly influenced by *cinema vérité*, in the collage method of the opaque 9.5-hour "modernist" documentary *Shoah*.[51]

Celan was drafting a revised version of the step → route → breathturn → progress trope in "The Meridian." Writing inscribed by January 20 is composed "toward the (needed) and inalienable (real); it is en route there; from this direction does its meaning open up for it—open up for us."[52] As the language of the Wannsee protocol was determinative, slamming closed the semantic door, so the radical lyric documentary response of the survivor, memorializing a lost chance at *Mitwelt*, must be opened up, unfixed. In "The Meridian" Celan is arguing for an open documentary art made from an experimental sense of history. That thesis leads him finally back to the dreaded charge of hermeticism, to which, as we have seen, he was extremely sensitive. From this point a successful response will be to embrace the term. Hermeticism in the postfascist context means closing off normative forms of aesthetic value in order to "open up" art to testimony of the real, a new *vérité*. He jotted this in his notebook: "Hermeticism, today: to close oneself to the (conventional) (compromised) 'beautiful,' in order to open up to something true [*Wahren*]." This is how one can "remember in the poem—remembrance as absence." It affirms a turn toward surviving: "I would speak here of hope," he adds. Whence the hope? "'Survival is everything'—that is singular in its context; it cannot, like the poem, be translated [by others] into cynicism."[53]

Thus did "The Meridian" call for a poetics of testimony. What's more: in its affirmatively hermetic manner, it is *itself* a survivor's testimony. Celan saw "witnesses" as "the (vocal) things, to whom man gives (himself) (the I) as consonant [*Mitlaut*] into another time." The word "witnesses" here comes with an asterisk, and the footnote reads: "as I-carrier."[54] The will to bear witness—the "I" being carried along, at least somewhat reluctantly—does not moot the modernist subject but only seems to do so. It focuses attention on the extremely narrow space through which the surviving *schreibende Ich* carries itself forward into the living world of the reader while not resisting the urge to speak nonsense commensurate with the unreality witnessed.

In "The Will to Bear Witness," Des Pres theorizes the writer as implicated observer for whom "*some* margin of giving and receiving is essential to life in extremity."[55] The impossible—and linguistically mystical—idea of the "I . . . as consonant into another time" produces a deliberate narratological problem. But it is not impossible when one considers the cotemporality required by deep memory. The survivor speaks in two times. "I try to remember and I can't," says Marceline Loridan-Ivens, the Auschwitz survivor whose applied postcolonial psychosociology is the focalizing center of the very first instance of *cinéma vérité*, *Chronicle of a Summer* (1961). "I try, but it's like a deep hole and I don't want to fall in."[56] Yet the present tense of "I try to remember" for Marceline—just then as she is being filmed, unscripted, in Paris in August 1960 by Jean Rouch and Edgar Morin with their innovative handheld, sound-synchronizing camera—is the moment when she gathers with radical industrial workers, French intellectuals agonized about the Algerian War, and West African students reckoning with the recent history of intra-European mass killings, over cigarettes, coffee, and wine at a rooftop restaurant, whereupon they collaboratively although awkwardly discover the interlocking sequencing of diverse personal testimonies and create new ties between anticolonial sentiment and holocaust narrative. *Chronicle* marks the invention of what Michael Rothberg (for his book about representations of decolonization) has called "multidirectional holocaust memory,"[57] in images capturing the moment in which an anti-Semitic nation moves from postwar promise to postcolonial reality. Witnesses like Marceline present their words within just such a vexed *now*, in the time *after*—Langer calls it "common memory"—of speaking or writing (and later the here and now of audience viewing or reader reading). But concurrently these signifiers exist in the silenced or unworded traumatic past, *during*—the unspeakable X of reseeing in the mind's eye the unreal real—and as such cannot ease us into their unfamiliar world through familiar linguistic devices. In testimony, then is now and also not now. Soliloquizing as she slowly walks through 1960 Paris, Marceline speaks directly to her father, who died in Auschwitz: "And *then* here I am *now*." "The war, the postwar," writes Rothberg, "intersect with little transition."[58] It has been said of *Chronicle of a Summer* that "it is not simply France that is changing here, it is the medium itself."[59] *Cinéma vérité* discovers the Auschwitz survivor turned pro-Algerian activist as Celan's "I-carrier," and, as with Celan, that "I" will seek vocabularies unmoored from belief in their meanings. Marceline, *after*, insists that she had been unable to "believe" the words of others or even of herself, yet somehow she belatedly learned to apply the unreality of *during*: "Not as much," she emphasizes, "as [in the death camp] I believed in a tomato or an onion. Words had deserted us." Fifteen years later, when contemplating a democratic republic's censorship of criticisms of its North African policies in relation to the ongoing social censorship of survivors' experiences with genocide, that disbelief reawakens into a politics: "I don't believe a word of the official history written by France."[60] Cotemporality becomes a mode risking an abridgement of social decency that is more a source of torment for the witness than edification for the recipient of the representation.[61] This is Celan's agonized poetics of survival, "this 'still-here' of the poem."[62] In a manner that only later (in the 1970s and 1980s) scholars studying survivor testimony such as Des Pres, Laub, Langer, LaCapra, Shoshana Felman, Saul Friedlander, Geoffrey Hartman, and Henry Krystal would theorize, Celan described the survivor's violation of expressive codes through what Krystal discovered in his study of prolonged traumatization was a lack of capacity to symbolize readily and what Langer in *Holocaust Testimonies: The Ruins of Memory* calls "humiliated memory."[63] In anticipating thus, Celan had to pioneer refutations (ahead of their time) of the assumption that a surviving victim's testimony yields therapeutic value and thus was beneficial for everyone and worth extracting despite the psychic cost. "Actually now that I remember those things," one survivor observed when he was asked to put the precarity into words, "I feel *more horrible* than I felt at the time."[64] Celan first attempted in drafting "The Meridian" to work out this disabling paradox through what was already, in the short fifteen-year history of survivor testimony, a pious cliché, for instance: "Survival is everything." But he soon dissented: "'Survival is everything.'—no, it is not everything: (no, to survive is indecent, as survivor one has to write for one's life even more so)," or else "from artistry there is just one step to posthumous whitewash."

When Celan referred to "process" he meant the transition from unutterable X to difficult yet usable language, and of course argued for self-consciousness— for "thinking what we are doing," to use Auden's phrase, as opposed to Pollock's "When I am in my painting, I do not know what I am doing." "Witnesses of a process," Celan argued, we are all responsible for the contemporary history of nonresponsiveness and irresponsibility from 1945 to the moment of the speech. He was rarely this straightforward in his notes as when making this point: "We have been, each in his own way, witnesses of a process, which has led us to this circumstance from that which only fifteen years ago still lay true and heavy on our heart: talk of the turning [*Unkehr*] instead of change itself, supposed engagement and commitment instead of real responsibility, cultural busy-ness rather than simple attentiveness." Here was Celan's clearest affirmative statement of the need to judge. He was typically more negative, unwilling to forgive those whose postwar art merely evinced correct "cultural busy-ness," for they were now just as guilty as the guilty bystanders during the war. Bystanders are not witnesses. They "are not present." "Only the victims of what the bystanders call history know something about it," and by "it" he means history itself. An almost prosecutorial attentiveness—in the writing and toward the writing and, as inscribed in the written words, to "all our dates"—formed the basis of this postwar aesthetic from which one could perceive both a counterholiness and a new sense of responsibility. This particular kind of attentiveness is not objective but a function of active subjectivity; it is "not [merely] a technique of observation."[65]

To prepare for "The Meridian," Celan read Walter Benjamin's 1934 essay on Franz Kafka (written while Benjamin was "living under Hitler, Year Two," an assessment shaped by the rise of Nazism and by an intense correspondence with Gershom Scholem in Jerusalem).[66] Celan seized on this assertion: "Attention is the natural prayer of the soul." "Real responsibility" would be harder to derive for the victim than for the unscathed bystanders. But because of the latter's abdication, their easy art talk, their righteous and pious politics, their "*supposed engagement*," it would have to be the witness who wrote the disaster as "we lie beneath the ruins of the scales, on which we *could* have weighed."[67] This was the scale of aesthetic judgment and also of ethical-judicial verdict, and it was in the basic groundwork of Celan's *ars poetica* presented in Germany, especially at the moment of Eichmann's reappearance, that these two things became one. "The Meridian" is a postdisaster Defence of Poesy with a radically renewed sense of Sidney's "unelected vocation."[68] It constitutes an apology for language fully in spite of words having been corrupted.

# Part 2

---

## The End of the End of Ideology

# 4

# Absurd Judgment

## Auden, Arendt, Eichmann, and the Kafka Revival

## A Reexamination of What We Think We Mean

Meanwhile in Manhattan, Arendt and Auden, intellectually an unlikely pair, became friends after discovering their mutual concern over the obligation to defend language against forces that had corrupted it. They joined together in such a defense but soon they disagreed. Arendt insisted on distinctions between ethical and judicial judgment, while Auden saw them as categorically merged.[1]

In November 1959 Auden had published in *Encounter* his interpretation of Shakespeare's Falstaff. The essay, smoothly argued otherwise, interrupts itself to digress on forgiveness and pardon (*there* Auden stressed the distinction). The digression was prompted by Auden's positive response to Arendt's *The Human Condition* (1958), in a commentary also published in *Encounter* and, as noted earlier in chapter 1, given the title "Thinking What We Are Doing." For Auden such self-awareness was always essentially linguistic but now, after the recent disaster, needed to be redefined as such. We "can never manage" this attention to "Doing" "unless we can first agree about the meaning of the words we think with, which, in its turn, requires that we become aware of what these words have meant in the past." Auden believed Arendt to have contributed her essay to the field of etymology, "a re-examination of what we think we mean."[2] Saying so was the closest Auden would ever come to a real affirmation of Make It New, but here in an ethical rather than a poetic context. Arendt's definition of ideal

political power—not power of the kind that wields violence but its opposite—
also starts with language. She has imagined, Auden notes, a politics realized
"only where word and deed have not parted . . . when words are not used to veil
intentions" and when deeds following such words "are not used to violate and
destroy, but to . . . create new realities."³ Auden's Falstaff essay devises such a
prelapsarian and, in effect, a pretotalitarian mode in which the word-world relationship remains undestroyed, where pardon and forgiveness are "forbidden to
calculate."⁴ Arendt obtained a copy of the November 1959 issue of *Encounter*
and wrote her long letter of February 14, 1960.

To what in particular did she respond? "The command to forgive is unconditional," Auden had argued. He noticed the failure in dramatic writing to
distinguish "the *spirit* of forgiveness" from "the *act* of pardon." When forgiveness necessitates action, it thus requires something that would not occur if
there were no forgiving. "This means that my enemy must be at my mercy"—
not ideal, given that, for Auden, charity is a disposition and should remain
separate from "judicial pardon," which is necessarily an act. Distinctions
between disposition and act have failed in literary representations of judgment
"because silence and inaction are undramatic."⁵ Auden's understanding of
Arendt's position was that it favored a "temporal justice" that "demands the
use of force to quell the unjust" and "a practical reckoning with time and
place" and "publicity for its laws." He argues rather for "Charity," which for-
bids force and repudiates any judgment specific to "time and place." Thus "we
are *not* to resist evil."⁶ Auden did not know Arendt well at this point and presumably had no idea how so strongly identified as Jewish this insistent position
on charity would make her feel. It was just a few months before the overdeter-
minations of the Eichmann moment, yet the rebuke of "publicity" seems to
have struck a nerve. Although without any mention by Auden of the modernist moralities of Franz Kafka, it was a drastic, adverse re-reading of capricious
state-sponsored justice of the sort encountered in works such as "In the Penal
Colony" and *The Castle*—and seemed to be the beginnings of a Christian postwar antimodernism, which set Arendt off. In her view, to the contrary, "both
blessing and forgiving imply a hierarchy." The judicial outlook cannot be overcome. Moreover, were literary representations of "silence and inaction" really
"undramatic"?⁷

Auden's doubt about the value of public justice is also, to be sure, exactly
opposed to the conclusion drawn by Celan, whose writing as we have seen
"shows a strong tendency toward silence" in a complex theorization of

obscurity that makes for an entire drama of writing that nonetheless openly defends language against corruption and produces judgment *not despite that but because* the scales of judgment have been destroyed. In her long, dense reply ("I just read the Falstaff piece, . . . " she began), Arendt disagrees: "the 'command to forgive is <u>not</u> unconditional,'" following which criticism her letter speculates on the distinction between "forgiveness and judicial pardon." It is only pride, not historical reality, that "insist[s] that that power of judgment remains unimpaired." Judgment can indeed "be destroyed in the act of forgiving." Pondering the "absurd position of the judges during the Nuremberg trials who were confronted with crimes of such a magnitude" as to render punishment nearly meaningless, she posits a theory of forgiveness that "does not aim at destruction but on the contrary at the restoration of the persons involved."[8]

This confidence would not quite extend, during the following year, to Arendt's sense of the Eichmann trial, to the irredeemable Adolf Eichmann himself. But owing to Auden's prompt, Arendt develops a hope drawn from her ethical anti-totalitarian etymology. Such hope required, as Auden put it, "that we become aware of what . . . words have meant in the past" *if and when* the goal is "reexamination of what we think we mean." That, rather than personal rehabilitation, is what she meant by restoration. Linguistic responsibility of this kind must be widespread and by no means limited to the perpetrators. Such notions of responsibility, of abilities to respond, coincided with those of artists and intellectuals considered in this book, especially here now in part 2 (chapters 4 through 10), as we observe each in the act of seeking some sort of return to an examination of prewar reexaminations of how meaning gets made. These renewals happen also to coincide with a wave of new postwar-style reencounters with the work of Kafka. Certainly, then, it is worth asking: Why the resurgence of Kafka (particularly in the United States) just then?[9]

One new encounter was Frederick Olafson's "Kafka and the Primacy of the Ethical," published in the Spring 1960 issue of the *Hudson Review*, which was largely taken up by a new reading of the Barnabas family episode in *The Castle*. Olafson, a moral philosopher, sought to challenge the generally accepted interpretation of "a morally submissive and acquiescent Kafka" by establishing how K. achieves critical detachment from the language of the Castle bureaucracy and of the village in order to achieve the fate, usually ascribed to him, of "helpless victim."[10] This cautiously argued *Hudson Review* piece, published just as

Eichmann's extradition stirred daily media coverage and extended conversation about perpetrators and victims, emerges as a parable of postdisaster
reconsideration of modernist skeptical ethics. Olafson revived focus on the villagers, who witness the abuse of K. by Castle administrators. They are guilty
bystanders. By disclosing their complicity, Kafka was creating a text of linguistic moral self-ownership. The daughter of the Barnabases, in rejecting a dishonorable proposal made by a high official of the Castle, brings down a punishment
upon the whole family, but, as Olafson writes, "this punishment is not inflicted
by the Castle" but by the villagers themselves, an extreme ostracism. Kafka's K.
has aligned himself with the Barnabas family. The novel's language, describing
activities, customs, projects, and mutual affirmations that characterize village
life in the shadow of the indecipherable totalitarianism of the Castle, in a sense
ostracizes and deterritorializes *readers* as they struggle to know what's going
on. Of course it does the same to K. as he becomes trapped inside Celan's alien
homeland, along with the Barnabas daughter, who is shunned for her exercise
of "independent moral initiative."[11]

Back in 1937 it had seemed a strenuous interpretive matter—a presumptuous
critical imposition even at a time when Nazi intentions to segregate and con-
centrate Europe's Jews were widely understood—for Max Brod in his biography
to interpret *The Castle* as a story "tangibly, straight from [Kafka's] Jewish soul"
about a Jewish citizen who "cannot make himself at home," who is always a
"stranger . . . looked upon with suspicion." Brod had pushed hard at this claim
in spite of the fact that "the word Jew does not appear in *The Castle*."[12] It was
going to be easier of course, after the genocide, to make such a reading. The villagers of *The Castle* as Olafson now redescribed them are unwilling to perceive
their internalization of the "cultural busy-ness" that the Castle's organizational
language has generated—to return to Celan's bitter phrase for bystanders' art
talk, by means of which "they say art and mean irresponsibility." Olafson reads
K. as, in Celan's terms, a "victim . . . of what the bystanders call history."[13] Celan
and Kafka (in *The Trial* and especially in *The Castle*) offer readings of history
more radical still: again, as Celan put it, it is *only the victims* of what the bystanders call history [who] *know something about it.*"

Unless one deems the political philosopher who covered the Eichmann trial
herself a "victim" in Celan's sense, a *survivor*—it's certainly a tenable designa-
tion, insofar as Hannah Arendt had been stripped of her German citizenship,
had been imprisoned by the Gestapo, had been saved through an illegally
obtained visa, had helped otherwise doomed children emigrate—her formulation does not place the victim-witness so urgently at the center of the creation

of a new history. Yet it enacts a similar and, in context, controversial shift of focus from the grand perpetrator, an individuated interpreter of invincible language rules, to the guilt of the normalizing majority. "The trouble with Eichmann was precisely that so many were like him," Arendt would soon write, "and that the many were neither perverted nor sadistic, that they were, and still are, terribly and terrifyingly normal. From the viewpoint of our legal institutions and of our moral standards of judgment, this normality was much more terrifying than all the atrocities put together."[14] This statement aligns with the Auden-Arendt debates on judgment of 1959–60, and with her discussions with Karl Jaspers of the legal issues entailed in the trial during their exchange of letters throughout 1960.[15] The correspondence with Jaspers coincides with her sense that the "failure" and "conspicuous helplessness" of the Israeli judges were necessitated by their narrow judicial charge, that of "understanding the criminal" rather than fully engaging victim-witnesses for the purpose of understanding the deep nature of *testimony* about the crime and its scope as legally (not just emotionally) actionable, or the particular history of the language that enabled both— that history languaged quite precisely of "our January 20th." In psychoaesthetic terms, Celan's "mindful[ness] of such dates" is the equivalent of the positive ethical terms of Auden's "Thinking What We Are Doing." The duty to witness is both socially reasonable and complexly personal ("To attend this trial is somehow, I feel," Arendt wrote, "an obligation I owe to my past") and yet, she felt, *absurd* when projected as obligation upon an individual.[16]

As Arendt explored new relevant connotations of absurdity with Jaspers and Auden, Albert Camus was killed in a horrific automobile accident—on January 4, 1960. The many remembrances unsurprisingly never failed to mention *The Plague* of 1947: its absurdist position (in Sartre's tribute forms of the word "absurd" appear five times in 962 words),[17] its status as an allegory of dehumanization in Nazi-occupied France. It was a book to which "our era responded." So the *New York Times* editorial board put it when commenting on the news of the Nobel laureate's death with its "grim philosophical irony."[18] "Our era" indeed, for the dangers seemingly surpassed remained latent. As the citizens of Oran celebrate the end of the war fought against the pandemic "*he* knew what these jubilant crowds did not know:. . . that the plague bacillus never dies or disappears for good; that it can lie dormant for years and years."[19] The fascism-pandemic analogue becomes at times nearly explicit in *The Plague*, especially when citizens, in particular French Algerian "humanists," disparage recommended mitigation practices. "When a war breaks out, people say: 'It's too stupid; it can't last long.' But though a war may well be 'too stupid,' that doesn't prevent its lasting."[20] Obituaries reminded readers of Camus's dangerous service in the French resistance, his brave pieces for *Combat*, and his childhood experience of poverty and witnessing injustice in Algeria. They invariably cited instances of absurd optimism.[21] "In the midst of winter," one assessment quoted, "I learned that there was in me an invincible summer."[22] "In the darkest depths of our nihilism," the *Times* noted that Camus had once contended, "I have sought only for the means of transcending it."[23] "The track he followed," William Faulkner in his memorial comment insisted, "was the only possible one which could *not* lead only to death."[24] It happened that just then, too, a new edition of Stuart Gilbert's translation of *The Plague* was published by Penguin.

The novel's strangely legible idea of absurdity drew directly from Kafka. Both writers understood Sisyphus to be "powerful and rebellious" and "know[ing] the whole extent of his misery."[25] Camus appended his "Hope and the Absurd in the Work of Franz Kafka" to the second edition of *The Myth of Sisyphus*. He cleverly nodded in *The Plague* to the influence: he made sure to include a character, the voluable profiteer Cottard, who during intermittent self-quarantine busied himself misreading *The Trial* as a detective novel. "I've been reading that detective story," this blowhard reports to the doctor protagonist. "It's about a poor devil who's arrested one fine morning, all of a sudden. People had been taking an interest in him and he knew nothing about it." The narrator informs us without editorializing that Cottard, who had previously held liberal views, now in the midst of the pandemic became skeptical even of the tardy and lax official remediative response and read only the conservative newspaper. Conservatives in Camus's Oran tend to believe that the pandemic will magically end through the assertion of individual reason, not government-designated quarantines, travel limits, bothersome diagnostic tracing, and socially distanced funerals. Oranians like Cottard pride themselves on "lucidly recognizing" things and thus "dispelling extraneous shadows."[26] Camus's narrator, like Bachmann's in "Everything," turns in extremis to the idea of a language of shadows and casts doubt on the sufficiency of logical recognition, giving only "the *appearance* of being clear and straightforward . . . in the tight, feverish . . . style he had adopted" in order to give shape to his formative Algerian experience. In doing so he refuses the "pleasing rationality" of "noncontradictory" writing (as Édouard Glissant has explained in a passage on Camus's underrecognized nontransparency)[27]— effecting overall a Kafkasque style of which logic and lucidity are its relentlessly ironic surface qualities.

*The Chicago Review* in its spring 1960 issue published Heinz Politzer's implicitly personal and transferential essay on Kafka and Camus, subtitled "Parables for Our Time." Born in Vienna, Politzer had been forced to flee Austria in 1938 at the time of the Anschluss, and wrote this piece in order to understand the "fascination" Kafka and Camus together held for "the European generation . . . who were young after the second World War." He was talking not about his cohort, those who had personally experienced fascism as the foundation of its own antifascism, but about the generation born around 1930. He seemed to have read Camus in a way mostly forgotten in later decades—Dominick LaCapra, studying history and memory after Auschwitz, has been a rare exception—as "one of the few major writers who addressed the Holocaust, which until recently [this was the late 1990s] has played an allusive, indirect role in the work of major structuralists and poststructuralists."[28] Politizer in 1960 was discovering that their particular fascination, a modernist openness, "arose from the questions" posed by Kafka and Camus rather than solutions provided, and derived from a resistance to plain mimetic rendering. Modern to the end, neither writer was ever "satisfied with copying reality in simple terms."[29] The monstrous bug Gregor becomes is and is also not a bug. The rats rising from Oran's sewers are and are also not rats. The three choices in response to the fascist existential threat allegorized in the virus were suicide, taking a "leap of faith" to choose belief, or embracing the absurd and thus inventing one's own estranged meaning. Camus had commended the third, the Kafkaesque choice, the first being uninteresting cowardice and the second just a moral lie.

## The Stubborn Integrity of the Fragment

By way of Kafka in 1960, then, we arrive at a special variation on the definition of the modern for the new moment: absurdity and personal historical consciousness can merge in a text without lessening (or, for Arendt, dismissing as merely personal) a sense of the absurd. Here is a key question now being posed: "Would [Kafka] have made the problem of guilt seem so primary and developed it so carefully if he meant it all to be read as mere neurotic distortions?" So asked theorist of fiction Murray Krieger in his book *The Tragic Vision* (1960). Or: Would Kafka have disclosed in such detail the court's hypocrisies in *The Trial* "if he merely wished to emphasize its apparent absurdities"?[30] Krieger's Kafka gives modern people an open, enigmatic, absurdist Aesopian text in which guilt can still be reliably read from the bottom up—"approached from below, from the details of the novel."[31] Reading guilt in Kafka "resists *systematic* interpretation" yet does not resist interpretation overall. As Suzanne Clark in *Cold Warriors* has put it in summarizing Krieger's complicated postwar relationship with modernism: the tragic vision follows from "'the modernism that is characterized by fragmentation' rather than synthesis," and such vision was formed at the historical moment when, in Krieger's words, "Justice has passed from the universal to the rebellious individual."[32] Krieger implicitly decries the fashionable existentialism of the moment through a formula assessing recent aesthetic and political histories together:

prewar modernism + genocidal world war = absurdity

As we discover the "disingenuousness of straining to marshal [textual details] to prove an argument, we rather consign them to the miscellaneous absurd."[33] To contend that modern writing resists synthetic, unfragmented interpretation is not the same as "obscurantism." When a minor court official blathers on about its infallibility and insists that the judiciary "never go[es] hunting for crime in the populace, but, as the Law decrees, are drawn towards the guilty,"[34] it should not indicate the ultimate indecipherability of such "apparent contradictions and claims" so much as the need to shift the register of reading. The "mystique of hierarchy" itself can and must be read, and guilt will be disclosed as no less specific. This approach coincides almost exactly with Arendt's interpretation of the problem of interpreting the guilt of Eichmann.

How in an era when ideologies were supposedly outmoded was one to understand responsibility without "any abstract doctrinal guilt"? Krieger was an anti-ideological critic-theorist who intellectually came of age in the academically conformist 1950s—*The New Apologists for Poetry* of 1956 is his classic work—and now reached an impasse. The political reading, that of a vague straw man Marxist, which he dismissed from the start—K.'s "frequent awareness of his guilt . . . is not a sign of the Court's justice by a symptom of K.'s brainwashing by the ruthless organization that has badgered him into submission"—turned out to be most logically persuasive as the result of Krieger's own methodological merge of modernism's openness and his commitment as a critic to textual detail. He wanted "the social and metaphysical levels [to] be urged at once" in this approach to the modern novel but in the end his formalism mastered the metaphysical while his inability to cope with the social created the only urgent, dramatic agony in an otherwise competent, rule-abiding monograph: an uncharacteristic, sprawling 643-word footnote that plunders two-thirds of the bottom space across two pages. If critics seek a seamless move ("without a leap") from literal to symbolic levels of reading, what will prevent it is Kafka's "failure to relate" two versions of the Court (they are described in contradictory ways in the novel). Krieger conceded that he himself cannot "do more than dodge this obstacle." His need for semantic sense, which should have been mitigated by his commitment to the value of the modernist fragment, led to blaming Kafka for reaching "the point where [his] aesthetic incompleteness shows." Krieger could only repeat his hope that "the world of social-economic reality and of nightmarish fantasy"—again here identified as "the political and metaphysical levels"—would have "a single narrative source," directly contradicting his defense of literary opacity and difficulty if they can be supported by detailed close reading, a defense his work effects.[35]

Pondering a Kafka apt for 1960, I seek a way of comprehending Murray Krieger's exhausted formalist existentialism. The ultimate question in poetics of this time—it applies to *The New Apologists for Poetry* and *The Tragic Vision* equally, where for a theorist the term "poetics" emphasizes the aesthetic within any genre—is whether the "impractical, non-propositional structure" of the modern poem can "help us understand ourselves in our world a little better." Wesley Morris, in "Murray Krieger: A Departure Into Diachrony," helpfully poses the question in this way: "Should we ask the poem to function more immediately in the realm of political action" if its obscurities inhibit the realization of literature's representational function?[36] Morris is not especially interested in biography, or psychology, yet in his discussion of the limits of Krieger's theorizing he contends that it is "a projection of a World War II *Weltanschauung*" in expecting modern writing to "imitate existential reality" while recognizing that "it is the poem's own Manichean vision that establishes the mask that it is said to imitate."[37] Krieger's undergraduate years at Rutgers University were interrupted by unusually long service in the armed forces during and after the war, including a tour in India at the volatile pre-postcolonial moment, and such experiences do help explain the intensity and uncharacteristic overwriting in Krieger's perhaps unwitting confusion of two kinds of histories that find their way into modern literature—history as "the 'stuff' of the poem insofar as it is lived" ("the living, felt, pulsing history of breathing men," as Krieger sentimentally put it) and history that is "the static formulae of ideology." In recent years the general objection to Krieger's theorizing has been that its "existential vision is out of date." The crass version of this complaint might run as follows: in the postwar 1950s existentialism was all the rage, and Krieger's formalist training merged with and was compromised by his war experience and readings of Gide, Camus, and Sartre. Morris points out that this is itself a "historical judgment." If the effect of the putative end of ideology is made manifest in the Manichaeanism drawn from a wartime sense of guilt and victimization—and in the way that exclusive focus on the "ideal of a recurrent assertion of individual freedom" but not of "political or collective action" blinds his theory of imaginative writing to "a vision more terrifying and more incomprehensible [even] than the remembered mad horrors of World War II"—then our historical reading of Krieger's historical reading of Kafka takes us momentarily to the *end* of the end of ideology. There the improbable, non-syllogistic structure of modern writing, "contemptuous of the practical world," produces art that is "subversive of those veils of cognitive distortion"[38] and thus reveals what Krieger, describing *The Trial*, calls "a convincing dossier" evidencing a guilt quite specific, a case readable even by those who do not believe in universal "notions of original sin shared."[39]

Even leaving aside Morris's particular critique of a critic's projection of the World War II experience onto a theory of modern reading, it is hard not to read about Krieger's Kafka for the 1960s without thinking about that suggestive anachronism that has been offered almost to the point of cliché in classrooms and belle-lettristic essays and dialogues hosted by earnest citizen reading groups encountering *The Trial*, *The Castle*, "In the Penal Colony," or *Amerika* for the first time: to wit, that Kafka was not just generally a prophet of totalitarianism but predictor of genocide with what George Steiner later called "detailed clairvoyance."[40] In 1960 this was by no means yet a convention, despite Arendt having passingly connected Kafka's prescience to a micro-origin of totalitarianism. "He trusted his great powers of imagination," she wrote, "to draw all the necessary conclusions and, as it were, to complete what reality had somehow neglected to bring into full focus."[41] Some of the delay in what would seem an obvious postwar revisionism was surely due to complications of the Cold War, a reaction to the totalitarianism Arendt was investigating.[42] Then there was the ghastly deferral of popular understanding predicted by Walter Benjamin in the late 1930s in his letters to Gershom Scholem—delay due to the slowness of accessibility to detailed information about the genocidal mechanisms and bureaucratic structures. "Kafka's world," Benjamin wrote to Scholem, "is the exact complement of his era which is preparing to do away with the inhabitants of this planet on a considerable scale. The experience which corresponds to that of Kafka, the private individual, will probably not become accessible to the masses until such time as they are being done away with." We read Kafka's fictions as idiosyncratic expressions of *self*-annihilation only until the moment finally arrives when they properly stand for the facts of mass murder on the social scale far, far beyond neurosis.[43] That had been 1938 and this finally was 1960. Was it now the terrible moment of accessibility Benjamin via Kafka had predicted?

Krieger's projection was not at all unique by the very end of that epoch. Nor were those of the heretical mythographer and World War II combat veteran Eliezar Aaron ("Leslie") Fiedler; the queer surrealist poet-critic of avant-garde film Parker Tyler; the expert on nihilist dialectics Peter Heller—a mix of U.S.-based commentators, all of whom published on Kafka in the year 1960, unified by what struck Fiedler as a timely "assent to the unforeseen lucidity of the obsession, the stubborn integrity of the fragment, the irreducibility of meaning maintained like a martyrdom." Commentary now on Kafka's predicament seemed "almost obligatory."[44] Heller's elegantly argued analysis of ways in which Kafka's main theme and, at once, the texture of the writing always trace the reduction of spiritual people to "something less than human," to debasement and barbarism, turns on the notion of a special form of alienation and strangeness: that of the assimilated western Jew attracted to "the Eastern Jews" only to find "the way back to their community . . . barred."

Heller's contention that Kafka's manner of "treat[ing] as normal an *essentially* alienated and *pervasively* dehumanized world" is uniquely powerful depended on his stipulation that "we have grown *accustomed as historical fact*"—my emphasis—to "systematic terror, . . . the genocides, and the methods of total warfare" and that "*even at present*" can imagine "still greater disasters." The fact of there having occurred a disaster is elided with the "fact" of our finally having grown accustomed to it as fact. And all this depended in the first instance on the quality of prophecy inhering in the kind of mediumistic modern writing that is itself, like human life lived in extremity, a "perennial 'process' and 'trial.'" Traditional narrative, with its word-world alignment, its commitment to circumstantial realism, does not predict forward in such a way. Rather it was—we do well again to notice a dependence on the rhetoric of facticity—"the fact that Kafka's 'concrete universals' invite simultaneously questions on all possible levels of discourse," the openness and opacity of the text itself, that enabled Kafka to be writing in the 1910s and 1920s about the totalitarianism of the 1930s and the holocaust of the 1940s, and rather than this being *less* historical as an approach to modernism in 1960 it was being offered as *more*. "A few years had passed after Kafka's death," writes Heller in "The Autonomy of Despair" for the

*Massachusetts Review* in its winter 1960 issue, "when his visions seemed to come true in the mass murder of the Jews (in which all of his relatives were killed)."[45]

Heller himself had escaped from the Nazi ascendancy, fleeing from Austria first to Britain and then entering the United States. He had been in a four-year analysis with Anna Freud starting at the age of nine (1929–32), later marrying the daughter of Anna's companion. Much later his experience with Freudian practice was published and studied as a major psychoanalytic case (we have his book *A Child Analysis with Anna Freud* and Anna's book *The Technique of Child Analysis*).[46] Heller's Kafkaesque "vision" is intensely personal, although in ways probably not evident to the casual reader of the *Massachusetts Review*. To *read* Kafka just at this moment, Heller suggests, is to experience an ordeal *oneself* like that of the survivor-witness. He concedes that of course "the reader will not be executed at the hands of two strangers," unlike K. in *The Trial*, "but as he [yes, *the reader*] emerges from this literary ordeal"—surviving the trial of the text itself—"he may have to ask himself whether the work and the summons were meant for him or, indeed, for any reader." This is not meant as metaphor. Kafka was being reread as a reluctant survivor whose anticipatory will to bear witness was tortuously ambiguous—a dreaded state of being to be described later by Des Pres as making the witness-survivor's predicament like that of the modernist writer and the modernist writer's predicament like that of the survivor.[47]

After suggesting that readers of Kafka endure their torment as a version of unwarranted summons, Heller reminded us that Kafka's final wish was that his writing be destroyed. He then asked: "Did he not disavow the wish to communicate his essential experience?" Des Pres describes such disavowal as the result of an "unexpected ambiguity": "As a witness the survivor is both sought and shunned; the desire to hear his truth is countered by the need to ignore him."[48] The unsayable experience of the survivor defies representation and *that* is the condition that, if nothing else is possible, needs bearing witness. Readers and hearers of testimony sometimes reject the veracity of the story *together with its form of telling* in order for the survivor, habituated to the incompleteness and fragmentation of the effort, to feel that *something* of the ordeal's unreality has been conveyed.[49] Heller comprehended this aspect of Kafka's writing: "Kafka does communicate an essential experience of irrevocable rejection, the experience of an ultimate non-arrival."[50] Such incessant "non-arrival" Celan theorized as a function of, or an analogue to, the way in which European Jewish life, because of its particular internal linguistic and cultural exile, has *historically ever* had about it, predictively, certain modern attributes, chief among them indeed this travail of "ultimate non-arrival." It is the figure of the Jew as always already modern. "To <u>remember</u> in the poem," Celan wrote in his notebook for "The Meridian" "—remembrance as absence." He jotted those key phrases after copying out a passage he found while reading Jean Paul's *Das Kampaner Tal* (1797): "as on the houses of the Jews (in memory of ruined Jerusalem), something always has to be left unfinished"—a likening that yokes together (1) violent dispersion and diaspora, (2) the familial home as memory (Celan's obsession, as we know), and (3) the written fragment.[51] Heller quoted a Czech friend of Kafka, Janouch, who distinctly remembered Kafka telling the story of a blind Jewish poet of Prague whose eyes had been damaged in brawls with Germans and non-Jewish Czechs. "He lost his eyesight as a German," Janouch recalled Kafka saying, "as something he never really was." He was "a pathetic symbol of the so-called German Jews of Prague." Writing as memory, remembrance as absence, internal exile as ongoing modern incompleteness: Kafka's situation—living among Czechs, participating in German intellectual literary heritage, "belong[ing] to neither community," considering oneself "part of a Europe that survived only as a community of letters"—was to embody an incompleteness and liminality in a place "that kept the memory of its ghetto alive" even as its liquidation was predictable.[52]

Despite Fiedler's annoyed tone in "Kafka and the Myth of the Jew," published with other essays in a section called "Three Jews" in *No! in Thunder* in 1960—the same year as the critical blockbuster *Love and Death in the American Novel*—his aim was to treat seriously the phenomenon of "the dignity of [the Jew's] ultimate exile" and "the noblest metaphor of the Outsider." Still, he ridiculed the emergence of the facile identifying gestures of sympathetic respondents to Kafka after the war. " 'Yes, it is like this!' we cry. 'Yes, *I* am like this!' " And further mockery: " 'We are all Semites.' " Fiedler seemed just as bothered by the ready acceptance of Kafka's modern style: it's the "stubborn integrity of the fragment"[53] that in the first place should induce rapture over the difficulty *we all* claim to face. The deradicalization of such a modern style was being managed, lamentably, in the name of sentimental postgenocide philo-Semitism.

Fiedler wanted to clear the critical terrain of liberal overidentification in order to assess Kafka's effective radical linking of the "eternal . . . expulsion from Paradise"—the current Jewish condition—with a certain innovative way of writing. That exilic status is "final," Kafka wrote (so Fiedler quoted him), and yet there is (just as Celan observed too) an "eternal nature of the occurrence" that makes possible the kind of art in which "we are continuously there whether we know it or not."[54] "There"? Where? Celan in "The Meridian" answered: *in the writing*. That indeed was the whole point of his talk. Fiedler's Kafka answered: in "the unforeseen lucidity of the obsession," in "the irreducibility of meaning maintained like a martyrdom." The "essential Jewishness of Kafka" just now was that he had tenaciously held to this double connection: on one hand, a specific homelessness or internal exile; and, on the other hand, the qualities of modern writing. Fiedler's complaint was that the particular Jewishness of this situation has made it possible—at a time when "public word on Kafka is a piety, almost obligatory amongst us, to the Zeitgest," even a "focus of love and fashion"—to forget that the "essential Jewishness of Kafka" inheres in the way he transformed a commitment to the haggadic method in which love of wisdom (content) is indistinguishable from, and, radically, less important than, the love of story (form). So "to call Kafka a Jew is not . . . to deny that he is a heretic." Kafka's modern radicalism lies in his demand that the "intolerable conditions" of faith at a time of systemic bureaucratic protofascism "be explained in terms of his *own* reason."

Fiedler argued that Kafka's genius was that he came to the very edge of leaping into the void but could not leap. He was on the verge of a flight from reason altogether, yet clung to a language coherent at the level of the sentence, on the threshold of its utter failure. Fiedler admired Kafka's "refusal to leap to faith where reason eventuates in anguish." From the perspective of a decade and a half after the total disaster he was said to have predicted, to look back at Kafka's "refusal to leap" was to imagine such anguish even further intensified. The question became who was in a position to observe the specific effects of the victim's agony. The "fashion" of "Semitism" created out of victimization a critical ideology. Judeophilia was a false latitudinarianism that tended to disguise the heretical elements of a style that had been conveying what cannot be readily known. Fiedler was less interested in such liberalism as was entailed in embrace of the noble outsider than in the radical "negative orthodoxy" that results when historical Judaism enforces its tendency not to "disown . . . its great heretics completely." The modernist "irreducibility of meaning maintained like a martyrdom" must not become merely obligatory if intolerable conditions are to be comprehended in an "unforeseen" clarity in this terribly unclear writing—writing so obsessively reasonable it becomes an aspect of a dreamlike surrealism. The leap beyond reason is an uneasy, daring next step.[55]

## Life Under the Perpetual Rule of Accidents

Parker Tyler's Kafka is the uneasiest of all, a figure who seems to have already taken that next step. This was according to the montaged argument of an irregular book, *The Three Faces of the Film: The Art, the Dream, the Cult* (1960). For Fiedler, Kafka could not undertake the final flight from reason, and the result was a style of grim logic that made it—happily, in Fiedler's view—impossible for facile, wisdom-seeking readers (Cold War–era Americans in particular) to fathom its form; thus its radicalism remains latent in its "unforeseen lucidity." For Celan, reconsidering Kafka as he prepared "The Meridian," the eerie language was a matter somehow of possession (or lack of it), not being; "being" seemed to be for Celan a synonym for the kind of postdisaster attentiveness to which he now aspired. (In his notes he kept mulling over this formulation: "Kafka: / Language means to have, not to be.") Celan sought to venture in writing himself where Kafka could not go, perhaps because the earlier artist did not live through the disaster toward which the "having" of his writing inclined. Celan's leap in "The Meridian" indicates a getting through and then beyond, from languaged world as compassed, to language as known somehow otherwise—a breathturning from the world in order to get back into it. "To get oneself through language," Celan wrote, "which—Kafka!—is only a having, into an accurate relation with one's Being—"[56] For Parker Tyler in *The Three Faces*, Kafka *had already made the leap* when in his first incomplete novel, *Amerika*, he had experimentally resituated the body of the guilt-ridden K. from "its European constriction" to the "legendary openness" of the United States.[57] This was a pathology of the nonrealist horizontal body in space that became for Tyler the key to understanding a new hero for the 1960s emerging in avant-garde film.

Tyler's experimental fiction back in the 1930s had been influenced by Gertrude Stein and Djuna Barnes. He had cowritten a comic novel about gay life in New York in a style consciously imitating that of Barnes. His surrealist dream-poems in *The Granite Butterfly* (hailed by William Carlos Williams as "the best long poem produced in America since the disaster of Eliot's Waste [Land]")[58] discovered an avid avant-garde readership toward the end of the seven-year run of *View*, the left-surrealist magazine Tyler coedited. Many of the contributors to *View* had taken refuge in the United States during the war, and brought to New York, through *View*'s special issues and antic social energy, the ideas and practices of European avant-gardes.[59] Tyler had spent part of the 1930s and the early war years in Los Angeles, where his modernist projects converged with an interest in movies; his thirty-year relationship with underground filmmaker Charles

Boultenhouse also shaped his turn toward film. *The Three Faces of the Film* was the first of Tyler's books to bring together all three fascinations: Euro-modernism's quixotic open-endedness; the constrained exilic experience of guilt-ridden innocence encountering American vastness; and action as less an experience than a dream. "The Dream-Amerika of Kafka and Chaplin," an experimental essay-chapter at the heart of the book, investigates all three issues at once.

As with Olafson, Krieger, Heller, Camus via Politzer, and Fiedler, Tyler's sense of the relevance of Kafka pertains to the way in the writing "the innocent [is] inextricably fused with the guilty." In each fiction, K. is written from legal judgment, the "'undesirable alien' of Kafka's Castle-land." Tyler's analysis, too, was a postholocaust reconsideration. His focus on *Amerika* makes sense as an augmentation of analyses in 1960 of *The Trial* and *The Castle* as predescriptions of fascism's effect on the spectral Jewish body. The early novel was also known as *The Disappeared* (*Der Verschollene*); Tyler's interest is in the lost "Dream-Amerika," the "fantasy 'Amerika' that we find difficult to keep separate from the real one."[60] He presented not just a postwar experience of rereading Kafka but that of many contemporary avant-garde artist's accounts of *wartime* annihilation. Why did Tyler now pair Kafka with Chaplin (as Arendt had been the first to do in "The Jew as Pariah," written during the war)?[61] Because in each "there is the 'crime' of being a Jew." Yet whereas Chaplin's tramp "cannot be aware of anything as a crime," Kafka's K. is "very much aware of *a* crime but he cannot identify *what* crime he has committed"[62]—and this makes all the difference, Tyler implied, between the homeless picaro wandering innocently through a guilty world, on the one hand, and on the other the undesirable alien acting out of guilt to face the surrealism, or superrealism, of social judgment. Notwithstanding his critiques of the rise of totalitarian hate—and the racist vilification in Nazi propaganda of the peculiar walk, flat feet, and furtive posture of the Jew,[63] and of the damnable Blackness of "this chimp in human clothing" with his "monkey business" and transgressive sexual "knowledge of . . . the beautiful blondes"[64]—Chaplin is for Tyler by 1960 a throwback. Kafka, however, will have greater influence on the postwar scene as the new era begins.

"The chief imaginative trend among Experimental or avant-garde film-makers is action as a *dream*, and the actor as a *somnambulist*," Tyler wrote in an eccentric, poetic caption called "The Dream" placed under a still photo taken from Stan Brakhage's film *Reflections on Black* (1955). The "'exotica' of pathology and supernaturalism" is Tyler's provocative phrase for what happens when action in art is permitted to occur "without the restraints of single-level consciousness, everyday reason, and so-called realism."[65] This was what he found so compelling in Kafka's *Amerika*. A surrealist anthropometry and anamorphism—the use of anamorphic photography, a technique Tyler locates in avant-garde films of the late 1950s, achieved through distorting images made by a special lens—indicate a desire to represent compression as a quality of dream, especially of the body of the undesirable alien trying to retain verticality, to remain honorably standing, across a broad landscape, which was what Tyler believed is the novel's greatest power. Kafka in *Amerika* momentarily managed to survive the constraint of "his situation" by, in effect, *going wide* even as affect is flattened. "He converted his own personal myth," Tyler writes, "with its European [geographic] constriction and metaphoric girth (the 'fairy tale' land of *The Castle*), into a common myth with a legendary openness . . . America itself."[66] "Openness" here has a double meaning for Tyler's eccentric book. The horizontality of the Dream-Amerika sets the human body in a contrast starker than ever, and is a matter of thematic, national setting. A nonrealist art, as a matter of aesthetic practice, leaves meaning undetermined even if the "land of phantasmal mechanisms" seems no less otherwise fascistic.[67] Thus when elsewhere in *The Three Faces* Tyler writes about recent films, he often returns to the experimental anthropometry of the Kafkaesque body wandering "amid the chaos of great cities."

Tyler meditates upon Peter Weiss's film from 1959, *The Mirage*, for instance, in which the protagonist, leaning precariously off a rickety wooden scaffold, gets a high view of "industry's 'daymarish' labyrinth," and stands ready to make his leap into the void (figure 4.1). This "illustrates the very spirit of Kafka's novel, *Amerika*." The impending leap qualifies him as the "new hero" of a new art. Son of a Hungarian Jewish father, himself a wartime exile from Germany, and later creator of the documentary play based on the Auschwitz trials, *The Investigation* (1965), Weiss in *The Mirage* expressed the influence of Wolfgang Staudte's film *Murderers Among Us* (*Die Mörder sind unter uns*, 1946), his first screening of which in 1947 provoked in Weiss a sense of film's capacity after genocide to make use of the "inexhaustible stock of painfully realistic, oddly dreamlike and surreal, shocking, accusatory, and thought-provoking visions."[68] Tyler observes in *Three Faces* that Weiss's character in *The Mirage* is caked in drying cement, markings of his hard alienated labor. His leap is a Kafkaesque/postmodern/ New Left updating of the old proletarian industrial martyr who falls—or maybe dives—headlong into and is monumentally entombed in a vat of cement in Pietro diDonato's wild modernist-communist novella of the 1930s, *Christ in Concrete* (made into a film in 1949, its director and lead actor then blacklisted). By presenting the still photograph from *The Mirage* as he does, Tyler emphasized a new socioaesthetic relationship guided by Kafka's self-destructive,

**4.1** A page from Parker Tyler's *The Three Faces of the Film* (1960) includes a still from Peter Weiss's 1959 film, *The Mirage*, in which the protagonist, leaning precariously off a rickety wooden industrial scaffold, gains a view of "industry's 'daymarish' labyrinth." A. S. Barnes.

pregenocidal "situation." It established a connection between the extreme impetus for the making of a work of art and the urge to plunge beyond reasoned interpretations of transcendence—what Thomas McEvilley (in discussing Yves Klein's art of self-endangerment) calls "the meta-hermeneutics of the Leap";[69] or what Arendt, in Kafka's sole appearance in *The Origins of Totalitarianism*, describes as the effect of life "under the perpetual rule of accidents, the inevitable tendency to read a special superhuman meaning into happenings whose rational significance is beyond . . . knowledge and understanding."[70] Celan, pondering how to write and read while living such a pariah's life ruled by accident, was referring to the annihilations of the war with greater personal specificity than Tyler or Klein—or even Weiss and Arendt—when he contemplated what he must now do in order to create, to "Leap—as entrance into the poem."[71] Yet at the same time, Tyler's Kafka, one of the modernist saints of the renewing avant-garde, helped viewers understand the special unreasonable "new hero" of *The Mirage* and similar figures in other such projects with

the same sort of "simple attentiveness" as that called for by Celan in preference
to mainstream "cultural busyness." Similarly, Yves Klein's attempts to explore
the "magico-artistic function of 'supporting birth into the tangible word,' "[72]
while situated in an art world seemingly far removed from Celan's (although
both of course were working in Paris), befit the sort of alternative "entrance
into the poem" Celan and others sought at the very end of the fifties.

# 5

# Oppose the Anti-Everything

## Zero Art and the Hopeful Leap

### Daring to Look at the Sky

The most assiduous interpreter of Yves Klein's art as a specific postwar phenomenon, Thomas McEvilley, contends that Klein's *Leap Into the Void*, while it seems an idiosyncratically mystical (even Rosicrucian) expression of one artist's obsessions with dreaming, flying, and dematerializing, is part of an effort to make of art a swerve "from worldly chaos into a beyond that is still characterized by unchanging verities."[1] Citing James Webb's histories of occultism as reactions to specific historical crises, in *The Flight from Reason* and other books, McEvilley outlines a parallelism between the modernist Orphism of Kazmir Malevich's avant-garde impetus (and that of Marcel Duchamp, László Moholy-Nagy, Piet Mondrian, and others) and the resurgence of artists in the late 1950s, and especially during 1960 and 1961, who signed the sky as an artwork (as Klein did), who presented matte monochome canvases slashed with a knife (as Zero-affiliated Argentine-Italian artist Lucio Fontana did), who made "fire paintings" with the burnt residue from flame throwers, Bunsen burners, and various flaming objects (Otto Piene, Henk Peeters, Jef Verheyen, and again Klein). "Periods of massive social and historical stress and disruption tend to foster Orphic thematics," and in this special sense the avant-gardism of 1960 sought restoration of the "reaction against the very method [of the so-called Age of Reason] which had brought success, a wild return"[2] to the "negative orthodoxy" that Fiedler, with seeming illiberalism, saw in Kafka's prophetic modernism, and that Baraka, through an awakened radicalism, sensed was demanded by the "new peoples" he began to recognize after applying his critique of American reason. In studying Yves Klein's art and ideas, McEvilley concludes that the "'flight from reason' [which] recurred with greater force" after World War II—greater still, he means, than in the previous postwar era (1919 to circa 1922) that had actuated high modernism—helps to interpret the *Leap Into the Void* as "a historical" "moment of going beyond all codes and interpretations, into the void where . . .'one stands firmly because one stands upon nothing.'"[3]

Not one "moment" in 1960, to be more precise, but at least three. On January 12, Klein gave a "practical demonstration of levitation" and leaped from the second-story ledge of a colleague's house at 67 rue de l'Assumption, apparently without a net and no witnesses.[4] On October 19 and 25, the leap was repeated (this time apparently with a net) and photographed. And on November 27, 1960, one of the pictures, after some photo-montaging, was published in a four-page faux daily newspaper, *Dimanche, the Newspaper of a Single Day*, and became the sensation of the Parisian art world (figure 5.1).

*Dimanche* exactly reproduced the layout and fonts of a Parisian daily and was distributed to newsstands that Sunday morning. The metahermeneutics of *Dimanche* and *Leap* were not one-offs for Klein as he variously explored the new radical aesthetics of the postwar body and expounded upon the relation between levitation, transcendence, and liberty, between "the void and fire"— and generally upon the "poetics of space."[5] His infamous performance piece "Anthropometries of the Blue Age," a Fluxus-like happening enacted before a seated audience at Galerie Internationale d'Art Contemporain on March 9, 1960, conceived of people as "living brushes." When the dance-painting was finished, the "Anthropometries" were exhibited as "'ashes' of the process." As McEvilley suggests, these were not "parodies of the traditional craftsmanly art of the figure." If they seemed to be antiart, it was in the way they returned to the aesthetic while still rejecting the fetish of the painting by drawing attention to the process as producing "ashes," figures of living beings finally arising out of destruction.[6] Soon Klein would combine the technique of painting with fire and the Anthropometries, wetting a canvas applied by bodies and then flaming it, thus outlining the human shape with "ghostlike traces."[7] Otto Piene's dark flame-orange canvas bears a seven-by-five grid of thirty-five round burns, its title, *Seventh Attempt to Burn the Night* (1960), suggesting a repetitive, perhaps even obsessive, campaign to reclaim the gloom by cauterizing it.[8] It is plausible to read Henk Peeters's *Pyrography: 8 Lines* (1960, soot on paper, 50 x 70 cm) as

**5.1** Yves Klein, *Leap Into the Void*, photographed by Harry Shunk and János (Jean) Kender, 1960. Yves Klein Archive. Reproduced by permission of Artists Rights Society.

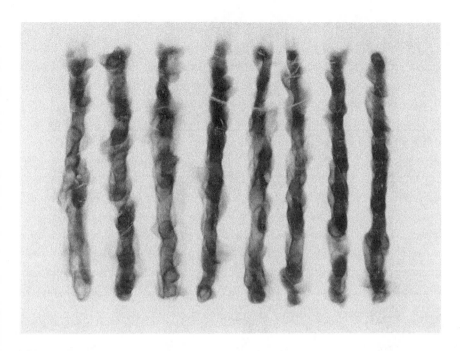

5.2 Henk Peeters, *Pyrography: 8 Lines* (1960, soot on paper, 50 x 70 cm). Courtesy Tijs Visser. O-Archive/o-Institute, ZERO Foundation.

a quasi-figural representation of immolated people laid out (figure 5.2). The pyrographies seem to convey Peeters's response to his own wartime apprehensions—he and his father printed newspapers for the resistance inside the family cigar factory and harbored Jewish friends,[9] and Henk then became active in the antifascist Dutch Communist Party[10]—as a method commensurate with the modernist imperative that the artist's attention should always turn "in upon the medium of his own craft"[11] yet now seeing process, additionally, as the making of ashes, limning ghostly absences of the body-gone-up-in-smoke.

Burning the painter's historically cherished canvas with flamethrowers, the artists of 1959, 1960, and 1961 affiliated with the Nul (artists mostly Dutch, some Italian, one Japanese) and Zero (mostly German, some French, Italian, American, Argentinian) movements explored an avant-gardism that might not be readily understood as deeply affected by the war's destructions, or indeed as postfascist. Yet aesthetically as such they are the cousins of Celan's verse absences and Bachmann's "learning the language of shadows" in prose, of Tyler's rereading of the Dream-Amerika as witnessing "The Disappeared," and of Rod Serling's sense (bespoken by Serling himself at the end of the *Twilight Zone* episode about Dachau) of the bizarre postdisaster world fifteen years later as a grave-yard of ashes "into [which] they shoveled all their reason, their logic, their knowl-edge."[12] If Yves Klein's art had a postwar politics, it was, as I have said, a post-logic or postknowledge negative orthodoxy, a rejection of the rejection of politics in a reaffirmation of modernism's flight from reason. McEvilley is surely right to see in Klein's conceptualist works of 1959 and 1960 his "act[ing] out the estab-lishment of a postgovernmental age." Of course his venture into parodic fake news, the four-page fictive newspaper, expressed such an intervention. In Novem-ber 1960 it momentarily disrupted codes of reasonable daily journalism and descriptive practices. Reading it (as no doubt many astonished Sunday readers of the news did) alongside the normative journalism of the day was an experi-ence very much like that of reading Celan's poems written opaquely from "our January 20th" alongside William Shirer's *Rise and Fall of the Third Reich* with its assumption that fascist effects could now be described with transparent final-ity. The headline above the *Leap* photograph ran "THEATER OF THE VOID" and the caption read "The Painter of Space Hurls Himself Into the Void." The "lead story," written by Klein himself, urged readers not to mistake this for a mere metropolitan conceptualism. It was his attempt to thwart dismissals of the stunt as neodadaist gag. The negative orthodoxy was strange yet sincere and hopeful. "The theater which I propose is not only the city of Paris, but is also the countryside, the desert, the mountain, even the sky. . . . Why not?"[13]

Otto Piene, who with Heinz Mack had founded the Zero group and whose *Pure Energy* (1958; exhibited at MoMA) had been inspired by László Moholy-Nagy's modernist *Light Space Modulator* (1930), sought as Klein did to sign the sky. What Piene later called "Sky art"—the term coined when he came to teach at the University of Pennsylvania at the end of the 1960s[14]—had begun in 1958–61 with his plan to "rid the night sky of its negative associations with wartime destruction by transforming it into a site for creation,"[15] to work art into the great-est realm, "light and space," "without being driven by fear and mistrust."[16] Dirk Pörschmann, writing about Zeroist utopianism, historicizes this experimental sensibility as a renewal of original modernist energies. First there was the flow-ering of the avant-garde from dada to Bauhaus in "expressive societies" of the interwar years; then in the 1940s "the collective madness of one people and the attempted annihilation of many others"; and, finally, in the late 1950s and 1960, the "revival of hope in places and lives that had been reduced to rubble." Zero movement artists, the generation born around 1930, "once again dared to look to the sky, the earth having shown itself to be intolerable."[17] During metamechanist

Jean Tinguely's first solo show in Germany, Zero-sponsored, he staged a post-constructivist action in which he tossed manifestos calling for "static" ("Be static! Movement is static!") from an airplane,[18] instructing recipient readers below his sky to "Live in the present" for an "absolute reality."[19] Piero Manzoni, whose outrageous Zero-, Nul-, and Fluxus-affiliated conceptual works of 1959–61 are seen as a critique of the hypercapitalism of the so-called postwar Italian economic miracle,[20] announced in 1960—an intensely productive year for him—that he would build a *Placentarium*, a spherical, pneumatic plastic theater to house Otto Piene's *Light Ballet*.[21] For Klein, "the sky as transcendence" meant both engagement and extrication for people disoriented by the situation on the ground.[22] In one of the "articles" published in *Dimanche, the Newspaper of a Single Day*, Klein responded to news of Russian cosmonauts' impending intrusion into artists' sky: "Today anyone who paints space must actually go into space to paint . . . he must go there by his own means."[23] The artist's "own means" (here distinct from and better than institutionally mobilized Soviet rocket science) meant not just DIY constructions, improvised tools on hand for making art, crude assemblages—a launch without boosters—but also a basic posttraumatic sincerity about the politics of this unique avant-garde moment: write, paint, sculpt, create like an artist having endured a coming of age amid mass murder, yes, but respond in such a way as not to reproduce any aspect of the same old vocabularies of guilt—neither competitive rehabilitation, nor left-to-right recrimination, nor insane space race. A teenager during the war in industrial Lübbecke in northwestern Germany, directly under the flight path of Luftwaffe sorties to England, Piene wrote in "Paths to Paradise" (for the third issue of *Zero* magazine, published in mid-1961) that his "greatest dream" was the "projection of light into the vast night sky,"[24] a postwar searchlight *not* deployed the least bit defensively. "Making empty space," as Francesco Lo Savio wrote in 1960, constituted the "first act of a process aimed at the affirmation" of reality. The process entailed recovery, a lessening of anxiety, not through therapeutically coming to (old) terms with horrors rained down from the skies, but aesthetically taking back the sky once "owned"—the cliché term preferred by journalists and military historians[25]—by the Luftwaffe. Who now *owned the skies* over Europe? Zero did. So Zero was liberationist: if previously "freedom of action" had "seemed precluded," now the new artistic "freedom annuls the anxiety of the end and offers an experience that will be able to live into the future."[26]

Heinz Mack and Otto Piene had begun at art school together in 1950 in Dusseldorf. As Mack recalled later, they were "surrounded by ruins" and "enclosed by a cultural cemetery," cut off from historical knowledge that might help form connections back to artists who had previously felt the urge to innovate as they now felt—a total evacuation of art context that was "unimaginable" in later decades. Valerie Hillings, assessing the postwar aesthetic disorientation felt by Mack and Piene just before they founded Zero, describes the movement as a response like that of the New Young German Poets, Zeroists' contemporaries, as Jerome Rothenberg encountered them—a response, that is, to "the Third Reich's efforts to eradicate the prewar avant-garde, including the exile and murder of progressive artists, dealers, art historians, and critics," which created an "information vacuum" (so Mack understated it) that "left Germany with a paucity of concrete links to experimental art of the late nineteenth and early twentieth centuries."[27] In 1957 Mack and Piene had begun to hold their nighttime gatherings at Piene's studio in order to teach themselves and their new colleagues how to redraw those lineages. So linking back to modernism for this generation turning thirty in 1960 was a *content* goal of an alternative art education. But the *form* of these evenings expressed an aim just as vital: Mack and Piene aimed to alter the very idea of exhibition—the gatherings were called "Evening *Exhibitions*"—into an "ephemeral configuration," a "performance, an event in real time, without the long-term consultability of fixed objects."[28] Hillings adds that such art happenings, because they eschewed post-facto "consultability," also meant "the ability to once again speak openly about progressive ideas."[29]

Avant-gardists now had three choices according to Piene: first, "splendid resignation" (the pleasure of "decay and decadence, the pleasant tortures of insisting on a ruined world"); second, participating in postwar art profiteering (by producing conventional "sculptures of motherhood and brotherhood on public plazas"); or third, optimism. When they chose the third, "the absurd position of optimism," Zeroists were reestablishing one of those connections that had been severed, bypassing the unhopeful existentialism that was fashionable—and indeed that earned some postwar philosophers and novelists some of the easy money available to those who made the second choice—in favor of the sort of ethical absurdism that Olafson and Tyler rediscovered in Kafka, Rothenberg explored in Duncan's take on Scholem, Baldwin outlined in "Notes" motivated by his "blind[ly] optimist[ic]" anti-anti-Semitic response to the pessimism of Roth and Cheever, and Celan worked through in "The Meridian" when writing about how postwar responsibility could be discovered through "homage to the majesty of the absurd." It marked an end of what Pörschmann in telling the Zero story calls "the political and social caesura" that followed the conclusion of World War II.[30]

Yes, I dream of a better world
Should I dream of a worse?

—wrote Piene in verse in "Paths of Paradise." Thus art's looking toward light, upward to sky: "Pictures are no longer dungeons." And thus the restoration of counterintuitive avant-garde "intimacy": "We treat pictures as neighbors or friends."[31]

Pörschmann describes the Zeroists' choice of absurd optimism as having "required courage" and contends that its source in many respects can be found in the "principle of hope" delineated by the unorthodox Jewish Marxist Ernst Bloch in three volumes of theory, the third of which was published in German in 1959 (though the whole project had been composed in the United States during Bloch's time as a refugee from Nazism).[32] *The Principle of Hope* argued that a humane art and culture depended on a rereading of the psychoanalytic idea of the unconscious, with a new preference for the terms "Not-Yet-Conscious" or the "Not-Yet-Become." The latter formulation in the original is *Noch-Nicht-Gewordene*, that which has "not even (yet) broken through as a word,"[33] the word as *during* never reaching its *after*, the aforementioned unsayable X of witness. The focus on "process" in Bloch's theorizing expresses his belief in the openness of the world: mutability, provisionality, motion, constant development.[34] Latent but unavailable traumas repressed can emerge when one redefines the unconscious as "forward dawning" and thus can repudiate Carl Jung's emphasis[35]—which Bloch deemed fascist—on unified, collective prehistories. On the basis of Zeroist aesthetics, Pörschmann has found Piene's comments to be directly influenced by Bloch's principles of hope. As young artists coming to maturity, although still plentifully angry, they wanted to make a new promising *alternative normalcy* out of extreme strangeness without repressing the humane. Sometimes the trauma of wartime youth was silent in their statements. Sometimes it was openly part of the contention, as in this moving remark: "It is not normal, after all, to send adolescent children to war at fifteen. Out of resistance to the war and against the duress of the Nazi period it is understandable that one might desire something different and better and clearer than such chaotic and constrained conditions. Hence the vision of a better, constructive, and more humane future."[36] The statement comes from an essay titled "Where Nothing Was Reflected as the Sky." As we have seen, the sky for Yves Klein was the space into which one leaped in order to instigate true art, like Celan's "Leap—as *entrance* into the poem." "Nothing Was Reflected" up there, yet it was *not* a nullity, but rather an open possibility for meaning. This correlates with bearing witness as it might be modified now by the principle of hope: the "negative space" of witnessing that is nonetheless productive, described by researchers such as Anna Neumann who study the "unworded stories" of the war-traumatized. Their metatexts, testimony as process, can "exist untold and in unrealized . . . form in the present day of its enactment."[37] Zeroists chose to create just such "a zone of silence," to use Piene's phrase, but again it was not a negation of the importance of having witnessed what happened. Zero, rather, signified "pure possibilities for a new beginning."[38] Henk Peeters, who met Klein in person in 1960, coauthored a "MANIFESTO AGAINST NOTHING" to help launch the Nul group; these artists called for the disbanding of art circles ("No art trade is just as functional as art trade"), true, but they were also saying through a typical Zeroist double negativity that they weren't against anything. "Something is almost nothing (not something)."[39] When Nul-affiliated Dutch artist Herman De Vries made 120 copies of a book comprising twenty blank white pages and a white cover (*Wit Is Overdaad*, Arnhem, Netherlands, 1960), he was contending that the reader should not consider the pages empty but should try to read them.[40] We are thus compelled to read into the void. This is Anna Neumann's realization about responsibility (as an ability to respond) toward what the witness saw but later chooses not to represent. "How do untold stories manifest themselves?"[41] Lo Savio's idea of "making empty space" meant the diminishment of "anxiety of the end," yet that emptiness—rather than a repressed absence, a refusal to tell, a neurotic gap, or forgotten negative—indicated new meaning. It is difficult to come any closer to a description of Celan's writing and Bloch's theorizing as emergent from the fascist night of the word. "The present of the poem," Celan wrote in his notebook, is that which "can <remain> unsaid because perhaps un unsayable—" even as the "porous poem it stands into time."[42] The "zone of silence" experimental artists now sought to enter was the opposite indeed of what Des Pres decries as "a 'conspiracy of silence' . . . undermin[ing] the survivor's authority"; on the contrary, as Des Pres argues, it aimed to reverse the doubting of expressions produced in response to mass suffering "so radically unique that the theory of neurosis is inadequate to deal with it."[43] When Celan observed that "The tendency to fall silent cannot not be hard,"[44] he was compounding a summary of much experimental art in the twentieth century with the urgency of its notorious "difficulty" at the end of this special "political and social caesura"—the "caesura" of 1945–60 having been itself a compounding of silence terrifyingly enforced in wartime. As with Celan, Bachmann, Karl Krolow, and others among those represented in *The New German Poets*, the Zero artists did *not* set out expecting to feel better as a result of this doubly negative—in other words, positive—difficulty.

When Mack and Piene visited an art show in Rotterdam, they objected to work they saw that "was burdened with an excessive psychological ballast."[45] Color was at the center of much of Zeroist and affiliated anti-Tachisme projects, most famously in Klein's monochromatic blue paintings, yet color was not seen by these people as psychologically symbolic. Even Bernard Aubertin's use of canvas-fields of red *opposed* "the universe of violence that the color red generates as a psychological force." Color, he added in an essay for *Zero* magazine's third issue (published in 1961), was not "intended to liberate the accumulated emotional tensions of the human being."[46] Color was gestureless presentation. It was not pictorially semantic; it was space. Zeroists opposed Art Informel or Tachisme as expressionistic. Tachisme was to Zero as dark is to light. Yet light in these works was not any more symbolic than blue or red. It meant, wrote Piene, "the space of action and movement, of life itself."[47]

## Destruction Construction

If these artists were antitherapeutic and antisymbolic, disrupting abstract expressionist angst, how can we possibly discern the real politics of their avant-gardism? Well, for one thing, they certainly did not shy from making political statements. They decried the lack of contemporary relevance in the work of Art Informel. Their conceptual writing and publication strategies, as Johan Pas observes, sought to raise the artist's concepts "to the level of world news,"[48] with Klein's *Dimanche* being an obvious instance of this ambition. In response to Germany's rearmament, and the creation of a "minister of shooting," Piene in a speech proposed a national organization headed by a "minister of creativity," just as France in 1959 had appointed novelist and art theorist Andre Malraux to lead its new Ministry of Culture. Zero movement art, so difficult to read politically if one uses the established ideological vocabularies of the late forties and fifties, intervenes at the moment when the end of ideology is reversed. Piene, in emphasizing Zero's absurdly optimistic opacity, made the point as succinctly as any artist readers will encounter in this book, except perhaps Baldwin in his "Notes": "The present does not need any 'anti's' to better it, but rather a 'for,'" Piene wrote. "Like many of my friends, I choose to oppose the 'anti everything'

with a 'for everything,' or more precisely a 'for everything for,' though negativity has become the empty-headed fashion of our time."[49]

Such "brave hopes," as Heinz Mack put it when describing his utopian *Sahara
Project*, depended on the complete erasure of distinctions between nature and
artifice and a fearless embrace of technology in spite of its associations with fascist warfare. In this sense, too, Zero and its Nouveau Réalisme established continuities from the dynamic devotion to the revolutionary newness of modernist
integrations of the natural and the technological such as those of William Carlos Williams and László Moholy-Nagy. There might be a technoindustrial dynamism to a Williams springtime, an electro-metallic intrusion from sea or into
air in a modulator constructed by Moholy-Nagy, who was a direct influence on
the "artificial garden" Mack proposed to create. In 1960–61 he formulated his
proposal for "a vibrating pillar of light in a desert." He and others were seeking
a vibrancy with "intensity" so extreme that it "necessarily demands a new environment."[50] In posters and leaflets advocating their ideas, Mack, Piene, and Günther Uecker urged once again that "Zero is the beginning" but added this: "Zero
is beautiful, dynamo dynamo dynamo. The trees in springtime, the snow, fire,
water, sea."[51] Here they were recalling in part the way in which the various
"Dynamo" poets and artists of the 1930s had called for an integration of modernism and political radicalism in celebrating operative industrial intensity and
contemporary energy as a new kind of nature.[52] Piene, Mack, and others felt they
were staging a return in two ways: to the electrical and photogrammic industri-
alism of Bauhaus modernists like Moholy-Nagy, to a revival of constructivism
that aesthetically bypassed the early 1940s; and to an ideologically unapologetic
use of technology while rejecting and severing its connection to technologies
of war. Piene later recalled for *Art in America* that "Artists after the war turned
against technology, because war is technology," but no longer was such psychic
avoidance or political timidity sufficient. "Zero was about the pure possibilities
for a new beginning." "Dynamo dynamo dynamo" *and* "trees in springtime"—
both of these at once—enabled a new politics of industrial technology in art.
Assemblagists saw a true new realism in thingy accumulations. The question
was "not one of removing an object from its utilitarian, industrial, or other underlying context." Jean Tinguely, Arman (Arman Fernandez, the French-born
American whose *Zero* #3 essay "The Realism of Accumulations" is quoted here),
Sari Dienes (a Hungarian-born Polish-German-Serbian artist in the United
States, cut off from Europe since the second day of the war), and Raphael
Montañez Ortiz were all paying homage to, not denouncing, the restoration of
the industrial, technical object "to its proper context on a surface sensitized to

the nth degree by its multiplied presence." Multiplicity meant hypersensitivity, an "obsessional and emphatic aspect," making a postwar ethics not just of "automation" and "assembly-line production" but also of the rapid obsolescence or "discarding" that follows. Through her assemblages of New York discards, rubbings of manhole covers, etc., Sari Dienes developed this anti-aesthetic aesthetic view, similar to that of her friend John Cage. "It's not," Dienes said, "a question of whether it's going to be good, or bad, or interesting. It has to happen. It's like life."[53] The debris-strewn yet capacious, living city was going to be one of art's answers to war's negating hatreds. A poem Dienes wrote on December 6, 1944, during her exile from the world war engulfing every one of her previous urban homes, begins with this hope: "The world is wide. / This city is a wide point in it."[54]

Positive "discarding" was the key to the urban metamechanics of Jean Tinguely's assemblages. On March 17, 1960, before an audience (and NBC cameras)[55] in the sculpture garden at the Museum of Modern Art in New York City, Tinguely displayed, and then destroyed, his piece *Homage to New York*. He worked with people whose expertise as artist and/or engineer merged. Among them were Robert Rauschenberg and Billy Klüver, a U.S.-based electrical engineer and art-and-technology (and computer) pioneer, an early instance of artist hacker. Tinguely and Klüver together visited public dumps in Newark and Summit, New Jersey; at such sites, Klüver observed, "Jean behaved like a tourist seeing the Grand Canyon for the first time. To him the landscape [of the dump] was extremely beautiful."[56] Klüver, present at the event on March 17, provided an eyewitness account for *Zero*'s third issue. Such witnessing was crucial to the human freedom Tinguely wanted to achieve. The deconstruction of the artwork, its main formal aspect, coincided with the viewer-participant's experience of extirpation. "What was important for me was that afterwards there would be nothing, except what remained in the minds of a few people," he said in an (unpublished) interview for the *New Yorker* two years later. "This was for me very liberating."[57]

*Homage to New York* brought to an undestroyed city and to its ascendant undestroyed art world the postwar idea of creation about destruction, a concept that long after World War II remained "starkly relevant in an age of perpetual war."[58] For Tinguely it was the opposite of the petrification of the fixed and exhibited work of art exactly as "it was the opposite of the cathedrals."[59] That the attending public browsed the remnants of the machine for debris to pick and bring home made this not a mockery of Gothicism's fetish of ruination but an affirmation of "the energy of a city that keeps rebuilding itself time after time" as an example of "the different and sometimes conflicting conceptions of artists and engineers on how machines should work."[60] Destructivism was meant to be miraculous. Billy Klüver, the early art-happenings A/V operator, felt that this was the art that would commensurately respond to the actualities of life in the postwar city. "Jean's machine was conceived in 'total anarchy and freedom,'" Klüver reported for *Zero* magazine, quoting Tinguely, and continued: "New York has humor and poetry in spite of the presence of the machine. . . . This experiment in art could never fail."[61] Making her own art experiments "mostly out of found objects" in New York, the perpetual refugee Sari Dienes rejoiced in the real that was to be distinguished only by eschewing the typical intense *searching* for art: "If you are really concentrated on looking for something, then you miss all the things you are not looking for."[62] That "over the *ruins* of Hitler's psychotic Reich," as Rothenberg noted, would "emerg[e] . . . a new avant-garde" was "a miracle." That "through the contemporary *rubble*, heaped up daily before us, the poem comes . . .," as Paul Celan wrote on October 9, presents us miraculously with "everything necessary for life."[63] Through the lens of such counterintuitive aesthetic optimism one can sense kineticism in the breathturn.

Some commentators—still operating, I would argue, in a 1950s postwar mode—described the dismantling of the artwork as a kind of suicide. In the context of the survivor's writing constituted of rubble "provid[ing] [us] with everything necessary for life"—and given this book's idea that there was a moment when experimental art reached the end of the night of the word while intensifying rather than losing its innovative impetus—it will not be surprising to learn that Jean Tinguely disagreed with the view of his work as self-slaughter. The redistributive act following destruction was spontaneously communitarian. "It wasn't the idea of a machine committing suicide that fascinated me primarily; it was the freedom that belonged to its ephemeral aspect."[64] "Destruction construction" was constructive but not destructive.[65] "I do not interpret the self-destruction of Jean's machine as an act of protest against the machine or as an expression of nihilism and despair," wrote Klüver in his wittily titled report of the MoMA evening, "The Garden Party." "The self-destruction or self-elimination of the machine is the ideal of good machine behavior. . . .'L'art ephémère' . . . creates a direct connection between the creative act and the receptive act of the audience."[66] When Lucio Fontana slashed his monochrome canvases, he believed this was a gesture toward "purity" rather than extinction. It's true that his plane-slicing response to the traditional medium was to offer a nothing, but his "Spatial Concept" series—including several famous canvases of 1960, such as *Spatial Concept "Waiting,"* now at the Tate Museum in London (figure 5.3)—meant "not a destructive

**5.3** Lucio Fontana, *Spatial Concept 'Waiting'* (1960, canvas). Tate Modern, London. Lucio Fontana Foundation (Milan). Reproduced by permission of Artist Rights Society.

nothing, but a creative nothing."[67] "My cuts," he declared, "are above all . . . an act of faith in the infinite."[68]

Klüver and Tinguely contended that when the urban machine eliminated itself, a crucial creative community was sustained. This was not a paradox. Destructivist art, sculptor Raphael Montañez Ortiz now realized—in notes he wrote between 1959 and 1961[69] that would be finalized as "Destructivism: A Manifesto" (1962)—made the rediscovery of human integrity only when, through the disintegrative *process* by which it was "actually worked out in the actual world with actual people" in community, "actual things occur[red]."[70]

Ortiz attended a workshop in Colorado led by a woman who treated the post-traumatic stress effects of child survivors of the holocaust, and this not only led to two of his most famous works—"Monument to Buchenwald" (1961; paper, earth, shoes, mixed media on wood destruction; figure 5.4) and "Children of Treblinka" (1962; children's shoes, mud, paper)—but also directly influenced his notes on Destructivism. The art of destruction was a counterintuitive turning back toward life. "Our screams of anguish and anger will contort our faces and bodies, our shouts will be 'to hell with death.' . . . The artist's sense of destruction will no longer be turned inward in fear . . . for as it gives death, so it will give to life."[71] Ortiz's three main concerns at this time were (1) a study of ritual "psychic excavations" in an ethnopoetic "quest for the authentic," resulting in art as "a sacrificial process" exactly concurrent with Deep Image and the gnostic final stage of folk revival in the 1950s;[72] (2) historical and contemporary destructions in art as related to human experiences with violence (the holocaust in particular, but also personal histories of racist brutality, childhood injuries, etc.);[73] and (3) Zeroist use of urban refuse and the removal from artmaking of the constructive element. This third interest led Ortiz to the influence of Arman and Yves Klein, especially the latter's contribution to the shift away from Abstract Expressionist values. Ortiz's piece "De Kooning Is DeKleining" (1960) was an homage to Klein.[74]

Thus did Jean Tinguely, Sari Dienes, Raphael Montañez Ortiz, and other assemblagists and destructivists choose "to oppose the 'anti everything' with a 'for everything'" and often did so through formal presentations of urban detritus. The gesture meant engaging and turning toward rather than away from the reality of cities' destruction in the very act of "liberating" existing art vocabularies. Klein was seeing that those vocabularies—the frames it set up, the supposed emotional intensity it invested onto what are after all the traditional flat surfaces of the painterly canvas, a linearity that had not shaken free of the timidity the fascist years had imposed—are the "lines, bars, of a psychological

**5.4** Raphael Montañez Ortiz, *Monument to Buchenwald* (1961), burned shoes, nails, paper, dirt, and synthetic resin on wood, 29 7/8 × 28 × 6 7/8 in. (unframed). Menil Collection, Houston. Photograph by Paul Hester. Courtesy Chicano Studies Research Center, UCLA, and Raphael Montañez Ortiz.

prison . . . are our chains." And so with his miraculously unsuicidal leap he "refuse[d] more and more emphatically . . . the transient psychology of the linear, the formal, the structural." Klein made it clear that structure was not merely a term of art. It was "our heredity, our education, our framework, our vices."[75] If "every structure left to us by history expresses the spirit of its builder," as Alexander Kluge wrote in the prefatory captions to his experimental film *Brutality in Stone* (1960), "even if later used for *other purposes*," the problem of art, now that the rubble dust had settled, was to decide what those "other purposes" would be. How can we be sure that a retrospective antifascist interpretation of such purposes is warranted? How, to take an example from chapter 2, can we have confidence in an interpretation discerning antifascism (as distinct from ideas of fascist techno-utopian indoctrination) in Bachmann's description of the wartime schoolchildren in "Youth in an Austrian Town" from *The Thirtieth Year*— that they had been "allowed to forget their Latin and learn to distinguish between the sounds of the engines in the sky"?[76] Was not the talent for such discernment damaging to the children and detrimental to art representing that damage?

Kluge's utopian experimental films and theories help make this distinction, just as does Tinguely's oddly idealistic obsession with technology. Kluge's *Brutality in Stone*, also known as *The Eternity of Yesterday*,[77] a twelve-minute movie in black and white, works with Yves Klein's idea that structure is "our heredity, our education, our framework, our vices" by presenting scenes of empty, inhumanly scaled Nazi buildings—weeds now growing through cracks and marble edifices pocked with fifteen-year-old Allied artillery fire—juxtaposed against a contemporary Zero-style voice-over narration telling of negative spaces (for instance: "Imagine mud huts or holes in the ground"; figure 5.5). All this is mixed with archival audio recordings: snatches of martial music, sentences recited from the diary of Auschwitz's Rudolf Höss implying claims for the grand structure of Nazi language. *Brutality in Stone* goes far beyond an Ozymandias-like dramatic irony. Kluge, a critical theorist,[78] was interested in postfascist problems of education and socialization, an obsession, actually, made evident in *Teachers Through Change* (*Lehrer im Wandel*, 11 mins., 35 mm, b&w, 1962–63), which presents various forms of repressive traditional schools and "pedagogical institutions" through montaged depictions of three teachers.[79]

*Brutality in Stone* anticipated by two years the New German Cinema or German New Wave (founded through the Oberhausen Manifesto of 1962), and perhaps it is the first postwar German film to stand so overtly against the commercial cinematic amnesia of the 1945–60 interregnum. Kluge and colleagues decried "Papa's Kino" of that era—as in "Papa's Kino ist tot," *dad's movie is dead*. Here again we encounter a hopeful avant-gardism, expressing "a social utopian wish" and founded upon the inauguration of an open inquiry into the Nazi past.[80] Toward the end of *Brutality in Stone* footage of neoclassical models of buildings Hitler and Albert Speer planned to create for the city of Berlin after it was renamed "Germania" front a soundtrack of Allied bombing. National Socialist material arrangements, including the grounds of the 1935 Nuremberg Rally (which Leni Riefenstahl used as a shooting set), remain visually present even as

I can imagine mud huts or holes in the ground,

5.5 Still from Alexander Kluge, *Brutality in Stone* (1960).

the story of destructive victory over such a framework can be heard. Kluge means that those ideas of structure remain our "psychological prison . . . our chains . . . our education." "The Utopia of Film" (the title of Kluge's first essay) requires, first, reckoning impeding structures, followed by, second, an "orient[ation] toward cognition," whereupon, third, paradoxically, an "anti-defeatism" can emerge from materialism.[81] *Brutality in Stone* is meant to be antidefeatist despite its depiction of debris. Its narrator is the voice of the generation that needed to come of age before it could know itself to have been damaged so utterly by those remnant structures. When Bachmann's third-person narrator, in that jarring epiphanic volta, suddenly reveals that "*I* was among [those] children"—the children who had learned to hear the precise, distinctive sounds of the different war planes overhead in the sky *they* now owned—her writing, an attempt overall to defy the fact "that everything was as it was, that everything is as it is," becomes a search for a counterword even if (or perhaps because) that word "doesn't exist." It supposed a new practice of close listening. The murderous structural grandiosity Kluge's 1960 documentary depicts is sadly "*our* heredity"; it should not require Baldwin's intervention on October 22, or Fanon's citation of Césaire in his Tunis lectures, to specify that the first-person possessive pronoun "our" in "our heredity" meant that of white Christians, but the disjunctive form of Kluge's film itself is in any event precisely such heredity's opposite, just as Bachmann's counterword was not the already used word but the finding of its alternative and Tinguely's destruction of creativity *as* creativity was hardly the demise of the city but, on the contrary, its hopeful future—just as illogically hopeful as Baldwin's feelings about Harlem despite its gaps and eliminations. Kluge's *Teachers Through Change* was in this sense a sequel to his 1960 short on Nazi architecture. "The main reason I employ montage," Kluge said, "is to destroy images. Through the mutual destruction of two images in montage, there emerges a third term: an epiphany."[82] What has been said of Kluge, the belated "adamant modernist," should I think be said now of the Zeroists: through avant-garde techniques they sought to "bring forward all the lost utopian aspirations of past political and aesthetic projects, all the wishes and hopes that history has left unrealized."[83] They actually believed in realization as counterhistory. "Zero: wir leben," read a "Proklamation" that appeared on television in 1961.[84] In spite of nothing, or because of it: *We live.*

# 6

# Adjustment and Its Discontents

## Aleatory Art vs. Cold War Deradicalization

## To Silence Debate with Lullabies

"It was in 1960," said Sari Dienes, "that I finally came to the conclusion of what I consider art is doing and what it is about. . . . Art is . . . humanity's expressing, giving form to their understanding of the reality of the moment."[1] "I started in 1960–61," said Jackson Mac Low, "after about 6 years of making poems and plays by chance operations and making poems by deterministic method, to make performance pieces in which the performers had a great range of choices in realizing them. . . . This was for me a double encounter with contingency."[2] And in that year, as we will see, these two convergences converged.

First, *Sari Dienes*: the pioneer feminist assemblagist who would show with Jean Tinguely and others in MoMA's momentous "Art of Assemblage" exhibit in 1961. She lived and worked in "the collage environment," as the *Art of Assemblage* chief curator put it.[3] Initially during her wartime exile and then in the late 1940s and 1950s, Dienes developed an artistic practice that moved against the machismo gestural registers of Abstract Expressionism toward an "indexical appropriation of the environment."[4] She once encountered Jackson Pollock at a bar, who turned to her and said: "I hate you and I hate your work." And "besides, you cannot paint without balls." "Jackson," she later recalled responding, "that is your problem, not mine."[5] Dienes was a significant influence on Jasper Johns, who also overheard Pollock's campaign for "really painting with two balls"[6] and

**6.1** Jaspers Johns, *Painting with Two Balls* (1960), Philadelphia Museum of Art. Reproduced by permission of Artists Rights Society.

countered in *Painting with Two Balls* (1960), a sliced canvas, like Lucio Fontana's, proclaiming its own materially inclusive "objectness" as a means of repudiating overconfident ideas of art's transparency, and directing attention, as Dienes did, toward the artwork as made *like* (and also *of*) mechanisms (figure 6.1).[7]

Dienes had left Hungary bearing her Polish family name Chylinska. She moved to Paris, where she studied with Fernand Leger, and then ventured to

London and Wales with the mathematician-poet Paul Dienes.[8] In New York she befriended John Cage, Yoko Ono, and later many of the American and visiting European Fluxus artists. Her assemblages predated Tinguely's *Homage to New York*, but that event in March 1960 in MoMA's garden served to galvanize art-world interest in a cutting-edge practice that was said to be "closer to everyday life than either abstract or representational art" and evinced, according to "Art of Assemblage" curator William Seitz, a "new realism" similar in spirit to the Nouveau Réalisme co-founded in 1958–60 by Zeroists Tinguely, Piene, Klein, and others, and aligned (as noted by Kaira Cabañas) with Klein's visual immediacy and "performative realism."[9]

This interest in ordinariness coincided with three developments in Dienes's work: her increased attention to pacifist elements of Zen Buddhism beginning in her exilic war years, an intellectual and then political commitment that led in the 1950s to close associations with Cage and others; her creation of the large-scale series titled *Sidewalk Rubbings* in the mid-1950s, made of geometrical compositions combined with rubbings of manhole covers, subway grates, and other elemental pieces of the urban streetscape (her own homages to New York; figure 6.2); and her two-year visit (1958–59) to Japan, where she studied print-making and other art traditions amid aesthetic and urban environments permanently altered by wartime disasters, including those wrought by the two atomic attacks of 1945.

And then *Jackson Mac Low*: there were two sources of his revelation about nonintentional language and performance in 1960—his initial attempts at composing by deterministic methods, including acrostic "reading-through text selection" back in 1954 and 1955;[10] and his active involvement in protests against atomic civil defense preparations back in 1955. As New Yorkers had begun that summer to celebrate the ten-year anniversary of victory over Japan and, in the view of many artists on the left, as the celebrants repressed or understated the role nuclear mass killings had played in that triumph, members of the Catholic Workers, the War Resisters League, and the Fellowship of Reconciliation—plus Mac Low, who explained to newspaper reporters that he "was not a member of any of these groups"—refused on June 15, 1955, to participate in mandatory civilian descents into bomb shelters during a "theoretical H-Bomb raid." The front page of the evening edition of the *New York World-Telegram* featured four articles above the fold about the drill, three of them covering the arrests of Mac Low and thirty others, while below the fold was a photo of the thirty-two-year-old writer being led away by a policeman while holding a placard reading "LET'S FACE / THE TRUTH / THERE IS / NO REAL / CIVIL

**6.2** Sari Dienes, *Untitled* (rubbing of manhole covers), c. 1953–54, ink on Webril, dimensions unknown. Copyright © 2021 Sari Dienes Foundation/Licensed by VAGA at Artists Rights Society (ARS), NY.

DEFENSE / *AGAINST H BOMBS*" (figure 6.3).[11] Then on August 5, to mark "the 10th anniversary of the dropping of the A Bomb on Hiroshima," as he told *Poetry* magazine editor Henry Rago, he would "testify . . . to our shame & sorrow for the Hiroshima bombing," call an end to war, pay respects at the Japanese Consulate, and commence a ten-day fast.[12]

For five years Mac Low's experimentation with aleatory verse and his activities as an anarcho-pacifist (the pacifism more or less lifelong, the anarchism originating at the end of the war in 1945)[13] progressed separately and engaged him in distinct activities with two nonoverlapping networks of people and organizations. But in 1960, through the creative explosion of 172 poem/performance pieces later published under the title *Stanzas for Iris Lezak*, he discovered the convergence of avant-garde art and political action well summarized in the title of a later talk, "The Poetics of Chance & the Politics of Simultaneous Spontaneity."[14] In a 1961 letter to Rago at *Poetry*, he described his work "written in the years 1938 through 1959" as having been written generally by "intuitional

**6.3** Page 1 of the *New York World-Telegram*, June 15, 1955.

rather than chance-operational methods," marking the break at 1960.[15] Now poem scores were determined by chance operations but with a democratic difference: "the realizations were, within explicit limits, entirely up to the initiative and imagination of the performers." The writer thus "encounter[s] the performers as makers as they chose among the wide range of possibilities given by my scores."[16] Mac Low realized that these poetic experiments could move him and colleagues toward utopian ideas about a "society without a coercive force pushing everybody around" and into experiments in art that could invent models of a "free society of equals which it is hoped the work will help to bring about." Consistent with his and others' longing to return to prewar modernisms prior to postwar deradicalization, Jerome Rothenberg believed that through this synthesis of political and poetic heresies "Mac Low's art returns to something like the stance of an earlier avant garde (Russian Futurism, Dada, etc.) for which artistic, spiritual & political renewals were all part of a single impulse." (Rothenberg added his opinion that "in no contemporary does [such renewal] show through as clearly, movingly" as in Mac Low's.)[17]

It took this same five-year period before Mac Low would artistically reflect on his response to Sari Dienes's 1955 show at the Betty Parsons Gallery, whereupon he produced the visual poem/score "A Piece for Sari Dienes" (1960), which enabled just such an intersubjective cocreation, as we will see. Mac Low assiduously recorded every iteration of his aleatory method, but it is still difficult to piece together the reasons for the half-decade delay in the realization just described, the basis of nearly all his work from 1960 until his death in 2004. Yet the point of this cultural history is to present the end of the 1950s and start of the 1960s in such a way as to make these synthesizing moments explicable in the context of the art and politics of the avant-garde. And some reconstruction is possible. The prolific writings gathered later in *Stanzas for Iris Lezak*, 396 pages of pieces all composed in 1960 "between sometime in April or May & Halloween Week,"[18] were the result of strategies often devised during the daily subway ride between Mac Low's home in the Bronx and his various jobs in Manhattan. Each rewriting or appropriation hinges on the postwar antiauthoritarian idea of hopeful social cocreation like that which Tinguely deemed "liberating" when the ephemerality of *Homage to New York* as audience-involved Happening encouraged witnesses' impulse—in an act the very opposite of art's suicide—to help dismantle and literally to carry away the installation. It is also akin to that Zeroist absurd optimism longed for in the life-affirming leap enabled in public responses of astonished readers construing Klein's *Dimanche* as actual world news, which made it no less journalistic. To use Mac Low's phrase, there was now a newsworthy "politics of simultaneous spontaneity."

That is to say: there was a politics *in* (content gotten from sourcetexts) and also *of* (poetic form) the aleatory method itself. The act of writing-through was a rewriting miraculously adding *point of view* nonauthorially. The method was ideological but the sourcetexts were just out there, ambient in the panoramic gathering of news, reviews, magazine features, letters, broadsides, and brochures of 1960. There was of course also a politics in the *choices* of texts that now needed rewriting. During this (un)creative spree Mac Low wrote through texts about, among other topics, new approaches to city planning (criticism of Robert Moses's beltways supposedly requiring demolition of neighborhoods); "Forbidden Marriage," racists' dread of "miscegenation"; Nicholas Berdyaev's connection of Christianity and anti-Semitism; "The Myth of the Two Germanies"; white colonialism and apartheid in sub-Saharan Africa; useless efforts to plan surviving nuclear attack; Cuba after the revolution of 1959; the crisis in the Congo in that hopeful moment following the declaration of independence on June 30, 1960, by Patrice Lumumba; Adlai Stevenson's stump speech condemning Richard Nixon, candidate in the upcoming November 8 U.S. presidential election. Most of Mac Low's book consists of aleatory responses to texts producing the day's news.

Reading *Stanzas for Iris Lezak* is a way—albeit an eccentric one—of learning, without the aid or detriment of commentary, about events and crises of 1960. It is a truer account of 1960 than this book. Then again, the quasi-nonintentional mixing, sampling, scrambling, cutting-up of the words of Adlai Stevenson's comments on Nixon as prospectively the next President of the United States could be said also to offer keen critical analyses and judgments—not only, for example, Stevenson's judgment of Nixon but Mac Low's of Stevenson's Nixon. Innovative art as itself criticism was the point. Stevenson's speech is to Mac Low's "Text of Stevenson Speech at Dinner Here Condemning Nixon on World Affairs"[19] as Rogers and Hammerstein's *The Sound of Music* (opened on Broadway in November 1959) is to John Coltrane's modal "My Favorite Things" (recorded in October 1960). Mac Low doesn't disagree with Stevenson about Nixon, nor does Coltrane dissent from Hammerstein's libretto of antifascist resistance, but each obviously has meaningful doubts about the efficacy of a mainstream mode (in Mac Low's case, the rote stump speech; in Coltrane's, the sentimental Broadway pop song) and has something much more to say—a completely different New Thing, as would be said of avant-garde jazz—through an alternative method. How exactly we deviate from Stevenson's plain national liberal rhetoric to Mac Low's seemingly illegible, anarcho-pacifist aleatory rewriting, as Mac Low contended (repeatedly over the years), models how people might deviate from war to peace. First they will reassess the conventional relationship of truth to freedom. "Today," Stevenson stumped a few weeks before the Nixon-Kennedy contest on November 8:

> the truth is **arbiter** not **only** between **free**dom and tyranny but between life and death. "The world," a revered clergyman said, "has become too dangerous for anything but the truth." . . . Mr. Nixon and Mr. [Henry Cabot] Lodge [Nixon's running mate] disagree and say that to talk that way is unpatriotic and dangerous, that it downgrades America, that it gives aid and comfort to the enemy. What's more, they say, it isn't true [that America isn't strong enough to fight tyranny] and America has never been stronger. . . . And I say that to silence debate with **lullabies** and irrelevancies is to smother **democracy**. . . . The Western tradition is worth preserving at any price [and] we will, as a nation, have the

counter-dynamic required to meet and defeat the totalitarian out-thrust. That time Hitler and Mussolini drew the sword—and they died by the sword. This time we must find a way to defeat the out-thrust without war. We must attack war itself.

And so on. Mac Low's severely restrictive chance-operations-generated rendering of this vintage 1950s-style Democratic Party text produced, to take a small sampling, these lines:

> only now
> world overwhelming Republican lullabies democracy
> accusation faces free arbiter identical[20]

—"identical," hard to distinguish, but ultimately, Mac Low and his aleatory art colleagues believed, a substantive challenge to Republican Party hegemony. The *détournement* suggested not that such challenge had truly been in Adlai all along, through eight Eisenhower years, but rather that turning slogans of the liberal system against themselves, a modest form of culture jamming, would produce the remonstrance against Nixonian deceit of which Adlai was, especially by that point (two thumping losses to centrist Republicanism later), no longer capable. Ahead of presidential contestation in which both Democrats and Republicans had nominated staunch cold warriors, Stevenson talked about the need for a "counter-dynamic" but of course does not attempt to supply one in the form of his own statement of its necessity, desperate as he felt that need to be by then. Recalling World War II as a tale of two maniacal totalitarians who "died by the sword" becomes itself part of the somnambulistic "lullaby." To "attack war *itself*," truly, one needed to move beyond the language of attack that rendered partisan accusations unfree, nay indeed "*identical.*" This is not the end of ideology, per Daniel Bell's thesis presented in *The End of Ideology* (1960), with its claim that partisan content is monotonous; on the contrary, as I have noted in other contexts, it augers the *end* of the end of ideology. Needless to say, too, as a piece of political writing, Mac Low's Stevenson poem would have been illegible to a writer like Bell.

The term "simultaneous" in the key formulation "simultaneous spontaneity" refers first of all to time, an underlying present tense created by the application of the writing-through process. It also refers to the status of two texts in dialogue, side by side, something like the translation that draws dynamism from moving forward and back from the original version—Coltrane elucidating by elaborating upon "My Favorite Things," Mac Low transposing Stevenson's set-piece party politicking. Interestingly, Mac Low did not supply any of the original texts, nor did he even cite them in notes or epigraphs. His readers would either have to recall the sources from the journalistic ambience of the day or they might altogether miss the specific sourcetext referent. In either case readers are left to *imagine* the simultaneity and to work from the translation back to an original in theory.

Consider "Good-by New York New York Prepares for Annihilation," the title of two textually related performance writings in Mac Low's book. "Good-by New York (I)" consists of passages culled from an article Dan Wakefield published in the August 1960 issue of *Esquire* on civil defense preparations and then worked over by nonintentional chance operations. The antinuclear positions taken in various pamphlets Mac Low had retyped (and in some cases wrote himself) and then mailed in letters to editors back in 1955 are now defamiliarized, their authorship reverse engineered. Whatever ideological antiwar stance one ascertains from these aleatory performance scores signifies only from the unintended juxtapositions created in the scissoring of the sourcetext's phrases. Here are the opening three lines of "Good-by New York New York Prepares for Annihilation":

> *Geese can quickly end this island fantasy*, of mortality is part of
> New York now; Defense Commission had just finished
> showing a visitor the series of slides that illustrate the complex
> operation of New York's elaborate plans for survival in the
> nuclear age. Been portrayed in pictures, York City?
> " 'New York.' " Earth is portrayed in a huge mural on the walls of
> the reception office in the New York State Civil Defense
> Commission headquarters, with orangish flames and gray
> smoke painted into the buildings and the sky.
> York City? *Of mortality is part of New York now*; return they
> could ask from their money is an accurate inscription on their
> tombstone. "Killed" in the simulated attack.[21]

Wakefield's readable, entertaining essay, full of dramatically ironic detail, describes a terrifying slide show that is somehow nonetheless dull, led by a Colonel Frank Pearson of the New York State Civil Defense Commission, presenting various plans: mobile hospitals ready to be set up in New York City high-school gymnasia, the Canadian radar installations of the Distant Early Warning

System, instructions for guiding children to honor "the 'Duck' command by huddling under their desks." *Question*: How would these plans be enacted if the city was directly hit? *Answer*: "Well, it would just be—'Good-by, New York.'" Wakefield's tone is *Esquire*-snarky. When he visits the New York State Civil Defense Commission headquarters at 124 East 28th Street, he sees the panoramic mural of the city, painted (further dramatic irony) in flaming orange and smoke-grey. The colorful description is accidentally but meaningfully pulled into Mac Low's performance piece. Wakefield notices that the mural's prognosticating label has not been upgraded for the new decade: "U.S.A . . . 195?" "We have some-how made it through that decade, but no one had got around to changing the date of our approaching extinction to '196?.'"[22] It's 1960 now! Must be a new epoch. The effect of Mac Low's writing-through is not to intensify the sardonic irony, even though Mac Low shares Wakefield's skepticism about these expen-sive, useless preparations. The random method of extraction, answering the arbi-trariness of nuclear civil defense at the structural level, creates a desperate sin-cerity of tone (this tone is classic Mac Low). The "simultaneous" reading of the two texts leaves one feeling that Wakefield, a writer on assignment, was jour-nalistically going to play along with the likes of Colonel Pearson. Wakefield quotes a recent report, dated November 1959, admitting that the problem of what New Yorkers should do in the event of an attack on the city should be "better left in the hands of Almighty God"—a piece of strangely frank official wording that Wakefield calls, in the essay's most obvious irony, "heartening." When the word "heartening" gets extracted from the text, in order to compose Mac Low's, it is of course *not* heartening. Nor is it heartening, despite the moral resistance involved, when New Yorkers express resentment toward "the notion of living like moles." "'What you people don't understand,'" Wakefield quotes a cham-pion of spending "approximately $6,000,000,000" on fall-out shelters, "'is that the shelter becomes your *home* after the blast. Why, I've seen people in Germany still living in bomb shelters fourteen years after the war.'"[23] After Mac Low's simultaneous spontaneity, what linguistically survives of this man's view (alarm-ingly affirming stubborn German revanchism) is "Negative-thinking New Yorkers, negative-thinking New Yorkers." The random process turns the poli-tics around, forming a true counterdynamic. "Nuclear explosion has been judged economic unfeasible by most authorities."[24] The sourcetext had reported, of course, experts' view that defense against such explosion is prohibitively costly.

And what of the striking natural appearance of the geese in Mac Low's open-ing line? That line is accidentally lyrical, "poetic": *"Geese can quickly end this island fantasy*, of mortality is part of New York now." An inexplicable conclusion to the urban pastoral. Wakefield began his article with an epigraph from E. B. White's legendarily exquisite essay about the city, "Here Is New York" (1949). Wakefield was right to reinterpret White's piece retrospectively as having about it an immediate postwar dread, despite its deserved reputation as a paean to the city's beauty and resilience. Yet "for the first time in its history, [New York] is destructible." Then White adds this: "A single flight of planes no bigger than a wedge of geese can quickly end this island fantasy, burn the sewers, crumble the bridges, turn the underground passages into lethal chambers, cremate the millions. The intimation of mortality is part of New York now."[25] Not literalized poetic geese, then. Rather, a figure of planes in terror formation. Once Mac Low renders Wakefield rendering of White's reverse-pastoral, the poetic geese are what survive. Note that although the Soviets acquired an atomic weapon in 1949, the year White's essay was published, the piece was *written* in the summer of 1948, at a time—a moment still of temporary yet widespread relief—when the United States was the sole proprietor of the bomb, and so White's dread of fire-bombing and civilian cremation must actually have been that of World War II: Hiroshima, Nagasaki, Tokyo, and Dresden—and I'd bet on Dresden as White's intended reference, for that city was bombed in massive wedge formations.

Here was one of those situations when Jackson Mac Low the aleatory poet "c[a]me up with this kabbalistic idea of 'saving the sparks,'" as he later described it. There were, after all, *some* radical sparks in Adlai Stevenson's otherwise predictable liberal speech and in Dan Wakefield's sane liberal explication of insane preparations for nuclear annihilation. If not, by definition, Mac Low would not have experienced the prompt when encountering them. An assiduous method, in any event, was required to see the sparks, thence to fan them. Mac Low's definition of this art action or intervention almost exactly coincides with Zeroist hopeful skepticism. "Saving the sparks is saving the creator spirit's spirit," Mac Low said. When an artist subjects a sourcetext that is ethically problematic (not benign Stevenson or congenial Wakefield), or appropriates such a text as a chance-generating medium, even then the venturesome combinist can "somehow rescue these sparks of spirit."[26] An example: Mac Low creatively repurposed the RAND Corporation's *A Million Random Digits and 100,000 Normal Deviates* (figure 6.4), a book initially made at the behest[27] of the "mad, paranoic and extremely depressive"[28] U.S. Secretary of Defense James Forrestal—"a consummate salesman of ideas"[29] whose war plan of 1948 had called for a strategic air offensive against Russia using atomic bombs—to enable rational

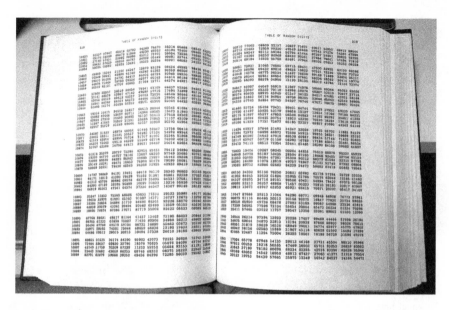

**6.4** Two pages from *A Million Random Digits with 100,000 Normal Deviates.*

strategizing for horrific military probabilities, sometimes based on crypto-graphic "nothing-up-my-sleeve numbers," eventually including MAD (mutu-ally assured destruction). When once describing his early mediumistic uses of RAND's *Million Random Digits* in his first acrostic text-selection poems (including some of those we have been considering here), Mac Low conceded, just as the secular spiritualist Zeroists would, that "spirit [is] a word I never use" and that the discussion "is awfully spooky."[30] He had wanted to redeem the inscriptions of "good mathematicians" whose positive genius survives in a seed text that can serve as a device for un-deradicalizing and reversing doomsday language. He likened this move to nonintentional acrostic rewritings through the *Cantos* of Ezra Pound in his *Words nd Ends from Ez*—"saving them in some way" from that poet's prewar and wartime fascism.

What Mac Low achieved with his "realization" of 1960 was similar to that of other artists encountered in this study: a method of extending meaning-making, not of eschewing it—"not," as Louis Cabri has written of Mac Low, "a rejection but rather a rethinking of representation" itself in relation to life lived in extremis. Cabri, who has described how Mac Low's ideological commitments "link to the formal level of his texts," traces the poet's anarchist philosophy back to the nineteenth century but observes that the particular postwar politics the artist encountered as he invented his process constitutes "a confrontation with the limits of the modern." Because, as Cabri puts it, "the limits Mac Low confronts within anarchism are in fact limits of the modernist understanding of political action," his efforts of 1960—for instance, writing through Wakefield's essay as a means of retracing the same strange terrain of Civil Defense—caused him to revisit his own antinuclear protest in 1955 with renewed confidence in the subversive effects of merging (rather than separating) political and aesthetic modes.[31]

Like Tinguely, Piene, Mack, Fontana, artist-engineer Klüver, and others, Mac Low was learning not to cause technology's association with fascist authoritarianism to deradicalize the concept of what art could do in response to such ideas. Whereas Mack's and Klüver's ideal appropriations were in the realm of wired electronics and artificial light, Mac Low's main concern was military informatics, tabulator technologies, and data collection. He had seen Sari Dienes's show of paintings, objects, and assemblages in the Betty Parsons Gallery in New York in late 1955. He preserved and often reread the printed notice or flyer from the show. Then in 1960 he decided to make this flyer into a visual poem-score. He placed an IBM computer punch card over the back of the flyer, held both at various angles, and rubbed a pencil point over the tiny rectangular holes in the punch card.

The score Mac Low produced by this act of (re)drawing, using an IBM punch card to inscribe upon the underlying text about Dienes, was created over two days in December 1960 and then given the title "A Piece for Sari Dienes" (figure 6.5). Performers to this day may play the piece on any instrument or object that produces sound, including hands, voice, etc., and may perform for any duration so long as "the production of auditory phenomena" corresponds to notation-like details in the sketch. The further from the original rubbing photocopies of the score get (the original card has been lost), the more the pencil marks resemble notes on musical staffs. Mac Low's "Instructions" for this poem/drawing/production insist that the use of "photocopies of photocopies" are "quite adequate for performance,"[32] visual opacities indicating further performative and auditory blur. The score was composed, as noted, at the end of 1960 and the first performance of the piece was done in Yoko Ono's Chambers Street studio in early April 1961, and again on July 16, 1961, at the downtown artists' café Les Deux Mégots.[33] One later performance, featuring Anne Tardos and Mac Low himself, was recorded and has been made available for download at PennSound.[34]

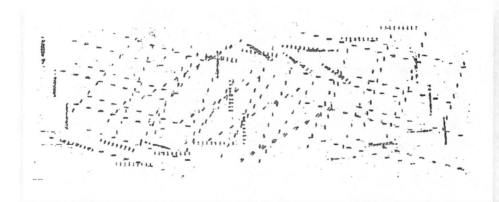

**6.5** Jackson Mac Low, *A Piece for Sari Dienes* (1960), photocopy of rubbings on an exhibit flyer from 1955 created with an IBM punch card. Source: Anne Tardos. Reproduced with generous permission from the estate of Jackson Mac Low.

No one who witnessed Mac Low's elaboration of Sari Dienes's work in 1960 and 1961—certainly not Yoko Ono, survivor of the Tokyo fire-bombings, or anarcho-pacifist John Cage, or German-born antifascist Judith Malina of the Living Theater—would have failed to understand the political significance of the use of the IBM punch card in this homage to the Hungarian-born Polish-Serbian-German artist-in-exile. The punch card symbolized—indeed, was the material tool of—fascist mass informatics. IBM had worked closely with the Nazi regime to build and run card-sorting operations that underwrote the census that, through new people-counting and registration technologies, identified every Jew in Germany (400,000), and then tracked them, along with their employers and associates; these card-sorting systems were eventually established at every major concentration camp. Edwin Black, author of *IBM and the Holocaust: The Strategic Alliance Between Nazi Germany and America's Most Powerful Corporation*, describes the IBM-Nazi relationship as enabling "the automation of human destruction"[35] and shows how IBM's invention of—and total (profitable) manufacturing monopolization of[36]—the punch card was at the center of the fascist story.[37] With "A Piece for Sari Dienes," here again in 1960 the fascist medium was the antifascist message.

That Dienes herself participated in several performances of "A Piece for Sari Dienes," and at least once painted a new visual representation of this protodigital representation of her 1955 show, by dipping her feet in paint as she moved according to the computer-card-shaped score and then "walking on a greatly enlarged copy of the notation on canvas"[38]—think of Yves Klein's *Anthropometries* happening in Europe at the same moment—suggests the new nonparadoxical relationship between ephemerality and the collaborative community they sought, just as Tinguely, Klüver, and their Zeroist colleagues were attempting in Paris, Dusseldorf, and New York. Inasmuch as there was nothing more or less real than the "New Realism" of Dienes's rubbings of urban streetscape technologies, which were a response to Zen pacifism, an unforgettable extended visit to ground zero of the atomic age, and permanent dislocation from her husband (caught in England on September 1, 1939, and never reunited with her),[39] so there was also a new realism, and indeed not an iota of abstraction, in Mac Low's collaborative cocreative synthesis of many of Sari Dienes's concerns with his own willingness to use the devices of the Cold War in the service of an art that resisted authoritative reading and, in doing so, actively supported shared nonconformity.

## Deradicalizations

Mac Low once mailed *Poetry* editor Rago a copy of a *Commonweal* essay on "The Rights of Non-Conformity." Sincere and unironic as ever, Mac Low was not, it seems, dropping a hint about the timid neoformalist verse appearing in the magazine's pages. It was part of a campaign in 1955 to goad *Poetry* editorially into endorsing protests against the way the end of the war was being celebrated ten years after. He also sent a copy of *Operation: The HUSH-HUSH Story of the H-bomb*, the pamphlet published by the War Resisters League; an appeal from the Provisional Defense Committee to help pay legal fees for those arrested during antiwar protests; and the typescript draft of a pamphlet Mac Low himself wrote, "You May Be Paying for Your Own Death," which made the same point that he would find, and nonintentionally write through, in Wakefield's *Esquire* piece.[40] Rago replied a few weeks later, politely declining to mention any of Mac Low's projects in the pages of *Poetry* (where other poets' activities, including some that can be described as political, were sometimes mentioned in the "News Notes" section), and explaining that *Poetry* was simply nonpolitical: "It is not a question of taboo; it is a question of what the job of this magazine is, i.e. what job it can claim to do COMPLETELY."[41] Mac Low might reasonably have felt that his poetic art was taboo. He once wrote to Rago that he had been submitting his writings to *Poetry* since he was fifteen, "and pretty often too," without any acceptances. In 1955 he sent seven more poems, including the now-anthologized "Glass Buildings," a calligram representing the poet's "attempt at expression by means of multiple ambiguity where all possible meanings are 'meant' by the poet." Tweaked a bit, that description of "Glass Buildings" aligned well with claims being made about verse appearing in *Poetry* by poets friendly to the New Criticism. An editorial red-penciling on Mac Low's incoming letter that time reads "REJECTED." Extremities of ambiguity surely count as a version of ambiguity, then a mainstream trait; extremes of non-intention are surely a version of avoiding the intentional fallacy. Not that Mac Low's experiments in aleatory writing would in any case find a congenial home in *Poetry* as "the place to say something about your activities," as Rago had put it in declining Mac Low's radicalism, but Mac Low might have been forgiven for wondering what "the job" of doing *poetry* "COMPLETELY," instead of politics, could mean if an entire exciting new world of postwar art was to be excluded.

*Poetry* would not publish an aleatory poem for decades. There were many problematic considerations, even leaving politico-aesthetic taboos aside. During the prolific mid-1960 months that produced "A Piece for Sari Dienes" and the many pieces in *Stanzas for Iris Lezak*, Mac Low, in an exuberantly creative mood, tried Rago again. He described his momentous realization as now leading to "the production of simultaneous poems for group reading," and submitted another typescript for publication.[42] He seems to have sent *Poetry* a copy of "A Piece for Sari Dienes"![43] The confusions it promulgates—its very status as poem (a punch card?), its nonsingular authorship enacted by "readers" as performers, its blurry relation to the underlying text of which it is a material rubbing, its essential ephemerality—challenged almost every mainstream premise. On February 19, 1960, Mac Low had written Rago to describe new poems and this time submitted thirty-seven of them for publication in *Poetry*. The only indication of a response in the *Poetry* archives is another red-penciled "REJECTED." In his cover letter, Mac Low had admitted: "I've pretty much despaired of publication during the last year or so." If for various conceptual, methodological, political, and orthographical reasons publishing poems in established venues was mostly closed off to this artist, despite his persistent efforts to be deemed very much a poet in a way that would be legible to a respected editor like Rago—he who had a reputation otherwise for open-mindedness—Mac Low realized he had better focus his attention on the emergent performance venues and collaborative conceptualist performative communities such as those gathering in Yoko Ono's loft and other Fluxus-friendly spaces, at clubs and coffeehouses, in John Cage's classes at the New

School (1957–60), and at the Living Theater established by Julian Beck and Judith Malina.

Mac Low had heard Malina many times advocate the idea of the Living Theater as an expression of collectivist, experimental antifascism. They lived in the same 14th Street building. At one point in 1960, Mac Low collaborated with John Cage and Malina as codirectors of a chance-based theater piece.[44] Malina's German father had tried in vain to warn Americans of Nazism in the 1930s. At twelve years old in 1938 Judith, now a German immigrant in New York, had helped stuff thousands of leaflets titled "Do You Know What Has Happened to Your Jewish Neighbors" into shampoo packets, which were then mailed back to Germany.[45] The Living Theater production of Bertolt Brecht's *In the Jungle of Cities*, performed in 1960, which Malina herself directed, explicitly meant to restage this parable of brutal mob hatred in a theatrical environment that would not be stopped by a "violently aroused audience"[46] of antimodernist right-wingers angered by "less and less coherent happenings on the stage,"[47] as had actually happened in Munich back in 1923. It was the restaging of this Brecht play just now that caused Malina and Julian Beck to radicalize even rehearsals, making them collaborative, and Beck to "resign . . . from his authoritative position"—as director—in which he was supposed to tell actors what to do.[48] There was an inevitable structural invisibility in efforts by artists like Mac Low, whose renewed antifascist urgencies required precisely the nonauthoritarian modes, like those of the Living Theater, that many if not most established art media, magazines, venues, and frameworks could not accommodate.

We have seen examples of the hopeful reradicalizing, constructive effects of such marginalization. Still, the main problem was the way in which exclusions strengthened centrist consensus in the world of poetry in particular (although the same issue could be said to plague nonfiction writing, theater, jazz, and even, though to a lesser extent, painting and sculpture), where accessibility shaped reviewing, curating or anthologizing, and overall trend-spotting. It could be argued that this stifling cycle circa 1960 was no more or less inhibiting then than it ever was or is. But I believe the pattern made it particularly difficult to read avant-garde reassessments of the war's necessary effect not on thematics but on language, medium, subgenre, form, and method, as we will shortly see through the instance of John Ashbery's poem "Europe" (1960). This tendency of the mainstream distorted paths of reception even for artists and critics whose own intense wartime tribulations *and* open-ness to modernist experiment nonetheless blinded them to the new convergence. The resolute, negative generalizations of Alain Bosquet present an instructive instance.

Bosquet was a French poet with an interest in twentieth-century American verse. He had fought the Nazis in the Belgian army and then with remnant French forces, then fled with his family to New York (where he edited a Free French magazine), and later advised the occupying Allied mission in postwar Germany. In 1960 he published with Gallimard a bilingual anthology he edited and translated, titled *Thirty-Five Young American Poets*. In featuring poems written after 1939, by poets of the first generation after modernism (among them, Stanley Kunitz, Robert Penn Warren, Theodore Roethke, Elizabeth Bishop, Randall Jarrell, John Ciardi, Richard Eberhart, Richard Wilbur, Peter Viereck, Daniel Hoffman, Merrill Moore, William Jay Smith) along with a few of the "New Americans" (John Ashbery, Allen Ginsberg, Barbara Guest), Bosquet created the clear impression for his Francophone readers that the contemporary poet of the postwar United States was, as one reviewer summarized, "a solitary individual," and reinforced the stereotype being typically put forward by the sociological assessors of the whole 1950s in which even artists were said to evince an "anti-intellectual attitude." While it was Bosquet's sense that "the American poet is in revolt against his country [and] feels that he is an exile in America," the writing, he contended, is nonetheless isolated and individualistic.[49] Given the collaborative art-making we have been encountering—and the abundant theorizing at the very end of the 1950s about the radicalizing social effects of such collaboration—the assumptions here of solitariness and anti-intellectualism raise a cautionary flag.

The reversal of Cold War deradicalization in networks of innovative writers—the Mac Low/Dienes/Living Theater/Fluxus/Zero/assemblagist nexus being only the most recent example offered here—are not anywhere legible in the opinionated introduction Bosquet wrote for his anthology. The American poet "rarely sees his colleagues." "Alone, he reacts against the crowd." Nor are the intense circulations and alt-publishing communities found in this overview. Rather, "the American poet publishes . . . poems scattered in university journals or the literary reviews of New York." (Consider, in contrast, how the independent magazine *Big Table* emerged when administrative officials and some faculty at the University of Chicago decided its predecessor *Chicago Review* was too heretical.) Bosquet's incorrect assessment, in any case, tends to support the conclusion that these are just the venues he surveyed to make his selections. From the anthologist's vantage, the postwar poets were longing for paperback anthologies of the sort sold from racks in train stations and drugstores, and such are "like complete but timid reference manuals" (his own gathering obviously meant to be otherwise). This is because American poems written after 1939 are themselves timid and outmoded. "Their verses are only slightly less ancient than the thinkers that they build upon" and stand as the "last descendants of the colonial and provincial poets." Its memories and new fears of annihilation far from inducing risk or counterintuitive unruly hopefulness, postwar writing works in a "panic but tight grip." If "the word has never come naturally" to U.S. poets, then now the situation was still worse. They might "go . . . against the grain; but from a distance." Formal experimentation in post-1939 American poems? These writers "consider the word as a tool, indispensable but with limited prerogatives." To the extent that Bosquet's poets are influenced by William Carlos Williams, it is "more from his [personal and professional] generosity than from his body of work." Modernists' invention of an "elliptical American language" deriving from "jazz and speed" has apparently fallen on contemporary deaf ears. Whitman and Dickinson, the two most powerful nineteenth-century American influences on the poetic avant-garde encountered in this book, are "only precursors in [the contemporary poet's] eyes, fossils best suited for a museum."

Bosquet expends several pages of his introduction describing the importance of the experience of the war. But its view is aligned with an immediate postwar perspective, not a contemporary one. "The poems that Karl Shapiro, Randall Jarrell, and Peter Viereck brought back from the Pacific and European fronts are among the most hopeless ever written." These three poets had by 1960 little to no impact on the new experiments—except perhaps Shapiro, but his influence, by way of the acerbic antimodernism of *In Defense of Ignorance* (1960), was provocatively negative. Bosquet's prose grows bitter: "Pages upon pages of losers and victims." And: "Not for an instant do these poems give you the impression that they were written by soldiers of a victorious army. Not for an instant do they sing of a happy future after the war."[50] Unlike the great modernists Stevens and Eliot of the first postwar period, the innovative early 1920s, contemporary U.S. poets do not inscribe into their writing the problems of the medium itself, do not "think about the poetic act as such"—the very thing that our experience with worldwide war should have forced upon the politics of form: greater metapoetic reflection, not less. Thus "*not one* [of the 'New' poets] has written anything (about poetry) which might interest a foreign reader."[51]

To be sure, Bosquet had left a position teaching at Brandeis University for a two-year stint in 1959 and 1960 back in France at the University of Lyon, and thus edited his anthology while far from the U.S. poetry scene. Nor back at home does he seem to have had any contact with the theoretical trends that were leading just then to the Oulipo and *Tel Quel* groups, both founded in 1960, or with the surrealist elements of the Situationist International—movements that would have a great effect on the developments of aleatory writing, literary post-structuralism, and poetry as counterspectacle, respectively, through the decade.[52] His sense that the war had inspired guilt and negativity in these writers, that they were anti-intellectual, and that they were in retreat from modern self-referentiality rather than more than ever drawn to it tells us of a disconnect that went far beyond such momentary dislocation, and I would argue that it is fundamentally akin to Henry Rago's bafflement. How relevant a stance was Bosquet's? A contemporary reviewer decided to put the term "New" inside quotation marks: the book contained "'*New*' Poetry and Poets." Had he encountered them, Bosquet might have made little sense of works like "A Piece for Sari Dienes" or Duncan's "The Maiden"—or Zukofsky's thirteen years compiling *Bottom: On Shakespeare*, or George Oppen's return after a long hiatus to poetry and war trauma in new poems such as "Survival: Infantry" and "Blood from the Stone," or Charles Reznikoff's *Inscriptions*, or Rukeyser's Akiba poems (she was represented in the anthology by straightforward work such as "Suicide Blues": "Are you able to imagine truth?")[53]—whereas the French anthologist had to content himself with producing generalizations about American art at the start of the 1960s from Robert Lowell's "The Dead in Europe," a poem of 1946 in which the fallen souls of World War II seek intercession from Mother Mary at the day of resurrection. "The Dead in Europe" is written in the dense, iambic Anglo-Saxon conventions of Lowell's *Lord Weary's Castle* (1947), as far in form from the "jellied fire" of flame-throwers and "planes unloaded" as a modern poem about modern warfare can get. It is not even a work Lowell himself chose for his ample *Selected Poems*. We cannot know exactly why "The Dead in Europe" was chosen for *Thirty-Five Young American Poets*. Did it serve the anthologist's purposes categorically as indeed "a war poem"? It had certainly been understandable, back in 1947, that *Life* magazine celebrated this very poem in its big spread on Lowell ("A SHY, AMIABLE YOUNG MAN") and put forth the conclusion that Lowell's pious and nondisjunct writing was "of a highly graphic and suggestive order."[54] But thirteen years later? Was it chosen because in response to the war it staged a return topically to original *American* sin (a special obsession of Bosquet's), a gesture, *notwithstanding* the traumatic realities of war, that tended to affirm his notion that contemporary art in the United States was isolated and only inwardly responsive—and in Lowell's case that isolation was a matter of record, for he had registered as a conscientious objector *against* the war. Bosquet did choose a few poems by John Ashbery ("Sonnet" and "The Painter," early, relatively accessible works), but he just missed a chance to pair Lowell's "The Dead in Europe" with Ashbery's ground-breaking poem "Europe"—a poem that Paul Carroll (editor of the breakaway *Big Table*) received from the poet in February 1960 and immediately celebrated in a letter to Robert Creeley ("remarkable. Such a peculiar haunting imagination. . . .")[55] and that Frank O'Hara that year pronounced "the most striking thing since The Waste Land."[56] That lines befitting the war-poem genre such as

> And somehow the perfect warrior is fallen

or

> The roar of the engine, of course,
> Rendered speech impossible[57]

would have appeared after arbitrary cutting-and-pasting made this the new antic, avant-garde *French* Ashbery, not the sullen Harvard graduate of a poem like "Sonnet."

Ashbery's "Europe" was constructed of 111 cut-up, collaged numbered extracts from a World War I–era aeronautics YA novel for girls, *Beryl of the Biplane* (1917), which he had "picked up by accident on one of the quais of Paris."[58] By way of this dadaist and Oulipian experiment (nothing close to either mode is to be found in Bosquet), Ashbery was now saying that the very choice of text to cut up for collaging honored the operation of chance—was itself, in short, devotedly European in topic and method. No surprise that for O'Hara—who in a letter to Ashbery on July 14, 1960, wrote that "Europe is carrying all before it,"[59] punning on poem title and new postwar trend—the work was an impious effort of an American expatriate in France to make writing responsive to the terrible, dizzying randomness and inexorable digressions forced by war's effects still unaddressed. In "Europe" "a whole culture of terror emerges from [its] fragments, poetically and plastically assisted to yield their truer, totalitarian impulses," as David Sweet has written about the poem. It is a work that manages simultaneously to reassert for its own time a relationship to the then-new Oulipean constraint-based devaluation of inspiration, to Duchampian iconoclasm, to Eliotic postwar multivocality, to the "whole culture of war" including its technologies, *and* to the connection between a vibrant American version of the "New Realism" and that of Europe in the most current of ways. (Sweet mentions the Nouveau Réalisme of Yves Klein and Jean Tinguely in connection with Rauschenberg and

Warhol.)[60] The "haunting" quality Paul Carroll read in Ashbery's new "Europe" exactly expressed for him the contemporary avant-garde poet's response to war.

How best, then, to comprehend Alain Bosquet's and Henry Rago's and others' disconnect from such radical haunting of war's belated effects in writing of the day? As such things go, when placed in the larger context of cultural politics of a moment in time, the belatedness made for relatively unharmful biases and incomprehension, perhaps no more than just typical fears of the new. Still, there abounded significant, available interventions—Donald Allen's *The New American Poets*; the momentous 1960 issue of Carroll's *Big Table*, which included new translations of European surrealism (André Breton) and the most unruly Beat language experiments (including Kerouac's *Old Angel Midnight*); Anna Balakian's *Surrealism: The Road to the Absolute*, insisting that that movement had been and still was "a way of life" at a time when "too much . . . tolerance of 'avant-garde'" threatened to dull the idea of psychic automatism as real social protest;[61] issues of the new *Echo*, featuring seven-inch 33-1/3 flexi-records bound into the magazine so its "readers" could listen to Salvador Dali talk about mispronouncing words *and* European folk lyrics sung by the Trapp Family Singers; the sixth number of Baraka's *Yugen*, which productively juxtaposed Tristan Tzara's dadaist "Wheat" and work by Michael McClure, Robert Creeley, Larry Eigner, and Deep Image poet Rochelle Owens; the *Evergreen Review* all-"Pataphysics" issue, edited by an American professor of French, Roger Shattuck; Rothenberg's *New Young German Poets*, of course; and the widely distributed *Beatitude* anthology from 1960, which included Bob Kaufman's Afro-Beat "Jail Poems," to which we will return. These projects would certainly abet formally experimental responses to the postwar situation to gain traction throughout the year. But again, to be sure, remnant 1950s-style critical and editorial assimilationism and adjustment—neomodernist Cold War formalism, the deradicalization of prewar modernism, whatever we choose to call it—and its sometimes unintended relationship to conservatism and outright antimodernism, were the merest expression of a much larger campaign to forget or repress the deep effects mass deaths of the world war were still having on contemporary culture. The realization of that impact is what marks the start of the 1960s. Fifties-style sociological generalizers, for various complex reasons, several of which we have already explored, missed these effects while somewhat suddenly films, plays, television series, mass-market novels (including sci-fi) and literary fiction alike—we will soon, beginning in the final section of this chapter, widen our generic scope to include these along with poetry—seemed to proceed by ignoring those generalizations or counteracting them in scene-by-scene or phrase-by-phrase creation, and then turned to face directly the old issue of the war with surprisingly much the same new spirit as Rothenberg, Tyler, Arendt, Ortiz, and Mac Low tried to comprehend the effects of the radical instabilities and devastations felt by Celan and Kafka and wrought by Eichmann and IBM.

## Adjustment and Its Discontents

This would hardly be the first time that literature and the arts moved ahead of political sociologists and sociological psychologists, and journalistic cultural commentators, in surveying the contemporary scene in search for a way to connect instabilities and fragments to represent such terror and totalitarian impulses (to cite again the framing idea of Ashbery's "Europe"). When Harvard sociologist Daniel Bell praised how in the 1950s the U.S. economy not only fully revived but also became permanently resilient, due largely to reliable corporate reinvestment—from 1946–48 onward corporations reinvested 62 percent of their profits, compared with 41 percent in 1936 and 31 percent in 1929—he knew full well that after expressing such lavish confidence he should at least have a brief glance at the minor "minus side": the "instabilities." In this Bell demonstrates the steadfastness of his focus on what he deemed natural, self-regulating, and nonpolitical adjustments made possible by triumphant centrist culture. *Adjustment* was for him always the operative term. It worked better on the econometric side of his argument than on the cultural side. Still, Bell reasoned, corporate reinvestment was a reliable litmus test: if the extent of postwar corporations' need to spend profits is on the "plus side of the ledger," "on the minus side, new instabilities are being introduced into the economy mostly by political countervailing forces." Note the phrase "countervailing forces." It was the key to Bell's centrist stance. Such forces had to have originated *somewhere* and at *some time*, of course, yet this passage comes in one of only four moments, in a book of 440 dense pages, when Bell even so much as mentions World War II, two of them just in passing.[62] In this first passage he begins by debunking the "myth" of the "total war economy." Advocating this unusual view, he stipulates that we know "how inefficient and haphazard the German war economy was"— an assumption that has been challenged many times in the post–Cold War historical correction led in fact by scholars of the holocaust, starting in 1961 with Raul Hillberg in *The Destruction of the European Jews*.[63] No, Bell argues, it's the *postwar* economy—the peacetime market—that is, if anything, successfully totalizing: the economy of the 1950s had become resistant to shock. Here is where the passing "minus side" enters: volatility is introduced by partisan political forces, yet even these are said to be "countervailing" or compensatory. And Bell does not mean the government, which he sees as "inevitably" providing "balance." Again: this is one of a very few passages about the recent world war in this book and about the supposedly minimal instabilities postdating it.

The two blockbuster sociological books about the whole 1950s that were published in 1960—Bell's *The End of Ideology*, from which I have been quoting, and Paul Goodman's *Growing Up Absurd*—indeed make essentially no reference to World War II, let alone the myriad forms of instability still felt fifteen years later fully despite (and perhaps in part because of) the now-permanent robust economy Bell commends and Goodman decries. One book is about the "exhaustion of political ideas" and the other is about an entire generation experiencing absurdity. But in each the seven years of world war just preceding these megaphenomena are off stage at best, irrelevant to exhaustion, disquiet, and absurdity at worst. To be sure, Bell and Goodman intended comprehensive descriptions and analyses of the 1950s, not the 1940s. Yet the new generalist mode of multidisciplinary public intellectual—the sweeping yet scholarly (or quasi-scholarly) thesis-driven treatise of deep but plain social description, consisting of what we now call "think pieces" stitched together after separate publication in quarterlies and magazines of opinion—created for their readers an absence, a misleading feeling that U.S. culture had transcended the uncertainty, irregularity, and anxiety of the global war and its mass destructions, that the rebuilding Bell described (and praised) had adjusted, stabilized, organized, and regularized, and had spread across all areas of life and thought, emanating from political economy outward to work, family life, adolescence, culture, and aesthetics.

In one of just two references to the war in Goodman's *Growing Up Absurd*, his traditionalist's lament over postwar know-nothingism leads him into several ironic parenthetical tales. Here is such a tale: once, in 1948, Goodman himself was lecturing on Kafka, before a classroom full of veterans whose tuition was reimbursed through the GI Bill, and was disconcerted to discover their frantic protest against reading this "psychotic" writer who "had no relation to reality—they [Goodman adds] who had lived through some of the *Trial* and were even then roaming under the *Castle*!" The anecdote serves as a doubly ironic parable in this work of Abnormal Sociology[64] of how "shell shock" causes cultural "conventionality" as a "defense" against "the war and the bomb." But the story took place in 1948, while the book about the 1950s suggests at all points that its theorizations point forward into the 1960s[65]—it is deemed "one of the

defining texts of the New Left"[66]—and yet these defensively antiexperimental-
ist war veterans, just two or three years demobilized, are supposed to help us
understand "political apathy" among students as *we have now passed through
a decade,*" the entire fifties. "Hipster skepticism," Goodman claims, is postideological. The cause of "the present political apathy" is the "dishonorable radical
leadership" of the 1930s and 1940s. The Beats (Goodman makes forty-eight references to them in his book) "now believe that *all* political thinking is a sell."[67]
It is doubtful that Goodman knew about the radicalizing effect the Beats were
having on the antifascist European generation too young to have fought in the
war. Examples abound. Walter Buchebner, for instance, an Austrian born in 1929,
had been just old enough for the desperate last Nazi teenage drafts and had gone
underground in 1945 rather than face conscription. In and out of menial jobs
through the fifties, all the while searching for a postwar voice and frustrated by
the conventional romantic poetry he was producing then, Buchebner found
Ginsberg and Burroughs and Beat jazz writing and then created what he called
"active poetry," seeking from it a way to revivify "dead" Austrian culture. This
was hardly dead-end hipster skepticism but, if anything, its hopeful and constructive opposite.[68]

The other mention of the war in *Growing Up Absurd* comes at the beginning
of Goodman's chapter "The Early Resigned," about the supposed attitudinal resignation of "The Beat Generation." Making no detailed contextual connections
from the Beats to Black Mountain aesthetics (although he bitterly ridicules Black
Mountain College)[69] or to the New York School or to German-influenced Deep
Image or dada-influenced cut-ups and aleatory collaborative performance art
(although it was right up Goodman's alley as a New York-based anarcho-pacifist),
or to the greater San Francisco Renaissance, *Growing Up Absurd* teaches us that
Beats are "too hip to be attracted to independent work." His cultural conservatism led to a critique that even T. S. Eliot and "even the Southern Agrarians might
have endorsed": Americans "floundered with 'manly' work." Goodman's leftist indictment of "our abundant society" merged with a reactionary lament that
such abundance "corrupts the fine arts." And he sincerely meant "fine." His work
typified the rise after the war of a "humanistic left that broke sharply with the
economic ideology of the old 1930s left" and as such it can be paired, Casey Nelson Blake has observed, with Bell's *The End of Ideology* in believing that dehumanization superseded exploitation as the greatest threat to ordinary people.
The Beats we meet in *Growing Up Absurd* are not contributing to the fine arts
even as their own rejections align with Goodman's complaint that "Everyone
talks nice." The Beats don't talk nice, for sure, but generally, per Goodman, "At

most there is some unruliness and dumb protest." The analysis is confused—in a way that other figures we encounter in this book were working through. The question Goodman cannot answer, despite his title, is this one: What constitutes unruliness sufficient to qualify as unabsurd? For an observer such as Lawrence Lipton in *The Holy Barbarians* (1959), that Jack Kerouac in writing sentences "makes mistakes as if they were discoveries" is itself a productive, improvised radicalism, a sincere absurdist's rule-breaking.[70] Lipton, a Łódź-born Jew, was still thinking about the war, and embraced the Beats in part because they pointed toward the sound of art as an alternative to mass death, a reasonable peaceful potential for which it was worth violating sane norming: "When the barbarians appear on the frontier of a civilization," Lipton was arguing, "it is a sign of a crisis in that civilization. If the barbarians come, not with weapons of war but with songs and ikons of peace, it is a sign that the crisis is one of a spiritual nature."[71] Goodman's topic was that very spiritual crisis, yet for him it is as if the modernist revolution had never occurred (whereby unruliness can enter the *form* of a fine art without compromising its status as painting, film, sculpture, score, novel, or poem). Nor, it would seem, had World War II occurred other than as an interruption of now-irrelevant 1930s leftism. It certainly is relevant that, as Blake notes in part to explain this anarchist radical's cultural conservatism, Goodman had opposed U.S. involvement in the Second World War.[72] Lipton's survey of Beat culture in *The Holy Barbarians* takes seriously the counterculture's derivation from the experience of global conflict. "The veteran of World War II," Lipton writes, "was a tough customer. He knew his lost years were gone forever, but he demanded everything in the way of compensation that he could squeeze out of the politicians." It was a serious postwar stance. Its "anti-fascis[m] . . . cut across all party lines from Left to Right."[73] For Goodman, though, the emergent literary countercultures of the late 1950s "are a phenomenon of the aftermath of World War II" in this ironic sense: their careers, potentially inside the Organization, were merely "*interrupted* by the draft," and that interruption was, we are to suppose, both in effect reactionary and incidental, as Beat culture actually "belongs to the middle status of the organized system" even as it stands "in a defensive ignorance of the academic culture"—and yet, paradoxically, also "reject[s] . . . popular culture."[74]

*Growing Up Absurd* offers scant recognition of the complexity of the Beat relationship with popular culture. Allen Ginsberg does not simply despise *Time* magazine. It is more complicated than that, for "every week" he obsessively reads *Time* and sees his American face mirrored in its cover.[75] A few minutes' look at the *Beatitude Anthology* (1960) discloses unironic affection for subway posters, camping equipment displayed in department store windows, lunch trucks, watching TV as a means of "trying to forget" pain, powdered Nescafé, and the nighttime view of Hollywood from the hills.[76] Goodman is implausibly astonished that Ginsberg, at a poetry reading Goodman attended, spoke with awe about visiting the Grand Canyon and he satirizes the notion that next the shaggy poet will join the Circle Line cruise up the Hudson.[77] (Had he no idea of the lineage from Whitman's visionary Americanism to Ginsberg's?) The satire draws from a selective, conservative misreading of Ginsberg. *Growing Up Absurd* is sometimes perceived as auguring the youth counterculture of the 1960s, and also as a continuation of Goodman's anarchism—which Jackson Mac Low often mentioned admiringly[78]—but a close rereading of this 1960 classic suggests otherwise, as Casey Nelson Blake has observed.[79] In fact it suggests that the plight of the youthful dissenter and that of the youthful conformist are essentially the same. One hardly recognizes here the radicalism, the utopian dream of experimentalism's social effects, and the belief in converged historical and aesthetic continuities, of American figures such as Bob Kaufman, Joseph Heller, Raphael Montañez Ortiz, James Baldwin, or Jerome Rothenberg—or, most of all, the way in which such people emerged through the fifties with a new understanding of the war and its connection to indecipherability, Baldwin's capacious "something more implacable" than whatever *A Tree Grows in Brooklyn* chose to witness. In this respect, Goodman's poetics are essentially antimodernist. Part of his attack on the ignorant "American young" (this too includes beatniks, we must suppose) is that they do not even know "the correct name for what they in fact do."[80] Correct name?

The End of Ideology can be similarly misread. By no means does Bell truly decry the "exhaustion of ideas." Imitating Eliot's triadic ideological parallelism, protesting too much about his open-mindedness, Bell described himself as a "socialist in economics, a liberal in politics, and a conservative in culture."[81] But cultural conservatism is what dominates his book. The locus of his argument comes in the first section of the chapter titled "The Mood of Three Generations" (there is apparently a singular "mood" for each). In this survey of artists and intellectuals of the 1930s, the 1940s, and the 1950s ("the Once-Born, the Twice-Born, and the After-Born [sic]"), Bell tells the history of the depressive effect political positions have had on art. So he begins to draw his book's overall view of where this history has led by 1960: not just to a refutation of intellectual and aesthetic extremity but also to its final irrelevance, to "an end to chiliastic

hopes . . .—and to ideology." He chooses Dwight MacDonald to illuminate the
1940s, and MacDonald's magazine *Politics* (1944–49) provides the context for
the only other mention of the war in Bell's book.[82] The writers of the modernist
period, such as the dadaists, drew their adversity from "scor[ning] bourgeois
mores," and the radicals of the 1930s had "fought 'capitalism,' and later, fascism."
But "*today*, intellectually, emotionally, who is the enemy that one can fight"?[83]
Apparently there are none. This grandly assumes that the war has been completely won, that dadaist scorn is obsolete (since neodadaists are bourgeoisified)
and political rebels, now without cause, will find traces of fascism nowhere. Het-
erodoxies of modernism and of radicalism obsolesced identically.

Bell's model for how this situation followed from the 1940s can be found in the
logic of the "most extraordinary article" MacDonald ever published in *Politics*,
Bruno Bettelheim's account of "behavior in extreme situations." (The *Politics*
article was an early version and section of *The Informed Heart: Autonomy in a
Mass Age*, published in 1960.) Bettelheim argued that in terrifying, desperate
circumstances men and women regress to "childlike behavior." The survivor
lives through "deep, infantile, regressive aspects in one's own nature," as Bell
summarized it, and "willingly take[s] on the hideous mask, stance and code of
the" fascist SS. This, Bell observes, is perhaps more disconcerting than evidence
of Nazi sadism.[84] Prisoners, Bettelheim had claimed, were "particularly sensitive to punishments similar to those which a parent might inflict on his child."
The punishment of a child is normal, and concentration camp inmates needed
signs of normalcy; so "they reacted to it not in an adult, but in a childish way."
They regressed, "develop[ing] types of behavior which are characteristic of
infancy or early youth," such as in response to the "strictly regulated" system
permitting "defecation."[85] As Terrence Des Pres and others who have debunked
this "case for infantilism" of the holocaust survivor point out, Bettelheim read
defilement as a function of the psychoanalytic metaphor of the individual's stages
of maturation (akin to toilet training during which process feces is first a stubborn possession maintained by immature selfhood). But, as Des Pres describes
through the study of a hundred survivor testimonies, excremental assault was
overwhelmingly *literal* in the camps, and "in extremity symbolism *as symbolism* loses its autonomy." The "shit-smeared" bodies of the survivor do not indicate regression, or childlike identification with a racist enemy.[86] On the contrary,
intended victims can protect or cover even with excrement the preservation of
human dignity and slow emergence of resistance. This psychoanalytic reading
of concentration camp inmates Bell displaced onto his general argument against

meaningful extremism. If at the end of ideology there is no longer an enemy to be found, and if resistance is causeless, it evinces elemental rather than contingent behavior, marking the triumph of the therapeutic over any real politics of genocide—such as planful political resistance, which, in the case of the Nazi camps, Bettelheim explained away.

## "It's Sort of Peaceful Now"

What is remarkable about the renaissance of responses to the war fifteen years later, and is especially surprising, perhaps, when it includes popular genres, is the extent to which these representations resist the therapeutic reading and, in some cases, assume a downright antitherapeutic stance toward posttraumatic testimonies of wartime life in extremis. Mac Low's "A Piece for Sari Dienes" celebrates a survivor, after all—and can be said to constitute an attack on fascist data-gathering—without a hint of sentimentality, although we can be fairly certain that Malina and Ono, upon seeing "A Piece" performed, were greatly moved. Yet the point now, in this coda to a chapter that began with the aleatory avant-garde, is that accessible, popular examples are plentiful. Are they as available to this analysis as Mac Low's esoteric geese—derived from the *New Yorker* via *Esquire*—assembled in a wedge formation that could "quickly end" Americans' fantasy of postwar safety? Yes. The television viewer who happened to be reading *The End of Ideology*, and on the evening of May 20, 1960, watched Rod Serling's *In the Presence of My Enemies*, a play about people involved in the Warsaw Ghetto uprising, could have sensed the same key difference as that between Dan Wakefield and Mac Low or between Adlai Stevenson and Mac Low. Bell's enlistment of Bettelheim, in the midst of a section on postideological art and culture, forms a striking negative psychological answer to the question "Today, intellectually, emotionally, who is the enemy that one can fight?"[87]— while Serling and others whose representations of the war we will survey in the balance of this chapter and in the following two present such enemies amply, and often as a powerful analogue to the postwar present, refusing the refusal of extremity in testimonies of absurd dignity, resistance, and unspeakable nonconformity. Presenting ghetto life as "*indescribable* torture of living death,"[88] by a frankly radical figure who especially from "1959 to 1961 [was deemed] television's prophet outcast,"[89] and called "TV's Angry Young Man,"[90] the play had first been rejected by CBS for *Playhouse 90* and in mid-January 1960 was picked up by the more progressive public broadcast station WNET (channel 13 in the New York area), for its "Play of the Week" series.[91]

A former paratrooper in the South Pacific theater, whose postwar "un-American" activities as a Jewish leftist have been somewhat obscured by McCarthy-era erasures,[92] Serling reinterpreted the war's lasting effects variously in 1960: in the TV play about the extermination of Warsaw's Jews, and in several episodes during the first season (1959–60) of *The Twilight Zone* on CBS, most famously in "The Odyssey of Flight 33." What Christopher Vials in *Haunted by Hitler*, using trauma studies, calls Serling's "trauma-informed antifascism" helps explain the persistence of a postdisaster cotemporality in the teleplays, his return again and again to the holocaust but also his congruence of anti-Semitism and racism (and speciesism).[93] He had transposed his own atrocious World War II experience (atop Mahonag during the desperate Battle of Leyte in late 1944) in order to create a teleplay for *Studio One* back in 1954, "The Strike," in which the commander of a decimated regiment, facing extreme options, makes a nonrational yet ethical decision. It was this writing about war that occasioned Serling's turn toward mature work and, eventually, to the politics of mass war deaths in *The Twilight Zone*.[94] The preseries episode (something of a pilot) that first focused CBS producers' attention on the *Twilight Zone* format, "The Time Element," featured a man who experiences recurring nightmares of the Pearl Harbor attack, and receives no practical help from his psychoanalyst, who dissuades the fellow from any literal interpretation of time travel in the dream, whereupon, in the final twist, the doctor suddenly finds his couch empty and learns later, at a tavern, that his patient had actually been killed years ago—on December 7, 1941. Whose interpretation of the former sailor's anxiety is the unexplainable one? In all of Serling's writing, not just his science fiction, those who conform to conventional therapeutic modes of interpretation soon understand nothing. Yet dozens of popular representations of the war during the 1950s reward conformists who, as Peter Biskind puts it, "toe the organizational line."[95] Not so "The Time Element"; in fact, the organization losing its way turns out to have been the network—CBS—that had bought the script and then shelved it for two years. This is not how a network and its corporate sponsor wanted to imagine the posttraumatic stress Pearl Harbor continued to cause.[96] Under the heading "The Organization Man Goes to War" in *Seeing Is Believing: How Hollywood Taught Us to Stop Worrying and Love the Fifties*, Biskind identifies film after film in which battles won are thematically secondary and even irrelevant; what is primary is almost always the victory managed by the Organization—victory over enemies, yes, but more relevantly over nonconformist figures. Surprisingly, conservative films of the 1950s, along with liberal ones, tolerate submission of the individual to the victorious functioning of the organization. In 1960 these representations begin to change. It's not simply that Serling's Organization Men become trapped in the nightmare of incomprehension. Even a happy celebrity-showcase film such as *Ocean's 11* (a "Rat Pack" summer blockbuster released on August 10), seemingly an affirmation of irresponsible glitz and consumer excess, has something significant to say about the war.

The "11" had fought together in the 82nd Airborne division, and the movie records a reunion of war buddies. The elaborate theft of five Las Vegas casinos is a mission intended to revive a sense of the uncanny and the absurd—paratroopers' repetitive heroic but insane leap into the void. These airmen do not want a reunion for *talking* about bygone ethics of undertaking worthwhile life-or-death risk; they want to *act* as a form of testifying to an otherwise inarticulate, inaccessible sense of responsibility. In such a "vehicle" film, set in the heart of these actors' favorite site of postwar glut, it is hard to imagine any subtext of nonconformity and regret, let alone trauma. But Danny Ocean's crew's military-style mission—the entire language of the plan is spoken in World War II–specific military vocabulary, a movie-long allegorical conceit—is an elaborate restaging and constant remembering of the honorable thieving of thieves that had been purposefully charged and ideologically coherent (and celebrated as necessary and triumphant) a decade and a half earlier. "What's wrong with the plan?" the group asks one temporary skeptic among them about the new venture. "For one thing," he replies, "fifteen years. This ain't a combat team, it's an alumni meeting." "Why waste all those tricks the army taught us," Danny Ocean observes later, "just because it's sort of peaceful now?"

Ocean and the other veterans of the 82nd Airborne come to realize the basis of their selfless selfish behavior and learn to hold two irreconcilable thoughts in mind at once: first, that "the brave ones don't come home" (whereas of course these people *have*—and then thrived) and, second, that, having survived, "there's only one thing you have, and that's danger. Cliffhanger." Cowritten by an antifascist modernist poet—Harry Brown—who had helped produce an experimental documentary featuring first-person testimonies of Allied soldiers in Europe with scenes from Belsen and Buchenwald,[97] *Ocean's 11* has more in common than one might think with the two neorealist films about World War II made in Italy in 1960, Vittorio de Sica's *Two Women* and Roberto Rossellini's *It Was a Night in Rome*. De Sica's film, an adaptation of the 1957 novel by Alberto Moravia, is an intense study of putative neutrality and selfish ambivalence among Italian civilians, and the sexual brutality that indecision permitted, during the terrible chaos of the period dubbed the "Marocchinate," a politically liminal moment immediately following the Battle of Monte Cassino in the strategic space between the Allied landing site at Anzio just to the southwest and fascist-controlled Rome (the Allies' and refugees' destination) just to the northeast. *Ocean's 11* obviously has little of this overt topical seriousness. Yet Ocean and his mumbling combat colleagues become intermittently articulate about an ill-defined ethical moment, contrasting all that literal against-odds cliffhanging they had endured during the war. Contemporary reviews unsurprisingly emphasized Rat Pack dissolution and styles of "crushingly cool" detachment,[98] and the *Washington Post* reviewer, used to putting the Washington spin on serious political flicks, dubbed it an "amoral tale."[99] Yet from the context of belated postwar representations of antifascism, we can sense, first, Ocean's own anguish about risk and mortality (one of his comrades actually dies during the *new* mission) and, second, generally, that such a comedy is on the contrary a moral tale about witnesses to mass destruction mired in amoral lives, just what De Sica and Rossellini aimed to depict from the obverse point of view of the disorganized victims of fascist occupation. The "tart comments on post-war living" inscribed in the witty *Ocean's 11* script originate traumatically.[100] They act out two basic paradoxes of combat trauma (as mapped from the research of three trauma theorists for the journal *Traumatology*). On the issue of safety, contradictorily and simultaneously: both "Nothing can harm me" *and* "I never turn my back to anyone." As for risk-taking: both "It mattered over there" *and* "Nothing matters here."[101] The veterans begin to regret the way in which postwar selfish indifference inhibits the collaborative, collective memory of the liberation they had brought to fascist-occupied Italy. Indeed, they use "liberate" as a verb for what they are attempting together now—a comic usage, of course, because it's directed at greedy Las Vegas (is Vegas thus fascist?), but also an indication of the power of the memory of worthy danger and of their dawning belief in the applicability of historical techniques to what Ocean calls the "sort of peaceful" present.

As two of these eleven veterans remind us during a quiet conversation about whether doing one more mission is worth courting the risk—and as most adult viewers of this film in the summer of 1960 would know from the mere utterance of the place name *Anzio*, heavily sighed by Henry Silva from the script—the 82nd Airborne had landed and established a beachhead thirty-eight miles down the coast from Rome, at the town of Anzio, enduring days of artillery fire, unit sizes reduced to twenty, with devastating losses alike to landing Allied infantry and paratroopers, German soldiers, and Italian citizens.[102] The slaughter set off the waves of crises of antifascist conscience in that region darkly registered in Rossellini's and de Sica's films, in Heller's *Catch-22* (a novel derived from its author's experience of sixty bombing raids flown in the small B-25), and in the eccentric best-selling dystopia by Walter Miller titled *A Canticle for Leibowitz*. Remarkably, notwithstanding the relative legibility of the story, its idea about the survival of language after annihilation is just as devoted to theories of randomness and to the postdisaster restoration of democratic cipherment as Jackson Mac Low's.

# 7

# Disaster Defies Utterance

## Arts of the Unsayable

### Words Help Make the Silences

A tail gunner in the Army Air Corps, the creator of *A Canticle for Lei-bowitz* (1960) flew more than fifty bombing missions over Italy just as Danny Ocean and colleagues drop into Anzio,[1] Rossellini's trio of Allied soldiers elude fascist spies in Rome while awaiting liberation, and de Sica's protagonist Cesira and the daughter she tries to protect cower in the village of Ciociaria a few miles in between. Positioned in the tail gunner's exposed aerial outpost, that vulnerable front-row seat, Walter M. Miller flew the infamous mission that dropped fourteen hundred tons of high explosives onto the medieval Benedictine abbey at Monte Cassino. The bombing caused the total destruction of the building built in 529 AD as well as art, archives, and unique manuscripts the Germans had not (yet) removed—an atrocious tactical error (the abbey was unoccupied and served scant military purpose) that the Allies would not officially concede until 1961,[2] just months after *A Canticle for Leibowitz* was published. Even a devout antifascist diarist in Rome—her witnessing forms the basis of Rossellini's film of 1960—was appalled by news in December 1943 of the forced evacuation by the Nazis of the Cassinese people, who ahead of the American attack "had no choice and no time," and by photographs of the destruction placarded around the city in early 1944.[3] By every account, Miller suffered pervasive trauma as the result of this gratuitous bombing, and remained always thereafter "a tortured person."[4] He "was deeply

depressed by post-traumatic stress disorder, and had been for half a century"
(so a visitor to his home observed at the time of Miller's death).[5] This state of
mental ill health inspired but was by no means resolved through the writing
of the novel about a nightmarish ruined world in which survivors struggle piece
by piece to comprehend the language of the shreds of a remnant archive, which
has "been reduced to archeological ambiguity."[6] A new abbey is formed from
the ruins that had been caused by the great "Flame Deluge." The monks study
bits of survivor testimony, disjunctive ur-texts that Miller dubs "versicles." These
texts survive the demise of an ordinary twentieth-century Jewish engineer named
Isaac Leibowitz.

Walker Percy described *A Canticle for Leibowitz* itself as a "cipher, a coded
message, a book in a strange language." Yet, Percy contended, this language is
a code with a special atrocity-caused difference: it is about—and, as a work of
writing, is itself—a secret that cannot or does not want to be told. The book is a
survivor's X. "Telling it ruins it." (Percy meant "ruins" in every sense.)[7] As "the
medieval reprise"[8] emerges from slow increased "mastery of pre-Deluge English,"
the postholocaust reconstitution of a writing culture becomes the central theme.
Miller's novel seems itself to be such a reconstitution. It could be said to be—
and to be about—the new, necessarily disjunct language that must survive
destruction. Focus on the infelicities of the old language is acute and at times
darkly comic. "But what of a triple appositive like *fallout survival shelter*?" the
apprentice Brother Francis muses upon being led to versicles inscribed in an
ancient shelter whose bland Cold War–era organizational American English
("once sealed, the hatch will be automatically unlocked by the servomonitor system when, but not before, any of the following conditions prevail") puts the lie
to the doomed notion of a "Sealed Environment." The phase called "the Simpli-
cation" was necessary. But syntheses, hybridities, and interoperabilities, Miller's main modes, will succeed. The will to bear witness is strong in Miller's vision
of the cultural effect following the flame deluge of Monte Cassino and like
destructions. For the composer of the versicles constituting his novel, writing is
a matter of survivor testimony: "The miraculous contraptions of the ancients
were not to be carelessly tampered with, as many a dead excavator-of-the-past
had testified with his dying gasp."[9] As in testimony to genocide, it is about "*Something* That Happened," in Walker Percy's phrase for the book, an opaque Jewish
*something* discoverable along "Jewish coordinates," an esotericist's "gnosis"[10]—
that which cannot be properly said and is best left improper and unruly.

Among the several interoperabilities obsessing Miller was the generic. His
book "about" World War II, another of the many war novels of 1960, defining

that global conflict as the origin of the concept of total disintegration, belongs as much to the tradition of political allegory—the same tradition preoccupying Arendt when she wrote *The Origins of Totalitarianism*—as to science fiction. The novel's relationship as allegory to the death of humanism and paltry possibilities of its revival might have struck audiences seeing Orson Welles's direction of Eugène Ionesco's play *Rhinoceros* in the spring of 1960 (or readers of the Grove Press publication, also published in 1960) as eerily aligned with the parabolic conversions in Miller's book. *Rhinoceros* was similarly "about" the war in retrospect and the utter failure of humanism. As we will see momentarily, *Rhinoceros* restages Camus's *The Plague* (in which the spread of a pandemic is equated to that of fascism) by merging deadly serious political allegory with an absurd fantasy of transmogrification in which centrists moving rightward turn into rhinos. In *A Canticle for Leibowitz*, there are absurd fabulistic aspects— and, following Mary Shelley's *The Last Man*, its global crisis is likened to a human sickness that reduces world population to one shepherd, and thus, like *The Plague*, it encoded a postwar life as a pandemic's aftermath.[11] Miller's fable is signaled with the appearance of the old Wandering Jew, who might be Isaac Leibowitz himself, saying in a stereotypical "nasal bleat" the blessing over his tiny piece of bread (Ha-motzi) in a language the Leibowitzite acolyte recites but doesn't comprehend (Hebrew).[12] As in Rod Serling's work, the strangeness of whose allegories always turns in the end on a darkly comic pun, misprision, or parapraxis, and as in Ionesco, whose rhino fascists are monsters that don't naturally belong in the French countryside unless animal life too has been altered by corrosive sociogeny, Miller's allegory of wartime and postwar culture extends the absurd idea that a middling Jewish engineer who designed (obviously malfunctioning) bomb shelters could be transformed into a saintly object of postholocaust messianic Jewish-Catholic hope. Such absurdist allegorical wartime readings remain wide open. "The anthropology . . . is both radical and overt," as Percy put it. The audience is aptly "uncomprehending."[13] These disparate texts of 1960 centrally thematize ideological interpretation itself. Historical understanding need not be thwarted by, and anyway cannot be derived from, linguistic disjunction or narrative misdirection. Ionesco's *Rhinoceros* is often read as an allegorical response to fascism as a social movement in the period immediately before the war.[14] By having citizens of a small provincial French town turn outwardly into rhinoceroses, rather than inwardly into fascists, the play explores its themes of conformity, culture, and mass movement. One citizen of the town, the persuasion of fascism coming over him, argues with an antifascist friend, screaming, "Humanism is all washed up! You're a ridiculous old sentimentalist," whereupon he transforms into a rhino and tries to trample the other.[15] Earlier, when the very first misplaced monstrous rhinoceros rumbles through the center of town, the man who would later become one himself, an incipient fascist concerned at this point "only" with law and order and with keeping the economy open, turns to his liberal humanist friend, seeking his response. The liberal says weakly, "Yais . . . yais . . . It shouldn't be allowed. It's dangerous. I hadn't realized. But don't worry about it, it won't get us here," at which point we already sense that the conservative is being pushed rightward and the mild antifascist is doomed.[16] Nor does "The Monsters Are Due on Maple Street," the most critically acclaimed episode of *The Twilight Zone* Serling wrote for its first season, aired on March 4, 1960, make any effort to hide the rhinos, as it were, of a small American village. Unlike Cold War sci-fi of the 1950s, whose political positions can almost always be read through anticommunism—in liberal sci-fi aliens are just different and sadly misunderstood, and turn destructive only if we fight them; in conservative sci-fi aliens would be destroyed if it weren't for foolish liberal tolerance—"The Monsters Are Due on Maple Street" reaches past the Cold War, and further back past the global hot war, 1939–45, back to the rise of fascism, and its use of the term "fallout" is the script's way of warning us against forgetting the lessons of World War II in our zealous fear of a Russian first nuclear strike. Unlike *Rhinoceros*, where the language, so to speak, always stays in character and the rhino is not revealed as a device for political reading, Serling steps out from the fiction at the end of "The Monsters," a human in a dark contemporary suit, deciphering rhinocerization for us, intoning: "There are weapons that are simply thoughts, attitudes, prejudices. . . . Prejudices can kill and suspicion can destroy and a thoughtless, frightened search for a scapegoat has a fallout all of its own . . . [a pause]. And the pity of it is that these things cannot be confined to [another pause]—The Twilight Zone."[17] Perhaps this openness to interpreting the postfascist analogue owes to the difference between highbrow European experimental theater and the unsubtleties of American television in prime time. Or perhaps, too, something more is going on.

Look closely at this Serling scene: a former RAF pilot, now gray haired, sits in coach on a commercial jet, on his way from London to New York, and then presumably to Los Angeles, where he now serves as military attaché to the British Consulate. Something seems wrong but he does not know what, and it comes out in a checklist of negatives. "No loss of power. No telltale shimmying. No flame or smoke. Nothing." No, no, no, nothing. Something has gone awry and if he could explain it, the phenomena of life would continue in the usual where-smoke-thus-fire denotative relationship.[18] But we cannot go back to that word-world

connection. Nothing remains of it. For this is the moment, as I have been arguing, when genre, in this case science fiction, converges with survivor testimony
as a fully developed mode of representation—where "silence became our guide,"
as the narrator of Aharon Appelfeld's halting memoiristic stories, uncomfortable
with language, says in that survivor's strange first collection, titled *Smoke*.[19] The
difficult silence Serling explores is that which Appelfeld struggles to create as he
writes through the annihilation of language. It is Otto Piene's Zeroist "zone of
silence" that is not in fact empty. It is that which, as Celan said, "can <remain>
unsaid because perhaps un unsayable" even as now the "porous poem . . . stands
into time."[20] For his book *Silence* (1961), an anthology of ways of saying "there is
nothing to say," John Cage included his "Lecture on Nothing": "There are
silences      and the / words      make      help make      the / silences," and added
a spooky note telling of a 1960 performance in which now, just then, finally, the
audience "got the point" and collectively "refrained from asking" any more of
the questions to which the lecturer gave preset responses. In the poem "Silence!"
Celan suggests that silence is shadowy rather than a set negative; it "mixe[s] the
Yes and the No."[21] The RAF officer's catalogue of "No" in Serling mixes with
affirmation and stands precisely into time (in Celan's sense) and is artfully not
meant to be an empty, resistant word (in Cage's). To his horror, the ex-pilot
realizes that his having "nothing to say" is "saying it / . . . as I need it." (With
Serling we consistently see the darkly comic irony of Cage's aleatory assurance
that "We need not fear these silences," a key new response to terrors of the previous era.)[22] The list of scarily confirming negatives is part of a new paratactic
language for sensing and then wisely confronting extremity.

Serling's once-authoritative person is here a passenger (not a pilot) on Flight 33,
in an episode called "The Odyssey of Flight 33," a teleplay written from a Serling
story in 1960 and aired on CBS on February 24, 1961. The strange sensation the
officer feels is a precise yet unimaginable *something*, immense speed without
any of the usual corresponding effects. As the pilot and crew also struggle to comprehend such acceleration and to contain it, the jet pushes through barriers of
sound and (somehow) of light. They are in radio silence, because they are flying
millions of years in the past. Lacking locating devices, the crew looks for Manhattan Island as a visual guide for landing at Idlewild Aiport. "How can it be
Manhattan? Where the hell's the skyline? Where are the buildings? . . . There
isn't any New York."[23] Soon they observe a dinosaur munching the island's jungle
flora. After pondering a course of action, they decide to repeat the maneuver and
ascend to catch the jet stream. The reverse move seems to work. They gratefully
see Manhattan again. But as they descend for a landing they notice that the air

controllers reached by radio seem unaware of recent advances in aviation and speak outmoded technical language. The copilot glimpses buildings of the New York World's Fair. It's 1939. "We came back . . . but dear God . . . *we didn't come back far enough!*"

Rod Serling's ultimate nightmare is returning to 1939, the moment before the beginning of the end. The length of the airport's old runways are insufficient to accommodate the landing of a jet, but this can't be the only reason why they decide to ascend again and does not explain their surrealistic desperation to regain the final two decades. The story-script Serling wrote for this episode makes the reason a bit clearer. Who in 1960 would knowingly return to the moment before the world war and be doomed to repeat that history? "Thirty thousand feet below," Serling writes, "it was 1939 and people gaped at the wondrous exhibits. There was the waterfall in front of the *Italian* building; the beautiful marble statuary that fronted the *Polish* pavilion; the exquisite detail of the tapestry and wood carvings shown by the smiling *Japanese*. And the people walked happily through a warm June afternoon, seeing only the sunlight and not knowing that darkness was falling over the world."[24] This is a facile politics of dramatic irony. Yet it makes for the one *Twilight Zone* episode in this period that ends with neither a final twist nor a resolution. Key otherwise to what was deemed the successful formula for popular sci-fi, the reveal here Serling meant not so much as a plot point as an observation about postwar epistemology—about what can and cannot be seen, known, explained—which is why perhaps the teleplay struggles to include the style of the story's final narration. The story's overt lyricism (spring/warmth/light) befits both the internationalist mood of wonder and a conventional sanguine focus on art. The reveal arrives in easily forgotten aesthetic detail as it constituted once a vista in the light: the artificial Italian waterfall, the Polish statuary, and the Japanese tapestry, all premodern, peacefully beheld by isolationist Americans (and one wayward British ex-pilot from the postdisaster future)—both the mode of art and the artwork itself all now gone, "disappeared" like New York City itself in the frightful humanless prehistory we glimpse mid-episode, invisible in the dark that not only preceded 1939 but followed. This is an "homage to New York" strikingly in accord with Tinguely's sense of the viewer's experience of urban extirpation and chance reassemblage. ("What was important for me," Tinguely said, "was that *afterwards* there would be nothing.") Serling's ending is meant to tie back to what the RAF officer had learned from the war about realizing illogical indiscernibles from negatives: "No flame or smoke. Nothing."

The American woman sitting next to the former British pilot on Flight 33, after castigating him for being from a tribe unable "to emotionalize anything," carelessly asks again, "*What* did you say you were?" Upon hearing his RAF rank repeated she pronounces it wonderful and informs him that a "Nephew of mine was in the navy during the Second World War. He was on a cruiser, or PT boat or something like that. Or was it a battleship?" The imprecision of her war remembrance further ironizes her criticism of her ally's alleged incapacity for creating emotional connection and experiencing therapeutic release; she had actually observed the Serlingesque truth that one can be outwardly, physically sickened by repression. The American's inability to describe her own family's wartime experience with even the most basic information—her forgetting the distinction between a patrol boat and a battleship—contrasts the RAF officer's inability to explain what has gone wrong. "There was this *feeling* [despite the 'awful coldness' of his people] . . . this *feeling* that he couldn't describe even to himself."[25] The two kinds of not knowing are different, and if you perceive them to be the same you are fated to an inability to mourn. One mode marks the failure of testimony and the other indicates its success. One is judged by Serling's tale to be causally irresponsible—hardly different from that of the blithe folks of 1939 living their warm June afternoon, thus doomed to repeat rhinocerization—and the other is affirmed as the necessary new Cagean pataphysics of saying while not saying.

The captain of Flight 33 fully shares the RAF officer's lecture on nothing. Immediately after giving the passengers an initial deceitful anodyne update— "There is no cause for alarm. We'll keep you posted. If we run according to schedule, we should be landing in . . . forty minutes."—he begins to despise his fate as the airline's Organization Man: "'Jesus God,' he said to himself, 'I should put on a gray flannel suit and sell toothpaste.'"[26] By the second update he is in full rebellion against allegiance to the Organization and to smooth centrist circumlocutious appeals to reason, and decides to use the positive negative language already affirmed in the RAF veteran by radical narrative perspective. "Disaster defied utterance," as Appelfeld wrote when recalling his posttraumatic experience with languages in the 1950s, just before he falteringly began to write stories. And after disaster, he continued, "smooth, fluent sentences leave me with a feeling of unclearness, of order that hides emptiness."[27] "Fragmentation," writes Blanchot in *The Writing of the Disaster*, "the mark of a coherence all the firmer in that it has to come undone in order to be reached, . . . for fragmentation is the pulling to pieces (the tearing) of that which never has preexisted (really or ideally) as a whole."[28] "What I'm going to tell you," the captain of Flight 33 says now to his passengers, "is something I can't explain." Quite aside from the dark comedy of a commercial airline pilot admitting he can't explain something, passengers and the episode's viewers experience the breakdown of traditional *I know/you don't* writer-to-reader narrative explanatory authority as the mark of a special, strange coherence. "The crew is as much in the dark as you are." He then asks them to look out the left side of the aircraft, where "those buildings down there *aren't* the United Nations." For the purposes of a representation of World War II in 1960, this antitautology, the opposite of sanctioned technical 1950s speech, has both logical-linguistic import and political valence. *If you are used to getting your postwar bearings through easy recognition of an internationalist landmark, please note that the UN Building you see is not in fact the United Nations, for its cooperativist assembly hasn't yet been urgently needed.* In the epilogue, Serling emerges to say, with perfect pataphysical nontransparency, that the humans of Flight 33 are still straying from New York somewhere, not searched for because "fearful of what they'd find."[29] It is unclear who "they" is. Are they other panicky humans who are afraid to search and do not know there are living beings to search for? Or our fellow citizens of 1960 who fall into repetition of the horrors of 1939–45? And what the RAF captain means when he "feels" that he "couldn't describe" what went wrong is a disastrous, mystically collective dissolution of the self in Blanchot's sense. "Each one restrains himself" in preparation for the fall of the disaster, "clinging to an other, an other who is himself and is the dissolution—the dispersion—of the self, and the restraint is sheer haste, panicky flight, death outside death."[30]

## To Make the Rest Participate

The vaunted "new language" of science fiction, as a version of writing disaster explored by practitioners throughout the 1950s, somewhat suddenly gains a new purpose—that of permitting esoteric yet avid testimony of unexplainable events while maintaining a commitment to ineffability. In the supposed lowbrow genre this of course originated at the heretical edges of science, with the epiphenomenalism, gnosticism, and pataphysics that fascinate and befall even diehard empiricists. But by 1960, once books like Shirer's *The Rise and Fall of the Third Reich* emerge with their unsaid methodological claim that the disaster of 1933–45 could be described with certitude after diligent effort, could be narratively arranged and in that sense rationalized, we begin to see work by artists inclined toward science fiction, such as Serling and Miller, whose interest is directed at the historical and political effects of worldwide war and are not primarily scientific. This is exactly how Mack's Zeroist Sahara Project, a vibrating transgeographic pillar of light, despite the mania for visual technologies, was meant not so much as technological sophistication as a straightforward utopian rejoinder to the constraints war's horrors had placed on time, space, and light. These two normally self-canceling concerns—urgent bearing witness, and the failure of language to describe historical occurrence—made for a convergence of high and low art genres, of the distinct arts of national cultures, of both grand and vernacular ambitions, of old and new media. We begin to see a strong thematizing of the needed postwar "new language," long idealized and advocated particularly by the sci-fi community, becoming accepted now not only across submodes of that increasingly popular genre—Serling and Miller both had a good deal to do with that success, as did Philip Wylie, Ray Bradbury, and Isaac Asimov, whose *Nine Tomorrows* of 1959 featured the metapoem "Rejection Slips," which could be said to have clinched the relationship between popular sci-fi and postmodern writing—but also in utopian installations (such as the assemblages of Dienes, Tinguely, and the holocaust-obsessed American sculptor Ortiz, and Piene's sky art), in art-house films (such as Rossellini's *It Was a Night in Rome*), in self-consciously literary fiction (such as Appelfeld was attempting just then in Israel with intense linguistic stubbornness) as well as, of course, as we have seen already in this book, in the work of postwar poets experimenting once again with language and form despite pressures to eschew ideological nonconformities. Sci-fi, fabulistic allegory, and other modes typically not otherwise associated with avant-garde art came together with experimentalists around a freshly radicalized acceptance of difficulty. The new ethical exigence of difficulty, connecting up an old lineage on the avant-garde side, converged in science fiction and fantasy with what Val Peterson had in the mid-1950s described as "the new language" required by anyone imagining total annihilation. Using that phrase, Peterson was quoting Dwight Eisenhower's speech to the United Nations General Assembly in 1953 as a new U.S. president: "I feel impelled to speak today in a language that, in a sense, is a new one, which I, who have spent so much of my life in the military profession, would have preferred never to use." (Eisenhower dated the birth of the "new language" at July 16, 1945, marking the advent of the successful Trinity bomb test.)[31] Peterson had associated the new language of science fiction—he was commenting on Wylie's *Tomorrow* (1954), a tale that influenced Serling's "The Monsters Are Due on Maple Street"—with the problems of representation worked through in testimonies to horror: "So difficult of comprehension is this new language to Americans generally" that the writer must "wisely" spend a good deal of effort "establishing the credibility of his witnesses."[32] "The tendency to fall silent," we recall Celan observing in his 1960 notebook, "cannot not be hard." "I am trying to be unfamiliar with what I'm doing," Cage wrote in *Silence* on Robert Rauschenberg's "empty" (white) canvases, *prior* to which "Conversation was difficult."[33] We have seen in our discussions of experimental art that the need for difficulty derived from representations witnessing threats of mass killing and mass extinction, circumstances that taught those who had already learned from modernism not just to understand nontransparent expression "resistant to immediacy and comprehension" but to comprehend various untranslatable styles as the crucial aspect of the "language-act most charged with the intent of communication, of reaching out to touch the listener or reader in his inmost"—George Steiner's definition of poetry in "On Difficulty." The writer facing such a circumstance, Steiner continued, "must literally create new words and syntactic modes" and must at all times make our language confusion, on top of everything else, itself centrally thematic.[34]

Roberto Rossellini's own new filmic syntactic mode was the use of the Pancinor zoom device. Indeed the central theme of the film in which he first fully used the device, *Era notte a Roma* (*It Was a Night in Rome* or *Escape by Night* of 1960), was the confusion of language as a form of antifascism truer and more real, counterintuitively, than that of immediate postwar neorealism. Exactly halfway through the film, Fyodor (played by Sergei Bondarchuk), a Russian sergeant who had escaped from a concentration camp, is suddenly overwhelmed by an urge to bear witness. He stands while his new friends sit at a makeshift Christmas dinner. For days they have been hiding from fascist spies and Nazi occupiers in a Roman attic and are desperate for the ritual continuity of the repast. Fyodor begins a simple toast in his rudimentary Italian. He wants his friends, a Roman couple, an American, and an Englishman (the latter two are, with him, survivors of the camp), to comprehend his love for them. This thought begins to challenge his ability in Italian and makes him think of the Russian language, of Russia, of home and remoteness from family. Distressed by problems of language and memory together, he shifts into Russian, first haltingly, then in a quiet burst, and finally in a vocal stream. We witness the secondary witnesses (the four at the festive attic table) watching this testimony as much as hearing it. Somehow they follow their friend in Russian. Here is part of his speech rendered into English: "I have a lot to say, we speak different languages but we understand each other. . . . We are surrounded by a war we never wanted which was forced on us. . . . Rivers of human blood have flowed. . . .

We became friends and I thank you but I can no longer sit here, I must return to drive out the enemy from our country with all my strength."[35]

The others comprehend not a word of this but the international ensemble of actors in the roles of Allied compatriots makes clear they comprehend. Rossellini provided no subtitles for his Italian audience. Nor in editions of the film for English-speaking audiences are English subtitles offered for Sergei Bondarchuk's speech. We are not to understand the words. We face the same difficulty as the gathered antifascists. The rivers of blood might as well be discerned only in the flow of these uttered words. The point is of course that quite particularly during the war "words had lost currency," as Appelfeld put it. "Words did not help one understand." Witness to life in extremis required "a kind of language that precedes speech." Neither the "wickedness" Fyodor experienced in the Nazi camp and in his sense of familial loss, nor the "generosity" of those who offer help (in Appelfeld's terms), "need . . . words." Fyodor's ecstatic speech—incomprehensible to addressees within the representational fiction of the film and to its recipients as artwork—befits Appelfeld's description of the process of survivor testimony: "These are extremely difficult feelings that appear to require detailed explanation [thus Fyodor reaches the limit of his Italian], but what can one do—the greater the suffering and the more intense the feelings of despair, the more superfluous words become." This, in Appelfeld's account, is followed immediately by a large historical claim: "It was only after the war that words reappeared."[36]

Peter Brunette has observed of *Era notte a Roma* that the "neorealist dream" of straightforward presentation of reality in the visual medium is challenged by "this language-subverting outburst" and succeeds because it comes in the context of the balance of "conventional linguistic signification."[37] The critic might have added that the neorealism movement founded in 1945 (the time of Rossellini's *Open City*, a precise predecessor of the 1960 film) as a direct response to the war is made problematic by, in Appelfeld's formulation, the *later* reappearance of words ironically conveying their insufficiency as documentary. Fyodor has momentarily gone into deep memory. His utterances evince cotemporality. He is simultaneously absent and present, reliving the past *and* conveying the current desperate feeling about memory (although not the content of that memory) to his colleagues, whom he knows also bear such memories.

*Era notte a Roma* tells the story of three escapees from the Nazi camp: Pemberton, a British Major; Bradley, an American pilot; and Fyodor, the Russian sergeant. The three are hidden in a loft by Esperia, an apolitical Italian who has mastered the ways of the black market, and her fiancé, Renato, whom she and we discover is active in the Resistance. Some contemporary reviewers—such as John Gillett writing for the July 1960 *Sight and Sound* review of that year's Cannes Festival films—were perplexed by the language confusions. Gillett admitted, though, that Rossellini's aim in "casting actors of differing nationalities to speak their own language" was "laudable."[38] Rather than limiting or contradicting Rossellini's documentary objective, the failure of semantic comprehension becomes a main feature of testimony as a kind of documentary. The document, as Ingeborg Bachmann noted, is to be found in "another language." The postfascist narrator of Bachmann's "Everything" discovers—just as, taken together, the multilingual Allies do here in this re-representation of frightful rhinocerization in Rome—that "it is all a question of language and *not merely of this one language of ours* that was created with others in Babel to confuse the world." Bachmann and Rossellini shared a sense that there was such a thing as the antifascist unconscious—that "underneath" "this one language of ours" there "smoulders another language that extends to gestures and looks, the unwinding of thoughts and the passage of feelings, and in it is all our misfortune." Discerned in a common ur-language of collective testimony, such misfortune extends beyond the hidden Allied escapees to the skeptical, unaligned Esperia. The more fascists and spies assume that their power enables them to extract sexual favors from her, the more her antifascist stance strengthens into a politics, but even as this progression is underway she needs to learn Bachmann's "another language." To reach the end of her apoliticism, to end her merely opportunistic life in the Roman black market, she will learn that the English officer Pemberton is not himself one of the raunchy men around her. Once, as she changes out of her nun's clothes (disguised thus she can safely visit illicit markets), Pemberton emerges from the attic hideout asking politely for "tea," but, striving to pronounce Italian vowels, he speaks a word Esperia deems "te." She believes him to want her ("you") rather than a hot drink, and defends herself with a knife. The Alliance is tenuous, and is constantly tested by connotative parapraxis, a shibboleth.

*Era notte a Roma* opens in documentary style. We view archival footage of Allied planes running bombing raids over the Italian landscape (later in the film we'll see footage of the landing at Anzio), while a newsreel-style voice summarizes the invasion, imprisonment of Allied soldiers in concentration camps, and protection given escapees by Italian citizens. Then the narration breaks from omniscience and speaks in grateful tones of "I" and "us" as witnesses to Nazi brutality in the camps and to the generosity of Italians. *Era notte a Roma* is structured as a survivor's story emerging from within documentary. Rossellini told a reporter that the movie is "an eyewitness testimony." Brunette compared it, part to part, with the September 1943-June 1944 diary of Nazi occupation, the pseudonymous *Inside Rome with the Germans* of "Jane Scrivener" (1945), and found the film of 1960 to be accurate down to the details.[39] The *mise-en-scène* sets up parallel and possibly contradictory film vocabularies, documentary synopses, and individual survivor testimony. "It was like a city of the dead," writes Scrivener in a typical entry.[40] Pemberton's later omniscient historical view based on his personal experience, information we understand—what again Langer calls "common memory"—is made possible by his having witnessed Fyodor's subjective testimony and by Esperia's preideological defense of herself against fascism's masculine power. The final objectivity, which in this case serves as a preface, is an effect of the realization of subject. Neorealism, so Rossellini famously redefined it in 1960, had been "the representation of authentic passions,"[41] but postwar politics had led to the suppression of discussions in the art of difficult problems, and to abusive depictions of "authentic passions" that were now "infantility" and "total vanity," mere devotion to "gratuitous acts of petty cruelty."[42] Realism between 1945 and 1960 had become escapism. *Era notte a Roma* stands as corrective: testimony to horror that is difficult rather than easy to understand; thematics focused on problems of representation rather than ticket-selling salacious immediacies of fascist barbarity, sexualized in what Susan Sontag would call "fascinating fascism" (exactly the opposite of Bettelheim's sense of survivors' "infantility"); and a revival of dignity rather than psychological abasement or debilitation in its depiction even of traumatic deep memory, as in Fyodor's agonized valediction.

The new use of the Pancinor zoom lens enabled Rossellini to take testimony without imposing the "psychological pressure" of earlier forms of tracking shots and, of course, of the sometimes jarring separate shot as a cut to extractive extreme close-up.[43] It supports Langer's sense of the cotemporality of survivor testimony:[44] the witness speaks from the past and *is there* while engaging (for the benefit of present company) common memory, recollections that can be shared only through at least minimal presence. As Andrew Sarris put it in an essay written in response to a Rossellini retrospective at MoMA (1964), "Long shot equals *then*. Zoom shot equals *now*."[45] The implication was something new to the visual theory of bearing witness. Only much later, in response to the development of systematic collections of video did the problem of the emotional tyranny of the extreme close-up enter discussions of representations of deep memory.[46] Yet here, right at the point of the invention of this single-shot zoom, Rossellini averts the problem, accepts transference (the auteur's own affective implication, by way of the lens, in the testimony and in Italians' role in the war), and circumvents the ideological contradiction typically otherwise effected by visually dictatorial close-up of the vulnerable witness in the act of reimagining war trauma. "Why . . . is the zoom so appropriate for Rossellini?" asked Sarris. "Because when Rossellini wants to establish the moral relationship between one character and another . . . he is not unduly concerned with the scenery in between." As Fyodor begins his toast in simple Italian, the lens is set to make a medium shot; we see the subject, not yet entering reverie, in relation to his casually attentive hearers—all of them easily comprehending. He says "I suffer" in Italian (words Sergei Bondarchuk, who generally could not communicate with the other actors, had learned on the set)—then "I suffer" again, now with greater semantic difficulty, and we are beginning, with a very slow zoom, to move ironically *away* from the community of sympathetic interlocutors.

Induced by what is created internally by memory of suffering and cannot be conveyed, the subject slips into deep memory, and disappears into the *during*—into the horrors of battle or of the camp, into his sense of distance from love and its loss, thus losing too the very people with whom his toast was meant to convey and share love. By the time he is linguistically alone, removed from the fictional friends, from the actual actors none of whom spoke Russian, and from viewers of the film, the Pancinor zoom has slowly excluded all others. As the untranslated Russian lamentation finally fully excludes us, the Pancinor backs out, gradually reconstituting the Alliance of English, American, antifascist Italian, and Russian (figure 7.1). It is "as though his very being," writes Brunette, "were expanding through love to encompass the others in the room as the lens movement ends as a group shot."[47] The formalist meaning of this close-up of a person incomprehensibly bearing witness is the very opposite of tyrannical. The ideological contradiction it avoids is that which Jackson Mac Low felt he could overcome when he began to "save the sparks" of authoritarian technique in performances that sustained the politics of antifascist authorial choices of constraint yet included other subjectivities in the making of meaning. The tyrannical close-up, no matter how sympathetic, can have the unintended consequence of undue psychological intrusion, creating a false hope of therapeutic outcome yet inducing a repetition of the trauma the testimony already sufficiently struggles to convey. Just as the prefatory voiceover is not the vaunted Voice of God (VOG), telling us that we are about to be told what history is, so neither is the camera recording Fyodor's recurrence of trauma itself an instance of the fascist aesthetic the film's evocation of translinguistic community is meant to repudiate.

The "desolating grief" Fyodor feels from testimony, to use a key phrase in Primo Levi's telling, is not primarily caused by the subject matter he recalls.

7.1 Still of Sergei Bondarchuk, as Fyodor, seen through the Pancinor zoom in Roberto Rosselini's *Era notte a Roma* (1960).

The content of memory provides the motive for themes, of course, but is not the source of the resurgence of traumatic intensity. The immediate cause is the detailed reconstruction of the isolation of a moment reflecting wartime agony, which Rossellini seeks as director in order to develop a revised neorealism and to protect opportunities in film for representations of such intensity. Again: the witnessing subject's isolation originates not from content but from *the fear of the failure to convey* that content, by a terror that witness-bearing will be met with indifference. No one anatomized that particular terror more assiduously than did Levi. He describes the "desolating grief" as a nightmare in which he is telling his sister and her friends first of particular phenomena of the death camp and then of the "intense pleasure, physical, inexpressible, to be at home" with them—for in his vision he is still enslaved at Auschwitz yet is imagining that he is back home. He realizes that his family and friends "are completely indifferent." Perhaps, he thinks, he has not sufficiently conveyed extremity. Perhaps they do not want to comprehend him. Perhaps the problem is that he voices an unrecognizable language. In any case, his hearers "speak confusedly of other things among themselves, *as if I was not there.*" *This* apparently inevitable failure of witness to extreme precarity—fear of absence *after* survival—not the phenomena of Auschwitz is what produces "pain in its pure state." The pain is "not tempered by a sense of reality," or "by the intrusion of extraneous circumstances." Consolation momentarily comes not from family or friends or sense of home but from fellow sufferers who indicate to him that in being thus alone he is not alone: this vision is the same "dream of many others," it turns out, "perhaps of everyone."[48] Fyodor's "immediate and violent impulse" to say he has "many things to recount," even though he lacks the signifying means to recount them, or indeed because of the lack, befits the pure pain Levi describes, and that purity is the source of the artfulness of many of the representations we encounter here. Whether from his own reading of Levi's account written and published in Italian in 1947, or otherwise, Rossellini shared a common goal of the experimental artist reencountering effects of the war in 1960: to retell the story of the disaster "to 'the rest,' " and "to make 'the rest' participate in it." Thus Levi in his original preface identifies and apologizes for the "violent impulse" of a writer otherwise modest and empirical. Because he seeks "an interior liberation" rather than an outward transparency—thus potentially contradicting his aim to "make 'the rest' participate"—he also feels he must apologize for the "*fragmentary* character" of his art.[49] Alfred Werner, reviewing Levi's book for the *Saturday Review* in January 1960, realized that Levi's "talent for terse statement" and his method as a writer " 'to build around himself a tenuous barrier of defense' "[50] were not contradictory. Indeed the two qualities, taken together, were the main reasons he survived. Werner's review indicates firsthand knowledge of the tenuous expository barrier. Himself a survivor—an Austro-Jewish art critic whose manuscripts were "destroyed when the Nazis entered Vienna" at the time of the Anschluss in 1938[51]—Werner mostly read German and now English, and here was celebrating the appearance of Levi's *If This Is a Man* (the proper title of *Survival in Auschwitz*) in English, translated by Stuart Woolf in close collaboration with Levi and published by Orion Press in late 1959.

Throughout 1960 ecstatic reviews along the lines of Werner's appeared in U.S. and British magazines and newspapers. The original Italian edition had only sold a total of fifteen hundred copies. Levi completed work on the German translation on May 13, 1960, the lively response to which would contribute to the perceived currency of his approach.[52] Levi's theory of the materiality of bearing witness, his acceptance of fragmentary telling, and his description of fascist irrealities as necessitating a new realism thenceforth permanently shaped the conversation about disaster, supplementing (but in several crucial ways differing from) Elie Wiesel's *Night* (1960). Max Henry Fisher's review for the *Times Literary Supplement* focused on Levi's contention—an unusual one at the time and again quite different from Bruno Bettelheim and other early theorists of survival—that people can "preserve a sense of reality."[53] It's from alignment with this sense in Levi, and from bitter disagreement with Bettelheim, that Terrence Des Pres later developed the idea that realism entailed not comprehension of reality but adaptation to it—that the myriad versions of the term "unreal" in testimony indicate not cliché but the paucity of premodern realist strategies. In Des Pres's critique of theories of survivor guilt he wholly revises a theory of responsibility: not the internal voice of authority (one's own VOG) that motivates will through social expectation and even self-loathing, but an externalizing "objective" ability to respond.[54] Survival preserves a sense of reality as unreality, and such a reality enables response. Thus responsibility is ipso facto formally innovative. It is not only Fyodor who emerges from the scene of his seemingly incomprehensible testimony with a renewed capacity for improvised feeling as a postwar form of responsibility. The antifascists gathered around the table, and we as viewers, are acutely aware of the experimental aim of Rossellini's use of language, as Levi put it, to "make 'the rest' participate." We are the rest, othered momentarily by the camera yet thus ultimately involved.

## The Smoke of War

One of Aharon Appelfeld's agonized early stories works through this distinction. Max, a survivor barely coping with daily life, is immobilized—cannot bear to remember yet cannot move forward—by the responsibility he feels after the burning of a synagogue into which his mother, father, and sister Zhani had been forced. An unnamed narrator recalls from Max's point of view that the "entire congregation suffocated there in smoke." So long as Max feels accountable for their deaths, and indeed feels the guilt of the lone survivor—did he deserve to live now while the rest of the family went up in smoke?—he is unable to open the "rucksacks" he hauled with him out of the forest in which he and a friend, Aryeh, had hidden during the war. The packs contain clothing of his parents and pieces of familial culture. The story, titled "Smoke," describes in a troubled language the halting process by which Max struggles to overcome a sense of responsibility and begins to reckon an ability to respond—to respond to Aryeh, now his sickly business partner in the butcher shop they jointly run, and to the larger meaning of the artifacts. Ill at home yet again on the day of the story, Aryeh can offer no help as Max labors in the shop. Max is angry at a supplier who, frustrated by the shopkeeper's stereotypical Old World dickering, has shouted at him. The narrator's language barely registers this as a shift in describing Max's thoughts and constrained actions.

Yet the narration here notably does switch for the first time to a "we" that refers to other characters in the fiction or to a larger empathetic community, indicating in either case the narrator's willingness to include himself and his writing in the awful turns of events. And soon after this shift Max decides to open the rucksacks. He returns to his small room, where he lives alone with his dog, Mitzi, opens the packs, and methodically lays their contents out on the bed. Zhani's jacket ("she wore it every Shabbat"), his mother's clothing, his father's clothing. He feels a compulsion to separate and arrange. The sense in this precise writing that "We need to keep them separate and not mix them" seems not so much a reference to kosher custom as to the challenges of confronting familial memories of self-organization, and both positively ritualistic and heinously ideological separation, a triggered response to the rediscovery of the family's "kitchenwares" that might otherwise seem superfluous, even neurotic. Appelfeld's displaced heartsick protagonist approaches the problem of the literal old burden with a "diligent discipline" that is also a new writer's promise and code; the story's generic unruliness is paradoxically consummately disciplined. Personal items and culturally significant objects (heirloom vestiges such as silver teaspoons) must be sorted, distinguished—cannot be left a "mess," certainly, but so too, Appelfeld as experienced survivor but novice writer sought for this to be a moment of psychological unburdening, or, to keep with the trope of the story and the therapeutic cliché, of *unpacking*. Max's reawakening capacity for responding to the memory of his parents and sister, and the connection of this exploration to his ghastly time in the forest, are internal while the narrative Hebrew prose remains stubbornly external. The objects inside the burden are, as it were, objectivities. Soon Max becomes so anxious that he cannot create categories for these memory-triggering artifacts, and flees with Mitzi to the roof of the apartment building. He then hurries out into the street to relieve a sudden craving for another cigarette (still more smoke). Walking the dark streets, seeking an open tobacconist, he comes upon the house of his companion Aryeh, observes his fellow survivor from outside lying ill in his room, and remembers how they had run through the forests fleeing local fascists—how Aryeh had had to carry Max on his shoulders.

"Smoke" is itself, at crucial moments, a messy text. As of this writing, it has not been published in an English translation. Ariel Resnikoff and Rivka Weinstock have identified in it some unidiomatic Hebrew, a self-consciousness about the cultural specificity of proper nouns, fragmented rather than seamless narrative movement, and in general an awkwardness that seems at times deliberate—such as somewhat unusual Hebrew word choices and diction, and inclusion of Yiddish and German slang—and at other moments the effect of a novice writer working in a recently acquired second language (or fourth, in Appelfeld's case).[55] Does the shift from "he" to "we" at a crucial emotional moment in Max's saga of responsibility, for instance, indicate a writer reaching the edge of his narrative ability or one gaining advantage from pronominal opacity?

Appelfeld's early stories engage all aspects of the disjunctions and maladjustments of the people appearing in them. These people are survivors of the war who (as he put it describing himself) bear a "mistrust of words," who prefer "stuttering" to lucidity, and for whom "words did not help one understand." Among the items Max has carried around unexamined for fifteen years since the war, a possession he cannot sort from the others, is an old (presumably ceremonial) plate, or perhaps several; he cannot tell which, as they appear now merely as plural "fragments of plate." The plate cannot be reconstructed, resisting Max's survivor's compulsion for categorical salience. The remnant is an objective correlative—each of the early stories has one—of Appelfeld's intransigent Hebrew *ars poetica*. The language of "Smoke" is that of a writer, like other child survivors, for whom "language had been completely torn from their throats." As a teenager in a displaced persons camp after liberation, Appelfeld had heard—and decades later could still quote verbatim—the testimony of another survivor telling of the "Pen," or "Keffer," an unspeakably dreadful space where Nazis had put one group of children to live with unfed German Shepherds. He has introduced this story by noting generally that "We children didn't know how to tell our stories." By the time the Russian army liberated the camp that maintained the Keffer, many of the children imprisoned in it had lost the ability to speak.[56] In the DP camp these children realized that "there were no words; the ones left over from home sounded hollow." When an adult survivor's language flowed from his mouth, the children realized that "the words he used [were] from before the war, and they sounded like coarse scraps, devoid of all taste." This is a trope of terror and of telling that Appelfeld's Max is still working through fifteen years later when he bickers with the meat supplier—"Smoke" is redolent of nonmetaphorical coarse scraps, "dripping water from all sides," flesh "changed into something else, and looked like scabs"—and when he has to learn to cope with the rucksacks' contained fragments. Having suffered multiple traumas during his many months of constant vigilance and frequent close escapes from murderous local anti-Semites and fascist militias in central European forests, Appelfeld himself was apparently not entirely mute at war's end, but he had lost his mother tongue and suffered from extreme reticence. It was during those transitional months that he realized how "disaster defied utterance." He eventually began to write in a diary that constructed "a mosaic of words," a collage of German, Yiddish, Hebrew, and Ruthenian fragments, adages, and quotations. Years later he returned to this diary and saw that the words were in fact just words, "not 'sentences.'" They were "the suppressed cries of a fourteen-year-old youth who'd lost all the languages he had spoken and was now left without a language."[57] The diary had become a "hiding place" in itself, where he could "pile up the remnants of his mother tongue." He turned from diary writing to poetry, and finally to fictional prose. The poems, which Yigal Schwartz has called a "necessary next step" from personal diary to literary stance, expressions of a speaker that is not him, gave him permission to explore a form in which nontransparency was a generic norm, where a "gloaming horizon" recalled from "alien lands" could redden either by autumnal coloration or by "sad[ness]" and "yearning" ("The Dovecote of Childhood," 1955) without explication or a story to be moved forward.[58]

"Smoke," as a fictive text, is a hiding place too, as opaque as any of the young writer's poems. It is an intentionally unhealthy suppression of suppression. Appelfeld later insisted that "the book is called *Smoke* because they're all chain smokers."[59] Certainly this is true—Max, his lungs already compromised by all other senses of smoke, is addicted to cigarettes—but it is also a witty misprision, to say the least: there is inferior meat to be smoked, there is the fog of war, there is machines' exhaust, there is the scent of clothing Max protected (as if a holocaust archive) against incineration, there is the "nausea of suffocation" from his dire heart condition, and there is just the frequent deployment of the titular word even when the context doesn't quite call for it. Smoke is everywhere. It cannot be fled despite Max's constant decamping from one situation to another. On his motorcycle, "He sped up, and a rushing scrim of smoke followed him." The resistant Hebrew of these early writings made for a metafictional quality in itself—word choice, diction, idiom, referent—through which the fog of writing *does* itself what it narratively *says*. If "*Smoke* . . . is about people who came to Israel after the disaster, . . . *continuing the life of the ghetto, of the camps*," then the language of smoke becomes literarily exophonic: a choiceless, inventive linguistic refusal to move on even at the risk of incorrectness[60] and, at crucial moments, "an almost cubist incoherence" (as Ariel Resnikoff puts it)—a strange experiment in welcoming parapraxis.

For Appelfeld, as for Celan, the idea of the mother tongue went far beyond the usual double meaning of matriarchal linguistic culture generally and emotional maternal attachment. These two were shaped as writers by the sudden

traumatic disappearance of their mothers—the unforgettable scene of instruction, as it were, in which the role of writer in each was born; even Appelfeld,
who was then a small child, seemed to know that the context of such killing was
a hatred by others of the very identity that had connected him to the lost parent.
Growing up at the edge of assimilated Jewish Germanic culture—both writers
were born and raised in Czernowitz in Bukovina, formerly in Austro-Hungary
and now in the southwestern corner of Ukraine near Romania—they received
from their mothers a cherished language legacy. Both, in writing, continued
always to face the paradox of what Celan called "the pain-laden rhyme"—the
horror of one's own resonant mastery, of harmony, conjunction, phrasal uniformity, verbal flow. We recall Celan's poem "Winter," in which the hibernal
weather, blowing from the Ukrainian east where fascists had taken his mother
to die, strokes across the "torn / strings of a strident and discordant harp," in
harp-poems sung askew by the son that enabled the Mother-muse to remind
him of his sweet lyric inheritance. Both writers resolved after the war to return
to what Appelfeld called an "inescapable dilemma" of "my mother tongue": "the
language had been German—the language of those who murdered my mother."
Like Celan, Appelfeld as a survivor of genocidal hatred recognized that "my German was not the language of those Germans but the language of my mother,
and it was as clear as daylight that if I met up with her I'd speak to her in the
language that we had spoken together since I was a small child."[61] Appelfeld,
younger than Celan, was a boy at the time of his mother's murder, but he, like
Celan, discovered only fifteen years after the war that the putative therapeutic
effect of bearing witness to severance from the mother was nil, and turned, at
that point, to imaginative writing, although nonetheless autobiographical, as an
experimental form of history. In doing so he indirectly contended, in his own
way, as Celan did in "The Meridian," that noncurative transferential (that is,
nonetheless affective) witnessing could positively constitute an inarticulate language radically responsive to terror—"a word against the grain, the word which
cuts the 'string,'" as Celan put it.[62]

    Older and somewhat more capable of willing himself toward a personal future,
Celan remained in Europe, as we know, and stubbornly wrote his poems in the
mother tongue. Meantime, just thirteen years old at war's end, Appelfeld was
gathered with other traumatized, stateless (and languageless) children into the
crowded holding camps, entered Mandatory Palestine on an illegal immigrant
ship in 1946, and then resolutely trained in schools "that molded these new arrivals in the image of the hardy *sabra* with no ties to their former lives."[63] Soon
Appelfeld "hated the people who forced me to speak Hebrew, and with the death

of my mother tongue, my hostility toward them only increased."[64] Revival of Hebrew as the Jewish language was a basic aim of Zionist ideology, "which suppressed or delegitimized Yiddish."[65] The intellectual and scholarly effect of such suppression, as we have seen, was to rationalize and deradicalize the tradition of nonrationalism in postwar interpretations of European Jewish culture. For the young Appelfeld in Israel after statehood, the enforced acquisition of Hebrew "was like being trapped in a protracted military tour of duty."[66] Israelis "cut themselves off from memory, and built themselves a language that was completely 'here,'" forgetting *there*. He heretically resisted, seeking a language that was not *here*, developing an odd idiomatic mélange of absence, a constant mix of *before* and *during*, composing what Blanchot in *The Writing of the Disaster* calls "demise writing" in which "the subject becomes absence"[67]—and what eventually resulted was strange writing like that of "Smoke." Appelfeld interpreted the postholocaust Zionist slogan "to build and to be rebuilt" as an "extinction of memory." Memory was linguistic.[68]

Against all this he set out on a radical course that could have been perceived then as reactionary. He was attracted to the old literary life of central Europe, the remnant folkways of which were to be encountered sporadically in the cafes of Jerusalem. A favorite haunt was Café Peter in the German Colony.[69] Young Appelfeld avidly studied Yiddish, Kabbalah, Hasidism, and other now "historical" forms of esoteric Judaic expression at Hebrew University, and even revived his childhood interest in the connections to the myth-driven Ruthenian culture of his mother's parents (who had lived on a farm, visits to which he had dreamily idealized). He connected with Gershom Scholem just as that intrepid revisionist was researching and writing the books about folkloric and kabbalistic interpretive traditions that would shape the postwar modernism of Rothenberg and others in 1960. Appelfeld was also deeply influenced by the Galician-born Israeli writer S. Y. Agnon. He became deeply absorbed in the writings of Kafka, and studied with Max Brod himself, Kafka's friend and keeper of the Kafka manuscripts.

The language of "Smoke" is Hebrew, to be sure, but the diction and setting have their hearts elsewhere. "Max" is not a Hebrew name. On the opening page, he arrives by motorcycle yet the second word deployed for this vehicle is not the standard "machine" but an English-Hebrew cognate, "motor," and the thing, starting up, somewhat unidiomatically "lights" or "ignites." Now inside his shop Max encounters a Mrs. Fuchs, who is German. She seeks bones to delight her "Hundi," an idiomatic German diminutive of hound. His landlady, we later learn, is a Mrs. Tischtuch, a German whose name means tablecloth and who sometimes brings him strudel and speaks with him in Polish. As Max closes up the stall, he sings to himself Polish and Russian songs. Foreign words, to be sure, were being commonly integrated into Hebrew. "Rucksack," a key word in this fiction, is a German word but might not have struck Hebrew readers as either unnatural or extrinsic; to this outsider's word Appelfeld adds the masculine Hebrew plural suffix, "-im," repeating *rucksackim* eight times in one scene.[70] Did Hebrew word choices at hand seem at times too rational or clean, insufficiently gnostic, for the intended disarray? We are several pages into the story before there is even an incidental reference to a Jerusalem place name (Nahalat Ahim Street) and only then realize for certain that the tale is set in Israel at the end of the 1950s. "Blood trickles in the streets" but we're not in a Polish, Czech, Austrian, or Bukovinian town, and it's not 1944. Blood runs because the meat suppliers are annoyed by having to deal with Max, and will drop their fleshy delivery on the shop's stoop, until one of them, claiming to understand Max truly, "thrust[s] his knife back in its sheath," calls for a peace in the negotiation, and permits Max's protest that "always I'm last." In postwar Jerusalem, where two ill survivors barely survive in business, the violence is metaphorical and the discrimination relatively trivial, just the cost of doing daily labor. But how can readers not think, paragraph to paragraph, that the setting is really Europe, that the "strange stabbing" Max's heart makes him feel, and the ongoing "smoke of war," are literal features? The embittered antagonism of content and form is disorienting. The "polyvalences are like Chaim Soutine," observed Ariel Resnikoff after undertaking the translation of "Smoke" used here—expressionist, dark, modern (and, for that matter, depicting bloody carcasses of beef). The Hebrew is a dislocated raw language just as the sociolinguistic theme is jarring displacement. "Smoke" is ultimately a central European fable, replete with hints of Polish and Russian ballads, except written in an intractable or begrudging, not fully learned diction, an anti–High Hebrew—as if the "protracted military tour" of compulsory instruction in the new language itself partly constructed of restored archaisms, inscriptions of the peremptory Zionist *after* and *here*, were being countered, as Appelfeld was becoming a serious writer, through a linguistic project of *during* and *there*.

From the mid-1950s through the end of the decade, Appelfeld devoted himself to a "routine of study and writing" (a curriculum disrupted once by a stint in the army during the Suez-Sinai conflagration).[71] Finally, in 1959–60, short stories began to appear in magazines with regularity sufficient to cause the literary establishment to take a little notice. Appelfeld in 2011 recalled the difficulties he had getting these recalcitrant, unruly tales published, given the aesthetic-ideological tenor of the Israeli situation.[72] His first collection of stories, itself called *Smoke* (*Ashan*; עשן), was finally published in 1962 after various false starts and delays.[73] Efraim Sicher suggests that Eichmann's extradition in May 1960 and subsequent trial in Jerusalem, which "swept" survivors "into the limelight," were in part responsible for the modest new tolerance of these survivor stories written against the grain.[74] If "rivers of words were already flowing about the war" by this point, the commotion surrounding Eichmann induced a still greater torrent. It was not survivor guilt, but its purported opposite, that caused survivors to "tell everything," fulfilling the promise to bear witness. Appelfeld found much of this writing "clichéd and superficial." Thus his career as a writer was launched on the basis of compounded negatives: dislike of the enforced language of *after*, and of its enforcers; the paradoxical urge to let flow a fluent rush of words about the disastrous past, despite the language of that past having been buried; and the problem of his personal traumatic loss of memory. Appelfeld decided that he "could not simply bear witness" because he "could not remember." "My writing began with a severe handicap," he wrote. This disabling amalgam—the maturing author who grew from the child whose mother tongue had been ripped from his throat was surely right to conceive of this as a disability—made for one of the significant literary experiments of the moment, although his later, more straightforward fictions perhaps have obscured this avant-garde aspect of the early work. If he could not bear witness, could not recollect that which written testimony *would* witness, then he needed to begin by writing about that very impediment to easy speech. He wrote in the chasm. His language of this time inhabits and expresses the aporia of 1945–60, the amnesiac space that is everywhere thematized in the first writings.

And he began with the horrifying spell as a parentless child lost in the forest. His memory of trying to motivate himself, alone in the woods, to create trails leading out of the darkness, by each day renewing belief in the fiction "that my parents were waiting for me," is told like a grim ancient ballad of the lost child, an epic picaresque, holocaust-era Hansel, doomed circuitously to hope for the way back to home and family. The magical thinking was this: "No longer would any omens mislead me, and there would be only one path that would lead me directly to my parents."[75] In Appelfeld's writing, the fog of war—that modern idea of fatal liminal misprision, of uncertainty in situational awareness—meets the ghastly mists of archaic folklore. Or, in one word: *smoke*, this young writer's first major trope of induction. When in the title story Appelfeld arrives at the point at which he must narrate Max's unpacking of the rucksacks, unexamined since 1945, he seeks to describe color (remarkably, the remains are unfaded) and to assign words to a peculiar smell. *Smoke* defined: a material thing of no apparent substance that nonetheless obscures or darkens understanding; an allusion to the biblical pillar of cloud in the wilderness (in Exodus), or (in Joshua) the whirlwind remnants of a destroyed city.

That biblical smoke gives connotation to the Hebrew word of a fluttering between states, as in the condition of the survivor's wartime rescuer, Reb Aryeh, who had borne aloft the injured doomed Max through the forests of Smolinka, and who now himself flutters between life and death. It's his reactive, stress-addictive quest for an evening's cigarette that draws Max back out onto the streets of Jerusalem, with its heretical pockets of preserved *during*. There in the dark he gazes at his failing guardian angel through a window. Max still badly needs a smoke; it's a trite realist fictive gesture, given the unexpressive protagonist. Yet of course the deeper craving, and yet another form of smoke, expresses profound esoteric iconoclasm. The folk memory—archaic, connotative, a radical form of historical response, entailing a readiness to embrace nothingness as legitimately forming a history—flutters between the categories and must be left unsorted. Far from Jerusalem but at the same moment, standing at the remnant site of the Triangle Shirtwaist Fire in lower Manhattan, peering back through the smoke of postwar time to contemplate contemporary intentional forgetting of the murderous hatred of immigrants, Louis Zukofsky similarly in 1960 resisted the merging of something and nothing as categories. Just as Max does with guilty reticence, the speaker of Zukofsky's "A" works out what memory constitutes when that which is remembered are burned corpses. Like Appelfeld, Zukofsky saw traumatic social memory as a movement *toward*. He wrote: "Memory can be a nothing towards something / A something towards nothing."[76]

# 8

# Thaw Poetics

## Folk Revival, Radical Unoriginality, and the Old Word Witness

## Thaw Poetics

Aharon Appelfeld's urge to resist Zionist aesthetics; his use of S. Y. Agnon as a model for the exploration of the conflict between traditional Jewish culture and modernity without relinquishing modern experiments in narration; and his sense from Kafka and Scholem of the power of the nonrational tale: these led him in the late 1950s back into the harrowing caliginous places betold in ballads and tales derived unoriginally from the oldest ethnographies of regions where those dark forests prevail. These were handed down teller to teller, of imagined spaces illegible to the disappeared innocents—strangely told predicaments of liminality, narrated across centuries, now to be varied and elaborated with the genocidal theme. At the same time, Primo Levi, a chemist and hardly by training an irrationalist—but whose survival taught him as a writer to contemplate the "deep-rooted and robust" folk traditions his scientific education in assimilated urban Italy had hidden from him[1]—began drafting his second book, *The Truce*. Using literary modes quite different from that of his initial socioeconomic observations of 1947, Levi's new manuscript would be about his circumnavigational, Odyssean return in 1945 from Auschwitz in Poland south and west to Turin in Italy by way of central and eastern Europe and Russia. Facing the problem of how to represent this uncannily indirect excursion, he experimented with a mix of genres (epic, picaresque, the gallant return-home tale, the sexual coming-of-age story, mock heroic, allegory, Künstlerroman or portrait of the artist as a youth, the travelogue, the slave escape narrative), depicting pan-European ethnopoetic encounters befitting the interlinguistic chaos of the moment. These and other representations of survival, liberation, and return—all suggesting, as the exuberantly cynical Greek figure Mordo Nahum tells Primo in *The Truce*, that "the war was not over" and that, on the contrary, "there was always war"[2]— aligned as modes with both local and international revivals of folk culture in such a way as to challenge conventional political explanations of why and how these concurrent recoveries pertained to memories of existential conflict. The "triumphant tour" on the festival circuit throughout 1960 of Grigori Chukhrai's film *Ballad of a Soldier* indicated not only that a war movie fifteen years later could seem relevant in its treatment of a soldier coming home as an exploration of the deep-rootedness of Russian folkways.[3] It also seemed to prove that the supposedly naive apoliticism of folk revival could somewhat succeed in the repressive Soviet Union, fully despite the policy of "unified national style," at least during this post-Stalinist "thaw" period.[4]

As an innovative form of cultural reaction, hiding in part behind its ancient unoriginalities, *Ballad of a Soldier* situated itself ideologically somewhat the way Appelfeld's early stories did with respect to an intense punitive pressure felt by writers to write only in the upbeat language of now. "Ballad" is a term Chukhrai deployed strategically. It coincided with, but also helped further launch, the Bardic or "authors' song" (авторская песня) movement within the Russian folk revival of the early 1960s and the quasi-sanctioned idea of "village prose," its focus on memory ("the radiance not of the future, but of the past") flying just under the radar of state control of culture.[5] Those trends directly paralleled the final stage—with its merge of defamiliarizing archaic intuitions and modern rational scholarship at once—of postwar folk revival in the United States, during which a countercultural figure such as Will Holt, graduate of the Dyer-Bennett School of Minstrelsy in Aspen, Colorado, could be featured on both the *Today* and *Jack Parr* television shows, indicating that "the growing popularity of folk music was a kind of news." Holt's appearance at the 1960 Newport Folk Festival, after a motorcycle tour of Europe, further revived the revival as he brought back European ballads rediscovered in the postwar period and old musical idioms he heard there.[6] In 1960 archivist-ethnomusicologist Alan Lomax produced the second of his now-famous "southern journeys," making the first-ever recordings of call-and-response work songs such as "I'm Goin' Home," publishing shape note hymns in Alabama,[7] recording Charley Everidge on the mouthbow and the songs of the isolated African American community on Sea

Island off Georgia.[8] While (also in 1960) visiting David MacAllester, the anthropologist studying Native American music, Lomax met MacAllester's student Victor Grauer and became fascinated by Hebrew incantation—*khazonus*, the cantorial art of improvised chanting—and by the emergent idea of a (then still fanciful) computerized relational database of sounds that could be used to search through a large corpus of oral folklore.[9] Lomax summarized one important aspect of his two decades of fieldwork in the May 1960 issue of *Hi/Fi Stereo Review*. He chose to focus on his European collecting. In *The Folk Songs of North America* (1960), a book of ballads, Lomax argued in the preface that innovation and tradition are convergent. His work of this period culminated in an application to the National Institute of Mental Health for a grant eventually titled "Folk Song as a Psycho-Social Indicator," in which he proposed extending phonotactics beyond the original Indo-European data set collected by Milman Parry and Albert Lord in the 1930s.[10]

Susan Montgomery reported from Newport that 1960 was the year when folk became "the property not of professionals" but of small anarchic groups of knowledgeable devotees who performed their own antiwar and pro–Civil Rights ballads while gathered "around fires built in holes."[11] These were fans who discovered countercultural innovation in "what could be done within the apparently limited form of the English folk ballad,"[12] who deemed their contributions to progressive culture to constitute a social-art experiment and their songs to be efficacious poetry, thus in a new way affirming Woody Guthrie's concept of the cheap portable folk instrument (namely, the guitar) that "this machine kills fascists"—returning to that spirit of wartime radicalism, we should note, nine months before Bob Dylan arrived at Gerde's Folk City in New York during the winter of 1960–61. A Cornell poetry class morphed into a semester of "Romp and Stomp," sessions about living folk balladry. When Peter Yarrow came to instruct by demonstration, the classroom was packed.[13] The song was again now a poem. But, crucially, the converse too: "the poem is, by this definition, a song."[14] That, anyway, is what Harry Levin said, the Jewish Joycean scholar of modernism at Harvard.

The heterodox definition Levin meant to convey was the one devised by Parry with his protégé Lord. Albert Lord published *The Singer of Tales* with Harvard University Press in 1960, clinching (and popularizing) the case against the academic and pedagogical habit of treating the *Iliad* and the *Odyssey* as written poetry and Homer as a writer. *The Singer of Tales* investigates the Homeric non-authorial style, through the oral-formulaic composition of sung Serbian verse, summarizing the Parry-Lord Theory that helped established oral tradition studies (and also to create what a half-century later would be called Sound Studies). The theory encouraged not just scholars but artists far outside the academy to take seriously historic and even prehistoric quasi-memorized chanting as sufficient reason to "re-examine the concept of originality." Lord's book suggested that "there may be other and better ways of being original than th[e] concern [dominant since the Renaissance] for the writer's own individuality." "In oral tradition," wrote Lord, "the idea of an original is illogical."[15] The "culture based on the printed book," Harry Levin said, summarizing Lord's heretical view while himself taking aim in 1960 at the conservative academy, has "bequeathed to us . . . snobberies." The study and teaching of literature were going to be empowered to use "folklore, anthropology, musicology, linguistics" and other supposedly nonliterary approaches in order to investigate—this time without mysticism in the method itself—the now-legitimate "quasi-mystical" idea of the "communal origins" of aesthetic expression.[16]

No surprise that Jerome Rothenberg, who had already been exploring archaic techniques of ecstasy, read *The Singer of Tales* "right after its publication."[17] He and his Deep Image colleagues began gathering "ethnopoetic" materials for volume 3 (compiled in 1960, published in 1961) of the magazine *Poems from the Floating World* (1959–63) under the subtitle "The Deep Image: Ancient and Modern." Their ambition was to suggest multinational, polygeneric, and unchronological relationships between and among old traditions on one hand and, on the other, renewed prewar modernisms after the war such as surrealism. Rothenberg's contribution to this issue, in addition to another rendering of Celan, was a translation of a sixteenth-century mystic, the *converso* Christian kabbalist San Juan de la Cruz. The summoning of this visionary poet was an inclusive gesture that Jonathan Mayhew interprets, in his chapter on Federico García Lorca's influence on Deep Image, as "contain[ing] hints of Rothenberg's incipient fascination with archaic and tribal poetries" such as would be fully expressed in *Technicians of the Sacred: A Range of Poetries from Africa, America, Asia, Europe and Oceania* at the culmination of the 1960s.[18] The term "Deep Image" was drawn from Lorca's "Cante Jondo" ("Deep Song").[19] Bolstered yet troubled exactly as Appelfeld was by his own encounter with Scholem's revisionism, Rothenberg sought a new understanding of archaic experimental traditions of poems as what Peter Cole calls "spiritual machines made of words," adapting the revolutionary phrase William Carlos Williams had used to describe the centrality of "formal invention" in modernist verse.[20] Rothenberg pushed the connection to this aspect of modernism harder and further back than did the West Coast Beats, but their interest in old oralities—poet ruth weiss called it "ear language" in her experimental film *The Brink* (1960)[21]—was at least a parallel if not overlapping effect. When Lawrence Lipton reported from Venice, California, in his chapter "Poetry and Jazz" in *The Holy Barbarians* that Beat writers dreamed of "a restoration of poetry to its ancient, traditional role as socially functional art allied with music in a single, reintegrated art form," he might have been outlining the trajectories of Deep Image and affiliated networks. So one timely, effective convergence with *The Singer of Tales* was Lorca's influence on Rothenberg (from the age of 16 or 17!),[22] and also on Creeley, Ginsberg, Baraka, Bob Kaufman, Michael McClure, Denise Levertov, and, earlier, Williams (whose interest in Lorca as an antifascist martyr, dating from 1937,[23] itself shaped Deep Image and a number of poets in *The New American Poetry*)[24]—especially the ideas that the *duende* is "a power, not a work"; is "a struggle, not a thought"; is not an effect of literary ability but "of the most ancient culture, of spontaneous creation."[25] Lorca influenced Miles Davis also, an effect combining with Davis's avid attention to Alan Lomax's Galician and Andalusian folk recordings to inspire *Sketches of Spain* (1960), an album that immediately began to encourage especially young American artists to seek "traces of a suppressed Moorish culture," the "dark knowledge" of a "secret history"—and, in the case of future poet Nathaniel Mackey, then just thirteen years old and obsessed with this album's "brooding, fugitive spirit," to start looking for "esoteric systems" everywhere.[26]

The influence of kabbalah was another convergence. In *The Poetry of Kabbalah* Cole shows himself to be a latter-day modernist kabbalist poet-scholar if ever there was one. His historical work to reconstruct a minor but persistent strain starts from the central conceptualization of integrated intuition and tradition. The synthesis is the basis of Lord's programmatic announcement of the recovery of orality's radical unoriginality. It made considerations of folk culture in 1960 variously available to the new aesthetics of modern extremity: Primo Levi's genre-altering ethnographic encounter with a liberated ur-Europe as a death camp survivor; Chukhrai's visual ballad of resilient home-front folkways; Louis Zukofsky's encounter with Rabbi Eliezer Pirke's ninth-century liturgy (resulting in "Peri poitikes," published November 1959, and its dictum, "Look in your own ear and read");[27] the widespread adoption of Zilphia Horton's 1945 version of Charles Albert Tindley's version of a little-known gospel ballad, "I'll Overcome Someday" ("We Shall Overcome") as a chant to support Nashville sit-ins from February to mid-May of 1960;[28] the trend toward the unoriginal ballad form in the writing of "war poets" fifteen years after the supposed cessation of conflict;[29] Oscar Hammerstein's invention of "songs they [Austrians] have sung / For a thousand years" in *The Sound of Music* as an expression of natural Alpine resistance against the Anschluss;[30] and Appelfeld's exophonic experiments in transcribing the smoke of war. Cole's historical premise is Scholem's derivation from the study of kabbalah—the "paradoxical emphasis," as Scholem put it, "on the congruence between intuition and tradition."[31] Levin sensed an impending major shift in academia. He recognized that audio and even filmed recordings were partly responsible for the demise of "presupposing the use of letters" in all professorial deployments of "the term 'literature.'" "The Word as spoken or sung, together with a visual image of the speaker or singer, has meanwhile been regaining its hold through electrical engineering." Levin meant, of course, the use of recording devices. "Look in your own *ear* and *read*" was, again, Zukofsky's way of channeling a visionary synesthesic rabbinical concept a millennium belatedly. Taking his own instruction seriously, Zukofsky one day in 1960 set up a reel-to-reel machine at home and made a rough, intimate recording of thirty-nine poems, including poem #2 of his *Barely and Widely* (1958): "You who were made for this music"[32]—addressing himself thus to readers *as hearers.*

In Lord's *The Singer of Tales* the poem as song meant that "its performer is, at the same time, its composer" and that "whatever he performs, he re-creates." Here is how Parry's former student Levin described Lord's breakthrough paradox in parallel to Scholem's: the poet's "art of improvisation is firmly grounded on his *control* of traditional components."[33] Just as John Coltrane in 1959 and 1960 became "more and more concerned with *structural* aspects of improvisation," and with "the *discipline* of composing in real time," he turned to ancient Near East and South Asian sources for melodic improvising and for the correspondence between scales and emotions, using a drone effect in the bass, trying out esoteric scalar mannerisms on his then-new soprano saxophone, and so on (beginning with *My Favorite Things* in October 1960).[34] Applying such a sense of structural modality to revelatory expression enabled Primo Levi in 1959–61 to recast completely the sources of his otherwise sober sociological recollections of liberation. The revelation had occurred on the evening of VE Day (May 8, 1945), to be exact, when Levi witnessed an elaborate makeshift folk performance given by Russian soldiers, officers, and doctors at the Soviet-run DP camp where he was thus far only slowly recovering his senses. Levi witnessed this theatrical performance as "unpretentious, puritanical, often childish." Yet that it "presupposed something not improvised, but deep-rooted and robust" made possible this classically trained Italian chemist's realization about his survival and his new writing without which the tragicomic, experimental, elemental allegory of *The Periodic Table* (1975) would have been impossible. It was a hard-to-define *something* he knew he had to explore. Displaced people flowed in and out. Most people in the camp were recovering in some manner. Supplies were scant. Various strategies for revenge and reconstruction conflicted. In this post-liberation camp it still seemed to be wartime. Thus when victory officially came, the Russian celebratory theater *had* to be spontaneous ("everything had been improvised, actors, seats, choir, programme, lights, curtain"). Yet the art of it all fell back on what the culture had long provided as readymade—not just the "Circassian costume and boots" for a "giddy dance" here, or only "the Arcadian manner" of a courtship dumb show with its ancient "twenty melodious strophes" there. The whole thing was sung and declaimed in Russian, of course. So it was "unfortunately incomprehensible"[35] to most of the Jewish death camp survivors in the audience, in whom it nonetheless—*as* untranslated and essentially untranslatable—reawakened with a jolt the strength of sexual longing and, more generatively, of *duende*, that "dark shuddering" in "search of new landscapes and unknown accents" Lorca had described for music, dance, and *spoken* poetry. These were the arts that "required a living body to interpret them," as Lorca had put it, the performative power arising from struggle rather than from thought.[36] Thus did these whirling dances and archetypal songs ultimately seem not "incomprehensible" at all, neither for the camp survivors who witnessed them then, in 1945, nor for Levi as he wrote through deep memory in 1960, recalling for the first time in his writing the urgent, random feelings presented by the scene in an open and more improvisatory genre. "The duende's arrival," Lorca had predicted, "always means a radical *change in forms*."[37] The Russian performance improvised an enviably robust aesthetic understanding of its exhausted, deprived audience—"the audience a long way removed from empty exhibitionism or intellectual abstractions, from conventionality or tired imitations." "Within its limits," *because* of such "limits," an innovative yet traditional art suggested a dynamic kind of witness to liberation that was "not commonplace, but generously free."[38] And this convergence of modes of witness served Levi as a new defense against the basic incomprehensibility of the story of Auschwitz he now felt he must keep telling at all costs.

*The Truce* describes Levi's first overcoming and then warm embrace of the already profound linguistic confusions exacerbated by refugees from many language cultures wandering through the Parry-Lord region and crossing in every folkloric which way. There was of course one sort of incomprehensibility, a state that intensified Levi's keenest traumatic fear from Auschwitz—that of his

testimony going misheard or unheard. But there was also another: the indecipherability of the European terrain itself. In a famous scene at Katowice, which we
know Levi wrote (and published separately) in 1959,[39] he attempts to exchange a
shirt for cash in the marketplace. He is standing among "Italians, French, Greeks,
etc." A Polish lawyer notices that Primo is still wearing his "'zebra' clothes" from
the death camp. The two attempt to communicate in Polish and then try German and French. Primo suddenly rediscovers in himself "a torrent of urgent
things to tell the civilized world," whereupon he naively hopes to use the Polish
lawyer as his translator, an intermediary for his testimony. But hearing the few
Polish words he knows in the lawyer's translation he reckons that the man has
uttered the word "political" rather than "Jew" in identifying the reason for his
internment. Levi realizes that the lawyer, presumably following the new Polish
line (communist and anti-Semitic), deliberately mistranslates the rationale for
his near-death. Here is the moment in the story when the supposedly amoral
Mordo Nahum, his transactional Greek companion, teaches him that "there was
always war." The lesson coincides with the resurgence of Primo Levi's worst
nightmare "of speaking and not being listened to, of finding liberty and [yet]
remaining alone."[40] Because *The Truce* itself reports the mistranslation in detail,
only the Primo reconstructed in this text, as he stood in the Katowice marketplace in 1945, is placed in the position of intense isolation. This is not quite like
the effect of Fyodor's untranslated urgent Russian speech in Rossellini's film,
for here the "torrent of urgent things" does of course get through to the *writer*
Levi speaking later in common memory, as it reaches us as *readers* of the belated
retelling. Later in the story, however, at the moment of the Russians' display of
*the duende*, all the key textual figures—Primo as he was then, Levi the writer-
witness at the start of the 1960s, readers of the account in the text's ongoing
present—have difficulty understanding the language spoken. That is the signal
moment when the survivor recognizes, in Bachmann's formulation, that
"underneath it there smoulders *another* language" emerging from the site of
intuition and tradition.

From this emergence Levi was able to reckon belatedly with the nightmarish
aspects of the European terrain through which he had wandered home as an
epic picaro in a book with many intentional comic likenings to the *Odyssey*.
Although the setting of his recurring bad dream had been Auschwitz, in this
text the awful phantasm coincides with Appelfeld's tormented imagining of endless pathless forests, following which, in Levi's postcamp experience, one seemingly never arrives back home to one's mother but instead "always remains at

the same place, as if in a nightmare . . . always the same steppe and forests on both sides . . . not a village, or a house, or smoke, or a milestone to show in some way that a bit of space had been conquered."[41] Alyosha, Grigori Chukhrai's sweet communist picaro, nodding toward Dostoyevsky's sensitive youngest brother Karamazov, learns to love in a landscape absent any such milestone. The film, which won best director prize at Cannes for 1960, brought together Chukhrai's experiences of the war, in which he fought on several of the most treacherous fronts in the Red Army's battles against Germany, and his fascination with surrealist film. (Two years later he would be ordered by the Central Committee not to award the Moscow Film Festival grand prize to Fellini for *8½*, but he did anyway, while Nikita Khrushchev, a Chukhrai fan, literally slept through the screening and then figuratively looked the other way.)[42] *Ballad of a Soldier* tells the intentionally undramatic story of the young soldier's departure from the Eastern Front in search of his mother after a rewarded (off-screen) act of ambiguous heroism. The loyal fellow spends all but ten minutes of an entire week's leave circuitously wandering the same sort of nightmarish terrain, but within the ambling structure of that quest, as in *The Truce*, loosely linked tales are told about people encountered by the cipher-like protagonist. Alyosha meets teenaged Shura, another wandering innocent, on a train. As they speak of friendship and love in purely generic terms—

> **Shura:** Do you believe in friendship?
> **Alyosha:** I do. On the front you'd be lost without it.
> **Shura:** No, I know that. Between a boy and a girl.

—*we see* momentarily what *they see* from the train, as it ambles forward in no known direction. Their chaste talk is formulaic. As such it is meant to be miraculous. They look longingly downward and then outward onto the passing ground in parallel. They and we see a landscape whose recognizable features have been nullified by war's destruction (figure 8.1). Nonetheless, they retain a sense of themselves as part of a country to which their set-piece folk romanticism either blinds them or causes them to adapt. *Ballad*, like *The Truce*, suggests that the way forward is the latter: adaptation. What Bosley Crowther for the *New York Times* and other reviewers notice about Alyosha and Shura, aside from obligatory nods at Khruschevite Thaw politics[43]—the *Times* subheadline "Film Is in Soviet Trend Toward Humaneness" finds no corresponding critical point in the review itself—is the capacity of these two death-savvy innocents for

**8.1** Side-by-side stills from a scene in Grigori Chukhrai's *Ballad of a Solder*.

accommodation to digression and joy experienced in the variation of contingent wartime and timeless epic patterning, both at once.[44] Its presentation of those qualities is the film's contribution to a "'Thaw' poetics," as a critic put it.[45]

When Vida Johnson observed that "*Ballad* walks away from the genre of war film as Alyosha walks away from the fields of war,"[46] she might have continued to describe what *Ballad* ventures toward: a new old kind of tale, armed by the experience of unprecedented devastation, that like Levi's earns its satisfactions from improvising upon, as Albert Lord put it, the "ever-changing phenomenon" represented by the "multiform." Crowther was right to focus on what is otherwise merely paradoxical phraseology of the newspaper review: the "swift, poetic way that the tragedy of it is concealed by a gentle lyric quality."[47] Because "we are not accustomed to thinking in terms of fluidity, we find it difficult to grasp something that is multiform," Lord wrote in a rare polemical assertion in *The Singer of Tales*. To those insisting on the conventional approach, "it seems . . . necessary to construct an ideal text or to seek an original." That is why some can "remain dissatisfied with an ever-changing phenomenon." Moving within the oldest of old forms, the epic of martial prodigal son returning home to maternity, Alyosha and Primo achieve purity as bearers of witness by accepting, in Lord's words, that there is no "single 'pure' form either for the individual singer or for the tradition as a whole."[48] By attaching his new two-part message about genocide's effects on survival—first, that from now on war is always; second, that the telling of the disaster is impossible yet must be performed—to forms of unoriginality, of a polysemy of genre, Levi discovered in this approach to bearing witness a kind of writing that is commensurate with the protean quality of his theme. ("Protean" is Lord's key term for the epic ballad singer.) The new mode of *The Truce* urges Levi's will to bear witness into a generic variation. In project

after project of testimony, in an ongoing writerly recurrence that will seem sufficiently fresh to the survivor himself, he will feel encouraged to push on in a
series of books, each its own genre, compelled to retell the same story. Thus did
the Parry-Lord Thesis match the postgenocidal situation. There could also, after
all, be located an unoriginal experimentalism. The Oulipians, forming themselves as a Workshop of Potential Literature officially on November 24, 1960, for
all their devotion to analytical newness and potentiality, discovered the ancient
excitements of constraints "as old or almost as old as the alphabet" and of their
keen "desire to recuperate and revivify traditional constraining forms."[49] Italo
Calvino, reciting the Oulipo story a few years later in "Cybernetics and Ghosts,"
used an analogy to "oral narrative, like the folk tale that has been handed
down . . . modeled on fixed structures" but nonetheless allows for "an enormous
number of combinations." Calvino observed that such a metaphysical formulary
is of course not "true only of oral narrative traditions" but can be extended to
writing.[50] Following this pattern of retrospective avant-gardism, the form of new
old telling is, in Lord's words, "ever changing in the singer's mind, because
the theme is in reality protean; in the singer's mind it has many shapes, all the
forms in which he has ever sung it, although his latest rendering of it will naturally be freshest in his mind." Thus, concluded Lord, "it is not a static entity."[51]
In addition to its relevance to structured improvisation—a major topic in its
own right just then, to which we return in the end—one can hardly think of
a more pertinent description of the problems of representation facing the
survivor.

Levi called his book *The Truce* (*La tregua*) to emphasize the ambiguous condition of mere cessation, a "queasy" state "before other future cruelties."[52] It is,
as Oulipian Jacques Rouboud put it, "both the story of what it recounts and the
story of the constraint that creates that which is recounted."[53] It is not a narration of devastation's end. The wayfaring picaro achieves no sense of liberation,
not even in the final scenes when after being embraced by his mother and sister
he sits finally at a clean table and begins the impossible task of permutating his
tale to "the others." *Ballad* makes the same point by setting its homeward ballad in the *middle* of the war—a soldier's leave rather than final demobilization.
But because the realm of folklife through which his leave takes him is never the
least bit separate from war's proliferating destructions, Alyosha is never truly
able to leave the front. His home front is the war itself. No progress away from
war or home or toward war or home signifies further development of his tale.
Yet the language of the film fully adapts. It ventures poetic harmony before permitting multiple discordances. "We fly like birds," a young peasant woman,

riding a train with her refugee family, dares to poeticize for Alyosha, "never knowing where we'll end up." Then, after a pause, a wizened elder comments: "Empty words." Suddenly all hear an explosion. "That's thunder," the hopeful young woman falsely denotes, persisting with her song of nature. The train stops. The bridge is out. Sitting targets, they are soon under attack from the air. So much for skepticism about the emptiness of words. In moments nearly everything is destroyed, including whatever "thunder" as natural description might once upon a time have signified. Alyosha survives, however. He and we see that the poeticizing refugee has been killed. *Ballad* gives its lyrical ballad as ballad, and then self-consciously takes it away—after which destruction, it is to be remembered.

*Ballad of a Soldier* is either shy about the idea of a tale having a program, or shrewd "thaw poetics." In any event it takes a stance against alleged aesthetic stances in urgent postwar calls for a clean, nonideological return to Make It New, deemed covertly strategic, thus suspect, in the contemporary reckonings with tradition we are surveying. The standards for describing and assessing experimental representations of the 1939–45 war's unprecedented destructions in the outbreak of art fifteen Cold War years later—high standards indeed, especially for poets in the United States, where experience of annihilation had to be beheld through far-flung deployment and exilic and even exophonic dislocation, or else through "home-front" imagination of great distances—can productively take cues from the availability of the Parry-Lord template for the "multiform" expression of newness as variation on the old. And it is in such multiple forms of art of 1960 where we can find, as we will now in turn, postfascist inventiveness in Muriel Rukeyser's *Akiba* commission and Charles Reznikoff's belated holocaust *Inscriptions* (in the balance of this chapter); and George Oppen's jarring nonnarrative new poems written after a two-decade hiatus, Barbara Guest's elucidation of the imagist legacy in her first book, *The Location of Things*, Louis Zukofsky's eccentric *Bottom: On Shakespeare* and "A"-13, and Bob Kaufman's ecstatic forms of Beat anti-neomodernist antifascism (all in the next chapter). Self-conscious as the singer was, the form of the telling might not noticeably be "ever changing in the singer's mind." It might leave few or no traces of the congruence between intuition and tradition. It might lack the aspect of re-creation to embody the Parry-Lord discovery that *whatever is performed is re-created*—of, in other words, innovation through formal alteration: the *thematizing of form* as an expression of protean shapes of topicality.

We turn thus to various projects of U.S. poets whose work of 1960 belatedly took up issues of survival, genocidal war, atomic annihilation, and traumatic postwar return, seeking in their attempts to renew with an avant-garde spirit some enactment of the "resistance" that R. N. (Ralph) Currey (in his anthology of 1960 titled *Poets of the 1939–1945 War*) felt should become more than subject matter in "the best war poetry in the correct sense of the term" (per T. S. Eliot in praise of Currey's book)[54] and indeed became a means of accommodating discordance, of adapting the modern ear to sounds of tales it might not otherwise hear—to "stories handed down, vague, unprovable, and marvelous" (the key phrase of Muriel Rukeyser), written in such a way as to convey those qualities. Primo Levi's revelation in *The Truce* and Paul Celan's in "The Meridian" offer an eccentric but revealing context. What was it exactly that Primo Levi now remembered he had gotten from the raw ethnic dance on VE Day of "twenty melodious strophes" whose semantic sense he and his Auschwitz companions could not comprehend as semantic sense but whose "deep-rooted" meaning they nonetheless knew to be the opposite of "intellectual abstraction" and could offer them the way forward?

# The Old Word Witness

Muriel Rukeyser, for her way forward, turned back to the life and work of Akiba Ben Joseph (50–132 CE). She did so because Akiba's life signified the association of the tortured body with the act of witnessing, and because of his Mishnaic hermeneutic system by which certain language is never mere formalism, each sign inscribing higher importance. Akiba, Rukeyser learned, was persuaded both of the purity of scripture's meaning and, at the same time, of the need for development and change in Judaism. He succeeded in synthesizing these opposites by means of a powerful interpretive method. In "The Bond," one of her Akiba poems, Rukeyser presents his biography in verse, conceives of it as a gift, and then theorizes the idea of give and take. From kabbalah she derives the scene of holy sparks emerging from vessels of creation,[55] the mystical form of presentation that can affect retellings:

> In giving, praising, we move beneath clouds of honor,
> In giving, in praise, we take gifts that are given

The spark from one to the other leaping, a bond
Of light[56]

In these poems the give/receive binary becomes an equivalence of survivor/
witness, and finally, in the poem called "The Witness," the relationship of
writer to reader is explicitly added. The Akiba poems evolve a ratio of postwar
subjectivity—

give, survivor, writer → receive, witness, reader

—where survivor and witness are transitive. For Rukeyser at this point "living
memory as a gift" became a political motive for art. In the Akiba poems Rukeyser explored a double legacy: a compelling "unverifiable" tale her mother presented to her, and the particular inheritance of witnessing descended from
Akiba's martyrdom. In one version of the doubled story, Rukeyser describes
Akiba in extreme terms—he supported an insurrection against an omnipotent
empire and "was tortured to death at the command of his friend"—and reports
her personal connection to this anti-imperialism: "The story in my mother's
family is that we are descended from Akiba—unverifiable, but a great gift to a
child."[57] Another tale about this telling emphasizes the method of mother's story
as a source of daughter's nascent poetics: "My mother . . . gave me a treasure
that I believe has a great deal to do with the kind of poetry I think of as unverifiable fact." This is tale as granting a mode. It signaled a shift in the poet's idea of
documentary poetics in practice. It constituted (in the title of this version of the
mother's story) the "Education of a Poet": "Now this is an extraordinary gift to
give a child"[58] for the development of her imagination. A third retelling appears
in a footnote Rukeyser provided after writing "The Witness." There the mother's bestowing of an "unverifiable" tale is an unsaid aspect of the poet ("oneself
as the one . . .") who has learned the responsibility of bearing secondary witness
to the "extraordinary gift" of the variable, retold story. "In 'The Witness,' we come
again from these scenes [Akiba's life and its contemporary effects] to our own
lives, with the knowledge of the past—of this one life, with its development and
transformation, its teaching, the belief in Bar Kochba [Akiba's revolutionary student whom the teacher defended at the cost of his life], the death; and then
oneself as the one witness to what has been given to us."[59]

In 1960 Rukeyser received a commission from the Union of American Hebrew
Congregations (UAHC) to write this Akiba series, which began appearing

serially in UAHC's magazine, *American Judaism*. An umbrella organization consisting of Reform synagogues and groups, UAHC aligned fairly well with Rukeyser in theological and pedagogical terms. UAHC members were tolerant of various unorthodoxies. The poet was assimilated and secular. Her identification as a "Jewish poet" had been mostly dormant. One mission of UAHC was to engage Jewish cultural and literary figures in the United States to emphasize the mainstream contributions to arts and letters of Jewish intellectuals. But UAHC's openness to unorthodoxy did not extend to the radical left, and Rukeyser in the late 1950s was emerging from a period of vicious red-baiting and even (rare in the world of poets) forms of actual McCarthy-era blacklisting.[60] The Akiba commission can thus be deemed to constitute a Thaw poetics. "The Way Out," the first poem in the sequence, takes up issues of exodus and diaspora, but another way to read it is as a response to the political disjuncture Rukeyser seems to have felt about the commission itself. A way out of Cold War–era suppressions of radical and ex-radical Jewish intellectuals—communists, Trotskyists, "premature anti-fascists" in the 1930s blamed as culture-destroying heretics and betrayers in the 1950s—could be found in archaic radicalisms of Jewish song.

"The Way Out" proposes the importance of "song" as a recollection of exile (outward movement) through internal change (indicated by variations in what Lord calls "the singer's mind"): "the world is a sign" itself, a *sign* in the linguistic sense; the world, an empirically known Out There, changes into "a way of speaking." Singing is finding, sounding out, discovering. This redefinition of art is based on variable modes and unverifiable retellings: "Energies, rhythms, journey. // Ways to discover. The song of *the way in*."[61] "The Way Out" offers itself as an exit from fifteen postwar years of centrist Jewish recrimination against those now-discredited revolutionary Jews whose idea of liberation was, as we would later say, intersectional. This first installment of the commission goes out of its thematic way to remind the readers of *American Judaism* magazine of the old ideological alliances that had made U.S. involvement in the fight against fascist racism possible and victorious. The "army who came to the ocean" seems to refer to the regiment of Exodus but it is also reminds us of the American invasions at Tripoli, Anzio, and Normandy. They are "the walkers / who walked through the opposites, from I to opened Thou," heading toward the liberation of camps the condition of whose inmates would shock and ratify the alliance—a dense triple allusion to (1) Martin Buber's *I and Thou* (Rukeyser had read it carefully),[62] (2) former slaves, Black and Jewish, precariously emerging from bondage, and (3) ideological unities of the Popular Front against fascism.

That moment of unity is recalled in the sentimental image of "the shivering children of Paris." Antifascism, communism (or now: anti-anticommunism, hardly less risky), anti-racism, and feminism (a major concern of the third poem in the series, "The Bonds") inform the "new song" being proposed and modeled here, just as "escaping Negroes" fleeing ahead of slaveholders, minority Communists outnumbered and pursued in a long march by the Kuomintang, Hebrews scrambling ahead of Pharaoh's army, and French children being force-marched by Pétainistes to the concentration camp at Drancy should not be expected to sing a single lyric but have indeed together "crossed over" into a positively innovative "Barbarian music: a new song." These are the ragtag armies whose song the Akiba commission chants: "All night down the centuries, have heard, music of passage" is one refrain. "Where the wilderness enters, the world, the song of the world" is another. The proposed "barbarian" aesthetic is surely in part a rejoinder to Adorno's dictum of 1949: "Even the most extreme consciousness of doom threatens to degenerate into idle chatter. Cultural criticism finds itself faced with the final stage of the dialectic of culture and barbarism. To write poetry after Auschwitz is barbaric. And this corrodes even the knowledge of why it has become impossible to write poetry today."[63] The Akiba commission contends that it is indeed *not* impossible, and updates the literary politics of the 1930s for the end of the 1950s to argue the point.

Back in 1949, the year Adorno's "Cultural Criticism and Society" was first published, Rukeyser was already engaging in an attempt to thwart Cold War revisionism of radical art of the prewar years. "Our drive," she recalled of the Old Left in *The Life of Poetry*, "was not for the old unity." Her generation of radical poets wanted "the work," of course, but, despite later conservative stereotypes, like Zeroists impatiently reckoning the same old ideological divides, they emphatically sought "the process." Rukeyser and her colleagues had been every bit as modern as before the disaster, committed to multivocality and in their art to a myriad sources (especially including the "idle chatter" Adorno despised)— neither aesthetically nor ideologically monolithic, despite the anticommunist, anti-Semitic, and anti-Black caricatures forming in the first years after the war as slanders against the 1930s. "We did not want a sense of Oneness with the One," she said, recalling the now-ridiculed leftist, "so much as a sense of Many-ness with the Many. Multiplicity no longer stood *against* unity."[64] Eleven years later, after this first postwar assessment, the centrist Jewish American community offered a communist lesbian feminist civil rights activist an opportunity to synthesize this anti-anticommunist view through a project reaching back, yet *much* further back than the prewar years—to the very origins of analyzing songs as midrash, the rabbinic tradition of retelling biblical stories, as Janet Kaufman has explained it in a major study of Rukeyser's Jewish sources. The synthesis brought the ancient materials together with a modern woman's familial story of multiplicity. What Ranen Omer-Sherman has written about Charles Reznikoff in this regard applies to Rukeyser's Akiba commission: both poets wanted now to "acknowledg[e] the multifaceted nature of identity without abandoning the significance of identity altogether," solemnizing the status of postwar art that would "never again be privy to the kind of unified vision avowed by . . . Orthodoxy."⁶⁵ A reviewer of Reznikoff's *Inscriptions* (1959) described the resulting composite as follows: the poet's "diasporism was as much a hybrid condition—formed in relation to Western/Odyssean tradition where it is the searching that counts, as it was a traditional Jewish concept."⁶⁶

Rukeyser was working through a keen consciousness of modernism's orientation to process ("the searching" rather than the searched for), an *un*-unified postwar condition; at the same time, she moved through her personal "multiple origins of nationality." Those complex origins: *Westjuden*, *Ostjuden*, secular, rabbinical—her father's German grandparents, her mother's Romanian family. "Her mother's 'gift,' " a critic has written, "represents a dynamic of Jewish diaspora simultaneous with connectedness."⁶⁷ Exactly to the extent that repressive expectations of unified identity are asserted to isolate and segregate (and then, in Nazi Europe, to exterminate), so responses witnessing oppression effected by such monological views should contrarily emerge, in Lord's sense at his most polemical, as multiform counterpoetics. When after Akiba refused to repudiate Bar Kokhba and cease teaching Torah, for which his flesh was torn away with iron combs, the revolt ended in a pogrom of ethnic cleansing, during which Jews in Roman Judea of every political disposition toward racist colonialism were profiled and brutalized by the ghetto police. Thus the "new song" of Akiba is also anachronistically that of the 1940s genocide, especially in the final poem in the series, "The Witness." If in "The Way Out" the sequence began with a "you" who is the poet, first adjusting to her role as witness to minoritarian suffering in order to open up to cognate oppressions, now in "The Witness" "*You who come after me* far from tonight," a plural, are her later readers. So the poem's readers are linked to the text in the chain of witness. "This moment" is the present of the writing, the commission of 1960—at the hoped-for end of the fifties' version of the antifascist thirties, when centrist Americanized reformed Jews might have "crossed over" to comprehensive or intersectional liberation theology (the politics that would fully emerge in the radicalized Jewish generation of the 1960s). But again the phrase "This moment" also signifies the perennial later time of readers' reading—our time. The poem ends as follows:

> You are made of signs, your eyes and your song.
> Your dance the dance, the walk into the present.
>
> All this we are and accept, being made of signs, speaking
> To you, in time not yet born.
> > The witness is myself.
> > > And you,
> The signs, the journeys of the night, survive.[68]

I take this to be a significant revision of Rukeyser's famous early dictum "Breathe-in experience, breathe-out poetry"—that famous leftist therapeutic theorizing of her first book, *Theory of Flight* (1935). The political views of the work of 1960 are unchanged from previous positions but the theory has made a turn. It is less about the poetic subject as medium than about the externalized languaging of the self. The Akiba commission marks a shift from inside-to-out self-expression (mind or heart to world) to a concept of secondary witnessing as enabling the transfer of responsibility from writer to reader, in a chain of multiple barbaric witness to ongoing genocides that alters the writer-reader relationship. That relationship once entailed a meeting of subject and object but now means survivor/writer/reader can emerge as linked intersubjectivities. In the grammar of these seemingly loosely written final lines, what "survive[s]"? The "signs" survive—the difficult word/subject/world encounter. The signified reader is urged toward the signifying act.

The sign requires "the bond" of testimony. "Martyr" derives from the Greek for "witness." Because the terms "audience" and "reader" and "listener" seemed to Rukeyser "inadequate" for the postwar situation, she chose "the old word 'wit-ness,'" the embrace of which indicated an epistemological shift: "knowing by personal experience" commits to "the act of giving evidence" against crimes. Now she stood with Charles Reznikoff against the poetics of what the latter cas-tigated as the "well-phrased eulogy," with its narrowing of who should mourn (with "faces politely sad"). Only from a repentant convergence of singer and victim—from "we" as survivors, "the remaining"—could be heard "The sentence [that] is sweet and sustaining." So Reznikoff wrote in his postwar *Inscriptions*.[69]

Witnessing permitted Rukeyser unapologetically to "announc[e] with the poem *that we are about to change*" while yet repudiating testimony's reputation for sentimentality.[70] The Akiba commission of 1960, with the endorsement of the mainstream UAHC, helps mark the end of witness to destruction as apolitical.

Reznikoff received neither political nor financial benefit from such a commission. Facing lack of interest and, for now, lack of patronage, he resorted to self-publishing *Inscriptions*. Nor in his verse was a sense "that we are about to change" ever made explicit. Yet in his ongoing project of documentary art, *Testimony*, he had already made the turn Rukeyser now experienced: the move from the written subject as medium (breathe in document, breathe out the signifying encounter) to the external languaging of engagé selfhood. "For Reznikoff," Ranen Omer-Sherman has observed, "a positive encounter is created whenever a culture has an inner, vital power that manifests itself as openness to elements from without" and the poet knows to involve such facticity in the writing. Omer-Sherman sees this mode particularly in *Inscriptions* and discovers Reznikoff's redefinition of desire there—as a yearning for postwar recovery.[71] Such a project, Michael Davidson has shown, "complicates our sense of high modernist formalism by relying on genres of folklore, documentary, oral history, reportage, legal testimony, and advertising." Yet of course it is nonetheless modernist, since "nothing could be more modernist than the introduction of nonliterary materials into the literary." In his book-length study of modern poetry and the "material word," Davidson describes how Rukeyser "can *incorporate* the document . . . by including testimony" and how Reznikoff learns to "write through the voices of multiple witnesses." This mode had irked the noncommunist modernist left, which criticized these strategies as dependent on verse presentations of "excrescences of capitalism" rather than, per proper Marxian theory, "the system's inner nature."[72] But that battle over the direction of modernism and the left had been waged in the 1930s, and the poetic impulse to "extend the document" (Rukeyser's phrase from *U.S. 1* of 1938) had been a merge of liberal WPA-inspired archiving (for that book she sampled language from the *Congressional Record*),[73] Duchampian appropriation, communist materialism, and folk unoriginality—a heterodox amalgam of aesthetic leftisms that *Partisan Review*'s influential anticommunist modernists would not embrace.[74] What Reznikoff wanted to do after the war, through the publication of *Inscriptions*, was to fetishize the fragment no longer but rather to present scraps qua scraps while observing others' valorization of it. He implicitly critiqued both malevolent and well-meaning commodification in the postdisaster context. The observing speaker of the four-line inscription numbered 24 in the book, for instance, addresses the fragment as if the writing were an urban leftist variation on the early imagist efforts of H. D.:

> Scrap of paper
> blown about the street,
> you would like to be cherished, I suppose,
> like a bank-note.

The fragment (not the poem but the object found in its slight narrative) is that worrisome "excrescence of capitalism" but itself remains innocent of seeking value (in the ironizing stance of "I suppose"). Early modernist objective austerity has been repurposed so that "system's [corrupt] inner nature" can be discerned as inscribed into the poem but not at the speaker's urging. When Kenneth Burke, the prewar era's most eclectic American leftist-modernist theorist, introduced Reznikoff's *Testimony* in the 1930s, he praised such austerity for "offer[ing] a salutary alternative to the world-historical syntheses" that were then fashionable.[75] *Inscriptions* updates that alternative to a time when the naturalization of the fragment (in, for example, the verse of H. D. or Williams) enabled another political take, but casually and almost lazily did not, as after the war, have to deal with its signifying the massive loss of subjects, by which point it was almost inevitable that a blown-about poetic fragment would be read as having possessed now-evacuated individuality. If William Carlos Williams in the 1930s, during his brief dalliance with organized Depression-era radical politics, could write this in one of his "proletarian portraits," describing a homeless couple strolling autumnally—

> Lost Ambling
> nowhere through
> the upper town they kick
>
> their way through
> heaps of
> fallen maple leaves
>
> still green—and
> crisp as dollar bills
> Nothing to do. Hot cha![76]

—then Reznikoff in *Inscriptions* had to face why world-changing tragedy inhered in "Another generation" of scattered, unvalorized leaves. This is the thirty-fifth inscription in full:

> Another generation of leaves is lying
> on the pavements;
> each had a name, I suppose,
> known to itself and its neighbors
> in every gust of wind.
>
> Now the wind
> taking, taking[77]

Williams's prewar sense of the Depression generation was cyclical and synchronic, and such urgent political actions as advocated by causes with which he was aligned when he wrote this and other proletarian portraits could be incorporated into the modern lyric through the figuration of economic and political downturn as seasonal. The fallen leaves might suggest a hard and perhaps lethal winter ahead (and in Williams's "The Yachts," which begins in terza rima, the falling leaves are Dante's, like Shelley's later, simile for the dead), but these were still green enough to generate easeful fantasies of wealth—money, we suppose, that seasonally grows on trees. The countless fallen dead of Reznikoff by the end of the 1950s "each had a name" and the wind of *Inscriptions* takes but does not restore. If desire is a longing for recovery, and if desire (at least in the appetitious Williams mode of modern subjectivity) is what produces language as parts of a world, then the challenge of Reznikoff's speakers in *Inscriptions* is how to cope with seeking a restoration of ambition when such words would produce a catalogue of names of the dead. Death here is historical and uncontingent. The mass death is unique. The naturalizing lyric can no longer suggest otherwise. And the problem with Reznikoff's new approach, as his friend and Objectivist colleague George Oppen wrote, was that "the effect can be very un-climactic."[78]

Crucial to the story of Reznikoff in 1960, Oppen was finally back in circulation, after his return to New York following many years of self-imposed exile in Mexico. During the summer, once Oppen had settled back in Brooklyn and accelerated his return to writing poems, he carefully read Reznikoff's self-published *Inscriptions*, which had become available in late 1959 and served to gather postwar writings. Oppen found the best poems in the book "overwhelmingly moving" and the verse to be "absolutely unique," and he immediately began

urging his successful half-sister June Oppen Degnan to subvene ("50/50 finan-
cially") the publication of a volume of selected Reznikoff. That project would
become *By the Waters of Manhattan* (1962), which included all but five of the
*Inscriptions* poems. On July 10, 1960, Oppen expressed concern that readers
of *Inscriptions* will ask "where's the whatsit, where's the whosis, where's the asso-
nance the dissonance the ambiguity the Eliot the etc." Such seemingly minor
writings (especially because they appeared in a small noncommercial volume)
nonetheless constituted a "major poetry." In the stylish assonance-discerning,
ambiguity-hunting New Critical mode, however, this was just the sort of work
likely to be ignored. To behold its radicalism aptly "would require," Oppen wrote,
"a new effort of sensibility, in fact a revolution of sensibility."[79] Lorine Niedecker,
another longtime Objectivist colleague, read *Inscriptions* too and it reawakened
her sense that the necessary revolution in sensibility had already occurred but
had been forgotten or suppressed. What was perhaps needed was a *reminder* of
the power of the poetics of radical concentration and condensation.

Niedecker wrote Reznikoff to say that in his new work she felt "a kinship
between us in the short poem"—that he was her "brother-in-poetry" and that
the two of them together were connected to East Asian aesthetic traditions of
contraction and implication. She used her response to *Inscriptions* to advocate
their mutual derivation from imagism of the first prewar moment, the mid-1910s.
Niedecker's response to Reznikoff—in which she points out "their shared attention to the ordinary and the intractable," as Stephen Fredman put it—suggests
several overlapping associations: imagism's and thus Objectivism's Japanese
sources; the relationship in the poetry of embracing common topics and figures
as a means of facing difficult facts that cannot be altered; the trouble now of producing and publishing such poetry ("hard to write and then get it printed");
and the use of poetry to discover that, in contrast with "the intractable" that
had afflicted people elsewhere, a modest hope is not unwarranted ("life is not
really too hard").[80]

We do not know how Reznikoff responded to Niedecker's reading of *Inscriptions*, but an educated guess is that it would have aligned with the favorable
review by Milton Hindus in *The New Leader*, where he observed that "the Japanese *haiku*" is one of the poet's "favorite forms" and that *Inscriptions* expressed
his continued association with "the Imagists (whose influence still makes itself
felt in some of his latest work)."[81] In all this somewhat nervous resituating of the
Objectivist movement of the early 1930s (Oppen, Reznikoff, Niedecker, Zukofsky, and Carl Rakosi) for the start of the 1960s, there was a latent, unmentioned
special historicizing, relevant to the way Reznikoff's verse inscriptions positioned

themselves as fragmented responses to genocide for the purpose of reassessing documentary modernism. *Inscriptions* is replete with what Omer-Sherman describes as "haunting juxtaposition[s] of extermination and continuity"[82]—in poems explicitly about Nazi murder such as the prefatory inscription (on the destruction of the Warsaw Ghetto) or those in which naturalization of "generations" of the named dead is rescued from lyric's dehumanization and thus given new historical context, such as number 35 ("Another generation of leaves is lying").

The postwar historicizing of the Objectivist movement as a form of modernism required the imposition of an unspeakable fate following a retold story of origin. If now it could be said that "Objectivism was born at the juncture between Jewish immigrant culture and Modernism" (as Burton Hatlen once put it),[83] then such an alternative narrative—*Inscriptions* was after all modestly just that—was to be updated to account for the poet's brave decision to "address a subject that would remain, for decades to come, an unmentionable topic, let alone a proper subject for twentieth-century lyric poetry."[84] Writing about "Reznikoff and the Holocaust" in the early 1980s—during a boom in books of holocaust testimony[85] that tended ironically to induce forgetfulness about the antithetical and always-already belated quality of the first efforts—Sylvia Rothchild provided a particular context for reading genocide into the form and content of *Inscriptions*. She reminded her readers of Lionel Trilling's unintentionally repressive conviction that "there would be no poems and no stories, only silence" and of holocaust scholar Lucy Dawidowicz's historiographical complaint that "survivors were prone to subjectivity" and "lacked the authority to speak for the community."[86] The views of Dawidowicz, an influential historian whose book on the holocaust was published in 1975, the same moment as Des Pres's *The Survivor*, Levi's *The Periodic Table*, and Reznikoff's *Holocaust*, should be deemed mainstream even at the time of Reznikoff's documentary poem, which was constructed of appropriated or sampled survivor testimony. Yet Rothchild wonders all the more at the radicalism of *Inscriptions*, published a decade and a half earlier. She marvels at the way in which his version of Objectivism—two decades still earlier—had already prepared him to be "the ideal witness and mourner."[87]

Reznikoff's *Inscriptions* can be said to consist of fifty-three ways of looking at possibilities of postsubjective mourning. Mourning here is fundamentally process, the "work done." Each "I" presents another decentered vocality. Each has a part in the collectivity of witness as massive loss is beheld through disparate scenes or specimens of urban diaspora. Even for the twenty-second inscription, the most oft-anthologized of them (titled "Te Deum"), the context made by the whole project casts doubt as to whether the figure who tells us "I sing" speaks for Reznikoff or for the survivor's subject position of any other part—other than this poem's metacommentary that all fifty-three witnessings come together, as it were, "at the common table." The *ars poetica* of "Te Deum" is a commonality and also an ordinariness. Thus in sum it implies Reznikoff's political view. Such conjoined connotation of democratic cataloguing is its memorable point: to sing "Not for victory / but for the day's work done"—*this* very inscription being an effect of that work, an inscribing that is constructed "as well as I was able."[88] Omer-Sherman is right to say that the poem quietly condemns insularity, bigotry, and indifference,[89] and Fredman is surely right to see the interrogation of "victory" as outlining a skepticism about the relevance of hierarchy and the effectiveness of projecting postwar "causes" onto the psychological work of mourning.[90]

Whatever liberation from perpetrators of cultural mass destruction might signify generates questions taken up by at least half of the fifty-three inscriptions. If the question is, *Which scraps remain?*—the answer is *these. Can the lost culture be made whole? No,* is the diasporic riposte. But the effort, a demand for reparations, for a making whole, underwrites "the work done." And ultimately: *Who was responsible?* Answer: to find out, "Look about me with a stranger's eyes." That is the retort of the nineteenth inscription. The speaker there has already died. The writing, consonant with Blanchot's theorizing in *The Writing of the Disaster,* presents an experiment in self-mourning. It begins as a gambit right out of Emily Dickinson ("I died last week, last year"), but quickly its source of uncanny communication with the living (the "many that I meet" although dead) shifts to a Celanesque traumatic lament, as haunting gusts carry words— perhaps the poem's very words—from deathly dislocation. "I bring a message from the wind and worms, / from darkness, dust, and stones; I wear a shroud." The dispatch from the dead either speaks "of trifles" *or* is "mute." *And who was responsible?* Is the supposed guilt or feeling of responsibility of a survivor an appropriate response for a mortified speaker—the remorse he feels over having died yet speaks trifles while others have lost the language? I take it that "trifles" also could include these verse inscriptions, seemingly inconsequential parts of a decimated world. Yet again the alternative is muteness, and that would negate the work done. "I have no word of blame, no stick or stone, / because I died. The fault, the weakness, / was mine, of course. Mine alone."[91]

*Inscriptions* directly faces what its inscribing is no longer capable of doing. "I have no word of blame," Reznikoff's speaker says at one point, not because blaming is moot but because the prospective blamer lacks the vocabulary for it.

Sometimes he seems reticent, minimalist. Yet here and there we find him searching for a mode that could give him the tools to manage the miracle of—to take
a wildly heretical instance—penning multiple sentences simultaneously with a
single authorial hand. Seeking such crazy heresy and marginality, Reznikoff consulted R. H. Charles's edition of the *Apocrypha* and *Pseudepigrapha*, and from
there was led to Simon Ockley's translation from Arabic of the apocryphal book
of Apocalyptic Ezra. Ezra was noncanonical but crucial to the development of
textuality during the transformation of the oral tradition in the first Christian
century, the time of Rukeyser's Akiba. Reznikoff was fascinated by the fact that
no whole Hebrew, Aramaic, or Greek original of the Apocalyptic Ezra existed.
Encountering the work of Joshua Bloch, chief of the Jewish Division of the New
York Public Library, Reznikoff made a poetic decision that might have seemed
to contradict tradition and yet in its quasi-aleatoric experimentalism was
emphatically aligned with the archaic multiforms. He would seek in an appro-
priative or uncreative remix of uncanonical Ezra a fresh means of inscribing
mourning. Bloch's job was to work with the many slightly differing versions of
Apocalyptic Ezra in extant Latin, Syriac, Arabic, Ethiopic, Georgian, and Arme-
nian translations, while reconstructing the fragments of the Greek version and
confronting the special elusiveness of the passed-down Hebrew text. Reznikoff
appropriated Bloch's hybrid translation, and then, for the strange fifteenth
inscription, transcribed "a rearrangement and versification" of the Fourth Book
of Ezra.

Yes, rearrangement. To be clear, the words of Inscription 15 are not those of
the postwar poet. Nor even can they be said to have been Bloch's, or even for
that matter Ezra's. But of course the selection and organization are Reznikoff's,
as are the lineations inserted into the appropriated phrases to make verse. The
opening lines of the poem, for instance, are sampled from Ezra as follows: first,
from chapter 3, verse 2; then from 3:31; then from the first two verses of chapter 4;
then a mash-up of verses 5 and 6 of chapter 4. Here in sumptuous Babylon, Jews
in exile are desolated. There then is a quick cut to Ezra's bitter comparison of
the two group's behaviors, which leads to angel Uriel's reply emphasizing how
little Ezra understands a larger plan. The metaphor for dim understanding is a
whirlwind *khurbn*, but in the post-holocaust Objectivist poem it is just one of
several metaphors offered. If you think you understand God's ways, Uriel argues,
"then weigh for me the weight of fire, / measure the blast of the wind."[92] Reznikoff's
sampled curation literalizes what is merely in Bloch's original a figure for human
ignorance, and implies Babylonian exile as allegory for the twentieth-century
postwar situation. It also suggests that Bloch's *original* effort was nothing of the

kind—rather it had itself been a variation and textualizing of an apocryphal story that had circulated multiformally and polylinguistically. This was the ideal choice for Reznikoff to make his point about postwar inscription.

So why Ezra of all possible figures? The story of Ezra the Scribe gives a view of that liminal moment just before authorship was instituted and when canonical decisions, seemingly random, included some tales and excluded others. Ezra after exile became the eminent includer, but the story of his argument with God about why Jewish people must be kept in misery, and why they must endure a destructive, incessant state of transition, remains apocryphal. This is the tale Reznikoff decides to clip for his art, and in it he asks, out of sequence, "If the world was designed / for the righteous, / why do they not have it?" And why are ethical people to be "ruled by a people" bent on destroying them? These are the problems of *Inscriptions* as pieces of a response to World War II. Arriving at the penultimate stanza of the cut-up inscription, Reznikoff, more aggressively than before, scrambles Bloch's transition of the myriad unfixed versions of the story of Ezra's precanonical textless homelessness: he draws from 8:41, 9:22, 8:55, 13:10–11—the nightmarish part of the Fourth Book of Apocalyptic Ezra, when the would-be scribe is told that in the cities "friend [will] suddenly turn upon friend" and the "fire will not cease to blaze." This is the applicable, radicalizing fate of the Jews in the "fiery furnace," both ancient and recent, that James Baldwin was just then finding so compelling as he pondered Hitler's impact on Black characters in his hypothetical fictions. What had been originally a metaphor of ignorance seemed now to predict nearly total racist annihilation and strongly hinted at the inscriber's duty to document it. And so mourning becomes secondary to the survival of the word, to the demand for a right to opacity, which in turn depends on alienation of the sort that finds its only home in that strange language. After the word "change[d] into winds and fire" and after "all was dark and silent," just before "the sun and moon were shining" again, "the voice of man was heard."

Reznikoff's reinscription of Ezra imagines a way of "Mourning not for the multitudes that perish" in deference to the possibilities inherent in its own eccentric anticanonical documentary art.[93] Inscribed mourning cannot own or singly authorize its textuality. The witness who "extends the document" finds estrangement from the language of victory, seeks to recover home in "the day's work done." "Vocabulary of alienation," writes Omer-Sherman, surely with Celan in mind, "is actually a profound claim to being-at-home."[94] The current home of *Inscriptions* was integrated New York City—as it was for Rukeyser and Zukofsky and now Oppen too. When poet A. R. Ammons reviewed *Inscriptions* for *Poetry* in April 1960, he made a list of "street scenes in New York" to be found in the poems. Along with two girls at the Automat, an old woman selling newspapers, etc., there is this odd figure: "the alien Jew alienated even from Jews." That last is quite an item for such a list. We can locate the poet's reference to the girls in the Automat by looking back through the poems. But the "alien Jew alienated even from Jews"? One has to wonder which inscription Ammons meant. Granted, he set aside just fifty-five words to discuss Reznikoff in a 1,002-word review. But the pairing of *alien* (diasporic displacement with a legal inflection) and *alienation* (via theories of disaffection and objectification) is not a convergence to be found in Reznikoff's work. To be sure, Ammons's overall judgment was that these poems were "winning." At the same time, they were "of slight artistic interest."[95] This was not a review likely to attract buyers of a self-published volume. In such neglect—and more profoundly, in such misreading of the thematizing purposes of Reznikoff's seemingly plain aesthetic—could be read in itself a relevant alienation. Milton Hindus in his review implied the connection between, on one hand, Reznikoff's "name ha[ving] largely escaped the rumormongers so that the fact of his accomplishment is almost a secret" and, on the other, the deceptive quality of the writing's "small compass" and the need for "a careful reader."[96] Robert Franciosi in "Reading Reznikoff" has argued that the central lesson Zukofsky learned from Reznikoff was how to suffer neglect, and Oppen felt that the neglect of Reznikoff was "a blessing."[97] In a letter dated May 16, 1960, after exclaiming over Cid Corman's publication of Zukofsky's modernist epic "A," Oppen expressed concern that the writing of such "an extraordinary perfection" would be ignored by the mainstream. "People are injured by nonrecognition perhaps." Oppen then pivots to his other colleague: "Maybe even Rezi, in limiting his experience and range. I don't even know what Rezi would have been if the world had invited him. Possibly less than he is." Oppen did not mean "limiting" as a criticism. As noted, he found the self-imposed constraints of *Inscriptions* "overwhelmingly moving."[98] No, limitation was an effect not of injurious misunderstanding but of an artist's subjectivity that, whatever its personal, ethnic, historical sources, managed to thwart simple projections onto survival and also to rescue the documented old song from its alienated status. Primo Levi by 1959–60 no longer suffered at least from physical injuries inflicted by Auschwitz, but rather from the neglect that had greeted his own first witnessing song. Now he taught himself to look back and see past assumptions of "conventionality or tired imitations" and to witness an old art renewed because "generously free and self-assertive" in a book crossing genres.[99] Reznikoff, Rukeyser, and Levi were each composing what Lord in *The Singer of Tales* identifies as the "return song." Lord outlined the pattern. There is, first and foremost, the "long and unsuccessful war." Then of course deceptions and wanderings.[100] Levi's pathway through the epic return song was his own experience, and needed only telling once the reversal of the derogation of folk, moving it from right to left (another Parry-Lord hallmark contention), had been achieved. Reznikoff and Rukeyser, from across the Atlantic, remotely found ancient and recent sources of alienation. But their return songs nonetheless converged old and new refusals of the alien.

# 9

# Abomunism

## Wars Within Wars in American Poetry

ABOMUNISTS DO NOT FEEL PAIN, NO MATTER HOW
MUCH IT HURTS.

—BOB KAUFMAN, "ABOMUNIST MANIFESTO"

## What to Know, What to Do

Insofar as Charles Reznikoff's appropriation of Ezra was an attempt to
unalienate the document, his writing of this period might be called an
Objectivist conceptualism. The curatorial method was a means of historically grappling with the holocaust as a dire interval when, in Ezra's
apocalyptic account, "friend suddenly turns upon friend" and the "fire
will not cease to blaze." This again was the shared fiery source of Baldwin's intense anti-anti-Semitic concerns and at the same time of his ultimate democratic vision. Louis Zukofsky deployed Ezra similarly, in a
piece titled "Nor Did the Prophet," the third section of a poetic sequence
titled "Song of Degrees" (drafted in 1953 and reworked in 1955). What concerned Zukofsky there was Ezra's role as "eyewitness to the return from
exile" at the end of the first Jewish diaspora and during the rebuilding of
the temple.[1]

Zukofsky had been reading the Bible and Hebrew commentaries. These were among the few possessions he had saved at the time of the death of his father, elegized as "Reb Pinchos" in the twelfth section of the ongoing epic poem "A." He had also been reading *The Pisan Cantos*, Ezra Pound's end-of-war addition to his epic, with its reactionary cultural nostalgia, its focus on rebuilding old Europe from the ruins, and its audacious (given his anti-Semitism) invocation of the reconstruction of the Temple in Jerusalem. Mark Scroggins argues that the figure we encounter in "Nor Did the Prophet" is both Ezra the Scribe and Ezra Pound. That confluence represented one way in which Zukofsky worked through the agonizing problem of Pound, whose modernist long poem *The Cantos* had inspired "A"; whose energetic support had brought sudden attention to the Objectivists in the early 1930s; whose fascist economic theories and anti-Semitism had, to say the least, troubled Zukofsky, and not just during the Depression when the younger poet's leftist and antifascist commitments had been acutest.[2] If Reznikoff's Ezra occurs in a sequence of writing about genocide, Zukofsky's Ezra leads him to assess, in Poundian verse, his original attraction to Poundian modernism in the context of, first, postwar diaspora and concepts of rebuilding and, second, his personal experience of having turned away, at the age of sixteen, from his father's religious culture—from his mother tongue and from Yiddishkeit generally—in order to embrace modernism as a secular radicalism and posttheological counterargument.

This swerve around the Jewish father can be read politically and psychologically—and also through the modern history of immigration and assimilation, although the aesthetic reading of the situation in Zukofsky's particular case will implicate all these categories. Scroggins's title is "Zukofsky's Holocaust Poetry" but his point is that such a thing is difficult to detect in the writing as writing. True, "A"-10, written in 1940, included a number of antifascist passages referring to Japanese, Spanish, Italian, and German authoritarianism, and specifically to the circumscriptions and impending fate of the Jews:

> Forbidden to telephone
> To telegraph
> To transact —
> Confiscated.

> . . . And the Pole go into the earth
> The Jew into middle Europe's rivers[3]

It is true, too, that *"A"*-12, the first postwar section of *"A,"* written in 1950, is "in part a eulogy" for Pinchos Zukofsky.[4] It expresses nostalgia for the life of the Lower East Side of New York in a way that projects upon the physically unharmed family residing in the United States a global Jewish mourning and a sense of the role of the secondary witness. It quotes passages from Martin Buber's accounts of Eastern European Hassidism as if they described a *living* culture. That continuity was to be embodied by the poet's son Paul, named for his grandfather. It praises Pablo Picasso's Gestapo-defying *Guernica* as "Ur-realist" ("Did you do this?" a fascist interrogator asks Picasso of that painting, to which the painter acidly replies, "*You* did").[5] And *"A"*-12 examines the ideological contradictions and betrayals—including that of communists, with whom Zukofsky, like other Objectivists, had been affiliated—and in that specifically political sense contemplates "The end of the known world."[6]

Everything about Zukofsky is complicated. Still, a typical thumbnail sketch of his career is not finally wrong to observe that after the war "the social and political concerns" that had previously preoccupied his writing "retreat into the background." Such overviews are generally right to cite "the fading of revolutionary hopes" and to limn "a re-centering of Zukofsky's life around home and family" in the immediate postwar period.[7] Of course this story of disillusionment expressed through domestic reinvestment is the oft-told tale of the conformist American fifties, Bell's notion of "the exhaustion of ideas" in *The End of Ideology* being just the most prominent expression of many commendations of homecoming and domestication. Was Louis Zukofsky's course through the 1950s not unique? Perhaps. But then came 1960.

In 1960 the overt antifascist themes of *"A"*-10, so seemingly then distinct from the complexities of Zukofsky's personal life, didn't fade into the background but revived and converged with the "personal" thematics ("life around home and family") as the poet turned toward the difficulty of writing his son's Jewish inheritance as a delayed postwar phenomenon. It was a dialectical moment. Scroggins's challenging project of locating Zukofsky's holocaust poetry per se is made only a bit easier by this synthesis, but the realignment could be said to have been affirmed by Denise Levertov's assertion in a key essay on *"A"* published in 1960 in which her starting assumptions were that Zukofsky "belongs to the tradition of Jewish scholars and thinkers," that he brings to literary reading "a Talmudist's attention to detail," and that among the *everyday* modes of his verse is the keen perception of "wars within wars."[8]

We will come back to Levertov's suggestive phrase. Meantime, yes: it was a momentous year for Louis Zukofsky. He finished composing *Bottom: On*

*Shakespeare*, another major work (of some seven hundred pages in all, thirteen years in the compiling), and published an excerpt from its eccentric "Alphabet of Subjects" in the December 1960 issue of *Poetry*. This was the year, too, when Lew David Feldman, an agent carrying blank checks from the Harry Ransom Research Center at the University of Texas, first came calling. The result was the invention of Zukofsky's archive, which necessitated the poet's rummaging around in files of his letters from Pound and Williams, and, at the end of 1960, led to a deal in which Texas would publish *Bottom: On Shakespeare*, a project one would have thought much less readily publishable than even *"A."* The entirety of *"A"* to that point, assembled in a single volume that he first held in his hands on December 25, 1959, circulated among readers and colleagues, yielded important responses (Oppen on May 16 proclaimed that the "verse . . . has an extraordinary perfection" and seemed "to be undertaking the impossible"),⁹ and was taken up by a few reviewers, including Levertov. The presence of *"A" 1–12* in one volume not surprisingly caused its author to reflect anew on the entire project. So in 1960 Zukofsky also began to turn toward the second half of *"A."* During the summer he wrote *"A"*-13, an unusual installment of the epic. This new poem was completed in September.

   *"A"*-13 in several respects did commence "a starting over" (in Barry Ahearn's phrase).¹⁰ It reset *"A."* It also told the story of postwar retrospective. Paul Zukofsky was sixteen years old, nearly seventeen, at the time *"A"*-13 was composed, a child of wartime's *after*. But the content of parental warning and advice in this poem expresses the stridency of *before*. That made for a disconnect. "Poetry, / For My Son When He Can Read," an essay the father had written in 1946, reflected on postwar poetic loss yet imagined the familial future. "To write poems may never seem enough when they speak of a life that has gone."¹¹ *"A"*-13 would be something else altogether. Readers of the whole of *"A"* are faced in its thirteenth part with a belated reckoning of prewar/postwar disjunction, a problem that had been available semantically, in "For My Son" and elsewhere, at the time of the end of the war (and of Paul's infancy). But for the sake of the wartime child's future it was more effective for having been delayed the decade and a half. Postwar belatedness in *"A"*-13 is the very source of its comic inwardness and its performance of pathetic emotional convolution. The reader senses that the Old School father freely dispenses advice while the teenager is not really listening. This creates a humorous tenor, rendering the prewar memories and sensibilities all the more poignant. The platitudinous admonitions the speaker offers range from clownish and fatuous ("To recover / Your coat don't / Lose your shirt" and "don't kick down / The ladder you stepped up")¹²—to aesthetic

and theological ("Intention betters contention" and "Don't be a stranger at the threshold").[13]

It is summertime in New York. A son and his Jewish father—the elder's mind freely associating around the city as it once was—take a long walking tour of Lower Manhattan, returning home to Brooklyn via the Brooklyn Bridge. The father bespeaks a cultural conservatism. But perhaps it's not really the fault of contemporary teens, rebels without causes. At NYU, along the way, oblivious "flocks of / Grandsons and Granddaughters who take courses eat" outdoors in Washington Square and have become learners of the mediated sort who read in the newspapers (rather than see nearby with their own eyes) which precious pieces of Old New York should be saved from downtown developers. The New York City of the father is "where today of its past I reappeared / A permanent fixture some sibylline hindsight praising the grille work / Of Worth Street," painted just as it was a hundred years before. In contrast, Paul and his generation are growing up absurd. "A"-13 is an associative scene of instruction inside a regretful tale of urban touring that which has been culturally displaced. What are the forces of displacement? One *must* learn what they are, and where. Instruction presupposes survival. And what sort of education? Paul himself was about to leave for college, so this need not be read as confessional; it is meant as a typical rather than particular parental concern about higher education and urban planning. "Extremes meet now," the father disappointedly observes about new-fangled remote teaching, "in the televised education of the University." As for art, and especially for music (the sphere of the son's talent): we listen to "Languidly precise Chopin" as played now "to Mickey Mouse / In a world (of the survival of the misfittest?)."[14]

"A"-13 satirizes such survival while yet testifying in all seriousness to "A dying they call civilization."[15] That doubled affect marks the turn from what a reader might expect, for we begin to realize that postwar children's absurd growing up can be linked to the failure of the poet's generation to have spoken effectively, when at all, of that dying. Paul's "father's rambling speech," Ahearn summarizes, "is thus the gist of a generation's worth of 'mute wisdom.' "[16] Father and son revisit the site of "The Triangle fire" (1911),[17] where 146 immigrants were incinerated or died by jumping to avoid the flames. What wisdom now to impart about "how many corpses" burned in the ghetto? What lesson to be conveyed such that "To *occupy* people / And keep them / Poor" remained relevant enough later to defend against apolitical absurdism?[18]

The visits to Duane Street, C Street, and Greene Street connect the twelfth part of "A" to the thirteenth after the decade's changes. Now the life-poem's urgency focuses on Jewish elegiac associations of Pinchos Zukofsky as they require the namesake grandson never to forget them, to form an unbroken chain of witness. But can the new generation truly reckon the scene, lost although still legible in the *Cantos*-like historical convolution and periphrasis of Pinchos's aging modernist son? Always conscious of his mortality and of his tendency toward convolution, the speaker of "A"-13 is aware of this problem. This poem imagines a history of its writing that had *not* expatriated, did not look to Europe for its models; rather its concerns had emigrated from Europe and then stayed home, had *not* rejected the father's mystical immigrant orthodoxies at sixteen— the very age the son's son is now—and need *not* now regret the loss of them.

Thus "A"-13 attempts a counterfactual history of ghetto occupation: an immaculate immigration story that walked that story back prior to genocide, a *Cantos*-style associative opacity minus the Poundian anti-Semitic botch, an inscription of "Inheritances [that] are *not* worth the hope." The father sentimentally ponders the son's old toys and admonishes him to "Arrange your house before // You go" off to college. Perhaps an inheritance worthy of hope can be found among revisited Old World remnants, such as the paperweight shaped like a bear that had been "your father's mother's heirloom." It is carefully and conventionally described, but denotation cannot last here for long, despite its being a poem seeking reliable witness to a gone world. And so this is what follows the heirloom: "It did not have. / That that world was bitter / Was world— // The grace of a madhouse—courtesy, *Thanks / for Passover delicacies*."[19] By the time Louis and Paul arrive at the Lower East Side, Yiddish phrases intrude, fantastical rabbinical figures move in and out of the text, and the poem's metrical signature, which had begun with a sincere iambic trimeter ("What do you want to know / What do you want to do"), has lost regularity and offers an astonishing modern prosody:

> On his pyjama seat lacerating
> Theological tarts and trembling hortatory
> Out of pseudepigrapha, Fathers and canon
> Contra bore with his dichotomy
> Dick and a cot and o me
> Isorhythm—I—so rhythm,
> Dominations and angelic orders and kings[20]

That Zukofsky's Joycean tendency presses against sense as sound ("Isorhythm—I—so rhythm"), to break every sententious dichotomy (here even the very term "dichotomy" itself!) into a whimsical postmodern nonbinarism, ironically *affirms* "Fathers and canon"—but only so long as such a literary order is influenced by the secret Jewish apocrypha.

Not many blocks from where Zukofsky was composing *"A"*-13 and finishing *Bottom*, Robert Duncan, on the visit from San Francisco described in chapter 3, was huddled with Rothenberg. It was, as we saw, a significant reciprocation. It marked a full circle, just as we too in this book have by now come full circle: Rothenberg enabled Duncan's first reading of Celan and Duncan introduced Rothenberg to Scholem's investigations into noncanonical sourcetexts making unheard-of things (to use Achebe's phrase for pushing English past known limits). Sixty years later Rothenberg could not forget what was triggered: a pivotal realization about the common mystical, pseudepigraphical sources of the "made place," as Duncan put it in *The Opening of the Field*, not just in Duncan's own writing but—and here was the turning point—more widely, across generations and movements, in various separate and collaborative remakings of modern art after disaster and resisting its repeat. Rothenberg now reckoned a parallel:

$$\text{Duncan} \rightarrow \text{Scholem} = \text{Duncan} \rightarrow \text{Zukofsky}$$

This was a triangulated "transaction" between archaism and avant-gardism—to use Stephen Fredman's helpful term[21]—in two senses: a transitive intellectual exchange, and an interanimation among types of available modes and materials. From a certain angle of approach one could see that these iconoclastic sources did enable Zukofsky despite Pound's influence otherwise or, at least, enabled Duncan's revisionist understanding of Zukofsky's project. "What was important to him [Duncan in his reading of Scholem], *as in his approach to Zukofsky*, was the connection he sensed to the old Jewish lore," Rothenberg recalls. "I think he was also encouraging me to explore all of that; he probably sensed it also in what I was then writing—much more than I did."[22] So what could writing as "a made place, created by light / Wherefrom the shadows that are forms fall," or the "secret" of "the source of the sun,"[23] possibly have to do with *Bottom: On Shakespeare*, Zukofsky's encyclopedic, *Arcades*-like epic or Joycean ("Wakean")[24] assemblage of writings on vision, perspective, gloss-as-gaze, and "optical delusion"?[25] After all, one was a work of condensed lyric permission, the other an unoriginal sprawling collage of quotations. Yet in each from its passionate gathering of doubted, eccentric sources the artist wanted to break through the post-disaster quietism with a poetics assuming that what ancient kabbalists called "peace in all worlds" could *only* come from illuminated reading.

Many of Zukofsky's sources for *Bottom* derive from the critical and textual Shakespeare canon, of course, but the immense "Alphabet of Subjects" also includes an amassing of passages from visionary parts of Isaiah and Job, from little-known medieval Jewish mystics, from the *Zohar* (thirteenth century) as miraculously glossing Shakespeare (seventeenth century), and from Talmudist etymologizing ("the word for *word* is also the word for *thing*"). *Bottom* was a kind of experimental Jewish autobiography confessing the discovery in "love : reason :: eyes : mind" that "Love needs *no tongue of reason* and the eyes are *I*—an identity."[26] The all-consuming alphabetic constraint of part 2 of *Bottom* might tend to affirm remarks such as James Rother's that Zukofsky is "a polymath afflicted with alphabetitis."[27] As Craig Dworkin argues in *Dictionary Poetics*, Zukofsky sometimes actually *quotes* from the dictionary; but, further, he seeks to "adopt and adapt the logic of the dictionary's own structure for his poetic ends," so that "the dictionary's fundamental mode of definition . . . constructs the very sort of transitive series exploited by Zukofsky to compose a poem."[28] Kabbalistic alphabetism liberates Zukofsky in *Bottom* from traditional categories of scholarly and interpretive relevance—and makes possible a different kind of whole thought. "An Alphabet of Subjects" writes out a utopian agenda, structured upon what Scholem calls "the world-process [a]s essentially a linguistic one, based on the unlimited combinations of the letters."[29] No doubt this is why, when Zukofsky prepared a sample sequence of passages for *Poetry*, for the December 1960 issue, he began with the *Zohar*, the foundational text of kabbalah with its focus on oral Torah as fluctuations of darkness and light. The *Zohar* passage selected for *Poetry* concludes with what happens when colorful ritual flame "attaches itself" to a white light: "Then there is peace in all worlds and the whole forms a unity."[30] This uncanny utopianism would seem to make little sense as the work of a modern poet on its own, but readers of *Poetry* who proceeded through passages about light and flame inside passages from Shakespeare's *Pericles*, Francis Bacon's *Novum Organum*, Descartes's *Meditations*, and Spinoza's commentary on intellectual emendation ("let us suppose . . . that this burning candle . . . burns in some imaginary space") would soon encounter *Bottom*'s theses strongly implied by the metatextual curation: first, "world-process" is essentially linguistic; second, textual illumination is a matter of learning to view the light; third, the "I" is always an eye; and fourth, such seeing is required for world peace.

As Bob Perelman writes in his introduction to the Wesleyan edition of *Bottom*, this is a work of "criticism that is nothing but quotation."[31] And if by publishing excerpts in *Poetry* magazine, still then the most important mainstream modernist venue, Zukofsky hoped to suggest this methodological essence, the

*Zohar* was indeed the perfect place to start. As Scholem explains, the *Zohar* "in its literary form" is itself a collection of sections consisting of midrashic statements and, in one part, is a collection of sayings and other texts.[32] *Bottom* presents its preference for the anatomical eye over the erring brain, and forces its readers to encounter its themes through the variety of their recurrences across different passages without annotating or intellectualizing them.[33] The relationships between and among curated topics—Judaism after its return from exile, Freud's psychoanalytic revisionist telling of diaspora in *Moses and Monotheism*, Kafka on Picasso, Isaiah on the strangeness of expulsion, the old Russian folk joke in which the czar seeks political advice from talmudists,[34] the applicability of the *Zohar* to Shakespearean presentations of the uninhabitable world, the letter "A" indicating the "implicit alchemy" of fission in the making of atomic weapons, and "F" indicative of "forgotten people"[35]—turn T. S. Eliot's proper notion of the proprietary tradition inside out, as Perelman observes,[36] by implying that only the erring interpretive brain would fail to put these wildly erratic pieces together to form a whole understanding of the disaster that had occurred. Kabbalistic flame, poetic pataphysics, and anti-anti-Semitism merge experimentally. Finishing a project that had occupied him almost the entirety of the 1945–60 interval, Zukofsky dates the moment of synthetic reckoning:

## 1960

If process is irreversible there is still a question: could science have looked forward to so much impact inside the head without feeding itself backward on sculptural *bodies*, tho they are cyclotrons, atomic piles—unintentionally they must hold the eye? Perhaps their sensuous embedded tonnage delights the technician as he looks to the point of making him forget the sublimed and subliminal cloudlike ends they are meant for.

He is referring to rational authoritarian suppressions of illumination—in both senses: light and commentary—that produce an attitude toward atomic warfare that heinously makes it more rather than less likely. The passage also conjures the role of science in the dropping of the bomb on people from above. It recalls photographic images sent back to the United States after Hiroshima and echoes uncanny testimonies to stunning views from the *Enola Gay*, puts one in mind of that deranged sun-like illuminating bomb hanging atop the tumultuous *Guernica* canvas, conjures a poem as itself approximating "embedded tonnage" such as the fold-out Concrete Poetry "Bomb" dropped on us from the pages of Gregory Corso's *The Happy Birthday of Death* (1960). The "cloudlike end" is the visual sublimity of the mushroom thunderhead masking the effect of mass-murdering "sculptural bodies." The implication, with corporeal terms like "tonnage," is the technician's sublimating vista from above such derangement—that which, despite prospects of mass annihilation, holds the postwar eye.

What then of the status of the postwar lyric, of art's own unwitting deleterious "subliminal cloudlike ends"? Composing "The Meridian" just then, Paul Celan made the same point about the effect of Hiroshima on the art of 1960. "The poem today . . . knows that there cannot be pure poetry . . . for there is . . . too much Strontium 90 in the air it breathes. . . . We have amidst the general loss of language a lyric Koine which, multiplying by fission, creates a 'chain' of lyric counterfeiters in the world."[37] What concerns Zukofsky is not that young lyric counterfeiters are being mainstreamed in public schools, trained on science-room oscilloscopes. Zukofsky's science found such tools compelling and not antithetical to art. No, the problem was rather that the training did not include ways of seeing "the substantial flickers of devotional tapers."

As Zukofsky finished both works in 1960, the apocryphal abecedarianism of *Bottom* naturally found its way into depictions of the postwar generational crisis in the new writing for *"A."* In section 3 of *"A"*-13 he will clearly insist upon a redefinition of writing but in a way, I am arguing, that had to come just when it did. He's more anxious here in the poem about his prewar and postwar Jewish family than in *Bottom* itself about its thesis. Perhaps the same skeptical filial listener ("Can I help it if you're my father?") will doubt the whole point, "as you may judge my Shakespeare theme—'*Love sees?*'"[38] And it is following this, precisely, that we come upon one of the most salient evocations of war terror that we will observe in a piece of writing by an American in 1960. Its sense of what Levertov, assessing *"A,"* called "the wars within wars" is equal in its linguistic perception of "the reconcilement of the abstract and the actual" of atrocity to the various acute reconciliations of George Oppen's "Blood from the Stone" and "Survival: Infantry," Bob Kaufman's "Jail Poems," Barbara Guest's "In the Alps," and Larry Eigner's "The Knowledge of Death" and "Human Humus." Pondering this range of poems responding to the war of 1939–45 in 1960, we note that just one of these poets, namely, Oppen, had seen the conflict at close range. *"A"*-13 is self-consciously a home-front art. The dozen or so lines calling for redefinition first contemplate night-before-battle jitters in *Henry V,* new rapid-fire shelling of modern warfare, bodies horrifyingly distorted in death ("the dead buddy, its boot stuck out"), the "instrument of torture" shown to those like Galileo who refute human-centered cosmologies, and, most affectingly—given the poem's overall concern about the fate of the college-bound teenaged Paul as the war-plagued sixties will commence—yet another assertion of eye-and-ear terrestrialism out-thinking the erring brain, an expression of empathy with the young soldier, aged by dread of war:

> It is in the earth of our hearts sometimes as in the world
> As with old faces of soldiers in their teens whimpering
> That tonight gone may bring peace.

After this climactic recitative in which somehow all the poem's themes are recapitulated in a single tercet, Zukofsky can personally historicize the effect of the world on poetry: "That was years before / The lyric poet made an art of violating." Because now "most anyone" who "Writes" bangs this big lyric drum, and because, on the contrary, now the prewar father of this postwar child knows himself to be only "moved / By the intimacy of one response," he can finally declare: "There will have to be a / Redefinition of writing."[39]

## When Hitler Became an Ordinary Policeman

What was it that had occurred "years before" the current mode—this fashionable lyric "art of violating" as it was now being taken up by "most anyone"? Doubtless Louis Zukofsky was referring to the trendiness of the Confessional Poetry. Perhaps specifically he had in mind Robert Lowell, whose *Life Studies* (1959) was garnering major attention and awards as Zukofsky was composing "A"-13 and still operated in the obscurity that Reznikoff was teaching him to tolerate, notwithstanding Corman's small-run publication of "A" 1–12. Earlier we saw how for Celan the "linguistically possible I-forms" specifically dated the crisis.[40] In "A"-13 Zukofsky is saying that the urgent need for reversing or rolling back "the rout of the senses" predates the Cold War–era trendiness of confessional lyricism. In calling for a "Redefinition of writing," as Celan did in "The Meridian" and Baldwin did in his prospectus for a new novel of spectral multivocality, Zukofsky now expresses the realization that any resurgence or counterrevolution would have its origins in the particular way in which the aesthetic ideologies of the 1930s (an effort to integrate High Modernism and antifascist politics) were then challenged by the total eliminations of the 1940s. And this was a story that could now be told through worries about a generation that must connect and remember despite those effacements. If the extreme adversities of emigration had not enabled sufficient foresight, then now had to be the time to revisit the *local* sites of murder, such as that of the vacancies along Harlem's postwar streets or of the Triangle Fire. "The red iron-doored windows which never opened" in Manhattan might seem at first to be the equivalent of Lowell's Boston aquarium in "For the Union Dead" (1960), where "Its broken windows are boarded." But what Lowell's speaker there wistfully remembers is a singularly unhappy privileged childhood (Lowell's *own*—"*I* often sigh still"), whereas Baldwin's perspective on "immense human gaps, like craters" is entirely social[41] and Zukofsky is showing his son the site where *others'*

> Fathers brothers and sisters
> Walked toward them
>     . . . six days a week
> As operators pressers and finishers

labored horribly in eugenicist "rat lofts" where windows were designed not to open when the fiery furnace raged.[42] The shuttered aquarium is perhaps the apt objective correlative of Lowell's overall feeling and aim. Our first encounter with his mood in that poem prepares us for his doom-saying political argument about civil rights and World War II. By contrast, because Polonius-like admonitions are both historically and personally self-parodied in *"A"*-13, we know how to read Zukofsky's view that "Inheritances are not worth the hope";[43] it sets up the poem's modified worldly yet *impersonal* collective aspiration. In Oppen, similarly, the vaunted "complete adequacy of the external to the emotion" (as T. S. Eliot phrased it in the essay deemed a founding document of 1950s New Criticism) was itself that which the dire experience of war defied in poems and paradoxically made them now possible[44]—rather *suddenly* possible, I should add, in the case of Oppen's homecoming after decades of exile. "There is a simple ego in a lyric," Oppen wrote in "Blood from the Stone," "A strange one in war. . . . / But all horror came from it." Indeed several of Oppen's new poems, after silence, testify to this horror.[45] Similarly in Barbara Guest's early writings in the New York School mode, which digressively recorded her movement between reconstructed Germany and Italy as she composed "In the Alps" for her first book, *The Location of Things* (1960), the fact "that one speaks after such a long time" should cause one to doubt whether "this [reinstatement of language] is a reason for happiness." And yet her poem, as we will see, presses forward then to rediscover the prewar modernist imagination.[46] Similarly, when Bob Kaufman in "Jail Poems" precariously vacates poetic subjectivity—"Someone who I am is no one. / Something I have done is nothing."—he nonetheless weeps tears over ethical, self-destructive "Beat-nik" acts, "yet believe[s]" sincerely.[47] Unlike Kaufman, incarcerated for all or some of the differences that he *is* (Black, Beat, Afro-surrealist, itinerant, too voluble or too silent, Creole-German-Jewish, socially as well as literarily improvisa-tional) rather than the noncompliant acts he has *done* (which is supposedly the American legal standard), Lowell's speaker is a priori very much already *some-one*. And the ease of that privileged subjectivity enters the rhetoric of Lowell's poem and enables its verbal flow in ways that can be said to contradict the poem's political stance against broken motives for postwar commercial devel-opment. Whereas the smooth language of "For the Union Dead" (to which we return at the start of the final chapter), even after a thesis-clinching reference to the disruption caused by the bombing of Hiroshima, might *itself* be said to "nose forward" and to "slide . . . by on grease," Larry Eigner's troubled, halting, difficult war poems—among them "The Knowledge of Death" and "Human Humus," both composed in January 1960—present partially worded vocalizations so dis-rupted that the reading experience sufficiently conveys the poem's accurate "knowledge of death." Here and in other poems of this period Eigner hinted at a special relationship between disability on one hand—the physical labor expended to perform the actions of writing (typing)—and, on the other, his powerful capac-ity as a postwar New American poet confined to the United States for extend-ing nevertheless "all over way to europe [*sic*]" in order to affirm hopefully rather than negate skeptically the necessary next aesthetic steps. Thus Eigner's poems of 1960 constitute a sharp anti-Adorno:

> yes but the actions
>     larger than words
>         the language
> might have survived[48]

George Oppen, Bob Kaufman, Barbara Guest, Larry Eigner: they had in com-mon Eigner's postwar discernment of the relationship between the survival of language and "actions / larger than words." Such signifying acts make it possi-ble for Eigner, notwithstanding confinement or indeed owing to it, to reflect knowingly on the war's human destructions. These writers rediscover the mate-rial qualities of language itself over its mere denotative effects. The connection between surviving war and finding alternatives to conventional representation, as we have seen in the case of many other artists also, is not accidental. And it will hardly seem surprising by this point in this book that a powerful anti-confessionalism emerged in the work of second- and third-generation modernists from the will to bear witness—that, as Zukofsky put it, the poet's aim "is not to show himself but that order that of itself can speak to all men."[49] Levertov quoted that line from Zukofsky's "For My Son When He Can Read" at the end of her review of "A" 1–12. She wrote: "How much the many young poets who are living on a diet of public confession, made without care for craft, and therefore being only on the edge of the art of poetry, might learn from Zukofsky of 'That order that of itself can speak to all men.'"[50] The effort to make primary a non-dogmatic form and a process of the art—"that order . . . of itself"—could be the means by which art responded to the experience and the aftermath of war's new and returning terrors, whether it be Celan's pain-laden rhyme, Rossellini's zooming close on pain's untranslatability, Serling's terrifying surreal fear of 1939, Baraka's elder narrator 64 in The System of Dante's Hell stuck in infernal 1947 ("I had the Kafka blues"),[51] Fiedler's Kafka's "irreducibility . . . maintained like a martyrdom," Levi's posttraumatic unfixing of genre, Bachmann's transposing into narration the memory of Austrian children "look[ing] up the words they don't understand," Baldwin's disquieting but hopeful "something more implacable," Mac Low's antiwar democracy disclosed by randomness, Zeroists's turn back toward life through an art of ashes, Tinguely's and Ortiz's reconstructions through demolition, Appelfeld's esoteric smoke as counterarticulation, Kaufman's Afro-Zen imagism as unruly and maladjusted riposte to neofascist brutality, Eigner's intrepid backtalk to disability, Fanon's permission granting patients' their own "insane" witness to widespread sociogeny, Marceline's shocking disclosure of her Birkenau tattoo for the Ivorian student Landry in the midst of a colloquy on African decolonization in Chronicle of a Summer, or Oppen's delayed PTSD poems of groundlessness.

"We crawled everywhere on the ground without seeing the earth again," recalls Oppen in "Survival: Infantry." The poem is written as a searing memory of his experience as an infantryman in France, where he miraculously survived a violent shelling. "And the world changed" is the poem's opening line. It had indeed, and the "And" provides a rather startling continuation of the poetic project after a quarter century of silence, now in media res. "Blood from the Stone" traces that history. The vector of its content is wartime → postwar (during → after), while as a matter of writing it inscribes prewar → postwar (before → after). It was composed in 1959 and/or 1960, probably in 1960,[52] and is in any case the very first poem Oppen wrote as he was (in Rachel Blau DuPlessis's phrase) "coming home" to poetry.[53] The long period of silence, a whole era of preoccupying radical political commitment and of horrifying war experiences, was truly a night of the word.

When starting out again to write in 1960, Oppen turned first to the labor of working out his ideas about World War II, and it felt like getting blood from a stone. "Blood" has four parts: first a homecoming, second a recapitulation of "The Thirties," third a halting account of "And war . . .—France— . . . Steel helmet. Monstrous," and fourth a fifty-year retrospective concluding with a turn back toward life and a final deliberate subjective historicism: "These were our times." The war for Oppen required the precontext of "The Thirties," its radicalized crowd and its stalwart "Belief," its momentary rejection of invention in favor of "just answer"—a preferred mode back then for accomplishing "all / That verse attempts." Kaufman, who served in the U.S. Merchant Marines but did not see combat and was younger than Oppen, similarly was a veteran of the communist movement.[54] Just as the sense of a permanently changed world in "Survival: Infantry" requires as a kind of preamble the historical contextualizing of the slightly earlier "Blood from the Stone" (which in turn recalls and belatedly justifies the objectivist-communist aesthetic of *Discrete Series* of 1934), so Kaufman's "Jail Poems" are a kind of modernist postscript to *The Abomunist Manifesto* (City Lights, 1959), which ecstatically recorded (and often shouted IN ALL CAPS) Kaufman's bemused disillusionment with the communist version of radical human behavior. "When attacked, Abomunists think positive, repeating over and under: 'If I were a crime, I'd want to be committed. . . .'" On daily political awareness: "ABOMUNISTS READ NEWSPAPERS ONLY TO ASCERTAIN THEIR ABOMINABILITY." On labor and political power: "The only office abomunists run for is the unemployment office." The critique of capital, of people who work for capital, isn't radical enough. The avant-garde can do better. "ABOMUNISTS DO NOT WRITE FOR MONEY; THEY WRITE THE MONEY."[55] Abomination is ultimately preferable to top-down communitarian normativity. "Jail Poems" reached readers in 1960 through the *Beatitude Anthology*, which curated work by poets who had been appearing in *Beatitude* magazine, cofounded by Kaufman at Cassandra's Coffee House in May 1959.

Abomunism, following the pattern of belated postwar responses we have seen throughout this book, was a revival of modern poetic radicalism that postdated communist commitment yet refused the end of ideology and instead ecstatically embraced it, standing fiercely against square anticommunist culture. It is said that Kaufman in 1959 alone was jailed thirty-nine times for disorderly conduct. Friends and allies deemed this a protest against conceptions of orderliness. Will

Alexander, a later poet-philosopher-pianist writing under the influence of Kaufman's visionary poetics, has argued that the detentions were "for poetic brilliance via bravura."[56] There are moments in "Jail Poems" when communist antifascism might seem to be deployed by rote as a matter of *content*, but Kaufman's mostly unironic devotion to the Beat *aesthetic*—the term "Beatnik" was supposedly coined by Bay Area journalist Herb Caen to describe Kaufman in particular[57]—affirms an always implicit but frequent claim that the relentless police brutality and racist profiling in North Beach narratively derived from World War II to align with, rather than separate from, other meditative imagistic parts of the thirty-five-section poem. When Kaufman tells a capsule history in the fourteenth section—

> One day Adolph Hitler had nothing to do,
> All the Jews were burned, artists all destroyed,
> Adolph Hitler was very bored, even with Eva,
> So he moved to San Francisco, become an ordinary
> Policeman, devoted himself to stomping out Beatniks

—it follows directly from his description in the opening section of what he can see with his eyes from his jail cell: an unobstructed "view of evil parallels." Caen's derogatory term "Beatnik" (coined April 2, 1958) might follow from the advent of *Sputnik* (October 4, 1957)—suddenly the big little "-nik" suffix was in the air— but I rather think it is also an expression of Caen's unconscious Jewish literary anti-Semitism: "The addition of 'nik,'" writes Norman Mailer in "Hipster and Beatnik" (*Advertisements for Myself*, 1959), "—'nik' being a pejorative diminutive in Yiddish—gave a quality of condescension to the word which proved agreeable to the newspaper mentality."[58] What was at stake in Caen's jibe about Kaufman and other Jewish, genocide-obsessed Beat writers such as Ginsberg was *who*—and which linguistic medium—would get to narrate this "view of evil parallels." The regular newspaper column spelling everything out regularly? Or the tiny verse inscription demanding its author's right to opacity? Kaufman borrows from antifascism to perfect what Maria Damon calls his "Afro-Zen koan[s]" and "rapid-fire aphorisms,"[59] in which he combined imagism, surrealism, anti-anticommunism, abomunism, and "a globally diasporic Black modernism" with jazz extemporizing[60]—a special synthesis and attitude toward oblivion that, with a few others attempting it, helped modal jazz and other forms of structured improvisation to explode onto the art scene in 1960, a version in minimalist verse of Coltrane's "trying so many things at once"[61] or his "sheets of sound."[62] Kaufman laments the fascist destruction of free heretical speech, or rather mourns its absence *out there* in the conformist, quietistic, impeccably liberal political sphere such as at Caen's daily newspaper.

James Smethurst sees in Kaufman's writing a thoroughgoing response to the Popular Front culture of World War II. By filling his poems with seemingly random references to key Popular Front figures and events (the Spanish Civil War, the poet Edwin Rolfe, and so on), Kaufman eschewed the conservative neomodernism, the counterrevolution of the word, that had forgotten or suppressed "the more 'extreme' and politically radical strains of modernism," such as surrealism as an extreme development of imagism.[63] As we have seen, this is a double-negative strategy of 1960: reject the rejection in order to embrace a prewar and wartime iconoclasm otherwise politically unavailable as an art strategy. Kaufman's possibly partly invented Caribbean ancestry was a means of proclaiming kinship with the Martinican surrealist poet and anticolonialist activist Aimé Césaire, whose agonized surrealism of the prewar years (leading to *Notebook of a Return to the Native Land* of 1939, which Kaufman read closely) was a major influence on the poetry Kaufman wrote in 1960, and whose founding of the literary review *Tropiques* during the war—surrealist André Breton, another key influence on Kaufman, befriended Césaire in Martinique during this time—informed the heretical stance and strategy of Kaufman's journal *Beatitude*.

Smethurst's application to Kaufman of a rigorous literary history of the international left—including both unionist and military left—enables emphasis on themes of incarceration. The operative pun on "cell" at work in "Jail Poems" comes to the fore: the prison space as a refuge from the hyperinterpretive sectarian life of the revolutionary cell. Its counterstyle aligns with Robert Creeley's sense of inhibiting aspects of the written sentence: "Oh yes, the sentence. That's what they call it when we put someone in jail."[64] Kaufman's "Jail Poems" relocate linguistic freedom exactly *here*, inside legal sentencing, in cells full of sane Beat vagrants deemed "defective" by authorities while judged by him to be poetic and persuasive:

> The defective on the floor, mumbling
> Was once a man who shouted across tables.

Kaufman's experimental project is on view in this two-line sentence. "Jail Poems" transcribes those mumblings. The Black Jewish poet, always sensitive to the Nazi/Beatnik-bashing police parallel, had a special talent for distinguishing—and then radicalizing by aestheticizing—remnants of political speech deemed

defective by racist and anti-Semitic squares. If in its file the FBI summarily identified him as "Negro, smooth talker"—in addition to plainly tagging him as a
"communist"[65]—Kaufman committed himself to the mumblings of the "defective" as shibbolethic abomunistic counterwords, innocent as the cellmate might
seem. Unsmooth "shout[ing] across tables" is always already politicized.

Kaufman and his jailed Beat comrades' "view of evil parallels" always
depended, as in a visual art, on light. His poems are photographic in that sense.
Conventional neomodernist poetry is that which "lacks EYES," as Cid Corman
wrote in a letter to Creeley in early 1961. "Jail Poems" has no lack of eyes. Surrealist via Césaire, Kaufman's verse deploys visual apprehension everywhere as
language. Its epistemological moments are the most striking. Serving a sentence,
a poet needs to know by what civilly disobedient radiance one sees such contrasts
in the "evil parallels"—an aim for a project that is a Beat version of Thoreau's
legendary contrapositional rejoinder to Emerson as the latter stands outside the
cell looking in ("the question is what are you doing *out there?*"). At such moments
Kaufman is sincerely at his most imagist, a bit of light coming in, wide eyes
looking out. For instance in section 15:

> Three long strings of light
> Braided into a ray.[66]

Notwithstanding every manner of brutalization (including involuntary
rounds of shock therapy),[67] the "Jail Poems" imply that the ultimate inhuman
brutality is the absence of color. There are moments when Kaufman seems to
have beatified not just American Transcendentalist *out there/in here* inversions
but also Wallace Stevens's faux lament over white suburban colorlessness, which
is disrupted by gauds of modernist imagination and, in a rare dream of longing
for an unruly antiracist poetry, liberated by the occasional vagrant veteran who,
having wandering into the somnambulistic suburb, "drunk and asleep in his
boots, / Catches tigers / in red weather" ("Disillusionment of Ten O'Clock").[68]
This itinerant outsider, the abomunist, has radical potential, for he has wandered
into the heart of imagism. In "Jail Poems" such aesthetically messianic figures
shift locales, discovering the ecstasies of light and color on the countercultural inside.

Barbara Guest's own fascination with the history of imagism led her eventually
to write a biography of H. D., an elaborate effort at getting back to the original
radical imagist impulse. We see hints of this effort in *The Location of Things*, in

poems such as "Russians at the Beach" and "In America, the Seasons" ("I incline toward you / like dead Europe") and "In the Alps." The latter poem asks "Where after the wars" one will locate a return of speech. Charlotte Delbo, working out the linguistic problems of postwar survival in "The Return," observed that "it was a matter of complete indifference to me that everything should be incomprehensible," and asked: "How could I reaccustom myself to a self which had become . . . detached from me?" And: "Was I alive to have an afterwards, to know what afterwards meant?"[69] And when "one speaks after such a long time," Guest wrote, the words seemed from "a fairy tale." Or, as Delbo put it, the postwar language she heard "came from another universe." The tale of *after* in Guest's haunting first poems is a "new-discovered place where one can dream / Of tigers with fair hair" and "houses whose hearths" are similarly unreal, made against suburbanized blandness, enforced normality. If Guest is summoning the imagistic Stevens here, it is in the service of reviving early modernist language as a strategy for renaturalizing spaces later contaminated by disaster—the same middle European terrain haunting Delbo's and Appelfeld's and Levi's writing just then too: "The forests resting from their struggles," observes Guest, "The streams with loads upon their icy backs."

Eigner seeks similar reconciliation of the "end / and the endless," the contingent real and the multiform tale perpetually told about nature: "The knowledge of death, and now / Knowledge of the stars."[70] For Oppen survival required accepting that "the world changed" during all-out global war, which in turn required an active memory in poems of things that "There had been," such as trees, fish in the sea, ground, rocks. "Where did all the rocks come from?" the survivor asks. And why must he ask? Because after all these years he can *still* smell the odor of explosives. His experience "In the same mud in the terrible ground" taught him what a poet might otherwise only imagine—that even the earth can shift, that even rocks despite confidently reported terrestrial origin can be moved by theoretical and *actual* groundlessness. Eigner's uncanny understanding of contingent death depends on his knowledge of stars' permanence, what he sees from his window. Guest knows "In the Alps" that she is "wandering" in the indestructible "blue" of the Alpine horizon, and in her first book seeks a postwar art that will "Let old lands speak their speech." This is a cousin, albeit formally a distant one, to Oscar Hammerstein's Jewish reinterpretation of this same terrain as uncontingently "alive" with words people "have sung for a thousand years," where there is always already at least a phonemic prompt, "one more sound, / One more thing that the hills might say."[71] "In the Alps" is Guest's adaptation of the dilemma faced similarly by Rothenberg in *White Sun Black Sun* and *New Young German Poets*: permitting such speech as the "old lands" of Europe bespeak is not the same as relinquishing antifascism, but rather suggests an emergence from the night of the word, the beginning of undoing deradicalization. Guest asks if that move can make "a reason for happiness." A sanguine instance would be a poem like this about a scenic European journey and its images, a tour of Maria von Trapp's therapeutic "favorite things." But in the end Guest is doubtful: "The air is freed of our crimes, / Lovers meet in the inns of our fathers." The pun on *sins of the fathers* indicates a strong irony. We are not freed of our crimes, despite the bracing air and "forests resting," after Appelfeld's, Alfred Werner's, George Steiner's, the von Trapps', Marjorie Perloff's (as we will see in chapter 10), and others' desperate escapes from central European fascism. The conclusion is practical, not bitter. The speaker-survivor in Oppen plainly testifies and affirms: "These were our times."

As we move toward a final encounter in this book with Lowell's confessionalism—with the problems of institutionalization, commercialization, monumentality, and memory—as a contrast to Oppen's and others' revived sense of surviving "our times," let us briefly return to Cid Corman's critique of the work of art "that lacks EYES." He was not writing to Creeley about Kaufman's carceral vision, but, to be sure, he was claiming solidarity with artists similarly abomunistic and officially designated as deranged. "This country, with its constipated egos and overadvertising, makes me sick," Corman wrote. "No wonder half the young people I've met have already been institutionalized (fucking word). There's no place to look but in, here. It's like so much of your own work that lacks EYES. You might as well be nowhere." The multiple eyes of "Jail Poems," like the multiple narrator-citizens of Baldwin's "Notes," are predicated on this invisibility. "*Something* I have done is nothing," Kaufman writes from jail. "Someplace I have been is nowhere. / I am not me." And he sincerely concludes: "Thank God for beatniks."[72]

By this point it was March 1961: Corman would visit and see San Francisco for himself, and he wrote Creeley about the counterculture generally; while doing so, he not so gently criticized Creeley's previous verse as apolitical. But this howl against repression and marginalization follows from a discussion of Zukofsky's "A." If Creeley was familiar with *Bottom: On Shakespeare* he would immediately have recognized the source of Corman's thesis: contemporary art must have "EYES." Corman told Creeley that his magazine *Origin* would be publishing excerpts from Zukofsky's new work, including, it seems, parts of *Bottom* (nearly all of it then still unpublished). Corman reports that he was performing from "A" at readings in the United States, Canada, and Japan. It is "the most mature piece of writing America has produced. . . . What EP [Pound] and WCW [Williams] talked about, Louis has done." The poem is political (he's been discussing its analysis of labor) and it is about love. " 'A,' " Corman writes, "is the most beautiful love poem in our canon." When Corman turns to excoriate American "egos" and "overadvertising" and curses the collective derogation of heretical young people as mentally ill, he is prepared to push Creeley toward a more politically engaged aesthetic stance on the basis of what he implies is *Zukofsky's* inspiration of the counterculture: "You recognize only yourself. And you have too much love to stop there. No theory will cover you, except with shame."[73] Because Creeley's verse "lacks EYES," it is narcissistic. This was exactly the challenge of the anti-confessionalism Zukofsky inscribed into "A"-13. Oppen's "Survival: Infantry" was similarly a turning point for the project of merging his political experience with a personal trauma in new poems without falling prey to confession's smooth assumptions.

John Palattella focuses on the ending of Oppen's war poem as a key point of nonconfession. Just prior to the final stanza, the poem is morosely self-expressive: "We were ashamed of our half life and our misery: we saw that everything had died." But then the turn, which begins with an "And" that functions like a "But," signaling the volta:

> And the letters came. People who addressed us thru our lives
> They left us gasping. And in tears
> In the same mud in the terrible ground

"The crucial word," writes Palattella, "is 'addressed.' Oppen does not say that people 'wrote' to him; they addressed him, spoke to him, through their words and hence through his life. . . . The letters, in other words, gave Oppen a language of survival."[74] This is the opposite of conventional first-hand testimony. His own primary experience is defined by other writers, other voices. That impersonal address is what deeply affects him: the memory of others' stories disrupting the process of groundlessness. And when Oppen, like Corman, wrote of his experience reading "the whole of 'A,' " he immediately understood the poem wasn't ultimately about Zukofsky. In a letter of 1960 Oppen wrote that "There are voices, people moving all thru it and a young man in N Y sort of wrapped in music." He found "A" "very much more moving" than in his earlier reading of "only the first 7 parts"—which indicates that he had not read *"A"* since *before the war*. Now he found the poem not just "more moving" but "very much simpler, than I had remembered."[75]

This was for Oppen a fate of postwar rereading, and we are edified by attempting a reconstruction of the readerly situation. Oppen barely survives a desperate battle. He then lives out a political exile. He returns home. In 1960, at the end of his very first poem about the war, he achieves a stance of posttraumatic impersonality. And *then* he finally revisits his friend's elaborate epic to find it affecting and simple. It cannot be determined if Oppen had yet read *"A"*-13, but no matter: he already understood the reasons for Zukofsky's move toward a special hope for the coming countercultural generation having grown up absurd—neither forcing his Old Left politics on them, nor even pressing his parenthood into the service of unironic paternalistic advice. Since we are turning now to Lowell's critique of postwar monumentality, it is apt to quote a passage from *"A"*-13 that captures Corman's and Oppen's sense of Zukofsky's new relevance:

> To rear the monument
> Of your own fame on the slob—
> If your children forget
>
> Your love is not unregarded—
> What is cold in the grave?
> To rely solely on friendship
>
> Is sad do not tax what holds
> Back[76]

By this point in the poem the speaker-father knows not to slip into top-down advice. The rhetoric of admonition is still here ("do not . . .") but it commends personal restraint. The poet wants to be heard by the children of the sixties. His aim of reaching them is in the sweetly modest double negative "Your love is not unregarded." The father will be seen, as the poem has EYES in the manner his poet-publisher Corman and his own *Bottom* advocate. Efficacy cannot be about "your own fame." Humility signals a theory of monumentality and memorialization in *"A."* *"A"*-13 inaugurates the parts of the modernist epic that will dwell on mortality and could be said at times to be a whole pre-elegy.

On the other hand, what sort of monument gets "rear[ed]" in erring testimony? Oppen now, fifteen years belatedly, sought an antimonumentalist memorial to war, an artwork declining to depict the soldier slogging through mud yet somehow otherwise conveying the addressing of others as radically ethical representations. In an interview about the complexities of representing genocidal war, James Young, the founding director of the Institute for Holocaust, Genocide, and Memory Studies, said the following: "There's a post-WWII generation that sees the monument as an essentially totalitarian form of art or architecture. It's a big rock telling people what to think; it's a big form that pretends to have meaning, that sustains itself for eternity, that never changes over time—it fixes history."[77] Yet "the world changed," observed the survivor of the horrific Battle of the Bulge: even the very rock of grounding, meaning's seeking of a basis, was altered by experience of the disaster. The art transformed by such transformation must itself of course be unfixed; it should not tell people what to think about extremity. Otherwise, as Zukofsky warns, "your children forget." In "A," postwar Jewish memory and "rear[ing] the monument" stand as opposites. Young has written *The Texture of Memory: Holocaust Memorials and Meaning*, and the first thing he undertook in that study was a summary of the case against traditional memorials: the monument petrifies history, and yet commits an even greater violation—it signifies an unstable cultural regime demanding prewar symbols before it is capable of modernity.[78]

# 10

## Favorite Things

*I know I will hear*
*What I've heard before.*

—OSCAR HAMMERSTEIN, II, "THE SOUND OF MUSIC"

## Stress Reactions: The Critique of Confessionalism and Memories of Anschluss

Monumentality and modernity: those were Robert Lowell's themes as he turned in the first six months of 1960 from the intensely personal apoliticism of *Life Studies* to "For the Union Dead," in which World War II–era pacifism is supposed to emerge as advocacy for civil rights. Here I am going to argue that the unstable cultural regime of "For the Union Dead" was confessional poetry itself—that the triumph of the therapeutic in the 1950s was problematic for art responding to the postwar situation; that this new poem by Lowell, in spite of concentrated thematic effort, stands among those grand "big forms," in James Young's phrase, that try to tell us what to think and are not yet capable of modernity, to cite again Young's summary of the shifts in postwar representation in memorial sculpture and architecture. The world of "For the Union Dead" has not fundamentally been changed in the way George Oppen now realized was crucial. Nor would the Afro-Beat "mumbling" of Bob Kaufman's beloved institutionalized activist be heard anywhere in the antimodernist discourse of Lowell's confession, notwithstanding his poem's progressive politics.

"When I finished *Life Studies*," Lowell mused, "I was left hanging on a question mark. I am still hanging there." The self-analysis was not private. He wrote those words to be printed in the program distributed to all attendees at the Boston Arts Festival in June 1960. From January to June he had been working on drafts of "For the Union Dead," and he then decided to declaim the piece at the festival. In Buenos Aires, Elizabeth Bishop learned to her delight that an audience of three thousand gathered outdoors on Boston Common heard the poem. She mentioned this remarkable fact to a friend and reported back to Lowell the friend's mildly mocking response, aimed at the poet's public reappearance (after debilitating rounds of mental illness) and mock-celebrating his renewed standing in the long line of literary Brahmins: "A Lowell speaks to Boston."[1]

Lowell had indeed been "hanging there." But the phrase did not refer to his feelings about Bostonian racism, as might be deduced from the poem. It was rather a version of his now-infamous binarism about the direction of contemporary poetry, presented in his speech on March 23, 1960, as he accepted the National Book Award for *Life Studies*. In the war between the neoformalist or well-wrought, "cooked" verse of *New Poets of England and America*—the anthology assembled by Donald Hall, Robert Pack, and Louis Simpson—and the "raw" poetry of Donald Allen's *New American Poetry*, Lowell now fantasized an aesthetic center. That moderation cleared a middle ground from which he could write within a great premodern and formalist tradition, boosted by New Critical acclaim, and yet somehow at the same time be able to continue in the supposedly "loose" or "loosened," "thrown together," "hurried, off-hand," "almost flippant," "lazy and anecdotal" mode of his verse of the late 1950s.[2] Lowell's biographer later said that "by 1960 the battle lines were clearly drawn," but Ian Hamilton was not referring to the civil rights theme of Lowell's declamation against Boston's urban version of the modern, performed in front of that large local crowd.[3] Hamilton refers not to a topical liberal-left, which Lowell occupied more or less unassailably in this new work, but to a popular literary centrism. "For the Union Dead" carefully declines to engage—or, as critic Marjorie Perloff would later suggest, indicates an outright ignorance of—concerns over the effects on the next generation of "rearing the monument" (a major anxiety, as we saw, in Louis Zukofsky's poetics), or of the belief that the experience of modern mass death changed the world and that the poem too must be included as an object in the world among those altered things (as in George Oppen's poetics), or of the sense that if "the language / might have survived" this survival was best conveyed in disjunctive art foregrounding its incapacity for facility (as in Larry Eigner's poetics). The center Lowell fantasized would not easily hold. On one hand there was the deferential and mildly negative language he deployed in his speech to describe cooked verse, which was "marvelously expert and remote," producing the poem as a "mechanical or catnip mouse for graduate seminars." On the other hand, raw verse seemed to him "like an unscored libretto by some bearded vegetarian Castro." The latter phrasing was loaded, satiric, antiradical, trading in routine ridicule of Beats and other New American outsider types.[4] It aimed its anger hardly less vaguely at the end-of-ideologists' straw man version of the new avant-garde left, and it was exactly the sort of duplicitous moderation that incited Baraka's Fanonian critique of American reason in the opening paragraphs of "Cuba Libre."

"For the Union Dead" seems to have begun from a straightforward, if naive, liberal historical position. Lowell's discussions with William Meredith just then (in late March) about their prospective collaboration on a staging of *Benito Cereno*—it would steer clear of any alleged "anti-negro" disposition in the Herman Melville original and would assume that "the tale is about the error of optimism"!—supports the view of Lowell's antiracist piety.[5] Early drafts of the new poem indicate this initial historical and political direction. A tentative title was "One Gallant Rush; for Colonel Robert Gould Shaw." Another typescript draft bears the title "Robert Shaw and His Men." "Colonel Shaw and the Massachusett's 54th" was another. Versions of one line, later excised, explicitly tied the cause of the Union in the U.S. Civil War to the nature of twentieth-century conflict: "The first modern war?" one typescript asks. "The first modern war perhaps," another speculates. The final version makes its quick, dismissive reference to World War II ("the last war") without the speaker's having substantively sought this connection. In the draft titled "Robert Shaw and His Men," Lowell permits the prefatory personal confession—his boyhood memory of the old South Boston Aquarium, now (in the present retrospect of the poem) in ruins, just as is the speaker's mind. But in the draft the historical divagation that follows is framed by a dream apparently dreamt by the adult Bostonian revisiting that once-happy scene of his childhood: "As I slept / {ONCE} [handwritten word inserted] my nose crawled like a snail on the glass."[6]

What might be called the Life Studies Effect took over in the drafting. The boy's nose presses against the glass. The daydream has the liminal quality of shapes moving slowly behind a nontransparent screen. In one version, even the "negro school-children move like fish" (they are elsewhere "compliant fish"; this wrong-headed parallel was later removed) and even news coverage as seen on a cathode tube by the sympathetic liberal Puritan speaker seems like "green ooze and glass." Another version—here the poem's final confessional focus is found, and it is given the title "The Old Aquarium"—makes boyhood remembrance, a Wordsworthian prompt, clear from the start; it begins "Remember how your {MY} [inserted handwritten word] nose crawled like a snail on the glass." The poem is devoted to a premodern concept of transparent language even as, at every turn, its tropes assume boundaries while calling out for opacity: the ooze and the glass separate liberal poetic subject from disenfranchised object.

The frame of local childhood memory remains through drafts of the poem. In one version we have:

> *Once* my nose, etc.
> *Later*, I marveled at, etc.
> *Later*, perhaps, as a statue, etc.

But despite the personalizing effect of the Romantic frame (*this was a dream of my youth and, feeling lost, I revisit it in this poem, and now we proceed*), in drafts there are intermittent confident claims to the authority of witness. Must one have lived into middle age to gain such historical perspective? "One has to have lived a little" is a phrase in the typescript draft titled "Colonel Shaw and His Negro Regiment." Notwithstanding these contentions, the statue representing Shaw has been rendered inaccessible by the avarice, presentism, and racist disregard of Boston's leaders and city planners in 1960. "He [Shaw's statue] is out of bounds now" is a line that remains in the finished version. The question, about the poem's composition as itself an aid to memory, becomes: How "out of bounds" should this memorializing mode properly remain? Lowell's hope is to speak ethically about what is "broken" in the social community well beyond what needs to be indicated by the objective correlative of the writer's mental state. The critique in "For the Union Dead" of Bostonian historical and contemporary anti-Blackness, and of a willful misremembering of the heroic abolitionist past and its association of postwar urban development and civic ignorance, is compromised by three factors: first, the questionable understanding of postwar monumentality, as already noted; second, a somewhat random, inexplicable assertion of the absence of memorializing "the last war"; and, third, its presumption of the privilege (for the purpose of earning authority through first-hand experience) of having a therapeutic encounter with one's personal history and current psychic ruination.

On May 19, 1960, as Lowell worked with final drafts of "For the Union Dead," a letter arrived from Bishop. She had been reading the poems of Anne Sexton. They reminded Bishop "quite a bit of you." But in the end Bishop insisted that she saw "all the difference in the world" between Sexton's confessional "simplicity" and "that of Life Studies." Sexton's "egocentricity" was "simply that." But Lowell's, in contrast, "has been . . ."—and here Bishop, unsure, pauses: "has been—what would be the reverse of sublimated." Whatever is indeed *unsublimated* is a quality that makes not just for "intensely interesting" verse but for a form of frankness that, instead of personal relevance, produces a pain rendered in words "applicable to every reader."[7] Stressing the universal relevance of these expressions of a friend's mania, a privacy made public, Bishop joined the prevailing critical assumption, shared far beyond Lowell's sympathetic circle. Nascent young critics such as Marjorie Perloff, for instance, then twenty-nine years old and the product in equal measures of liberalism and New Criticism at Oberlin College and recent recipient of a master's degree from literarily conservative Catholic University,[8] were stunned by *Life Studies*. The method of confessional poetry—in Lowell's *Life Studies*, Anne Sexton's *To Bedlam and Part Way Back* (1960), Sylvia Plath's *The Colossus and Other Poems* (1960), and W. D. Snodgrass's *Heart's Needle* (1959; winner of the 1960 Pulitzer Prize)—was all the rage. Even "cooked" poet-critics such as Daniel Hoffman (reviewing ten new books in the *Sewanee Review* in winter 1960, among them Robert Pack's well-cooked *A Stranger's Paradise*) conceded that Lowell provided "the boldest innovations in technique" whereas younger poets were still merely "assimilat[ing]" the modernist styles "of forty years ago." Hoffman, like Alain Bosquet in his French anthology that year, longed for Lowell's early work—of the 1940s—but that didn't mean he was ready to praise poets of 1960 who sought reconnection to the word-as-such revolution of the 1910s and 1920s. His recommendation of Lowell assumed a *break* with the modern and stipulated that such reaction and restoration were qualities indicating innovation.[9] Perloff and others of the generation born around 1930, tracking the trend at the start of the 1960s, might have encountered some expressions of misgiving (in newspaper and magazine reviews of Lowell, Plath, Snodgrass, and Sexton) from poets aligned against the cooked verse promoted by Pack, Hall, and Simpson; we have seen this in responses by Zukofsky and Levertov, and of course there were other skeptics. But only later did critics fully explore doubts about whether the confessional mode succeeded in representing postwar life on the historical (and international) scale. I interpret Perloff's later caustic reconsideration of "For the Union Dead," to which we return shortly, as inextricably connected to her own searing experience of wartime extremity, so let us first turn to that.

Hers was a refugee's story of sudden disruption and dislocation, then of counterreactive cultural nonalienation, and then, beginning around 1960, of persistent dissent from mainstream American literary critique. The effects of this stance, I believe, began to manifest themselves as—after a period of intense no-regrets assimilation—the young critic began to put to specific use her exilic antifascist sensibility, the influence of her parents' and relatives' preference for Kultur ("their true religion") over Kitsch,[10] and her commitment to multilingualism and comparativism in assessments of the status of the postwar avant-garde in the United States. In effect, she would begin to ask: How does a critic learn to test claims such as Elizabeth Bishop's chummy stance on Lowell's private pain that it is applicable to every reader? From what stance toward postwar culture does Bishop—per her jacket blurb for *Life Studies*—get the "chilling sensation of here-and-now, of exact contemporaneity"?[11] Moreover (even if it *does* refer contemporaneously): What indeed is "the reverse of sublimated" in postwar art? Is it candor? Is it sincerity? Psychopathological truth-telling? Directness of speech? The problem, of course, is that representation is neither transparent nor direct. Insofar as the emotional import of a poem must be brought through the *Sprachgitter*, or "speech-grille," that Celan at this time constructed and tried himself to write through (for Perloff this is a key figuration of nontransparency),[12] it connects what is otherwise deemed mere personal neurosis with, to say the least, a more significant state of loss, where "tidings" (including the poem itself) bringing news of lost lives are not just inscribed with one murdered mother and her one son but point more indicatively—and more powerfully—to "this world" ("Black Flakes").[13]

A sense of the opacity of *Sprachgitter* came later, as did the revised position on Lowell's contemporaneity. First she had to swerve from an avid faith in big-C Culture she had observed and (not without internal struggle) inherited from her family's assimilated, worldly Viennese (then émigré) community. The Kultur-Kitsch dichotomy might be reckoned through intensive study of the mixing of high and low in postmodernity. Its pertinence might be ascertained by learning to hold two ideas at once about the intellectual aftereffects of a family's story, always a simultaneous "yes *and* no" (in her phrase)—for instance, in her ongoing response to the kitschy version of the story of Austrian antifascism at the time of the 1938 Anschluss presented in *The Sound of Music*: enjoyed the scenery and the songs, but of course it was laughably "shlocky and absurd"; *and yet* always

"enjoyed it," and many decades later still recalled her very first reaction "exactly"—
and "still watches for a few minutes when it comes on" television.[14] Why? Perhaps
in part because the arduous, audacious Alpine getaway on foot of her maternal
grandfather, the eminent diplomat Richard Schüller—which she later called "his
*Sound of Music* mountain-style escape"—symbolized for her the "troubling" mix of
Austrian Jewish loyalty, ignorance, stubborn pride, resistance, and accommodation
of which the world of her parents was constructed, "a world so self-contradictory
*one can never quite describe it.*"[15] Thus does such ultimately impossible description become an ongoing project. Through a trilogy of works—first, a memoir,
*The Vienna Paradox*, in which a late-career critic returns headlong back into
that harrowing original source material, telling of its associated traumas; second, *Unoriginal Genius*, with its vivid defense of artists whose language fails "a
test for detecting foreigners, or persons from another district";[16] and finally
*The Edge of Irony: Modernism in the Shadow of the Habsburg Empire*, a study of
Austro-Modernism with the German invasion of Austria, the Anschluss, as its
culminating event—the refugee systematically applied her knowledge of Euro-
modernist political culture to the realm of a lifework as literary historian. These
works are critical correctives. They are also, in varying degrees, personal. The
title of a chapter on Celan in the third of these books is "The Last Habsburg
Poet"; he never wrote in a purely monolingual German context, encompassed
always by several languages, and was in many senses particularly *Austrian*. The
title of a chapter in *The Vienna Paradox* is "Losing Everything But One's Accent,"
a phrase that conjures the image of the intelligent European girl desperate to
Americanize. What do these things have in common? The idea of "accent" in
the memoir's chapter title is not difficult to consider. But in the reality of wartime
and immediate postwar daily life, as we learn, it was an agonizing travail—the
experience of finding refuge requiring focused linguistic effort for a Jewish, ex-
Austrian, *non*-German, native German speaker during a fiercely anti-German
era. Then there is the further problem of the experience hinted at in the phrase
"Losing Everything."

    What can we know about such loss? In this book we have seen its effects on
many. *The Vienna Paradox* describes ongoing phobias and posttraumatic
responses, although, because so much else of historical interest is being narrated
and because the memoirist's aim is furthest from confession, these glimpses of
conscious and unconscious depletion—how assuredly, after all, can one *feel* that
one has "los[t] *everything*," how can one yearn for a hardly known or never-
known negative?—are not so much understated as kept largely disconnected
from the main story. The emigration narrative has sufficient force without the

need for detailed scenes of dislocation and deterritorialization. Perloff opens her tale of the Anschluss not in Vienna but in Philadelphia's Thirtieth Street Station, and other dim, heavy-aired contemporary train terminals. When in such spaces, even decades later, she confesses to feeling *"unaccountably* sad." Even in Tokyo's clean, well-lit bullet train depot she feels "the same *familiar* twinge of anxiety." She quickly intervenes morbid self-analysis to note that she shares Ludwig Wittgenstein's doubts about Freud and will not go in for "psychological explanation." "But"—nonetheless—she then goes on to describe "my train phobia."[17]

These and others unabated fears have a precise etiology: the night of March 13, 1938. It was the crucial moment in the family's hurried flight from fascism, which was triggered by the Anschluss of March 12. Later in the memoir we learn also of her ongoing border anxiety. It comes after a passage about her intensely positive "feeling for America," most keenly realized whenever she passes through the border at U.S. Passport Control and Customs. She feels she is "home" then, far from "a threatening or threatened national border." When, conversely, traveling in Germany in the 1980s and seeing signs reading *Die Grenze* (The Border), she becomes again "acutely anxious" and "panicked and clutched my passport." She calls these experiences, in an uncharacteristic two-noun phrase that seems a touch clinical, "stress reactions." Notwithstanding the "fear of frontiers," in order to attend a conference (honoring her mother's work as an economist), she returns to Austria, the scene of actual crimes committed against her family, and feels strangely still ostracized, pushed into an atypical silence, made worse when she describes herself to her hosts as a "refugee" after being asked why she pronounced perfect German.[18] The question was hardly innocent, an anti-Semitic slip of the mother tongue.

Perloff's experiences and views are acutely contextual, and unsurprising as such. In archives such as those enabled by the work of Langer, Laub, Geoffrey Hartman at Yale University, interviewer-archivists at Yad Vashem and Stephen Spielberg's foundation, and other people and projects, and from research conducted by Beth B. Cohen for *Child Survivors of the Holocaust*,[19] we can now access hundreds of testimonies of survivors who were children at the moment of intra-European or external escape or deportation. Those who were already mature at the time have recalled traumatic memories, of course—the uttered yet ultimately unsayable X of seeking to denote what was witnessed—and when these stammer or struggle to speak or write, as we see in the cases of young adults Primo Levi and Paul Celan and preteens such as Beat poet ruth weiss—born Austrian in 1928, she was eleven at the moment of exile—it is because the disaster defies smooth utterance. weiss's *Gallery of Women* (1959), *Blue in Green* (1960), and the experimental film *The Brink* (1960) burst forth with "the wailing wailing wonder of the now" and yet are laconic and mordant—temporally composite but never lacking in confidence about what time it is: "now belonging is for now / then will tell of itself."[20] *Then will tell of itself*: it's clear from these and other writings and performances that ruth weiss remembered much from her Jewish family's desperate flight from Berlin to Vienna to the Netherlands to—in 1939—Chicago. But for younger children, such as Appelfeld, who become adults no longer able quite to recall frightful scenes of childhood, the problem is not primarily reporting the clearly recollected unsaid, for X was always already itself vague. In such cases bearing witness is doubly subject to problems of representation. Those then between the ages of four and eight typically have had a few clear memories but could still look accurately back at their own *misinterpretation* of events and behavioral patterns *at the time*. They don't forget everything they saw or overheard, but they don't remember or trust the memory of feelings and reactions. The scenes now present are cotemporal in the complex of survivors' before, during, and after: *after* told through stratifications of learned, authoritative historical retrospect; and also *during* told through innocent, immature perspective yet with details chosen for dramatic irony, which lends putative authority; and scant liminal images, typically family tableaux, of *before*. Postwar adult expectations further turned the narrative screw: "You were only a child, it didn't affect you," Beth Cohen quotes an interview with a child survivor who cites parental admonition, "and you don't remember anyway and what you remember is incorrect." "We were very young," another child survivor told Cohen, "we had no story to tell," but of course he *did*, and tells it as repressed glimpses—not in spite of but because of "some form of denial, always, always."[21] Faced with her own early writing in preserved letters (originally mailed to her father)—in which she delightedly celebrates the "huge strawberries" to be found during a final retreat at Vallombrosa just preceding the ordeal of emigration— Perloff later asks, "Was I really this unaware?"[22] Why had sudden exile seemed so happy and pleasurable? Was denial all around her so successful? Or was there intense suffering around her already *then* being successfully repressed by the young girl? What was the significance of mentioning these favorite things— things that could keep her from "feeling sad," as the song goes? On one side there were sweet berries and pleasant twice-daily visits to the beach. On the other ("sad" and "bad"), unfavorite things more painful than bee stings and dog bites. This, for instance, while on a train: she remembers a friend of her father, thrown off the transport immediately after it was discovered he held the wrong passport. She recalls this only because she can still conjure the horrified look on her father's face. Parents' reactions intermediate a crisis. Little children under duress do triangulate. She overheard talk of a girl who had contracted polio, had then become paralyzed during the course of the train trip, and was carried off—and "for years [thereafter] I had an irrational fear of polio." She received calming but even then confusing parental explanations. As they fled, her mother said simply that they would "no longer be Austrians."[23] Did the parents' protection of their children from much of the sudden discontinuity actually "save . . . us from a great deal of fear and trauma?"

Perloff argues that such safeguarding as a matter of parenting was "the right thing to do," but concedes that she and others who share her experience "were curiously unprepared for the future." Becoming a refugee at six years old, she was uprooted from home, removed from the site of the family's bookish culture, and dislocated from her language. Her brother, then eight and a half, might have been "more aware" of what their mother meant when she uttered the fateful instruction that they could no longer "be" Austrians. Perloff recalls finding this both plain and incomprehensible. She remembers not quite remembering, and that of itself constitutes a crucial memory of a child's overall experience with fascist horror. *The Vienna Paradox* is not so much an effort to make the drastic challenge to identity comprehensible now as it is an exploration of why memoir must be a "collage" of pieces of historical context,[24] and why constructed memory is the apt medium for representing loss suffered by a person whose professional work has advocated experimental art accessible to us despite its supposed incomprehensibility—not in spite of but *because* of the "dangers of nonengagement" and of "amnesia" and "the aporias of diaspora."[25]

The embrace of anticonfessional, nonnarrative fragmentation, assemblage, and collage as a mode, in the work of others—of Frank O'Hara's I-do-this-I-do-that parataxis,[26] of Samuel Beckett's postwar "shift . . . from 'merely personal expression of disadvantage' to 'an awareness of the communality of loss'" in response to the "sight of so much brutal activity" in Occupied France,[27] of the procedural personal impersonality of Lyn Hejinian's *My Life* as derived from Zukofsky and Oulipo[28]—but also in her *own* writing, has been her means of preparing herself for the "future" for which her parents' safeguarding did not. And what was that future? It was a then-unpopular version of the story of twentieth-century modernism accounting for wartime and postwar suppressions, forgettings, and disconnections, which in 1959–61 she intrepidly did not bother to ask permission to study and then described and advocated as an aesthetic partisan beginning in the late 1960s and early 1970s, following a digressive and at first unrewarded journey through misogyny and anti-Semitism in American academia. This future consisted of art adamantly New, defended by a constant promulgation of inventive modes and untried or misremembered forms and through rebuke of "scholars [who] have thrown up their hands and declared [passages written by writers like Stein and Celan] 'meaningless'"[29]—a project managed without regard to linguistic or disciplinary borders and launched, Brian Reed argues, the moment she began "Poetry Chronicle: 1970–71" by quoting and affirming the controversial assertion that "Robert Lowell is the least distinguished poet alive."[30]

Dining at the Café Sabarsky in Manhattan, the too-perfect simulacrum of a café culture that had never quite existed in Austria, Perloff felt it to be yet another "inevitable by-product of exile." The experience of Sabarsky's pea soup "triggered a Proustian recollection" of taste and smell from the "first six and a half years of my life."[31] The scene enables the memoir's first evocation of the appropriation of Jewish property, so much now there before her eyes in the style of the furnishings and artwork of an alluring Viennese urbanism surrounding her. Finally, however, the café is not really Perloff's aesthetic terrain but predates it. It simulates *early* modern Vienna, with strong hints of still earlier imperial styles. Her tastes run more to the starker and bolder concrete, glass, and steel late-modernist-style Austrian Cultural Forum, designed by Austrian-born architect Raimund Abraham. This structure is more congenial to the memoirist's memory-triggering motives than faux Hapsburg Style. The encounter provokes what is for me the key passage in the work. The Forum's outward friendliness to our critic-turned-memoirist is deceptive. Its website presents writings of Ernst Jandl, Cagean sounds, an abstract geometric design, a calendar of impeccably avant-garde events. Now *here* is an exilic Austria for the twenty-first century. Still, all is not well. The scene and analysis Perloff provides might remind us of the disposition of the experimental postholocaust novel *How German Is It* (1980) by Walter Abish, in which architecture constructs an assertive positive space atop traumatic holes in the ground dug during the preceding era. Monumentality fakes the impossibility of memorialization. Architect Abraham, only a bit younger than Perloff, can recall the "iron sky" of planes raining down bombs. Just before his Forum opened Abraham quoted modernist Adolf Loos: "When you walk through the woods and come upon a hole two feet wide, six feet long, and six feet deep, you know that is architecture."[32] The architect went on to say that his Austrian youth taught him how death is part of life. The Loosian conception of architecture is that spatially it inaptly fills, or more accurately cannot fill, the body-sized grave one encounters in what was for Abraham a childhood trauma of stumbling upon, and falling into, burial cavities in the Austrian wood. "No building," he continued, "can match the terrifying empty spaces of these original sites." What sites does he mean? "No Holocaust memorial," he continued, "ever succeeds in the end because no monument can ever be more monumental than a concentration camp."[33] Perloff reports that the resurgence of fascism in Austrian politics caused Abraham, creator of the official New York cultural center of his homeland, said to be the most significant piece of Manhattan architecture since the Seagram Building of 1958 and the Guggenheim Museum of 1959,[34] to renounce his Austrian citizenship. This work, with its modernist allusions and postmodern gesturing, its tilting zinc facade compared to the slicing blades of a guillotine, stands for the modernist memoirist in the shadow of the specter of "a dark politics that never *seems to quite go away*." And then, with only a meager transition ("Or at least I would like to see it that way," announces the start of a new paragraph), we come to the central story of name change: from "Gabriele," the given European name, to "Marjorie," the girl who "yearned only to be as American as possible." Nothing unusual, on its own, about this sentiment. She joined many immigrants for whom name change constructed fresh identity, a turn back toward life, and a first forgetting enabled by the shift of language and accent. Yet in the same spirit as a hole and a darkness that "never seems to quite go away," she continues to experience the self-consciousness of seeing the name in print (or feels the *absence* of "Gabriele Mintz") and is sometimes left "wonder[ing] who Marjorie Perloff is."[35] The Forum's architectural masking unmasks "dishonest decades." She quotes the Auden poem famously using that phrase to rebuke the 1930s, "September 1, 1939," as an aid to interpreting the building's design. It is vain to make monuments to such a past that will do it justice. We will retake dominion of the iron sky through work that experiments with designed or "made" forms, moving aesthetically upward and forward, but only as a leaping into that void, as a dreamt-of alternative to the death that had rained down. The Zero artists, most born as Perloff was in Central Europe and belonging precisely to her generation, would turn to that iron sky and seek to rewrite it—to sign it, as one does an artwork. The critic sometimes to this day sees her own name and recognizes it as a mask. And note that in the scene she's not looking in the mirror—the memoir admits no such therapeutic cliché—but rather at "the name in print," her byline, not permitting herself unambiguous pride of authorship.[36] The name forgets and retains. "Then will tell of itself," as the Austrian refugee ruth weiss put it, even in a name; thus on and

in her books, and in any mention in magazines and posters she could editorially control, weiss always adamantly spelled hers in lower-case letters. Why?
To insist upon the caustic irony about the supposed modesty and subservience
of Beat women, certainly, but also to repudiate the hierarchical German convention of capitalizing nouns.[37]

*The Vienna Paradox* narrates the transition from assimilated American postwar wife and mother of the 1950s to avatar of the avant-garde beginning in the
1960s, and is resistant to the psychological reading of the phobias and the traumas it nonetheless freely concedes. "Margie" has little patience, not just for the
dour *byunskys*—Austrian refugees who constantly complained how much better everything had been *bei uns* (with us, all together) back in Europe—but also
for their theorizing American descendants, those who "criticiz[e] all facets of
U.S. capitalism, technologism, and media culture." Her case in point is Theodor
Adorno. She laments in the Frankfurt School's exilic sociology the "paucity of
reflections and research on *American* democracy."[38] She wonders why such a per-
ceptive person could live in the United States for a decade and know so little
about how American culture works—and would theorize about it anyway. *The
Vienna Paradox* takes several pages to offer a reconsideration of Adorno.

Perloff had often taught Adorno's book *Minima Moralia*, which was written
in New York in 1944 and 1945. She admired it as an instance of literary hybrid-
ity, for its subtle fragments expressing the "damaged life." But for the purposes
of composing *The Vienna Paradox* the experience of rereading Adorno was a
belated shock. He, who might easily have suffered the fate of millions, complains
in *Minima Moralia* of the way in which doors in the United States are made so
as to be slammed loudly, "sliding frames to shove." This puts him in mind of
"the violent, hard-hitting, unresting jerkiness of Fascist maltreatment." Perloff
finds such analysis infuriating. The slamming of a door was not necessarily a
rude gesture. Inside her own family's modest refugees' home in the Bronx, exactly
when Adorno was writing, where life was constrained by tiny room sizes, doors
did constantly slam. That a reading of this American life as fascist could ever
have seemed "persuasive and appealing" suddenly seemed irksome. Given the
sharpness and, arguably, unfairness to the whole of *Minima Moralia* as this passage is, it seems doubtful that Perloff would have included Adorno in her autobiography if her main problem was a sensitivity to Americans' tolerance of
"unresting jerkiness." There was obviously much more being challenged for her
in the cultural citizenship of the radically displaced. "Every intellectual in emigration," Adorno had written, "is, without exception, mutilated, and does well
to acknowledge it to himself." And further: the refugee "lives in an environment

that must remain incomprehensible to him."[39] Who was he calling mutilated? Who was incapable of comprehending new surroundings?

The convergence of this critique of the critique of American commercialism and the critic's special sensitivity to matters of emigration and fascism—a difficult combination to interpret because it crosses typical American lefts and rights—afforded no catharsis. It was latent in works as early as her book on Frank O'Hara and soon found overt expression in her devastating essay on Wallace Stevens's ignorance of the effect of European conflict during wartime.[40] It is to be found also in the reconsideration of Lowell's "For the Union Dead," to which we now return. This was a review-essay written in response to the publication of Lowell's *Collected Poems* and tellingly coincided with the writing of the memoir. She began the review with a personal recollection. As Lowell worked on the many drafts of "For the Union Dead," he was, as we have seen, aware of ways in which *Life Studies* had shaken the poetry world with its smart frankness, and Perloff confesses to a strong memory of the moment she herself felt the shock: "1959 was the year my second daughter was born and I was having a hard time of it. Two children under the age of three, very little help, a physician husband who was rarely home, endless Gerber meals to serve, piles of baby clothes to take down to the building's laundry room, and . . . the conversations with Other Mothers in the playground that revolved around things like the parsley sale at the Giant supermarket."[41] Like so many others she had felt this poetry "authentically" to depict a real American husband and wife, Cal and Lizzie. Perhaps this sort of modern literature might become her métier, once the babies required less constant care. Was Lowell's verse a gateway—a connector to life as she had herself been living it in "'the tranquillized Fifties'"[42] and to her fierce drive to make complicated expressions of the American language intelligible? The critic who now recalls her own early misreading of Lowell's "For the Union Dead" works with memory in the same way as the memoirist who recalls young Gabriele Mintz in Italy awaiting emigration as she misreads placidity and relative safety in delightfully "huge strawberries" and frequent outings to the beach, a few of the favorite things that kept the Nazi thunder at bay. The essay on Lowell still found "distinct pleasure" in his pre-Confession lines. But when she turned to public verse in the confessional mode such as "For the Union Dead," she found Lowell's complaint about "crass commercialism" in present-day Boston presented in a metaphor that will not withstand scrutiny.

Lowell sees that they are digging ditches downtown. The monument to integrationist Shaw, the epitome of what Perloff commends as "New England heroism," must stand among acquisitive contemporary chaos as Lowell perceives it. Clever figurations of fish in the old aquarium are likened to Shaw's forgotten monumental bravery as it "sticks like a fishbone / in the city's throat." And cars, trendily "giant finned," move through construction-clogged traffic "like fish" themselves. Perloff concedes that she continues to be impressed, as the young housewife in 1959 was when first confronted with *Life Studies*, by the "masterly . . . interweaving" of these images as an "indictment of the debased present."[43] But she also wonders how well Lowell in 1960 understood the earlier histories he presupposed. Was the indictment warranted in context? She quotes the poem's climax:

> The ditch is nearer.
> There are no statues for the last war here;
> on Boyston Street, a commercial photograph
> shows Hiroshima boiling
>
> over a Mosler Safe, the "Rock of Ages"
> that survived the blast.

*Our* "Rock of Ages" is a safe made by the Mosler Safe Company, corporate maker of security equipment, preventer equally of employee embezzlement and global conflagration, guaranteed in a morbid postwar ad campaign to outlast any nuclear blast. Here the safe is accidentally and "mindlessly" juxtaposed on the dismembered streetscape against a photograph of the devastation of a Japanese city after the dropping of an atomic bomb. The big Boston dig, the prompt for this cleverly ironic meditation—following Ian Hamilton and others, Perloff dubs it a perfect New Critical poem—is "nearer," moving toward the space where World War II ("the last war") is *not* eulogized. "Nearer" than what? Now we can recall Celan's "Nearness of Graves" (from chapter 2), its four neatly parallel couplets creating contrast with linguistic self-loathing and "pain-laden rhyme"; the poet there is able to display individual poetic talent while not forgiving himself for proximity to the massing of death. The commercial crudity of Lowell's present, crowding out proper memorializing gestures such as that Northeastern anti-Confederate piety that gave rise to Colonel Shaw's statue, is connected to the constructive dig (for the unburial of a parking garage) and to gaudy fishy cars. Perloff finds the poem's cultural criticism pat and pious, Lowell's aim "to write a poetry of *witness*" a failure,[44] and her response should remind us of her frustration with Adorno's complaints about American culture. The touchstone is the survivor of genocide. Here are two paragraphs in the essay on Lowell:

In California, where I have been teaching since the late seventies, "For the Union Dead" never quite caught on. Here, after all, the automobile is a simple necessity of life. Innocent students are likely to ask, "Why does Lowell disapprove of those who drive cars? Why is theirs a 'savage servility'?" And this inevitably leads to such further questions as "Why is it a sign of moral decay to build an underground garage beneath the Boston Common? How *were* the members of the then growing work force, many of whom faced a long commute, to get to work downtown?"

Such questions, naïve as they may sound, raise important issues. "The ditch is nearer" is one of those lines that sounds profound, but what does it really mean? Was the ditch really nearer for the millions freed from the Nazis at the end of World War II? Or was their future just beginning? Again, the declaration that "There are no statues for the last war here" is questionable. The monuments for the last war, most people would now say, are the concentration camps themselves—Dachau and Buchenwald, Auschwitz and Belsen. Or the Holocaust museums around the world like Daniel Libeskind's new Jewish Museum in Berlin. Or the Holocaust narratives like Primo Levi's *The Drowned and the Saved* and Marcel Ophuls's great film *The Sorrow and the Pity.*

So Lowell's public piece is not really political writing at all. Its superficial complaint against "the very notion of industrial and technological progress" indicates that what passes for "public truth" here is "its author's private phantasmagoria."[45] That "unforgivable landscape" in the poem is not Boston's in the social sense;[46] it is that of Lowell's therapeutic postwar American imagination. When one loses everything including one's accent, the remnant language constitutes a resilient yet precious selfhood. The memoirist in *The Vienna Paradox* is wary of proudly performed public truths. It may be that her train phobias, border traumas, belated sense of repressed horror disguised by the sweetness of a favorite thing—those Proustian berries, a reversal of object loss—or irrational fear of paralysis, and relentless assault on critical claims of incomprehensibility, all form under the banner of so-called confessional writing an elaborate "private phantasmagoria" passing as historical analysis. The memoir as memoir is modest. But strident are its judgments about the "culturally pluralistic, yet divided, and markedly monolingual society," commended by those who forget or at least are not haunted by genocide, and this attitude makes possible the boldness of a chapter titled "Language in Migration" in *Unoriginal Genius.*

In "Language in Migration" Perloff tells of her respect for Caroline Bergvall's art project titled *Say: "Parsley,"* which takes a limited array of words in English and uses them to understand their potential for fresh political reckonings with linguistic disaster. Exophony, the practice of writing in a language that is not one's mother tongue, is essentially about translation, but it never leaves behind the first language in the relanguaging of the second. Perloff notes that for Bergvall, a French-Norwegian writer composing in English, the term "shibboleth" is fundamental—as it was for Celan, notwithstanding Duncan's misreading of that term as red-flagging communism. A psychoaesthetic triangulation is being made. The connotation of shibboleth, as noted earlier, is this (per Perloff): "a word or sound which a person is unable to pronounce correctly; a word used as a test for detecting foreigners, or persons from another district, by their pronunciation." She commends Bergvall's art-adjacent commentary on shibboleth, in which the poet grappled with the genocide of Creole Haitians under Rafael Trujillo in 1937. The massacred were first identified by their failure to roll the "*r*" in the Spanish word for parsley. When Perloff writes about these poets and their multilinguistic political concerns—Bergvall, Yoko Towada, and others—readers of *The Vienna Paradox* recognize the critic herself as something of an exophonic writer. "In a world of relentless global communication, poetry has begun to concern itself with the processing and absorption of the 'foreign' itself." In such an approach to this latest iteration of modernity, we can ask, "what happens when there is no more commanding voice to assess those fragments?" They are factual fragments rendered as such by daring to cross *Die Grenze* and are the remediless effects of life after painful dispossession and dislocation.[47] Codes, Elaine Scarry has written in *The Body in Pain*, "are attempts to make meaning irrecoverable, or . . . to embed that meaning in multiple tiers of arbitrarily sequenced signs in order to divert the opponent's energies into . . . incomprehension." Language in migration, Perloff's Bergvall contends, manages to flee its opponents by understanding the processes of what Scarry calls the "verbal unanchoredness inside war."[48]

What then was testimony without facticity? Lowell's poem sided with monumentality but did not seem to need to reckon with its own January 20. A phrase to be found in a "For the Union Dead" draft—"to tell how many died"—is not extant in the final version. Nothing in the poem comes close to such reckoning. While Perloff's dissent from this kind of postwar lyric subjectivity, this coded verbal unanchoredness, this suppression of the documentary in favor of the rhetoric of the personal, was then still nascent, she was of the new generation of Yves Klein, Aharon Appelfeld, Jerome Rothenberg, and Marceline Loridan-Ivens; the contexts their work of 1960 provides, taken together, make that emergent dissent discernible. The exophonic critic was in a position to meditate upon the convergence of war remembrance and literary experimentation—its return to a radical modernism, a critical aesthetic envincing awareness of its European predecessors—that has been at the heart of this book.

So the survivor (indeed just barely) of the Anschluss, now Americanized eighteen years later, and academically apprenticed (following her mother's path, though in literary studies rather than economics), completed her master's thesis. She wrote it in her second or third language (the topic was Bergsonian epiphany), gave birth to the second child in 1959, and then in 1960 made the decision to return for her PhD, a program she commenced in 1961. She "had shifted allegiances from fiction to poetry and poetics."[49] She had an unspecific plan to help open the field. She knew at least that "I wanted to become a different kind of Modernist," as she later recalled, "no longer the student of Anglo-American poetics from Yeats to Robert Lowell, but of the larger, early 20th-century world called the Avant-Garde."[50] As her fervor for experimental writing developed over the months and years after her encounter with Lowell's remembering-that-was-really-forgetting, her negative responses to thematic pieties, such as those expressed in Lowell's poem of 1960, were going to stand against literary and academic monumentalities—presented authoritatively yet abetting well-meaning but false closure, the sort of then-trendy representations that try to "do our memory-work for us" and thus "become that much more forgetful," as Young puts it when theorizing holocaust memorials. "In effect," Young continues, "the initial impulse to memorialize [traumatic] events . . . may actually spring from an opposite and equal desire to forget them."[51] Never forgetting became a major aesthetic subtext.

Perhaps the most memorable negative monument of the experience of terroristic Nazi annexation was the idea of the family library, the shock to the young reader of its sudden absence—"my parents' elaborate Library, which had taken years to build." The deprivation of an intellectual archive made deep spectral emptiness, paralleling for the portrait of the writer as a young girl Abraham's definition of his spatial art: "a hole two feet wide, six feet long, and six feet deep, [which] you know . . . is architecture." Perloff six decades later "still cringe[s]" at the memory of the precipitous loss of all those volumes, a crucial secular Jewish legacy[52]—its loss rationally explained by parents then, and by war historians such as William Shirer later, through information about victims' desperate haste and about the Nazi decree on severe limits imposed upon refugees' suitcases. How much more deeply it shaped postwar intellectual culture is difficult to calculate. The very idea of the territorial "solution" of the so-called Jewish Question applied with fanatical vengeance to the cherished libraries of intellectuals.

The six-year-old underreacted at the time, naturally, and then carried forward fears that manifested themselves only later—compensatory personal and also intellectual work achieved through *new* books not only *acquired* but ultimately *written* in an adopted place. Indeed, compensation is an apt word. Theorists of survivor testimony talk of writing as incessant "research" intended to locate a self that has been lost. In just this context Shoshana Felman quotes the speech Celan gave in 1958 at Bremen: "to orient myself, to explore where I was and was meant to go, to sketch out reality for myself." The act doesn't make that reality unreal or unrealistic.[53] On the contrary, writing makes a realistic presence out of absence, produces "mute objects of expression" in Francis Ponge's phrase for his own compensatory writing after a flight from the Nazis—he who wrote a book (*The Pine-Woods Notebook*) because, finding himself in sudden exile, he simply had no books at hand to read. This was the gist of the hopeful Zeroist response to the war: absurd, yes, but the "negative space" nonetheless makes a space.

## You Can't Hide Here: Finding the Antifascist Word in *The Sound of Music*

Perhaps ultimately less upsetting than the loss of a family's intellectual legacy, but still (with the right evidence) a prosecutable crime, was this one: soon after the Anschluss, the attendant or concierge of the house where the Mintz family had resided—a person who had glared maliciously at the Jewish family during their comings and goings—appropriated their furniture, household goods, china, silver, and artworks.[54] This person was an Austrian anti-Semite and doubtless welcomed the Anschluss. The Nazis themselves were surprised by the enthusiasm displayed toward Hitler in the days after annexation.[55] Most Germans in Austria greeted the Anschluss gladly; they deemed it to be completing the long-delayed job of reconciling all Germans into one state. Yet non-German Austrians welcomed it too, for a variety of reasons, among which anti-Semitism was obviously one. Jews were driven through the streets, their homes and shops plundered by Austrians. Jewish actors from the Theater in der Josefstadt were forced to clean toilets.[56] A stiff Reich Flight Tax was imposed,[57] as were myriad forfeitures and account seizures, which, along with many others, Gabriele Mintz's family incurred.[58] Soon 130,000 Jews left Vienna; of sixty-five thousand

**10.1** Salzburgers greeting the Nazi army during the Anschluss, March 12, 1938. Salzburg City Archive, Franz Krieger Photo Archive.

eventually deported to concentration camps and death camps, fewer than two thousand survived. In March 1938 alone, 220 Austrian Jews took their own lives.[59] In the plebiscite on April 10, the vote "For" annexation won 99.73 percent of ballots in Austria.[60] On March 12, one of the von Trapp children, Werner, had opened a window, letting in "heavy waves" of "the sound of numerous bells," including those of the same Nonnberg Cathedral whose abbey had sent Maria to care for the von Trapps. "The Nazis were marching into Salzburg," Maria recalled in *The Story of the Trapp Family Singers*, her memoir of 1949, and they were being ecstatically greeted (figure 10.1). Georg—Captain von Trapp, the antifascist who had declined to fly the Nazi flag and was about to refuse an admiralty in the German Navy—asked that the window be closed to keep out the cold. "He didn't want to hear the bells," Maria recalled thinking. Moments later, an Austrian's voice on the radio intoned: "Now we want the whole world to hear how the people in Austria greet their liberator. They rush to the church steeples, and all the bells in the whole town of Salzburg are ringing out of their grateful joy." The next day the children came home from school describing the city flying red-white-and-black swastikas, and again the radio announced: "The happiness of [Salzburg's] inhabitants is insuppressible."[61]

How did all this now look from the vantage of 1960? The close analysis of Eichmann's role at the Wannsee Conference, undertaken as his trial was planned, began to reveal that annexation had been the crucial "first stage" of genocidal process. Eichmann's Central Office for Jewish Emigration in Vienna created the initial "diplomatic" apparatus used to force Jews out of an occupied nation in massive numbers.[62] The Anschluss was a major event in itself, but it had also been, it was becoming clear, a testing ground. Partly in response to embarrassment over such deeper realizations of its pivotal role, what was now being taught in the schools was that Austria had been a "victim," and that Austrians were a special, not-German identity.[63] This was "Opferthese," the victim theory, by which all Austrians, including Nazi supporters, were deemed unwilling victims of the German regime and not responsible for its crimes.[64] For a while at the beginning of the 1960s Russians became the main villains against whom Austrians had fought in a just war.[65] Recent scholars have studied the revisionist historians who were reassessing 1930s appeasement in the late 1950s and early 1960s. "Newer views" about the prewar months that advocated "the rationality of appeasement"[66] as a political strategy began to appear in the late 1950s and were popularized by the early documentary research of Donald Cameron Watt and the strongly agnostic, interpretive writing of A. J. P. Taylor (culminating in *The Origins of the Second World War* in 1961). Ultimately Taylor's controversial work has been reevaluated as striking a blow, albeit a rude one, against settled postwar interpretations.[67] But at the start of the 1960s its approach aligned conveniently with "realistic," present-focused efforts to avoid the old left-vs.-right conflicts in postwar Austrian politics, to help reconcile differences and so avoid the paralysis for the Second Republic that had doomed the prewar First Republic. This approach required making the appeasement of 1938 seem in retrospect not unreasonable, "complicating" Austria's role during the Nazi era and thus suppressing or at least deferring discussions of purely ideological Austrian Nazism (including its anti-Semitism).[68] Such new challenges to the old plain liberal-left hatred of appeasement (Taylor described "a program for the pacification of Europe . . . devised by Chamberlain, *not thrust upon him* by Hitler") gave credence to the view that the Anschluss was the result of the victimization of Austrians at the hands of diplomatic failures on all sides,[69] not by virtue of their own racist sins. This view filtered down. A children's book published in 1955 presented Austria as a casualty of German military aggression *equivalent* to the disappointments of Poland and France (where in fact armies resisted).[70]

For context it does well to reprise 1955, antecedent days for the realizations described in these pages. Clement Greenberg was trying his hand at the first English translation of Celan ("Deathfugue"). Rothenberg, twenty-four years old, was still living in unreconstructed Mainz. Zukofsky was rewriting "Song of Degrees" but not yet ready to ponder postwar Jewish life in "A"-13. Baraka, on leave from his Air Force tour of duty at an airbase in Puerto Rico, was wildly entertained in prerevolutionary Havana as "the vice capital of the world," not yet capable of imagining "Cuba Libre" or the "shaken" "revelation" and radicalization he would experience five years later.[71] Achebe's Obi Okonkwo, still then in London, composed his poem "Nigeria," dreaming of the "unity" that would come from "Forgetting region, tribe or speech." Shirer couldn't get any publisher interested in his idea of a big narrative book on Nazism's rise. Camus, responding to Roland Barthes's critique of *The Plague*, insisted on its political allegory and warned that the pandemic/fascism analogy "can apply . . . to any tyranny" and that people will behave similarly "again, no doubt, when any terror confronts them."[72] Mac Low made first attempts at "reading through text selection" and got arrested for protesting civil defense on Hiroshima Day. Students writing the final exam in Arendt's "Political Science 1104" at Berkeley were asked to "Describe a Concentration-camp society" *or* "Explain why intellectuals can be so attracted by a totalitarian ideology."[73] Celan visited Germany and found the German spoken there alien to his. And the refugee Gabriele Mintz, now Marjorie Perloff, was visiting Vienna for the first time since the day after the Anschluss seventeen years earlier. Some of the city had been rebuilt by 1955, but "its drive was to restore the Imperial Vienna of Kaiser Franz Joseph, even as the prominent role that Jews had played in the *Kaiserzeit* was systematically wiped out." Austrian architecture had been *further* "Aryanized," even beyond the initial submissive remakes of 1938–39. She hadn't been following current Austrian politics but on this first return visit learned that Austrians "resent[ed] the ten-year Allied Occupation much more than the seven years (*sieben Jahren*) of Nazi rule that preceded it" and 40 percent deemed Nazism "a good idea" failingly executed.[74]

Almost a decade later, five years on the other side of our year, much was the same, to be sure, although with some key differences. This time the visitor was Robert Wise, director of the film version of *The Sound of Music*, scouting scenes and securing permissions in Salzburg. For the on-location shoots there would need to be many actors costumed as Nazis storming city streets. Salzburgers wanted nothing to do with such reconstructions, or with issues that would be raised again by the wide distribution of the von Trapp story. The city council voted to ban Wise from using swastika flags for his on-location shooting until the director threatened to splice into the film original newsreel footage from March 13, 1938, documenting Salzburgers' warm welcoming; at that point the council reconsidered its position.[75] On the scale of postwar reconciliations and forgettings, this was a relatively minor intrusion. The Hollywood *Sound of Music* (1965) certainly tells an antifascist story but Nazi presence on camera is quite limited (albeit surely menacing). The intellectual reason Georg calls off his engagement with the élite Viennese Baroness Elsa—in the musical it was because of her proappeasement politics—has been cut. From the libretto:

> ELSA: Georg—if they—if they should invade us—would you defy
> them? . . . I feel I know what's going to happen here. Can't you
> see things my way?
> CAPTAIN: No—not if you're willing to see things their way.[76]

In the movie, of course, the break-up is entirely about Georg's attraction to Maria. Then there's the tension created by Max Detweiler's and Elsa's advocacy of the position that there's "No Way to Stop It," "it" in the song's title referring to Nazi invasion and occupation. That lyric and another sung discussion among the adults about appeasement were dropped for the film from the Rogers and Hammerstein play. The movie's makers deemed "No Way to Stop It" "weak,"[77] *weak* doubtless a euphemism for ideologically complicating. Billy Wilder, upon hearing in the late 1950s that there was to be a Broadway production made of Maria von Trapp's memoir, with songs by Richard Rogers and Oscar Hammerstein, II, pronounced: "No musical with swastikas in it will ever be a success!"[78] Wilder's well-circulated quip—he was of course Austrian-born and his view of the project carried extra weight—was still in the minds of the makers of the movie when David Lehman, rewriting Howard Lindsay and Russel Crouse's book for the musical and even modifying Hammerstein's libretto, simplified the story still further by inserting the scene in which Captain von Trapp angrily rips up the Nazi flag upon arriving home with Maria from their honeymoon a few days after the Anschluss, there being no ambiguity at all now about how audiences should react to all those swastikas waving at them from the big screen.

Wilder was wrong about popular reception. The musical play opened on November 16, 1959, ran through 1960 and well beyond, won five Tony Awards including Best Musical on April 24, 1960, produced a cast album that remained at #1 on *Billboard*'s best-selling albums chart for sixteen weeks in 1960—and which somehow (no one knows for certain when or how) got into the hands of John Coltrane just then looking to try out his new soprano saxophone on existing lyric structures. Wilder was right, however, about the critics, whose response ranged from charmed indifference to loathing and who ridiculed the musical as "a cheerful abundance of kirche-küche-kinder sentiment,"[79] and as "too 'sweet' and 'saccharine,'"[80] and were "disappoint[ed] to see the American stage succumbing to the clichés of operetta."[81] I no more hesitate to investigate the firmness of the handling of antifascism in *The Sound of Music* than in my close reading for chapter 6 of triggered antifascist recollection in *Ocean's Eleven*. An earnest reading here is buoyed additionally by Julian Woolford's recent book published in a reputable scholarly series by Routledge on this work, arguing, among other things, that it "heralded ... the ... reinvention of history and biography" in musical theater.[82] The 1959–60 musical (not the 1965 film) interprets Austrian appeasement contextually, as both a matter for understanding the lethal capitulation of 1938 and a matter for tracking the start of the 1960s. In its absurdly hopeful way, it stands competently with other subtle, belated rereadings of antifascism. The Crouse-Lindsay-Hammerstein libretto consistently indicates a detailed comprehension not just of Maria and Georg's unusual resistance but of the particulars of how Nazism dismantled and then permanently distorted a receptive national culture from within.

Appeasement not in theory, or as the usual quick rhetorical dodge, but contextually is inscribed into the play's every adaptation of the genre and even dramatic devices, small and mostly unnoticed smart veracities marshaled to express a conscious popular counterintervention in the shameful legacy. Librettos' unhistorical plot turns abound in pop musicals. They are infamously forgiven (especially in opera) by audiences. One must somehow arrive at the next song. Yet not even the harshest critics of *The Sound of Music* found such maladroitness. Forgotten by most, surely, twenty-three years later as the libretto was being composed, was the decisive Austro-German Friendship Agreement of July 1936: Germany promised to forsake all claims to Austria and in return the (doomed) Austrian prime minister Kurt Schuschnigg agreed that his nation will "regard ... herself as a German State."[83] There were a number of reasons why this arrangement was disingenuous on both sides. For one thing, the Nazi leadership was not going to honor the forsaking of its intention to annex. Another subtle hollowness in the agreement had to do with the outlawed Austrian Nazi Party as a transnational entity. National socialism was supposed to operate only locally as an intra-Austrian group but instead received every order directly from Berlin. This hidden abrogation of the deal well befit the specific dramatic needs for the tension in the Rolf-Liesl romance and the flow of information from the stage to the play's audiences about the oncoming Anschluss, the key dramatic irony making *every* song both personal (the various romances, Maria's feelings for the children, etc.) and political (the impending Nazi invasion)—doubly signifying, which was Hammerstein's specialty in versification. Rolf, who visited the von Trapp house only when delivering official telegrams to Liesl's antifascist father, wanted to find a phony justification for returning to see her, notwithstanding Rolf's knowledge of Georg's resistance. The two young people plot. "I could come here by mistake," Rolf offers. This seems fine to her but audiences already know it is a terrible idea despite their cheering for the success of Liesl's crush. This is just prior to the Anschluss, after which German subterfuge would finally be out in the open, but Rolf, although "suddenly concerned" (per the stage direction) with what he is revealing to the innocent Liesl, knows that a German Nazi officer, one Colonel Schneider, will receive telegrams directly from Berlin, as he is in Salzburg staying with the hateful Gauleiter Zeller of the Austrian Nazis. "No one's supposed to know [Schneider]'s here," explains Rolf.[84] Though a teenager and at the bottom of the then-secret Salzburger Nazi hierarchy, Rolf through the middle and latter scenes of the play delivers crucial, always dramatically ironic information. This is complex plot devicing, meaningful because the precolonial Austro-German pact was being undermined in a particular way the librettists knew or learned.

And what of genre? *The Sound of Music* is sometimes mocked, and also praised, for its invention of the "kidsical."[85] But this too should be read, I think, as a rejoinder to the eve-of-Anschluss status quo. Why did Schuschnigg when desperately calling for a plebiscite before the invasion set the minimum voting age at twenty-four? It was an electoral counterstrategy designed to exclude younger voters, who represented overwhelmingly the generational concentration of Austrian Nazi influence. The young were scary. Liesl is "sixteen, going on seventeen"—adult enough, Hammerstein meant, to learn to resist loving a collaborationist. And audiences certainly wish *she* could have a say in her national future. The play's source, Maria von Trapp's memoir, is a relatively adult-centered story, a surprise surely to its readers today. The interjected centrality of children—those naturally allegiant to their terrain's beauty, aligned with the distrust of their antifascist elders at home, precociously fearful of the oncoming Nazi thunder (in the famous safe-space bedroom scene with Maria on her first night at the house), and intensely in need of their governess's new style of liberal parenting—innovates Broadway *and* generally the troubled history to that point of postwar representations of colonial annexation. Summarizing the changes to Maria's narrative brought about by writers Crouse, Lindsay, and Hammerstein, Woolford offers this clever yet accurate pitch-like overview: "Kindly governess battles a despotic father for the love of the children, and brings liberalism into the household."[86] The sentence well conveys the ideology of the work and refuses to concede its apoliticism. Maria arrives back from the abbey and sees that Georg has reverted to militaristic fathering. Pushing the patriarch a measure leftward, and not very sweetly in this instance, she suggests that his anti-Nazi politics must correspond to a concept of familial countersocialization—that the personal and political cannot not be interoperative. Maria observes the hypocritical backsliding as follows: "They [had become] just unhappy little marching machines."[87] While poring over Maria's 1949 memoir, Crouse and Lindsay found, in a phrase, her uncharacteristically figurative attempt to see the fearful swastika as one might encounter it innocently for the first time, and decided to adapt this figure for the libretto after transferring it to one of the children, Brigitta, who is (like the adults) disgusted by but also (like a child) terrorized by "the flag with the black spider on it."[88] How can one gainsay a child's arachnophobia? Fearing the fascist spider, the girl needs a favorite thing. The evening thunderstorm that draws the children to Maria's room is similarly terrifying, meant surely to suggest the oncoming march of overwhelming force—the anxiously imagined Blitzkrieg. (A stage production in 2011 affirmed this interpretation during the scene by projecting Hitler's face as it peers through the storm clouds.)[89]

Maria returns to Georg and the children because the Mother Abbess insists—improbably, given its execrable history of exclusion and denial—that the Catholic Church is a means of facing life as it actually is lived. "These walls were not meant to shut out problems!"[90] Maria Augusta Kutschera, ultimately as devout as any Austrian Catholic, had been abused as a child by her foster mother's son-in-law, the "uncle" who raised her. Hammerstein knew what kind of choice had been made when *this* woman's story was the one selected to be the basis of his own final, pre-elegaic libretto (he was terminally ill with cancer, and would die in July 1960). Mother Abbess is a character made to offer a woman's empathy; the historical woman upon whom the character is based, she who had managed Maria's investiture, surely knew something of the abuse in the background. She has plausibly created for Maria a haven, not a prison, where, unlike much of the rest of the Austrian Catholic structure, there would eventually be a safe space for the von Trapps as they prepared to flee into exile. In the musical, the initial singing of "My Favorite Things" is not Maria quelling the children's fears (as it is famously in the film). Rather, the lyric arrives early, when we are first introduced to Maria's relationship with the only person in the Catholic hierarchy we meet in the drama. She and the Mother Abbess sing this sanguine list-poem,

meant to help Maria cope with the detailed material memories of *her* childhood traumas in contrast with the generic child's gratifying "things," *her* need
to lyricize objects of natural cultural (as distinct from dysfunctionally familial)
continuities—the special impersonal yet powerful comfort offered by "songs they
[Austrians] have sung / For a thousand years." The most comforting thing Mother
Abbess could possibly say was that she shared Maria's experience, that she herself knew the reconstructive effect of those favorite compensatory things, a fleeting dark hint perhaps of Mother's own local reasons for being where she is
("Mother, where did *you* learn that song?" "I was brought up in the mountains
myself.")[91] Remembering these words, the canticle of hopeful enumeration, is itself
meaningful in the way the poetics of catalogue or inventorying is meaningful.
And, despite the parataxis, all those connecting, locating prepositions: "on,"
"on," "with," "of," "with," "on," "of," "with," "on," "into," "of." Mother pretends to
be not quite able to recall the words to go with the provincial things she can't
otherwise forget, and this faux memory loss makes for a startling therapeutic
moment, especially surprising so early in the story when we are meeting characters for the first time. "It's been on my mind, too," Mother tells Maria of "My
Favorite Things." "I wish you hadn't stopped [singing it]. I used to sing that song
when I was a child, and I can't quite remember—Please—"[92] Among Hammerstein's canniest lines in this work, "How do you find a word that means Maria?,"
sung one scene ahead of the Maria-Mother "Favorite Things," is a gesture toward
a permissive, liberal theory of language: *it's all right when we as adults, our
memories problematic, cannot recall the word for a thing, yet, still, such forgetting
is to be worked through as the source of the pain, so when "I simply remember" the
word-thing connection, there is ipso facto hope.* The hope Mother Abbess conveys
is not authoritative, nor the least bit authoritarian, notwithstanding or perhaps
despite the Catholic institution she represents. It follows from the process, which
she knows is necessary, by which disconnection between words and things can
sometimes be worked out.

The musical indeed touches upon what happens when the disconnection
between word and thing extends to the problem of the child's selfhood in the
authoritarian situation. Woolford's emphasis on Maria's introduction of liberal
parenting as a countersocializing ideology that shores up political resistance is
not wrong-headed. Looking back on the scene of childhood later—the audience
of *The Sound of Music* is always aware of this sad retrospective—we can see an
inexorable edging toward insanity that is being staved off by Maria's support of
the healthy development of the young Austrian "I," singing songs that are

materially what Ingeborg Bachmann in her talk "The Writing I" called "the obligations of the 'I' coming out of his mouth." Bachmann's stories in *The Thirtieth Year*—her narrators were the age of the teenaged von Trapp children in Austria during the war—describe the scene that would have obtained had not "favorite things"-style linguistic hope saved the day. Sentimental, yes, but that parenting and resistance coincided is the actual basis of the von Trapp story. The nightmare scenario averted in this one special positive case, smoothed over by Broadway in its chirpy celebration of resistance, is described through a horrifying anecdote Bachmann told in the middle of "The Writing I." The story reads like something of a cross between a scene of parenting Dos and Don'ts in A. S. Neill's *Summerhill* (1960), a ghastly extra damaged-ego backstory to Alfred Hitchcock's *Psycho* (1960), and a hellish tale of the young patient experiencing sociogenic neurosis during colonial occupation in Fanon's *The Wretched of the Earth*. The story Bachmann tells runs as follows:

> Once I saw a small child, whose mother was pressuring him to admit that he'd done something; he was obdurate at first, and perhaps didn't even realize what was expected of him. "Say that you did it," the woman prompted over and over. "Say: I did it!" And suddenly, as if a light went off, or he grew tired of remaining silent and refusing, the child said: "I did it," and then said it again, entirely delighted with the sentence, or even more so with [that] deciding word: "I did it, I I I!." He simply would not stop, but screamed and shrieked again and again, until he, laughing hysterically, wriggled his way into the woman's arms like an epileptic. "I, I, did it, I!" This scene was strange, because an "I" was being discovered and simultaneously being revealed, its meaning and lack of meaning, and a wild pleasure in the discovery of the "I" itself, to the verge of insanity, insanity like one will never again reach about it, when one is forced to say "I," when the word has been taken for granted for so long, worn out, an everyday word, until everything, that it should represent from one situation to another, degrades.

The parataxis of "My Favorite Things" offers a definition of associative creativity not so very unlike the "'I' without a guarantee" Bachmann calls for in her lecture, an "I" that "will have its triumph" because "when no one believes it" it still "gets a chance to speak . . . out of the silenced congregation."[93] This associative creativity is horizontal rather than vertical, as semantic word-thing connections are being made and the degradation of the nightmarish "I" of fascist pedagogy and parenting is being averted—yet lyrically and psychically a real working through. And so it nonetheless stands against the denotative hierarchy, against the suppression of transference (in Dominick LaCapra's sense—that is to say, the hiding of the full implication of the "I" in the process being identified). All this is supposed to have happened initially inside, and then adjacent to, the traditional conservative hierarchical culture of the Catholic Church.

The full story of Catholic institutional indifference toward victims of fascist hatred had not been told, not nearly, by 1960, but I believe a sense of the small, scattered local resistance to that indifference is discernible in the abbey's latitudinarian search for a—not the—word that means Maria. In general there was little mistaking such countervalence here in the overall context of Anschluss. Shirer noted that many Catholics in "this overwhelmingly Catholic country" were swayed by the "widely publicized statement" by Cardinal Theodor Innitzer welcoming Nazism to Austria.[94] On March 12, 1938, the Cardinal announced: "Catholics should thank the Lord for the bloodless way this great political change has occurred. . . . One of our missions remaining is a determined fight against communism. . . . Everyone should obey the orders of the new institutions."[95] Neither the historical novitiate Maria Kutschera, nor the Maria fictively invented in the libretto with her indefatigable "I," would obey such orders. And the Jewish Hammerstein, an antiracist activist since the 1930s, as he drafted his last verses, agonized over a meaning that could possibly be constructed for the Catholic abbey. His unpublished notebooks show him working through a song tentatively titled "Face Life." On the draft he scribbled a marginal question: "What does God want me to do with my life?" And on another sheet he wrote these words: "You can't hide here. Don't think these walls shut out problems. . . . You have to face life wherever you are. You have to look for life, for the life you were meant to lead. Until you find it you are not living." "Here" in the haunting sentence "You can't hide here" is, for one thing, the Jewish libretto itself, just as "you" might biographically be the mortally ill writer. These contemplations—the basis of what became in its final version the pragmatic nonidealism of "Climb Ev'ry Mountain," a song for the Mother Abbess to sing (a strange choice out of context, perhaps, but it should make more sense by now)—are about the counterintuitive *realism* of searching for a word to join a favorite thing. Facing life, or in other words *working through*, entails "climbing a hill," not nearer the fantastical, impossible "moon" of typical sentimental pop lyric, he notes, but a kind of realistic, step-wise coping, getting "closer to the *next* hill."[96] So there is the hill of the work of songwriting, parallel to the next hill of the von Trapp's escape route over Maria's natal mountain into safe Switzerland. "I couldn't be lost on that mountain," Maria testifies to Mother, "That's my mountain. I was brought up on it!" (And then hinting a bit darkly at the past, given the abuse the historical Maria as a girl had suffered and fled: "It was that mountain that brought me to you.")[97]

The draft note can be read as working through mortality and hierarchy. Its dejected resolution, "You can't hide here," does survive into the final version of Oscar Hammerstein's final piece of writing, though not in those words. His collaborators on the show, indeed most everyone in Hollywood, knew of his antiracist passion. Max Detweiler's end-of-ideological thinking—so current in 1960, what with Daniel Bell's centrist thesis among other forms of condescension toward the radical revival of antifascism—is here not neutrality but simply an abetting of hatred. Saying "I have no political convictions" in Austria in 1938 is in every sense an assertion of just such conviction. And what of saying it in the United States in 1960? On the eve of the Nazis' arrival, Max says he will do "what anyone with any sense would do—just sit tight and wait for it all to blow over."[98] "No Way to Stop It" was sung from a stage in New York City 1,443 times between November 16, 1959, and June 15, 1963, momentous months of crisis in the Civil Rights struggle, reinitiated in the spring of 1960 with the first wave of lunch-counter sit-ins, which were met by racist violence: "Be wise, compromise. / Compromise, and be wise! / Let them think you're on their side, be noncommittal."[99] There seems little doubt that Hammerstein intended a parallelism between fascism and anti-Blackness. His involvement with the Hollywood Anti-Nazi League—he was a founding member in the summer of 1936, and a member of its executive council—was always directed at "combating racial intolerance." He saw segregation in the United States and European anti-Semitism as aspects of one problem. In 1945 he led the collaborative writing of "The Myth That Threatens America," presented to writers, radio producers, advertisers, and people in the communications industry. This was for him the main lesson of World War II. It *can* happen here. It begins with the constant flow of microaggressions, including those well intentioned: "Even writers with no racist bias can inadvertently give support to prejudice and do more harm than hatemongers when they use the devices of stereotype as a lazy way of getting laughs and making quick characterization." In the late 1940s Hammerstein joined the Writers' Board for World Government because he was "distressed by racism and anti-Semitism." In 1957, as he first considered involvement with the *Sound of Music* project, he was planning to edit a book of antiracist essays, his own chapter to be titled "Dear Believer in White Supremacy," an uphill attempt to dissuade members of the Ku Klux Klan and White Citizen Councils from far-right ideologies.[100] Then came *The Sound of Music*: as Woolford summarizes the negative critical response, "its *only claim* to radicalism [was] that it brought Nazis onto the Broadway music stage for the first time."[101] Theatrical "radicalism": Stephen Sondheim, Hammerstein's protégé, deemed his teacher-mentor and "surrogate father"[102] to be an "*experimental* playwright" from beginning to end.[103] What was "experimental" about "My Favorite Things," for instance, was partly of course the way he and Rodgers set the parataxis into a waltz, and John Coltrane, although the pop song wasn't his field the way it would be Sondheim's, keenly sensed the same, deciding to dervishly whirl up the phrasal associativeness of 3/4 time into a runaway 6/8. The book with Hammerstein's planned direct appeal to American white supremacists didn't come off, but *The Sound of Music* libretto did reassess mass tolerance for fascism as a precursor to global war: another form of racist hatred requiring dissuasion. "Face Life," the titular phrase of the draft song, is not a dictum in support of Max Detweiler's accommodationist "realism," but its gnostic opposite. Its point, to quote one of the verses, is this: "A song is no song / Till you sing it."[104]

## So Many Things at One Time: Coltrane and the Beginning of Beyond

"Coltrane on Coltrane," published in the September 26, 1960, issue of *Down Beat*, is considered by some critics as, in the words of one, "Probably the most important statement he made."[105] "I want to progress," John Coltrane said, "but I don't want to go so far out that I can't see what others are doing."[106] Nat Hentoff noted not a diminution but an increase in the "fury" of the saxophonist's searching while at the same time a desire to make experimental jazz "more presentable."[107] On *Giant Steps*, recorded in March and May of 1959 and released in February of 1960, the piece "Syeeda's Song Flute," named for Coltrane's ten-year-old daughter, felt apt to him as part of the quest to "see what others are doing," not just other musicians and artists, of course, but immediate family too. "It reminded me of her because it sounds like a happy, child's song."[108] In March 1960 an interviewer in Stockholm asked him presumptuously (offensively?): "So you got an open mind, huh?" Coltrane responded patiently and sincerely: "I've been trying recently, to, uh, to *search myself*, you know, and try to find things that are reminiscent, that sound like those things." The word "those" has no antecedent in this remarkable statement. "Those things" bears a kinship to James Baldwin's visceral "something more implacable" as improvisationally outlined in his "Notes" of October 22. *Which* "something" Coltrane is not yet able to say any more than Baldwin can readily write in the novel he hypothesizes. They will both always be hypothesizing. Coltrane promised this reminiscence would happen imminently, although he didn't yet know how. "I'm really going to do some work on that soon."[109] *Giant Steps*, his fifth LP, is considered by many a masterpiece. The ballad "Naima," with its range of chords over a bass pedal, slow and restrained, is one of several cuts cherished by critics and fans. But Coltrane was disappointed with the album for particular reasons. It sounded to him "just like academic exercises, and I'm trying more and more to make it sound prettier. . . . Now I'm primarily interested in trying to work what I have, what I know, down into a more lyrical line, you know. That's what I mean by beautiful, more lyrical. So it'd be, you know, easily understood."[110]

Steve Kuhn, a young jazz pianist who was sitting in with Coltrane variously in 1960, himself "heard the Broadway" version of "My Favorite Things," but perhaps unsurprisingly made no mention of it to his colleagues. Could such music be relevant to their leader's current searching? And yet, as jazz historians have observed, this was the very moment, dubbed "the beginning of beyond," when an increasing sense of the rigidities of the harmonic framework brought about "the perpetual interpretation of traditional patterns,"[111] and for this inquiry a waltz would seem as such a special attraction and challenge. In August 1960, as the quartet Coltrane was forming—following his final departure from Miles Davis's group, back in April—played at Joe Termini's jazz gallery, Kuhn witnessed an audience member, probably a song plugger, approach Coltrane and hand him the sheet music to the song. McCoy Tyner recalled that soon Coltrane brought "My Favorite Things" to the group. The band was familiar with the sound but "weren't lining up to see the play" on Broadway. Asked later about attending *The Sound of Music* himself, Tyner laughed and said, "No, that's unimaginable."[112]

Coltrane's arrangement of "My Favorite Things," as noted, doubled the time signature to 6/8, so that the conjunctions holding together the paratactic parts fall away in the prosody, making the song somehow still more of an enumeration. "Raindrops on roses and whiskers on kittens" became, in effect, "Raindrops on roses whiskers on kittens." The transposition into sound of Hammerstein's repeated emphatic prepositions, syntactic glue that sets spatial relations and holds disparate things together, takes precedence over what in a pure waltz meter, 3/4, would have to have been the sonic equivalents of the conjunctions, the more conventional connectors (and beats the librettist needed to add lest he ruin mainstream prosodic expectations). "With vertical chordal movement reduced to a minimum," writes Ekkehard Jost on Coltrane's modal jazz, "there was room for freedom in a horizontal direction."[113] This, nearly the very definition of modal playing, led to several fundamental qualities of free jazz, but it also connects to the nonhierarchy of parataxis in writing. In Coltrane's cover the "associative creativity" I noted earlier of the musical's original—a creativity that is structured around the non-cause-and-effect catalogue of words-things connections (or now, sounds-things connections)—renders denotation still more open. The song still points to things-in-themselves in the world, *thematically*, of course ("favorite *things*" as *dingen an sich!*), but also does so formally. Indeed, the song remains devoted to referentiality. Coltrane's "beyond," his Kleinian leap into the void, still refers back to Hammersteinian life faced squarely. "Kinetic cumulation," even if interrupting "calm melody,"[114] need not be impersonal. Baraka, later recalling Coltrane's playing circa 1959–61, saw him as "leaping away from 'the given,'" but it was "life" even so ("the new blast of life that Coltrane carried"), utterly humane. For if Miles Davis's playing was "perfection," Coltrane—Baraka cited a poem about Coltrane's art by Amus Mor—"would come in 'wrong.'"[115] Coltrane's elaborations of 1960 furthered the work of releasing each—sound and thing—from logical or emotional dependence on another. Its multiphonics reach back to the multiphonemics of its libretto source. Meta DuEwa Jones reads Coltrane's "My Favorite Things" as a "stellar model" of that phonic/phonemic relationship and sees it as a "technique reveal[ing] features of jazz poetry of this period," into the 1960s and subsequently, through the post-soul Coltrane poem to the "moment's notice" of Nathaniel Mackey's epic ("long song") writing of the twenty-first century in which a wandering people, always "com[ing] in 'wrong,'" displaced and exilic yet worldly and humane, "knew *something*" yet remained "scared being scared," which is tantamount to "know- / ing's omen, moment's gnosis."[116]

"My Favorite Things" has a clearly defined A section and B section. The A parts present the happy things in the verses. The B part functions as a kind of chorus but sounds like a bridge. Jazz scholar and Coltrane biographer Lewis Porter describes the B part as "the first mention of negative experiences." (The bee stings, the dog bites.) The song's point, Porter notes—not only Coltrane's album *My Favorite Things* per se, but the song's overall situation in *The Sound of Music* too—is "perfectly sensible, [a] valuable message": "the good things help us to overcome the bad."[117] Coltrane's rearrangement plays the A section *eleven* times. No sad B to be heard. The B section is suppressed and then we realize has been deferred until the very end, a coda of a few bad things, at which point it feels as if he has (and we also have) earned the "simpl[e] remember[ing]." Notwithstanding so much else that has been altered, structurally this postponement of the B section constitutes the biggest change. The A parts limit harmonic activity and rely instead on modal explorations of a single chord or simple alternating chord pattern, lasting anywhere from nine to thirty-one seconds. Then the extended solos by Coltrane and Tyner, digressive and at moments dissonant but never contradictory, extend time vastly and yet are also restrained (especially in the initial studio recording). Even the longest solos in the recording of 1960— one is 148 measures compared with thirty-two at that point in the pop song— never venture very far melodically from the original. This extended duration (and surely it is listeners' strongest first impression of the song) seems to work out the generous—and, in connection with the astonishing synchronicity of the new band, aesthetically communitarian—*turn* toward the "lyrical" and "understood" sound Coltrane said he sought to make in 1960, toward what theorists of testimony call "the alignment between witnesses" as the very definition of art:[118] in other words, his not wanting "to go so far out that I can't see what *others* are doing." The song for Syeeda, his own child, had recently suggested for him this "search" for "those things" that are new and yet somehow "reminiscent." "Reminiscent" is a fascinating word choice, probably referring to the way early memories come back. Porter observes that the deferring of the sad B section is as serious as any other Coltrane composition, but "it's just that it uses examples *that a child would understand*, because in the [*Sound of Music*] script, the song is addressed to children."[119] Syeeda's sweet lyric is Coltrane's first adaptation of the new kidsical. And what children do understand, through trauma too often, is the stinging and biting of life faced head-on. The creative tension sought by Rodgers and Hammerstein in *including* as unsubordinated equivalences contrasting protective, resistant, familial adult tolerance *and* fascist thunderous hatred outside the domestic space, which motivates the final "simply remember" of the B part, gets worked out by Coltrane's unironic adaptation. This happens not through permitting the B part to intrude regularly as per Hammerstein's lyric language but by commensurate musical means: piano and bass together creating "simplified modal structure" and thus "a feeling of organized stasis" on one hand, exactly while, on the other, the active drums and soprano sax together create an opposite effect, which is the sense of chance occurrence—improvisation's intended nonintentional "moment's notice"[120]—following from the idea of exploration Coltrane kept mentioning in his statements of 1960.[121]

Qualities unoriginal, variational, and improvisational converge. Coltrane's version of scalar exercise might be conventionally deemed vertical but is horizontal in effect, equating rather than hierarchizing—the scale being the thing that provides the melodic tools one needs to make all tones. Rodgers perhaps knew little if anything about scalar structures being then tried as part of the jazz "new thing," but the point nonetheless of his and Hammerstein's "Do Re Mi" was musically to show Maria taking a first step toward a progressive countersocialization of the children. Young Brigitta pushes back against the very idea of the scalar exercise, complaining, "Is that what you call a song?" Maria's almost Oulipian metaresponse is this: "No. Do re mi fa so and so on are only the tools we use to build a song. Once we have these notes in our heads we can sing a million different tunes."[122] When Coltrane told his Swedish radio interviewer that his new urgent "searching" meant paradoxically "find[ing] things that are reminiscent, that sound like those things," he was speculating about something very much like Lord's contention in *The Singer of Tales* that in the long improvisatory tradition of orality "the idea of an original is illogical." This is what Hammerstein meant by the *sound* of music. Maria, feeling at home climbing the "next hill," sings out: "I know I will hear / What I've heard before."

Ingrid Monson, the Harvard ethnomusicologist, has argued that Coltrane's relationship with *The Sound of Music* is essentially critical. The song is a parody and "inverts the piece on every level."[123] In a 2010 radio documentary she is interviewed, and clarifies: the appropriation of show tunes by the jazz avant-garde does indeed produce a form of parody, yet it's "not necessarily funny, but thoughtful, self-conscious."[124] Porter has suggested that Monson "makes the mistake of assuming that Coltrane wanted to dress this song up because he must have thought this tune was silly. Quite the opposite, he took the song seriously, and saw things in it that the composer had not." Porter quotes Coltrane on unoriginality thus: "I would have loved to have written it, but it's by Rodgers and Hammerstein."[125] "My Favorite Things" became "my favorite piece of all those I have recorded,"[126] Coltrane said elsewhere. He had recently recorded Rodgers and Hart's song "Manhattan" (1958), and the *My Favorite Things* album includes other standards, such as the Gershwin-DuBose Heyward "Summertime." For the title song he respectfully retained the original key center of E even though, transposed for the soprano sax, it became a much harder key to play in. "The waltz," he told French critic François Postif, "is fantastic: when you play it slowly, it has an element of gospel that's not at all displeasing; when you play it quickly, it possesses undeniable qualities. It's very interesting to discover a terrain that renews itself according to the impulse you give it."[127] Coltrane emphatically insisted that he saw this renewal as an expression of hope—unlikely hope for an unlikely time, but hope nonetheless. The song plugger's sheet music would of course have included Hammerstein's words. Monson refers to "the emphasis on white things in the lyric" (girls in white dresses, silver white winters, etc.) and decides that Coltrane redid the song in order to "look . . . upon the lyrics with an ironic eye."[128] On the other hand, in speaking of the song's "valuable message" (that good overcomes bad), Lewis Porter implies that Coltrane fully considered the lyrics and melody in context. Whether that context included any sense of the Austrian situation—Coltrane's quartet would visit Graz in 1962 and performed an elaborately triumphant twenty-three-minute version of "My Favorite Things" as a second-set finale (greeted by ecstatic applause)—it's a fact that while Austrians lived under Nazi control for seven years, playing jazz was dangerous and could only be done in secret. Shortly after the liberation of Vienna "the jazz musicians crawled out of their basements, and . . . there was a surprising renaissance of the jazz scene,"[129] as observed by Oscar Peterson and others who visited Vienna and Graz and played with surviving Austrian musicians. Jazz had been part of the sensibility of an antifascist minority, suppressed as "degenerate art" and then reborn as a liberatory nod to U.S. (and particularly of course to Black) culture.[130] "My Favorite Things" might be heard, at least in Graz two years after its initial adaptation, as an affirmative nod of solidarity in return.

Coltrane in 1960 was adamant about "searching" for hope in "those things." Yet contemporaries persistently assumed otherwise. Why? Ben Ratliff has found "no evidence anywhere that Coltrane ever *tried* to be provocative," and demonstrates in great detail that he "wasn't interested in the shocking-diversion aspect of modernity."[131] Coltrane did hear something urgent in *The Sound of Music* as a sourcework in 1960, but why was the assumption promulgated that this response was ipso facto angry and nihilistic? Partly it is owing to the aesthetic radicalism of experimental jazz, its expectation or reputation as such, as compared with the reputational limits of his song's source—allegedly the "*only* radicalism" of Hammerstein's work, which was the thematic and historical (*rather than formal and literary*) encounter, albeit sentimentalized, with the century's immense history of systematic, ideological racist hatred. Just as with the assumption, as I argued in this book's opening pages, that James Baldwin on October 22 was not really intending to be the "blind optimist" in the conclusion of his "Notes for a Hypothetical Novel"—despite his outright saying it—so the critical cliché that

Coltrane was an "angry young tenor" seems essentially itself both racist and anti-modernist in context. John Tynan, who mostly admired *My Favorite Things*, wrote that "Slashing the canvas of his own creation, Coltrane erupted in a fantastic onrush of surrealism and disconnected musical thought" and is "best appreciated within the dark corridors of his personal psyche" and by our understanding of "neurotic compulsion."[132] Soon Tynan was tirading against "nihilistic exercises" and, with André Previn and others, the lack of "sequential development."[133] This idea alleging performative, avant-garde destructivism (to use Raphael Montañez Ortiz's then-new term), "slashing the canvas" as a dark, nihilistic act with a pathological origin, its expression thus putatively confessional, should put us in mind of Zero-affiliated painter Lucio Fontana whose slashed canvases in his "Spatial Concept" series were misread as anger and postwar depression. In fact Fontana and other Zeroists, as we have seen, saw such art as a rejection of the very negativity that assumed theirs, and delighted (through a productive "ambivalence" about artform and genre)[134] in blurring the distinction between the expected two-dimensionality of the medium and the three-dimensionality of some other artform being mysteriously activated beyond.[135] Coltrane aspired to just such delight. One critic asked him about the review written by another arguing that as an "angry young tenor" he backs himself into rhythmic corners on flurries of notes. Coltrane responded by saying that he just *seems* angry because he's "trying so many things at one time."[136] An interviewer asked point-blank: "Do you feel angry?" "No I don't . . . Um, I was talking to a fella today and I told him that the reason I play so many, so many—it sounds, maybe it sounds angry because I'm—I'm trying so many things at one time, you see, like I . . . I haven't sorted them out."[137] In a draft of "Coltrane on Coltrane," he wrote: "When I first heard the phrase ['angry young tenor'], I didn't know what the writers were talking about. My playing isn't angry."[138] If this book opened by pairing Baldwin's counterintuitive optimism about the prospect of a complete renaming and Celan's absurd hope for a linguistic mysticism that constantly calls itself into question, now we conclude with, on one hand, Coltrane's sincere insistence on the concurrence of modal or "spatial" playing (to use Fontana's term) and, on the other, a few favorite things he believed had the power to make us not "feel so bad." That is a compelling speculative convergence. Perhaps it is a main reason why Coltrane's song of 1960 continues to be so alluring as a model for innovating with existing structures. And then there was this additional bit of concurrence: Celan and Baldwin each presented on the evening of October 22, 1960, in Darmstadt and San Francisco, respectively, while Coltrane and his new quartet recorded "My Favorite Things" for the first time in an Atlantic

Records studio in New York the night before, October 21. I have been arguing that in 1960, through a deferred retrospective on an unresolved history of massive destruction activated by racist ideologies, many artists made the turn back toward life, however disjunctively and dissonantly; perhaps October after all was the pivotal month in that pivotal year. Michael Bruce McDonald summarizes the then-misunderstood idea of positive aspiration in Coltrane's art, which only stood against "*a facile, too easily won* hopefulness, a hopefulness that fails to acknowledge the ineluctability of dissonance in all that is audible."[139] Ultimately, though, Coltrane sought to express, as others we've encountered also did just then, an "abiding belief in the special restorative power that [art] can possess, the power to revitalize even a seemingly moribund culture."[140] "In a nation that buries the past from its children," Jerome Rothenberg offered as the year had begun, "the pain of their song is a triumph."[141] After burial so deep, that triumph had taken its sweet time.

# Notes

## Preface

1. Jerome Rothenberg, ed., *New Young German Poets* (San Francisco: City Lights, 1959), [3].
2. Hans Severus Ziegler, in a speech in February 1937 promoting an exhibition of degenerate music and theater that would parallel the "Degenerate Art" exhibit featuring the work of despised modernist painters and sculptors. Quoted by Michael H. Kater, *Culture in Nazi Germany* (New Haven, CT: Yale University Press, 2019), 48.

## 1. An Introduction to the Survivor

1. Robert Gutwillig, "Dim Views Through Fog," *New York Times*, November 13, 1960, 68–69.
2. Roth published his talk as "Writing American Fiction," *Commentary*, March 1961, 223–33. Quoted and cited here: 226, 227, 233, emphasis added.
3. Baldwin, "Notes for a Hypothetical Novel," in *Nobody Knows My Name* (New York: Dell, 1963), 154; first published by Dial Press in 1961.
4. Baldwin, 145, 154, emphases added.
5. Irving Howe, "On Harvey Swados," *Massachusetts Review* 24, no. 3 (Autumn 1983): 638.
6. He wrote extensively about the period. In the novel *Standing Fast*, Swados depicts in detail the inner life of anti-Stalinist left-wing groups during World War II.
7. Audio recording, "James Baldwin: October 22, 1960," San Francisco Poetry Center, Poetry Center Digital Archive: https://diva.sfsu.edu/collections/poetrycenter/bundles/223229; original emphasis indicated.
8. Baldwin, "Notes," 142.
9. Baldwin, 145.
10. Baldwin, 143, 147.
11. James Baldwin, "Letter from a Region in My Mind," in *The Fire Next Time* (New York: Vintage, 1962), 20.

12. Édouard Glissant, *Poetics of Relation*, trans. Betsy Wing (Ann Arbor: University of Michigan Press, 1997), 189.

13. James Baldwin, "Fifth Avenue, Uptown," in *Nobody Knows My Name*, 58.

14. David Leeming, *James Baldwin, a Biography* (New York: Knopf, 1994), 21, 18.

15. Leeming, 26.

16. Hilton Als, "The Enemy Within: The Making and Unmaking of James Baldwin," *New Yorker*, February 9, 1998, 74.

17. Alan M. Wald, *American Night: The Literary Left in the Era of Cold War* (Chapel Hill: University of North Carolina Press, 2012), 132.

18. Stan Weir, "Meetings with James Baldwin," *Against the Current* 18 (January-February 1989): 35–41. Weir's recollection was that Baldwin's main objection to the Workers Party was its attitude toward homosexuality, not its position on European fascism.

19. *The Congressional Record, Proceedings and Debates of the 82nd Congress*, Second Session, 98, 8 (January 8, 1952-March 5, 1952), A-1241. See also Wald, *American Night*, 176.

20. Baldwin, "The Harlem Ghetto," *Commentary*, February 1948, 170.

21. Hilton Als, "The Enemy Within," 74.

22. Julius Lester, "James Baldwin—Reflections of a Maverick," in *Conversations with James Baldwin*, ed. Fred L. Standley and Louis H. Pratt (Jackson: University Press of Mississippi, 1989), 228.

23. Baldwin, "Notes," 146.

24. Baldwin, "Letter from a Region," 36.

25. Baldwin, "The Harlem Ghetto," 169.

26. Herb Boyd, *Baldwin's Harlem: A Biography of James Baldwin* (New York: Astria, 2008), 106.

27. Baldwin, "Letter from a Region," 37.

28. Dori Laub, "Bearing Witness or the Vicissitudes of Listening," in *Testimony: Crises of Witnessing and Literature, Psychoanalysis, and History*, ed. Shoshana Felman and Dori Laub (New York: Routlege, 1992), 67–68.

29. It should be noted that much later Baldwin identified Cheever as one of the white writers of his generation who could be called a "witness" (high praise for Baldwin). "Somehow these lost suburbanites in Cheever's work are very moving. He engages your passion. His people are not remote." Lester, "James Baldwin—Reflections of a Maverick," 228. See also Adrienne Brown, "We Wear the White Mask: John Cheever Writes Race," *Modern Fiction Studies* 64, no. 1 (Spring 2018): 52–54.

30. Baldwin, "Letter from a Region," 37.

31. Baldwin, 53. Baldwin's assessment of distinctions between Jewish whiteness and Christian whiteness shifted over time (see "The Harlem Ghetto" of 1948, already cited, and "Negroes Are Anti-Semitic Because They're Anti-White," *New York Times Book Review*, April 9, 1967, 26–27, 135–40), but his view that African Americans in the United States were not surprised by the holocaust did not seem to change.

32. William L. Shirer, *The Rise and Fall of the Third Reich* (New York: Simon and Schuster, 1960), 966. Shirer is quoting from notes taken at the Wannsee Conference, January 20, 1942, from Nuremberg Trial documents.

33. Baldwin, "Letter from a Region," 52.

34. Baldwin, "Notes," 145.

35. Baldwin, 151.

36. Paul Celan, "The Meridian," in *Collected Prose*, trans. Rosemarie Waldrop (New York: Routledge, 2003), 44.

37. This is a paraphrase of a point Marjorie Perloff makes about Celan in "Sound Scraps, Vision Scraps: Paul Celan's Poetic Practice," in *Radical Poetics and Secular Jewish Culture*, ed. Stephen Paul Miller and Daniel Morris (Tuscaloosa: University of Alabama Press, 2010), 291.

38. James Baldwin, "Why I Stopped Hating Shakespeare," in *The Cross of Redemption: Uncollected Writings* (New York: Pantheon, 2011), 67.

39. Chinua Achebe, *Morning Yet on Creation Day* (Garden City, NY: Anchor/Doubleday, 1975), 103.

40. Paul Celan, *Von Schwelle zu Schwelle: Vorstufen—Textgenese—Endfassung* (Frankfurt: Suhrkamp, 2002), 117. Jerome Rothenberg, ed., *New Young German Poets* (San Francisco: City Lights, 1959), 18.

41. Allen Ginsberg, *Das Geheul und andere Gedichte*, trans. Wolfgang Fleischmann and Rudolf Wittkopf (Wiesbaden: Limes, 1959). See Gregory Divers, *The Image and Influence of America in German Poetry Since 1945* (Rochester: Camden House, 2002), 45.

42. Later, in the preface to *Revolution of the Word* (1974), Rothenberg referred to the lamentably "submerged" status of Crosby among those who should be given credit for the "re-explor[ation] of the idea of an avant-garde" starting in the mid-1950s—especially among those who helped the new avant-gardists connect to "the European and Latin-American avant-gardes that were at the heart" of what Rothenberg and his colleagues in the late 1950s and early 1960s were attempting to achieve. Crosby, thus, was on Rothenberg's list of crucial progenitors of the new "Counter-Poetics" (preface to *Revolution of the Word*, reprinted in *Pre-Faces and Other Writings* [New York: New Directions, 1981], 103).

43. Rothenberg, *New Young German Poets*, 41.

44. Rothenberg, *White Sun Black Sun* (New York: Hawk's Well Press, 1960), 17.

45. Jerome Rothenberg, "Khurbn," in *Triptych* (New York: New Directions, 2007), 153. "Practice your scream": "Dos Geshray (The Scream)," 161, emphases added.

46. Letter from Jerome Rothenberg to Robert Duncan, September 27, 1960; published in *Eye of Witness: A Jerome Rothenberg Reader*, ed. Heriberto Yépez (Boston: Black Widow, 2013), 56.

47. The anthology took a few years of gathering materials (1957–59)—with many selected poems dated 1952, 1955, 1957, etc.—and of course some months in production. Much of the correspondence between Allen and poets took place in 1957 and 1958. See Alan Golding, "'The New American Poetry' Revisited, Again," *Contemporary Literature* 39, 2 (Summer 1998): 180–211.

48. Dori Laub, "An Event Without a Witness: Truth, Testimony, and Survival," in Felman and Laub, *Testimony*, 79–80.

49. Jerome Rothenberg, *New Selected Poems, 1970–1985* (New York: New Directions, 1986), 70.

50. Jerome Rothenberg, preface to *A Big Jewish Book* (1978), reprinted in *Pre-Faces*, 119.

51. Jerome Rothenberg, preface to *Revolution of the Word* (1974), in *Pre-Faces*, 106.

52. Rothenberg, *Pre-Faces*, 105.

53. Jerome Rothenberg, "The Holy Words of Tristan Tzara," in *New Selected Poems, 1970–1985*, 95.

54. Jerome Rothenberg, "Khurbn and Holocaust: Poetry After Auschwitz," *Dialectical Anthropology* 24, nos. 3 and 4 (December 1999), special issue "Poetry and Ethics After the Holocaust," 281.

55. Jerome Rothenberg, "Dialogue on Oral Poetry," in *Pre-Faces*, 16.

56. Jerome Rothenberg, interview with the author, February 26, 2015. Austin Warren, *Continuity: The Last Essays of Austin Warren*, ed. George A. Panichas (Macon, GA: Mercer

University Press, 1996), quoted in Robert Drake, "Continuity, Coherence, Completion," *Mississippi Quarterly* 49, no. 4 (1996): 851.

57. Rothenberg, interview with the author, February 26, 2015.

58. René Wellek and Austin Warren, *Theory of Literature* (New York: Harcourt, Brace, 1949), 139–272. In most editions section 4 is entitled "The Intrinsic Study of Literature," including sections titled "Euphony, Rhythm, and Meter," "Image, Metaphor, Symbol, Myth," etc. "The 'intrinsic' approach," e.g., William Troy, "Limits of the Intrinsic," *Hudson Review* 2, no. 4 (Winter 1950): 620.

59. Jerome Rothenberg, preface to *Revolution of the Word* (1974), in *Pre-Faces*, 100, 103.

60. Rothenberg, interview with the author, February 26, 2015.

61. Rothenberg, interview with the author, February 26, 2015.

62. On the deliberate slowness of reconstruction in the French zone: Galia Press-Barnathan, "The 'Classic' Case: France and Germany from War to Union," in *The Political Economy of Transitions to Peace* (Pittsburgh: University of Pittsburgh Press, 2009), 134, 136, 153; F. Roy Willis, *France, Germany, and the New Europe, 1945–1967*, rev. ed. (Stanford, CA: Stanford University Press, 1968), 37, 46; Alistair Cole, *Franco-German Relations* (Essex, UK: Pearson Education, 2001), 5.

63. Erich Kästner, "Autobiography and Other Poems," trans. Jerome Dennis Rothenberg, *Hudson Review* 10, no. 4 (Winter 1957–58): 558.

64. Paul Celan, "Death Fugue," trans. Clement Greenberg, *Commentary* 19, no. 3 (March 1, 1955), 243. Michael Bullock also translated "Death Fugue" in the 1950s (John Felstiner, *Poet, Survivor, Jew* [New Haven, CT: Yale University Press, 1995], 32).

65. Rothenberg, interview with the author, February 26, 2015.

66. Rothenberg, "Introduction," in *New Young German Poets*, [3].

67. Rothenberg, interview with the author, February 26, 2015.

68. Rothenberg, interview with the author, February 26, 2015.

69. Jerome Rothenberg and Al Filreis, "Rothenberg Non-Adorno: Writing After Auschwitz," transcription prepared by Michael Nardone of a public interview held at the Kelly Writers House, Philadelphia, April 29, 2008; published in *Jacket2*, April 7, 2010: https://jacket2.org/node/187.

70. Sample of coverage of the German "economic miracle" in U.S. newspapers in 1960: "Germany and Economic Growth," *New York Times*, February 20, 1960, 22; Ernest S. Pisko, "West German Vigor," *Christian Science Monitor*, July 20, 1960, 9; "Economic Boom Spreads in West Germany," *Christian Science Monitor*, December 1, 1960, 6; Seymour Freidin, "The Tab" (a column about West German businessmen's expense account shenanigans), *New York Times*, April 7, 1960, 30. A poll of West German citizens taken in March showed that just 20 percent "Questions the 'Economic Miracle,'" *New York Times*, April 3, 1960, 21.

71. Numerous historians of criticism and theory have narrated the New Critical drive to "resolve tension." See, e.g., Steven Lynn, "A Passage Into Critical Theory," *College English* 52, no. 3 (March 1990): 258–71; David C. Greetham, *Textual Scholarship: An Introduction* (New York: Garland, 1994), 339–42; and Greetham, *Conversations: Contemporary Critical Theory and the Teaching of Literature*, ed. Charles Moran and Elizabeth F. Penfield (Urbana, IL: National Council of Teachers of English, 1990), 101–3.

72. Henry Cord Meyer, *Five Images of Germany: Half a Century of American Views on German History* (Washington DC: Service Center for Teachers of History, 1960), 49–53; quoted by Gavriel D. Rosenfeld in "The Reception of William L. Shirer's *The Rise and Fall of the Third Reich* in the United States and West Germany, 1960–62," *Journal of Contemporary History* 29, no. 1 (January 1994): 111.

73. Letter from Hannah Arendt to Gertrude Jaspers, January 3, 1960; in *Hannah Arendt Karl Jaspers Correspondence, 1926–1969*, ed. Lotte Kohler and Hans Saner, trans. Robert and Rita Kimber (New York: Harcourt Brace Jovanovich, 1992), 384–85.

74. George Steiner, "The Hollow Miracle: Notes on the German Language," *Reporter*, February 18, 1960, 36.

75. Celan, "Corona," 19; emphasis added. See Celan, *Selected Poems and Prose of Paul Celan*, 28–29.

76. Rothenberg, *New Young German Poets*, 18.

77. Ingeborg Bachmann, *War Diary*, ed. Han Höller, trans. Mike Mitchell (London: Seagull, 2018), 17.

78. Here Bachmann might have been expressing sympathy for Paul Celan specifically over the traumatic loss of his mother, a moment that haunts many of Celan's poems. In an early poem, in which is yet another agonized association of nature's ongoing cycle with the mother's disruptedness, Celan observes the seemingly white leaves of an aspen tree in the dark, only to remind himself that "My mother's hair never turned white." Paul Celan, *Selected Poems and Prose*, ed. and trans. John Felstiner (New York: Norton, 2001), 21.

79. Rothenberg, *New Young German Poets*, 42–45, emphasis added.

80. Rothenberg, [3].

81. Paul Celan, *The Meridian: Final Version—Drafts—Materials*, ed. Bernhard Böschenstein and Heino Schmull, trans. Pierre Joris (Stanford, CA: Stanford University Press, 2011), 172.

82. Steiner, "The Hollow Miracle," 36.

83. Steiner, 37.

84. Steiner, 37.

85. Maya Jaggi, "George and His Dragons," *Guardian* (London), March 17, 2001, 6–9.

86. George Steiner, "On Difficulty," in *On Difficulty, and Other Essays* (London: Oxford University Press, 1978), 18–47.

87. George Steiner, *Language and Silence: Essays on Language, Literature, and the Inhuman* (New York: Atheneum, 1977), a book in which some passages are devoted to *The Warsaw Diary of Chaim Kaplan*.

88. George Steiner, "A Remark on Language and Psychoanalysis," in *On Difficulty, and Other Essays*, 48–60; "covert meanings:" 51.

89. Steiner, "On Difficulty," 18.

90. Steiner, 34–35.

91. Steiner, "The Hollow Miracle," 37–38.

92. Robert Jay Lifton, *The Nazi Doctors: Medical Killing and the Psychology of Genocide* (New York: Basic, 1986), 172–74; and chapter 15, "The Experimental Impulse," 269–302.

93. W. H. Auden, "Thinking What We Are Doing," *Encounter* 12, no. 6 (June 1959): 76.

94. Hannah Arendt, "Social Science: Techniques and the Study of Concentration Camps," 1950; republished in *Essays in Understanding, 1930–54*, ed. Jerome Kohn (New York: Harcourt, Brace, 1994), 235. See Mary G. Dietz, "Arendt and the Holocaust," in *The Cambridge Companion to Hannah Arendt*, ed. Dana Villa (Cambridge: Cambridge University Press, 2000), 86–88.

95. Letter from Hannah Arendt to Karl Jaspers, December 23, 1960; in Kohler and Saner *Hannah Arendt Karl Jaspers Correspondence, 1926–1969*, 417.

96. Jackson Pollock, *Possibilities* 1, no. 1 (Winter 1947–48): 79.

97. Celan, *The Meridian: Final Version*, 145, 144.

98. Enrico Castellani, "Continuity and Newness," originally published in *Azimuth* 2 (January 1960), unpaginated; translated and republished in *Zero: Countdown to Tomorrow*,

*1950s–60s* (New York: Guggenheim Museum, 2014), 222. When asked in an interview in 1960 about the influence of American abstract expressionists, Henk Peeters, leader of the Nul group, said: "It's undeniable that Jackson Pollock and Rothko, De Kooning and Tobey have influenced us greatly, but the sizes of their works are like those of their cars, which you can never park." (Jean-Jacques Lévêque published the interview in the French art magazine *Sens Plastique*; Henk Peeters Archive, www.henkpeetersarchive.info/by-jean-jacques-leacuteveque.html).

99.   Joan Retallack, *The Poethical Wager* (Berkeley: University of California Press, 2004).
100.  Maurice Blanchot, *The Writing of the Disaster*, trans. Ann Smock (Lincoln: University of Nebraska Press, 1986), 58.
101.  Celan, *The Meridian: Final Version*, 105.
102.  Celan, 107.
103.  Celan, 137.
104.  Celan, *Collected Prose*, trans. Waldrop, 44, emphasis added.
105.  Celan, *Selected Poems*, trans. Felstiner, 24–25.
106.  Blake Bailey, *Cheever: A Life* (New York: Knopf, 2009), 283.
107.  Bailey, 284.
108.  Baldwin, "Notes," 143.

## 2. Pain-Laden Rhymes

1.   Pierre Joris, introduction to Paul Celan, *Breathturn Into Timestead: The Collected Later Poetry, a Bilingual Edition*, trans. Pierre Joris (New York: Farrar Straus Giroux, 2014), l.
2.   Paul Celan, *Selected Poems and Prose of Paul Celan*, ed. and trans. John Felstiner (New York: Norton, 2001), xx.
3.   Pierre Joris, introduction to Paul Celan, *Memory Rose Into Threshold Speech: The Collected Earlier Poetry*, trans. Pierre Joris (New York: Farrar, Straus and Giroux, 2020), xvi. Marjorie Perloff has written about the particular Austrian inflections of Celan's German in *Edge of Irony: Modernism in the Shadow of the Hapsburg Empire* (Chicago: University of Chicago Press, 2016), 129–36. One can also argue that Romanian was his first language, or, as per Dirk Weissman, that he possessed multiple "(M)other Tongue(s)." See Weissman, "Paul Celan's (M)other Tongue(s): On the (Self-)Portrayal of the Artist as a Monolingual Poet," in *(M)Other Tongues: Literary Reflexions on a Difficult Distinction*, ed. Juliane Prade (Newcastle, UK: Cambridge Scholars, 2013), 143–52.
4.   Paul Celan, *The Meridian: Final Version—Drafts—Materials*, ed. Bernhard Böschenstein and Heino Schmull, trans. Pierre Joris (Stanford, CA: Stanford University Press, 2011), 173.
5.   Celan, *Selected Poems and Prose*, trans. Felstiner, 8–9.
6.   André Schwarz-Bart, *The Last of the Just* (New York: Atheneum, 1960), 374.
7.   Celan, *Selected Poems and Prose*, trans. Felstiner, 8–9.
8.   Celan, 10–11.
9.   Celan, *Collected Prose*, trans. Rosemarie Waldrop (New York: Routledge, 2003), 48, emphasis added.
10.  Celan, *Wolfsbohne Paul Celan Wolf's Bean*, trans. Michael Hamburger (New York: Delos, 1997), n.p.
11.  Celan, *Paul Celan: Selections*, ed. and trans. Pierre Joris (Berkeley: University of California Press, 2005), 75.
12.  John Felstiner, *Poet, Survivor, Jew* (New Haven: Yale University Press, 1995), 171.

13. Celan, *Wolfsbohne*, trans. Hamburger, n.p.

14. Quoted in Eric Kligerman, *Sites of the Uncanny: Paul Celan, Specularity and the Visual Arts* (Berlin: Walter de Gruyter, 2007), 124. "Die Sprache, mit der ich meine Gedichte mache, hat in nichts etwas mit der zu tun, die hier oder anderswo gesprochen wird," English translation by Kligerman.

15. Interview with Jacques Derrida conducted by Evelyne Grossman, *Europe 861–62* (January–February 2001): 90–91; excerpted in Celan, *Celan: Selections*, ed. Joris, 203.

16. Günter Blöcker, review of *Sprachgitter* in *Der Tagesspiegel* (Berlin), October 11, 1959; enclosed with letter from Paul Celan to Ingeborg Bachmann, October 17, 1959, in *Correspondence: Ingeborg Bachmann and Paul Celan*, ed. Bertrand Badiou, Hans Höller, Andrea Stoll, and Barbara Wiedemann, trans. Wieland Hoban (London: Seagull/Goethe-Institut, 2010), 191–92.

17. Michael Hamburger's translation of "Wolfsbohne" into English was belatedly published in the *Times Literary Supplement*, May 16, 1997: www.the-tls.co.uk/tls/reviews/literature_and_poetry/article710387.ece. Some of the contextual information here comes from Hamburger's editorial comment. An informational translator's note serves as preface to *Wolfsbohne*, trans. Michael Hamburger.

18. George Steiner, "On Difficulty," in *On Difficulty, and Other Essays* (London: Oxford University Press, 1978), 33.

19. Celan, *Wolfsbohne*, trans. Hamburger, n.p., [4], [10].

20. Celan, *Selected Poems and Prose*, trans. Felstiner, 107.

21. "We are lost": *Wolfsbohne*, trans. Hamburger, [4]. "This world": Celan, *Selected Poems and Prose*, trans. Felstiner, 15.

22. Blöcker also wrote: "Celan has greater freedom vis-à-vis the German language than most of his poet colleagues. That may owe to his origins." John Felstiner convincingly suggests that Celan took the phrase "his origins" as indicative of anti-Semitism (Felstiner, *Paul Celan: Poet, Survivor, Jew*, 148).

23. Badiou, Höller, Stoll, and Wiedemann, *Correspondence: Bachmann Celan*, 193.

24. Badiou, Höller, Stoll, and Wiedemann, 195–96.

25. Badiou, Höller, Stoll, and Wiedemann, 207–8, 218n, 244, 221. The letters do not mention his having mailed it to her. And it remained an unpublished typescript, presumably in the process of revision. We can only presume that he showed it to her during one of their meetings.

26. Badiou, Höller, Stoll, and Wiedemann, *Correspondence: Bachmann and Celan*, 241–44, 246n, emphasis added.

27. Roth, "Writing American Fiction," *Commentary*, March 1961, 227.

28. Paul O'Neill, "The Only Rebellion Around: But the Shabby Beats Bungle the Job in Arguing, Sulking and Bad Poetry," *Life*, November 30, 1959, 115–16, 119–20, 123–26, 129–30.

29. Brion Gysin and William S. Burroughs, "Open Letter to Life Magazine," in *Minutes to Go* (San Francisco: Two Cities, 1960), 11–12.

30. Three poems by Holmes appeared in the March 1960 issue of *Poetry* and a review essay appeared in the May issue. Two of Holmes's poems had also been published by Rago in July 1957.

31. R. P. Blackmur, "Theodore Holmes: Dactyls and All," in *Outsider at the Heart of Things: Essays*, ed. James T. Jones (Urbana: University of Illinois Press, 1989), 262. Original publication: "Theodore Holmes: Dactyls and All," *Princeton University Library Chronicle* 25 (1963): 44–50. It was also published in *Seven Princeton Poets*, ed. Sherman Hawkinds (Princeton: Princeton University Library, 1963), 44–50.

32. Theodore Holmes, "Bertolt Brecht and Others," *Poetry*, October 1960, 55, emphasis added.
33. Jerome Rothenberg, ed., *New Young German Poets* (San Francisco: City Lights, 1959), [3].
34. Interview with Jacques Derrida by Evelyne Grossman, excerpted in *Paul Celan: Selections*, ed. Joris, 204.
35. Rothenberg, *New York German Poets*, 14.
36. Badiou, Holler, Stoll, and Wiedemann, *Correspondence: Bachmann and Celan*, 208n.
37. Bachmann, *The Thirtieth Year*, trans. Michael Bullock (New York: Holmes and Meier, 1987), 61.
38. Kristen Krick-Aigner, *Ingeborg Bachmann's Telling Stories: Fairy Tale Beginnings and Holocaust Endings* (Riverside, CA: Ariadne, 2002), 11.
39. Krick-Aigner, 9, 8.
40. Bachmann, *The Thirtieth Year*, 63.
41. Bachmann, 10, 59.
42. Ingeborg Bachmann, *War Diary*, ed. Hans Höller, trans. Mike Mitchell (London: Seagull, 2018), 7–9.
43. Bachmann, *The Thirtieth Year*, 3–5, 6, 8–9.
44. Bachmann, *War Diary*, 6–7.
45. Bachmann, *The Thirtieth Year*, 63.
46. Bachmann, 61–62.
47. Quoted by Krick-Aigner, *Bachmann's Telling Stories*, 9.
48. There is some small mystery about the exact date of this lecture, the third in the series. It was scheduled for December 9, 1959, but might have been postponed and presented some weeks later. I am grateful to Professor Daniel Dornhofer of the Institut für England- & Amerikastudien (IEAS) at Geothe-Universität Frankfurt in Frankfurt am Main.
49. Ingeborg Bachmann, "Das schreibende Ich," in *Werke*, volume 4, ed. Christine Koschel, Inge von Weidenbaum, and Clemens Münster (Munich: Piper, 1993), 237. Translation by Selena Dyer.
50. Bachmann, 234, 237.
51. Bachmann, 218, 233, 219–20.
52. Krick-Aigner, *Bachmann's Telling Stories*, 36.
53. Bachmann, "Das schreibende Ich," 217, emphasis added.
54. Gordon Craig, "Shirer's Vivid, Monumental Chronicle of Nazi Germany," *New York Herald Tribune Book Review*, October 16, 1960, 1.
55. "[L]ucidity, reliability, and compelling" are terms used by Gavriel D. Rosenfeld in his close analysis of responses to Shirer's book, in "The Reception of William L. Shirer's *The Rise and Fall of the Third Reich* in the United States and West Germany, 1960–62," *Journal of Contemporary History* 29, no. 1 (January 1994): 106.
56. "Shirer Crowns His Career with Superb History," *Chicago Sunday Tribune Magazine of Books*, October 16, 1960, 1.
57. See Christopher Browning, "German Memory, Judicial Interrogation, and Historical Reconstruction: Writing Perpetrator History from Postwar Testimony," in *Probing the Limits of Representation: Nazism and the "Final Solution,"* ed. Saul Friedlander (Cambridge: Harvard University Press, 1992), 22–36.
58. Bachmann, "Das schreibende Ich," 219–20, 217, emphasis added.
59. Gordon Craig, "Shirer's Vivid, Monumental Chronicle of Nazi Germany," 1.
60. William Birmingham, "Through Our Fault, Through Our Fault . . . ," *Cross Currents*, Winter 1961, 88, emphasis added.

61. H. R. Trevor-Roper, "Light on Our Century's Darkest Night: The Awful Story of Hitler's Germany Is Movingly Told in a Masterly Study," *New York Times Book Review*, October 16, 1960, 1, emphasis added.

62. William L. Shirer, *The Rise and Fall of the Third Reich: A History of Nazi Germany* (New York: Simon and Schuster, 1960), 90.

63. Quoted in Jessie Hohmann and Daniel Joyce, *International Law's Objects* (New York: Oxford University Press, 2018), 209.

64. Shirer, *Rise and Fall of the Third Reich*, dust jacket of first edition hardcover.

65. Stephan Landsman, "The Eichmann Case and the Invention of the Witness-Driven Atrocity Trial," *Columbia Journal of Transnational Law* 51, no. 1 (2012): 69.

66. Frantz Fanon, "The Meeting Between Society and Psychiatry," in *Alienation and Freedom*, ed. Jean Khalfa and Robert J. C. Young, trans. Steven Corcoran (London: Bloomsbury Academic, 2018), 526.

67. Albert Camus, *Resistance, Rebellion, and Death*, trans. Justin O'Brien (New York: Knopf, 1960), 6.

68. Letter from Hannah Arendt to Gertrud Jaspers, January 3, 1960, in *Hannah Arendt Karl Jaspers Correspondence, 1926–1969*, ed. Lotte Kohler and Hans Saner, trans. Robert and Rita Kimber (New York: Harcourt Brace Jovanovich, 1992), 384.

69. These phrases are used in *Truth and Reconciliation Commission of South Africa Report*, volume 3, chapter 6, October 28, 1998, 531–537, www.justice.gov.za/trc/report/finalreport/Volume%203.pdf.

70. "Fifty Killed in South Africa As Police Fire on Rioters," *New York Times*, March 22, 1960, 1.

71. "What They Commend in Mississippi," *Chicago Tribune*, April 15, 1960, 14.

72. Barbie Zelizer, *About to Die: How News Images Move the Public* (New York: Oxford University Press, 2010), 182–85.

73. Paul Ginsborg, *A History of Contemporary Italy: Society and Politics, 1943–1988* (Harmondsworth, UK: Penguin, 1990), 254–58.

74. See *New York Times* articles as follows: January 3, 1960, 4; January 5, 1960, 2; January 7, 1960, 2; December 28, 1959, 2; December 31, 1959, 1; May 5, 1960, 5. Rosenfeld ("Reception of Shirer's *Rise and Fall*," 104) provides an overview.

75. Rosenfeld, "Reception of Shirer's *Rise and Fall*," 119, 128n89.

76. See *New York Times* articles as follows: January 8, 1960, 3; April 8, 1960, 12; May 5, 1960, 5. On Oberländer, see Kater, *Culture in Nazi Germany*, 310.

77. "Nazi Murders Studied," *New York Times*, May 21, 1960, 11.

78. Deathcamps.org/treblinka/perpetrators.html [item 341].

79. Chris Webb, *Sobibor Death Camp: History, Biographies, Remembrance* (Stuttgart: Ibidem-Verlag, 2017), 343.

80. "Germans Arrest Nazi Camp Chief," *New York Times*, December 21, 1960, 5.

81. It had been written in 1946 while Höss awaited trial. The German text was not published until 1958. See Joost A. M. Meerloo, "Memoirs of a Murderer," *New York Times Book Review*, March 13, 1960, 3.

82. Rosenfeld, "Reception of Shirer's *Rise and Fall*," 100.

83. Robert Jay Lifton, *The Nazi Doctors: Medical Killing and the Psychology of Genocide* (New York: Basic, 1986), 257.

84. "Books and Authors," *New York Times*, July 5, 1960, 29.

85. "In and Out of Books," *New York Times Book Review*, July 24, 1960, 8.

86. "In and Out of Books," *New York Times Book Review*, September 18, 1960.

87.  Lifton, *The Nazi Doctors*, 358.

88.  I am using Dominick LaCapra's definition of transference, drawn from the psychoana-
     lytic models of implicated therapeutic subject-position. A succinct definition can be found
     in *History and Memory After Auschwitz* (Ithaca, NY: Cornell University Press, 1998), 11–12.

89.  Marius Turda, "The Ambiguous Victim: Miklós Nyiszli's Narrative of Medical Experimen-
     tation in Auschwitz-Birkenau," *Historein* 14, no. 1 (2014): 43–58.

90.  Fanon uses the number of deaths reported by Radio Cairo. The French claimed that one
     thousand were killed. Historians have put the number variously at between six thousand
     and twenty thousand.

91.  Frantz Fanon, *The Wretched of the Earth*, trans. Richard Philcox (New York: Grove,
     2004), 38.

92.  Fanon, 37, 36.

93.  Paul Hoffmann, "[Ralph] Bunche says '60 Is Year of Africa,'" *New York Times*, February 16,
     1960, 15.

94.  Fanon, *The Wretched of the Earth*, 36.

95.  Cynthia Young, "Havana up in Harlem: LeRoi Jones, Harold Cruse and the Making of a
     Cultural Revolution," *Science and Society* 65, no. 1 (Spring 2001): 12.

96.  Fanon, *The Wretched of the Earth*, 37.

97.  William Taubman, *Khrushchev: The Man and His Era* (New York: Norton, 2003), 657n1.
     Bill Nichols, *Representing Reality: Issues and Concepts in Documentary* (Bloomington: Indi-
     ana University Press, 1991), 117. Taubman's subsequent research led him to conclude that
     the shoe-banging did occur. Yet the photograph is of a speech given on September 23, two
     weeks prior to the infamous moment of impoliteness to which Fanon refers.

98.  Quoted in Peter Hudis, *Frantz Fanon: Philosopher of the Barricades* (London: Pluto,
     2015), 18.

99.  David Macey, *Frantz Fanon: A Biography* (London: Verso, 2012), 86.

100. Quoted in Alice Cherki, *Frantz Fanon: A Portrait* (Paris: Seuil, 2000), 10.

101. Macey, *Frantz Fanon*, 93. Sheryl Silver Ochayon, "The Jews of Algeria, Morocco and Tuni-
     sia," Yad Vashem, www.yadvashem.org/articles/general/the-jews-of-algeria-morocco-and
     -tunisia.html#footnoteref5_6z204l2.

102. Aimé Césaire, *Discourse on Colonialism* (New York: Monthly Review Press, 2000), 36.

103. Fanon, "The Meeting Between Society and Psychiatry," 527.

104. Fanon, 526.

105. Fanon, *The Wretched of the Earth*, 51.

106. Lawrence Langer, *Holocaust Testimonies: The Ruins of Memory* (New Haven, CT: Yale Uni-
     versity Press, 1991), 67.

107. Terrence Des Pres, *The Survivor: An Anatomy of Life in the Death Camps* (New York: Oxford
     University Press, 1976), 41.

108. Fanon, "The Meeting Between Society and Psychiatry," 518, 524.

109. Sylvia Wynter, "Towards the Sociogenic Principle: Fanon, Identity, the Puzzle of Conscious
     Experience, and What It Is Like to Be Black," *National Identies and Socio-Political Changes
     in Latin America*, ed. Mercedes F. Durán-Cogan and Antonio Gómez-Moriana (New York:
     Routledge, 2001), 30–66.

110. Fanon, "The Meeting Between Society and Psychiatry," 519.

111. Fanon, *The Wretched of the Earth*, 181, 184.

112. Donald Allen, ed., *The New American Poetry, 1945–1960* (Berkeley: University of Califor-
     nia Press, 1960), 424.

113.   Kimberly W. Benston, "Amiri Baraka: An Interview," *boundary2* 6, no. 2 (1978): 106.

114.   Fred Moten, *The Universal Machine* (Durham, NC: Duke University Press, 2018), 186.

115.   Jones, "Cuba Libre," *Evergreen Review* 4, no. 15 (November-December 1960): 139–59.

116.   LeRoi Jones, *Home: Social Essays* (New York: William Morrow, 1966), 11–12, 26.

117.   Jones, 39, 62.

118.   Jones, 61, 62.

119.   Young, "Havana up in Harlem," 12–38.

120.   LeRoi Jones, *Black Music* (New York: W. Morrow, 1967), 70.

121.   Werner Sollors, *Amiri Baraka / LeRoi Jones: The Quest for a "Populist Modernism"* (New York: Columbia University Press, 1978), 65; Staughton Lynd, "Toward a History of the New Left," in *The New Left: A Collection of Essays*, ed. Priscilla Long (Boston: Extending Horizons, 1969), 6.

122.   Letter from "LeRoi" [Jones] to "Rubi" [Betancourt], undated [August 1960], Leroi Jones/Amiri Baraka Collection, Box 1, George Arents Research Library, Syracuse University.

123.   Baraka's FBI file has been obtained by and made available by the Washington University libraries: http://omeka.wustl.edu/omeka/exhibits/show/fbeyes/baraka.

124.   William Carlos Williams, *The Collected Poems*, vol. 1, *1909–1939*, ed. A. Walton Litz and Christopher MacGowan (New York: New Directions, 1986), 76.

125.   Amiri Baraka, *S O S, Poems 1961–2013*, ed. Paul Vangelisti (New York: Grove, 2014), 38.

126.   Benston, "An Interview," 109.

127.   Amiri Baraka, *The Autobiography of LeRoi Jones* (Chicago: Lawrence Hill, 1984), 246.

128.   Baraka, 247.

129.   "At the same time," Baraka writes in the *Autobiography* (246–47) following paragraphs about the Cuban experience and "Cuba Libre," "I had begun a long prose work." He then describes *The System of Dante's Hell*. Contextual clues in the *Autobiography*—such as the birth of his daughter Lisa (b. 1961) and a move to a new apartment—further date the composition. I am grateful to William J. Harris and Aldon Nielsen for their guidance on dating the composition of *System*. A typescript draft of the novel, titled "HELL," is in the Baraka collection at the Moorland-Spingarn Collection at Howard University. It is undated but notes inserted into the notebook containing the draft provide further contextual clues as to the time of the writing. A note published in *Floating Bear* in 1961 describes a stage production of one section of the novel. Aldon Nielsen, *Writing Between the Lines: Race and Intertextuality* (Athens: University of Georgia Press, 1994), 92. The "Sound and Image" coda to *System* refers to the whole work as "what vision I had of . . . association complexes . . . around 1960–61." Amiri Baraka, *The System of Dante's Hell* (Brooklyn, NY: Akashic, 1965), 158.

130.   Nielsen, *Writing Between the Lines*, 89.

131.   Baraka, *The System of Dante's Hell*, 90.

132.   Jones, *Home*, 26.

133.   Nielsen, *Writing Between the Lines*, 83.

134.   Mercedes Mackay, "No Longer at Ease," *African Affairs* 60, no. 241 (October 1961): 550.

135.   Chinua Achebe, *No Longer at Ease* (New York: Ivan Obolensky, 1960), 49, 36, 93.

136.   Achebe, 7, 92, 104, 106, 7, 106.

137.   In this sense *No Longer at Ease* anticipates Achebe's major critical intervention twenty-seven years later: Chinua Achebe, "An Image of Africa: Racism in Conrad's 'Heart of Darkness,'" *Massachusetts Review* 18 (1977); reprinted in *Heart of Darkness, an Authoritative Text*, ed. Robert Kimbrough (New York: Norton, 1988), 251–61.

138. Achebe, *No Longer at Ease*, 106.

139. Achebe, 151, 49.

140. Chinua Achebe, *Morning Yet on Creation Day* (Garden City, NY: Anchor/Doubleday, 1975), 103.

141. T. S. Eliot, *Collected Poems, 1909–1962* (London: Faber and Faber, 1999), 99.

142. See Bahmin Zarrinjooee, "Dissemination of English in Chinua Achebe's *No Longer at Ease*," *Advances in Language and Literary Studies* 7, no. 4 (August 2016): esp. 237.

143. Ben Mkapa, "No Longer at Ease," *Transition* 3 (January 1962): 36.

144. Achebe, *No Longer at Ease*, 8, 36.

145. Philip Rogers, "'No Longer at Ease': Chinua Achebe's 'Heart of Whiteness,'" *Research in African Literature* 14, no. 2 (Summer 1983): 165–83. Rogers quotes the novel: "Sometimes one kernel was shiny-black and alive, the other powdery-white and dead," and adds: "The two halves of the palm kernel perfectly represent the two halves of Obi's divided life" (176).

146. Allister E. Hinds, "Government Policy and the Nigerian Palm Oil Export Industry, 1939–49," *Journal of African History* 38, no. 3 (1997): 459–78.

147. Achebe, *No Longer at Ease*, 36–37. Chima J. Korieh, *Nigeria and World War II: Colonialism, Empire, and Global Conflict* (New York: Cambridge University Press, 2020); Judith Byfield, Carolyn Brown, Timothy Parsons, and Ahmad Alawad Sikainga, *Africa and World War II* (New York: Cambridge University Press, 2015).

148. See Robert M. Young, "Deadly Unconscious Logics in Joseph Heller's Catch-22," *Psychoanalytic Review* 84, no. 6 (1997): 891–903.

149. Joseph Heller, *Catch-22* (New York: Dell, 1961), 328.

150. Aileen Pippett, "Something Went Wrong," *New York Times Book Review*, February 14, 1960, 4.

151. Glen Sire, *The Death-Makers* (Greenwich, CT: Fawcett, 1960), 57.

152. William Golding, *Free Fall* (London: Faber and Faber, 1959), 147.

153. Bachmann, *The Thirtieth Year*, 50.

154. Dominick LaCapra, *Representing the Holocaust: History, Theory, Trauma* (Ithaca, NY: Cornell University Press, 1994), 72; and *History and Memory After Auschwitz*, 11–12.

155. Lifton, *The Nazi Doctors*, 257, 350–51, 358–64, 366, 367–70, 378, 458.

156. See Lifton, 358 (on Mengele's "academic ambitions") and 269–302 ("The Experimental Impulse"), and passim.

157. Baldwin, "Notes for a Hypothetical Novel," in *Nobody Knows My Name* (New York: Dell, 1963), 154; audio recording, "James Baldwin: October 22, 1960," San Francisco Poetry Center, Poetry Center Digital Archive: https://diva.sfsu.edu/collections/poetrycenter/bundles/223229.

158. Achebe, *Morning Yet on Creation Day*, 103.

159. Fanon, "The Meeting Between Society and Psychiatry," 527.

160. Nelly Sachs, "Chorus of the Rescued," in *O the Chimneys: Selected Poems* (New York: Farrar, Straus and Giroux, 1967), 25.

161. Ingeborg Bachmann, "Dialects—for Nelly Sachs," in *Darkness Spoken: Ingeborg Bachmann, Collected Poems*, trans. Peter Filkins (Brookline, MA: Zephyr, 2006), 331.

162. See Emma Garman, "Feminize Your Canon: Ingeborg Bachmann," *Paris Review*, July 9, 2019; Marjorie Perloff, *Edge of Irony: Modernism in the Shadow of the Hapsburg Empire* (Chicago: University of Chicago Press, 2016), 138–40, 141, 142, 146–49; Badiou, Holler, Stoll, and Wiedemann, *Correspondence: Ingeborg Bachmann and Paul Celan*, esp. 211, 241–46, 311–38.

163. Bachmann, *The Collected Poems*, 331.

164. LaCapra, *Representing the Holocaust*, 72.
165. Fanon, *The Wretched of the Earth*, 181.


3. Openings of the Field

1. Pablo Neruda, *I Explain a Few Things: Selected Poems*, ed. Ilan Stavans (New York: Farrar, Straus and Giroux, 2007), 31.
2. Lawrence Langer, *Holocaust Testimonies: The Ruins of Memory* (New Haven, CT: Yale University Press, 1991), 1–38.
3. Paul Celan, *Selected Poems and Prose of Paul Celan*, ed. and trans. John Felstiner (New York: Norton, 2001), 75.
4. Paul Celan, *Memory Rose Into Threshold Speech: The Collected Earlier Poetry*, trans. Pierre Joris (New York: Farrar, Straus and Giroux, 2020), 144–47.
5. Jerome Rothenberg, ed., *New Young German Poets* (San Francisco: City Lights, 1959), 23–24.
6. Paul Celan, *The Meridian: Final Version—Drafts—Materials*, ed. Bernhard Böschenstein and Heino Schmull, trans. Pierre Joris (Stanford, CA: Stanford University Press, 2011), 184.
7. On Bukovina as once the eastern edge of a "vast oriental empire" before it "entered the great Middle-European Empire," see Irina Livezeanu, *Cultural Politics in Greater Romania: Regionalism, Nation Building, and Ethnic Struggle, 1918–1930* (Ithaca, NY: Cornell University Press, 2018), 54.
8. Shira Wolosky, "Paul Celan's Linguistic Mysticism," *Studies in 20th Century Literature* 10, no. 2 (1986): 191–211.
9. *Google Books Ngram Viewer*, "No pasaran."
10. Celan, *Memory Rose Into Threshold Speech*, trans. Joris, 144–45.
11. This was essentially the day the Nationalists won and is generally seen as the moment when Europeans could imagine what happened next on September 1. On February 27, as Britain and France recognized Franco, in the House of Commons the Labor leader, Clement Atlee, accused Chamberlain of "a gross betrayal of democracy, the consummation of two and a half years of the hypocritical pretense of non-intervention and a connivance all the time at aggression" (quoted by Hugh Purcell, *The Spanish Civil War* [London: Wayland, 1973], 110). I have found only one bit of evidence in Celan to support this reading of the date, a somewhat cryptic reference in his notebooks of 1960 to himself as "a belated child of the old Austria" followed by these coded antifascist jottings: "Communism—Viennese February—Oh fly, we are the workers of Vienna . . . how rare reversal (*Umkehr*) is." Celan, *The Meridian: Final Version*, 185.
12. Celan, *The Meridian: Final Version*, 8, 162, 144, 126.
13. Celan, *Collected Prose*, trans. Rosemarie Waldrop (New York: Routledge, 2003), 46.
14. Rothenberg, "Seeing Leni Riefenstahl's Triumph of the Will, San Francisco, 1959," *White Sun Black Sun* (New York: Hawk's Well Press, 1960), 17.
15. Jerome Rothenberg, interview with the author, February 26, 2015.
16. Robert S. Coale offers an instance of this pattern in the French postwar context, in "French Collaboration on Display," *Volunteer* 32, no. 1 (March 2015): 14.
17. Lisa Jarnot, *Robert Duncan, the Ambassador from Venus: A Biography* (Berkeley: University of California Press, 2012), 149.
18. Rothenberg, interview with the author, February 26, 2015.

19. For an overview of Duncan's interest in Scholem and kabbalah, see Norman Finkelstein, *Like a Dark Rabbi: Modern Poetry and the Jewish Literary Imagination* (Cincinnati: Hebrew Union College Press, 2019), 242–47.

20. See Scholem's section summarizing kabbalistic ecstasy in *Kabbalah* (New York: Penguin, 1978), 180.

21. Jerome Rothenberg, email to the author, February 27, 2015.

22. He was describing his interest in Jewish mysticism for Herbert Weiner, whose books helped introduce Jewish mysticism to American Jews. Quoted in George Robinson, *Essential Judaism* (New York: Pocket, 2000), 400.

23. Scholem, *Jewish Gnosticism* (New York: Jewish Theological Seminary of America, 1960), 6, 5, emphasis added.

24. Letter from Robert Duncan to Henry Rago, February 27, 1959, Poetry magazine papers, Regenstein Library, University of Chicago.

25. This is a line in a draft poem Duncan mailed to friends. It was later published in Michael McClure and James Harmon's *Ark II/Moby I*. See Jarnot, *Robert Duncan, Ambassador from Venus*, 150.

26. Dan Featherston, "A Place of First Permission: Robert Duncan's Atlantis Dream," *Modernism/Modernity* 15, no. 4 (November 2008): 682.

27. Featherston, 683.

28. Rothenberg, *Eye of Witness: A Jerome Rothenberg Reader*, ed. Heriberto Yépez (Boston: Black Widow, 2013), 55–56.

29. John Felstiner, *Poet, Survivor, Jew* (New Haven, CT: Yale University Press, 1995), 163.

30. Celan, *Collected Prose*, trans. Waldrop, 46, 40.

31. Celan, *The Meridian: Final Version*, 126.

32. Celan, *Collected Prose*, trans. Waldrop, 44, 40, 43, 40.

33. Celan, *The Meridian: Final Version*, 178.

34. Celan, *Collected Prose*, trans. Waldrop, 40, 44, 45, 47.

35. Celan, *The Meridian: Final Version*, 167.

36. Celan, *The Meridian: Final Version*, 142.

37. Celan, *Collected Prose*, trans. Waldrop, 48–49.

38. Celan, *The Meridian: Final Version*, 104.

39. Celan, 202.

40. Celan, 62.

41. Celan passingly referred in "The Meridian" to Büchner's figure of Lenz "who 'on the 20th of January' was walking through the mountain."

42. Celan, *Collected Prose*, trans. Waldrop, 47, 53, ellipsis in the original.

43. Celan, *The Meridian: Final Version*, 32, 67, 32, 55, 58, 32.

44. Celan, *The Meridian: Final Version*, 113, 114, 60 (emphasis added), 64, 144, 145, 207.

45. Hannah Arendt, *Eichmann in Jerusalem: A Report on the Banality of Evil* (New York: Penguin, 1963), 145.

46. Hanna Yablonka, *The State of Israel vs. Adolf Eichmann*, trans. Ora Cummings and David Herman (New York: Schocken, 2004), 24; Sergio I. Minerbi, *The Eichmann Trial Diary* (New York: Enigma, 2011), 14, 22–23; Deborah E. Lipstadt, *The Eichmann Trial* (New York: Schocken, 2011), 136–37.

47. Celan, *Collected Prose*, trans. Waldrop, 37.

48. Celan, *The Meridian: Final Version*, 67.

49. Celan, *Collected Prose*, trans. Waldrop, 48.

50. Celan, *The Meridian: Final Version*, 119.

51. Richard Brody, "Witness," *New Yorker*, March 19, 2012, 82. "Fiction of the real" is Lanzmann's phrase. "Modernist," describing *Shoah*'s disjunctive mode, is Brody's word.

52. Celan, *The Meridian: Final Version*, 119.

53. Celan, 149, 103, 149, 117.

54. Celan, 144.

55. Terrence Des Pres, *The Survivor: An Anatomy of Life in the Death Camps* (New York: Oxford University Press, 1976), 37, emphasis added.

56. Marceline Loridan-Ivens, *But You Did Not Come Back: A Memoir*, trans. Judith Perrignon (New York: Grove, 2016), 2.

57. Michael Rothberg, *Multidirectional Memory: Remembering the Holocaust in the Age of Decolonization* (Stanford, CA: Stanford University Press, 2009).

58. Rothberg, *Multidirectional Memory*, 186.

59. Sam Di Iorio, "Truth and Consequences," *Chronicle of a Summer* (Criterion Collection, 2013), 8.

60. Loridan-Ivens, *But You Did Not Come Back*, 12, 48.

61. Langer, *Holocaust Testimonies*, 18–20.

62. Celan, *Collected Prose*, trans. Waldrop, 49.

63. Langer, *Holocaust Testimonies*, 77–120. See Henry Krystal, "Trauma and Affects," *Psychoanalytic Study of the Child* 33 (1978): 81–116. On "the evolution of testimony," see Annette Wieviorka, *The Era of the Witness*, trans. Jared Stark (Ithaca: Cornell University Press, 2006).

64. Langer, *Holocaust Testimonies*, 65.

65. Celan, *The Meridian: Final Version*, 156, 169, 57, 163.

66. Jean Bollack, *The Art of Reading: From Homer to Paul Celan*, trans. C. Porter, S. Tarrow, and B. King, ed. C. Koenig, L. Muellner, G. Nagy, and S. Pollock, Hellenic Studies Series 73 (Washington, DC: Center for Hellenic Studies, 2016), chap. 20, "Benjamin Reading Kafka," https://chs.harvard.edu/CHS/article/display/6641.20-benjamin-reading-kafka. This essay was originally published as "Benjamin devant Kafka," in *Walter Benjamin, le critique européen*, ed. H. Wismann and P. Lavelle (Lille: Presses universitaires du Septentrion, 2010), 213–77.

67. Celan, *The Meridian: Final Version*, 9, 62.

68. Philip Sidney, "The Defense of Poesy," in *English Essays: From Sir Philip Sidney to Maccaulay* (New York: P. F. Collier, 1937), 8.

## 4. Absurd Judgment

1. See Susannah Gottlieb, *Regions of Sorrow: Anxiety and Messianism in Hannah Arendt and W. H. Auden* (Stanford, CA: Stanford University Press, 2003).

2. W. H. Auden, "Thinking What We Are Doing," *Encounter* 12, no. 6 (June 1959): 72.

3. Hannah Arendt, *The Human Condition* (Garden City, NY: Doubleday, 1959), 178–79. Arendt is quoted by Auden in "Thinking What We Are Doing," 74.

4. Auden, "The Fallen City," *Encounter* 13, no. 5 (November 1959): 29.

5. Auden, 28, emphasis added.

6. W. H. Auden, *The Dyer's Hand, and Other Essays* (New York: Random House, 1962), 201.

7. Julia Reinhard Lupton, "Judging Forgiveness: Hannah Arendt, W. H. Auden, and *The Winter's Tale*," *New Literary History* 45, no. 4 (Autumn 2014): 654, 642.

8. Letter from Hannah Arendt to W. H. Auden, February 14, 1960: The Hannah Arendt Papers at the Library of Congress, Auden folder, Correspondence File series, "1938–1976."

9. It was said that Kafka was "now being rediscovered in Germany and eagerly discussed among the younger writers" in the period 1946–48—the observation was made in 1949—but also that this rediscovery had not yet extended to the United States. "The ghastly impact of his native scene upon the European writer has been incomparably more disturbing than the equivalent pressure upon the American whose society is essentially intact." Victor Lange, "Notes on the German Literary Scene 1946–48," *Modern Language Journal* 33, no. 1 (January 1949): 7–8.

10. Frederick A. Olafson, "Kafka and the Primacy of the Ethical," *Hudson Review* 13, no. 1 (Spring 1960): 61.

11. Olafson, 68.

12. Max Brod, *Franz Kafka: A Biography* (New York: Schocken, 1947), 186–87. First published in Prague, 1937.

13. Paul Celan, *The Meridian: Final Version—Drafts—Materials*, ed. Bernhard Böschenstein and Heino Schmull, trans. Pierre Joris (Stanford, CA: Stanford University Press, 2011), 169, 57.

14. Hannah Arendt, *Eichmann in Jerusalem: A Report on the Banality of Evil* (New York: Penguin, 1963), 276.

15. Elizabeth Young, *Hannah Arendt: For Love of the World* (New Haven, CT: Yale University Press, 2004), 328–30.

16. Hannah Arendt, letter to Vassar College, January 2, 1961, Library of Congress. Quoted in Young, *Hannah Arendt*, 329.

17. Jean-Paul Sartre, "Tribute to Albert Camus," trans. Justin O'Brien, *Reporter Magazine*, February 4, 1960, 173–75.

18. "Albert Camus," *New York Times*, January 5, 1960, 30.

19. Albert Camus, *The Plague*, trans. Stuart Gilbert (New York: Knopf, 1958), 308.

20. Camus, 37.

21. E.g., "Albert Camus, Famed Author, Dies in Crash," *Oakland Tribune*, January 4, 1960, 1; "Albert Camus," *Sarasota News*, January 13, 1960, 4; "Late French Existentialist Understood Life Problems," *Southern California Daily Trojan*, January 6, 1960, 1.

22. Anthony Thomas Arlotto, "Albert Camus: Bequest of a Questionmark [sic]," *Heights* (Boston), January 8, 1960, 5.

23. "Writing of Camus Was Influenced by Resistance and Existentialism," *New York Times*, January 5, 1960, 4.

24. William Faulkner, "Albert Camus," in *Essays, Speeches and Public Letters*, ed. James B. Meriwether (New York: Modern Library, 2004), 113; first published as "Hommage à Albert Camus," in *La Nouvelle Revue Française*.

25. Albert Camus, *The Myth of Sisyphus*, trans. Justin O'Brien (New York: Knopf, 1957), 119, 121, 129.

26. Camus, *The Plague*, 57, 55, 40.

27. Édouard Glissant, *Poetics of Relation*, trans. Betsy Wing (Ann Arbor: University of Michigan Press, 1997), 116, 113.

28. Dominick LaCapra, *Representing the Holocaust: History, Theory, Trauma* (Ithaca, NY: Cornell University Press, 1994), 73.

29. Heinz Politzer, "Franz Kafka and Albert Camus: Parables for Our Time," *Chicago Review* 14, no. 1 (Spring 1960): 57.

30. Murray Krieger, *The Tragic Vision: Variations on a Theme in Literary Interpretation* (New York: Holt, Rinehart and Winston, 1960), 116.

31. Krieger, 117.

32.  Suzanne Clark, *Cold Warriors: Manliness on Trial in the Rhetoric of the West* (Carbondale: Southern Illinois University Press, 2000), 71, 101.

33.  Krieger, *The Tragic Vision*, 116.

34.  Franz Kafka, *The Trial*, trans. Willa Muir and Edwin Muir (New York: Knopf/Everyman's Library, 1992), 7. Quoted by Krieger, *The Tragic Vision*, 118.

35.  Krieger, *The Tragic Vision*, 138–40.

36.  Wesley Morris, "Murray Krieger: A Departure Into Diachrony," in *Murray Krieger and Contemporary Critical Theory*, ed. Bruce Hendrickson (New York: Columbia University Press, 1986), 105.

37.  Morris, 104.

38.  Morris, 106, 105, 104, 105.

39.  Krieger, *The Tragic Vision*, 122.

40.  George Steiner, introduction to Kafka, *The Trial* (New York: Schocken, 1995).

41.  Hannah Arendt, *The Origins of Totalitarianism* (1951; New York: Harcourt, Brace and World, 1968), 246.

42.  See Veronika Tuckerova, *Reading Kafka in Prague: The Reception of Franz Kafka Between the East and the West During the Cold War* (PhD diss., Columbia University, 2012). A special exception was Günther Anders (Hannah Arendt's ex-husband) in *Kafka, Pro and Contra: The Trial Documents* (1951), but Anders argued that Kafka's presentation of a world in which guilt and punishment are disconnected permitted Germans to deflect collective guilt for Nazi mass murder. This was not an argument that went over well anywhere for various, quite different reasons, and Anders had little immediate influence. See Kata Gellen, "*Kafka, Pro and Contra*: Günther Anders's Holocaust Book," in *Kafka and the Universal* (Berlin: De Gruyter, 2016), 283–306. By the late 1960s, writers such as George Steiner and Theodor Adorno reasserted Kafka's role as holocaust prophet. In "Kafka as Holocaust Prophet: A Dissenting View" (1986), Lawrence Langer argued that Steiner and others embraced "dubious evidence" in order to liberate "an urgent but misdirected modern need to find in past art (if not past history) 'logical' precedents for the unprecedented illogic of the Holocaust" (Lawrence L. Langer, "Kafka as Holocaust Prophet: A Dissenting View," in *Admitting the Holocaust: Collected Essays* [New York: Oxford University Press, 1995], 113).

43.  Walter Benjamin, "Some Reflections on Kafka," in *Illuminations: Essays and Reflections*, ed. Hannah Arendt, trans. Harry Zohn (New York: Schocken, 1969), 159–60.

44.  Leslie Fiedler, "Kafka and the Myth of the Jew," in *No! in Thunder* (Boston: Beacon, 1960), 98–99.

45.  Peter Heller, "The Autonomy of Despair," *Massachusetts Review* 1, no. 2 (Winter 1960): 245–46.

46.  Nick Midgley, "Peter Heller's *A Child Analysis with Anna Freud*: The Significance of the Case for the History of Child Psychoanalysis," *Journal of the American Psychoanalytic Association* 60, no. 1 (1990): 45–70.

47.  Terrence Des Pres, *The Survivor: An Anatomy of Life in the Death Camps* (New York: Oxford University Press, 1976), 3–26.

48.  Des Pres, 41.

49.  Lawrence Langer has explored the necessary "search," on the part of a testimony's audience, "for the inner principles of incoherence that make these testimonies accessible to us." Lawrence Langer, *Holocaust Testimonies: The Ruins of Memory* (New Haven, CT: Yale University Press, 1991), 16–17. See also 20, 29, 84–85, 100–101, 117–19.

50.  Heller, "The Autonomy of Despair," 232.

51.  Celan, *The Meridian: Final Version*, 105.

52.  Heller, "The Autonomy of Despair," 244.

53.  Leslie Fiedler, "Kafka and the Myth of the Jew," in *No! in Thunder: Essays on Myth and Literature* (Boston: Beacon, 1960), 98–99.

54.  Fiedler, 100.

55.  Fiedler, 98–100.

56.  Celan, *The Meridian: Final Version-Drafts*, 112, 197.

57.  Parker Tyler, *The Three Faces of the Film: The Art, the Dream, the Cult* (New York: Thomas Yoseloff, 1960), 94.

58.  Quoted in Marjorie Perloff, "The Granite Butterfly: A Poem in Nine Cantos," *William Carlos Williams Review* 22, no. 1 (Spring 1996): 103.

59.  See Alan Wald, *The American Night* (Chapel Hill: University of North Carolina Press, 2012), 127.

60.  Tyler, *The Three Faces of the Film*, 101, 95, 101.

61.  Hannah Arendt, "The Jew as Pariah: A Hidden Tradition," *Jewish Social Studies* 6, no. 2 (April 1944): 99–122, esp. 101.

62.  Tyler, *The Three Faces of the Film*, 100.

63.  See Liliane Weissberg, "Hannah Arendt, Charlie Chaplin, and the Hidden Jewish Tradition," *Jewish Studies at the Central European University* 6 (2007–09), ed. Adrás Kovács and Michael L. Miller (Budapest: Central European University, 2011), 89.

64.  "Charlie Chaplin: The Jewish Chimp in America," *Der Stürmer* 18 (May 1940): 3, translated and reprinted in *The Third Reich Sourcebook*, ed. Anson Rabinbach and Sander L. Gilman (Berkeley: University of California Press, 2013), 594.

65.  Tyler, *The Three Faces of the Film*, 97.

66.  Tyler, 94.

67.  Tyler, 97.

68.  Quoted by Andreas Wutz in "The Realism in Surrealism: On the Filmic Work of Peter Weiss," published in German in *Texte Zur Kunst* 87 (2012): 176–81. English translation by Wutz:   www.academia.edu/4761887/THE_REALISM_IN_SURREALISM_-_On_the_filmic_work_of_Peter_Weiss_-_by_Andreas_Wutz_2012. The quoted phrase appears in the English translation on 2. The source in Weiss: "Peter Weiss, Swedish Original," in *Biografbladet* 3 (1947); German translation by Jan Christer Bengtsson: "Peter Weiss über Film und Filmemachen," in *Peter Weiss und der Film*, exhibit catalogue, Nordische Filmtage Lübeck, 1986. English translation by Wutz.

69.  Thomas McEvilley, "Yves Klein: Messenger of the Age of Space," *Artforum* 20, no. 5 (January 1982): 41.

70.  Arendt, *The Origins of Totalitarianism*, 245–46.

71.  Celan, *The Meridian: Final Version—Drafts—Materials*, 207.

72.  McEvilley, *Yves the Provocateur: Yves Klein and Twentieth-Century Art* (Kingston, NY: McPherson, 2010), 151.

## 5. Oppose the Anti-Everything

1.  Thomas McEvilley, *Sculpture in the Age of Doubt* (New York: Allworth, 1999), 230.

2.  James Webb, *The Flight from Reason: The Age of the Irrational* (London: Macdonald, 1971), republished as *The Occult Underground* (La Salle, IL: Open Court, 1974), 7. See Marco Pasi, "The

Modernity of Occultism: Reflections on Some Crucial Aspects," in *Hermes in the Academy: Ten Years' Study of Western Esotericism at the University of Amsterdam*, ed. Wouter J. Hangraaf and Joyce Pijnenburg (Amsterdam: Amsterdam University Press, 2009), 62.

3. Thomas McEvilley, "Yves Klein: Messenger of the Age of Space," *Artforum* 20, no. 5 (January 1982): 41.

4. McEvilley, 48. Pierre Restany, *Yves Klein, Fire at the Heart of the Void*, trans. Andrea Loselle (New York: Journal of Contemporary Art Editions, 1992), 45.

5. Restany, *Yves Klein*, 45.

6. McEvilley, "Messenger from the Age of Space," 44.

7. Valerie Hillings, ed., *Zero: Countdown to Tomorrow, 1950s–60s* (New York: Guggenheim Museum, 2014), 142.

8. Reproduced in Hillings, 147.

9. Emails from Mattijs Visser to the author, March 2–4, 2020. Visser is a curator of art exhibitions, scholar of Henk Peeters's work, and Peeters's nephew.

10. Henk Peeters, *Henk Peeters On: Art, Life and Piero Manzoni* (Beetsterzwaag: Kunstruimte Wagemans, 2014), 7.

11. Clement Greenberg, "Avant-Garde and Kitsch," in *The Collected Essays and Criticism*, ed. John O'Brian (Chicago: University of Chicago Press, 1986), 1:9. Greenberg's essay was quoted by McEvilley in connection with the work of Yves Klein. McEvilley, *Yves the Provocateur: Yves Klein and Twentieth-Century Art* (Kingston, NY: McPherson, 2010), 60.

12. Rod Serling, "Death's Head Revisited," written 1960, aired November 10, 1961. Quoted by Mark Boulton, "Sending the Extremists to the Cornfield: Rod Serling's Crusade Against Radical Conservatism," *Journal of Popular Culture* 47, no. 6 (2014): 1229. Serling's opening narration makes clear that Gunther Lutze, once an SS Captain, has returned to the ruins of a concentration camp where he supervised "torture" and "slaughter" "some seventeen years ago," which puts the time setting of the episode at the present and the crimes at 1943–44. The person cast for the part of Lutze also played the Nazi-allied Austrian Gauleiter in *The Sound of Music*. Serling stipulated that the main cast was to have had personal connections to the holocaust. See Marc Scott Zicree, *The Twilight Zone Companion*, 2nd ed. (West Hollywood, CA: Sillman-James Press, 1982); and Bill DeVoe, *Trivia from The Twilight Zone* (Albany, GA: Bear Manor Media, 2008).

13. Quoted in McEvilley, *Yves the Provocateur*, 163.

14. Charles Darwent, "German Artist Who Was a Founder of Zero, One of the Most Influential Movements in Modern Art" (obituary), *Guardian*, July 24, 2014, www.theguardian.com /artanddesign/2014/jul/24/otto-piene. I am grateful to Samantha Kirk, University Archives/ Weitzman School of Design, for her assistance.

15. Valerie Hillings, "Countdown to a New Beginning: The Multinational Zero Network, 1950s–60s," in Hillings, *Zero: Countdown to Tomorrow*, 28.

16. Otto Piene, "Ways to Paradise," trans. Rory Spry, *Zero* 3 (July 1961): n.p., reprinted as "Paths to Paradise," in *Zero*, ed. Otto Piene and Heinz Mack, trans. Howard Beckman (Cambridge, MA: MIT Press, 1973), 149.

17. Dirk Pörschmann, "Where No Man Has Gone Before: Utopia Zero," in Hillings, *Zero: Countdown to Tomorrow*, 62.

18. "Static, static, static! Be static! Be static! Movement is static! Movement is static! Movement is static because it is the only immutable thing—the only certainty, the only unchangeable. The only certainty is that movement is static" (quoted in Guy Brett, *Force Fields: Phases of the Kinetic* [Barcelona Spain: Hayward Gallery, Museu d'Art Contemporani, 2000], 250).

19. Jean Tinguely, "Für Statik," trans. Pamela Lee, in *Chronophobia: On Time in the Arts of the 1960s* (Cambridge, MA: MIT Press, 2004), 106; originally published in 1959. Valerie Hillings, "Countdown to a New Beginning," 20.

20. *Art/Invest*, Manzoni biography, www.artinvest2000.com/manzoni_english.htm.

21. Germano Celant, *Manzoni* (New York: Gagosian Gallery, 2009), 195. See Pörschmann, "Where No Man Has Gone Before," 64.

22. McEvilley, *Yves the Provocateur*, 153.

23. McEvilley, 86.

24. Piene, "Paths to Paradise," 149.

25. See John Gooch, *Airpower: Theory and Practice* (Abingdon, Oxfordshire: Routledge, 2013), 15, 1st edition published in 1995; Philip S. Meilinger, *The Paths of Heaven: The Evolution of Airpower Theory* (New York: Lancer, 2000), 250; Alex Kershaw, *The Few: The American Knights of the Air Who Risked Everything to Save Britain in the Summer of 1940* (Boston: De Capo, 2007), 105 (Kershaw is describing the airspace over the English channel).

26. Francesco Lo Savio, untitled statement, Piene and Mack, *Zero*, 224, trans. Stephen Sartarelli; originally published in *Monochrome Malerei*, ed. Udo Kultermann, Leverkusen Wester Germany, 1960, unpaginated.

27. Hillings, "Countdown to a New Beginning," 17.

28. Lawrence Alloway, "Viva Zero," in Piene and Mack, *Zero*, ix.

29. Hillings, "Countdown to a New Beginning," 17.

30. Pörschmann, "Where No Man Has Gone Before," 66.

31. Piene, "Paths to Paradise," 148.

32. Pörschmann, "Where No Man Has Gone Before," 66, 67n38.

33. Ernst Bloch, *The Principle of Hope*, trans. Neville Plaice, Stephen Plaice, and Paul Knight (Cambridge, MA: MIT Press, 1986), 1:5–6.

34. Vincent Geoghegan, *Ernst Bloch* (New York: Routledge, 1996), 32.

35. One of Bloch's chapters is titled "Discovery of the Not-Yet-Conscious or of Forward Dawning," in *The Principle of Hope*, 1:114. See Richard H. Roberts, *Hope and Its Hieroglyph* (Atlanta: Scholars, 1990), 75.

36. Otto Piene, "Wo sich nichts spiegelte als der Himmel," in *Zero in der Dusseldorfer Szene: Piene, Uecker, Mack*, ed. Helga Meister (Dusseldorf, 2006), 23, trans. Dirk Pörschmann; quoted in Pörschmann, "Where No Man Has Gone Before," 67n41.

37. Anna Neumann, "Ways Without Words: Learning from Silence and Story in Post-Holocaust Lives," in *Learning from Our Lives: Women, Research, and Autobiography in Education*, ed. Anna Neumann and P. L. Peterson (New York: Columbia Teachers' College Press, 1997), 111, 110.

38. Otto Piene, "The Development of the Group 'Zero,'" *Times Literary Supplement*, September 3, 1964, 812–13.

39. Peeters, *Art, Life and Manzoni*, 10.

40. Cees de Boer, *Herman de Vries: overal stroomt mijn oog* (Uitgeverij De Kunst/Waanders: Zwolle 2014), 89–90.

41. Neumann, "Ways Without Words," 93.

42. Paul Celan, *The Meridian: Final Version—Drafts—Materials*, ed. Bernhard Böschenstein and Heino Schmull, trans. Pierre Joris (Stanford, CA: Stanford University Press, 2011), 113.

43. Terrence Des Pres, *The Survivor: An Anatomy of Life in the Death Camps* (New York: Oxford University Press, 1976), 40–41.

44. Celan, *The Meridian: Final Version*, 161.

45. Letter from Mack and Piene to Hans Sonnenberg, July 27, 1959, quoted by Hillings, "Countdown to a New Beginning," 24, 42n65.

46. Bernard Aubertin, "Sketch of the Pictorial Situation of Red in a Spatial Concept," *Zero #3* (1961), republished in Piene and Mack, *Zero*, 231.

47. Quoted by Hillings, "Countdown to a New Beginning," 25.

48. Johan Pas, "'White Is Superabundance': Zero Writing and Publications Strategies," in Hillings, *Zero: Countdown to Tomorrow*, 57.

49. Quoted in Pörschmann, "Where No Man Has Gone Before," 64.

50. Heinz Mack, "The Sahara Project," in Piene and Mack, *Zero*, 180–84.

51. Untitled text for poster and leaflet, trans. Edouard Derom, Hillings, *Zero: Countdown to Tomorrow*, 228.

52. See Alan Filreis, *Modernism from Right to Left: Wallace Stevens, the Thirties and Literary Radicalism* (Cambridge: Cambridge University Press, 1994), 106–7, 171, 205, 259.

53. Unpublished transcription of a compilation of five interviews with Sari Dienes, made available by Barbara Pollitt and the Sari Dienes Foundation. This statement is recorded at 20:53 into the forty-one-minute audio compilation.

54. Unpublished untitled poem by Sari Dienes, dated (in the typescript) December 6, 1944, Sari Dienes Foundation.

55. Some of the footage can be viewed in clips posted to YouTube by Stephen Conford, Giselle Zatonyl, and others.

56. J. W. Klüver, "The Garden Party," in Piene and Mack, *Zero*, 120.

57. Quoted in an unpublished interview conducted by Calvin Tomkins for an article for *The New Yorker* in 1962. Available at the "RUDY/GODINEZ" site: http://rudygodinez.tumblr .com/post/74978105271/jean-tinguely-homage-to-new-york-1960.

58. "A Homage to a Homage, Destruction at Its Core," *New York Times*, April 10, 2011, AR26.

59. Unpublished notes by Calvin Tomkins. The unpublished interview was conducted by Calvin Tomkins for an article for *The New Yorker* (courtesy Calvin Tomkins Papers, II.A.5. The Museum of Modern Art Archives, New York). See Michael Landy, "Homage to Destruction," for the Tate Modern, 2009 (www.tate.org.uk/tate-etc/issue-17-autumn-2009/homage -destruction).

60. *Mediakunstnetz*, entry on *Homage to New York*, www.medienkunstnetz.de/works/homage -to-new-york/images/2/.

61. Klüver, "The Garden Party," 120.

62. Unpublished transcription of a compilation of five interviews with Sari Dienes, made available by Barbara Pollitt and the Sari Dienes Foundation. This statement is recorded at 2:18 into the forty-one-minute audio compilation. She is combining Cagean aesthetics with Picasso's modernist dictum: "I never look for anything, I'm just finding things" (2:44).

63. Celan, *The Meridian: Final Version*, 121, emphasis added.

64. Unpublished notes by Calvin Tomkins.

65. The formal title of the piece for the March 17 art happening was entitled "Destructive Construction No. 1" (Klüver, "Garden Party," 120).

66. Klüver, 124.

67. Quoted in *Lucio Fontana*, exhibition catalogue, Palazzo delle Esposizioni (Rome, 1998), 246.

68. Quoted from a statement made in 1962 in Luca Massimo Barbero, "Lucio Fontana: Venice / New York," *Lucio Fontana Venezia/New York* (New York: Guggenheim Foundation, 2006), 23.

69.  Notes and drafts are archived among the Raphael Ortiz Papers, Chicano Studies Research Center, UCLA.

70.  Raphael Ortiz, "Destructivism: A Manifesto," in *Raphael Montañez Ortiz: Years of the Warrior 1960—Years of the Psyche 1988* (New York: El Museo Del Carrio, 1988), 52. I have consulted typescript drafts in the Raphael Ortiz Papers, Chicano Studies Research Center, UCLA.

71.  Ortiz, "Destructivism: A Manifesto," 52.

72.  Rocio Aranda-Alvarado, "Unmaking: The Work of Raphael Montañez Ortiz," in *Unmaking: The Work of Raphael Montañez Ortiz* (Jersey City, NJ: Jersey City Museum, 2006), 5–14.

73.  Kristine Stiles, "Raphael Montañez Ortiz," in *Years of the Warrior 1960—Years of the Psyche 1988*, 8–15.

74.  "Raphael Montañez Ortiz," in *Arqueologías de destrucción, 1958–2014* (Haverford, PA: Cantor Fitzgerald Gallery at Haverford College, 2015); Stiles, "Raphael Ortiz," 10.

75.  Yves Klein, "The Monochrome Adventure," typescript in the Yves Klein archive, quoted in McEvilley, "Messenger from the Age of Space," 40.

76.  Bachmann, *The Thirtieth Year*, 8.

77.  Stuart Liebman, "Why Kluge?," *October* 46 (Autumn 1988): 11; the issue was titled "Alexander Kluge: Theoretical Writings, Stories and an Interview."

78.  Christopher Pavsek has written of Kluge that "he is . . . an important critical theorist, the most interesting heir to the Marxist tradition of Benjamin and Adorno," whose *The Public Sphere and Experience* (1972) is a "veritable bible for many leftist intellectuals of the '70s" ("The Stubborn Utopian: The Films of Alexander Kluge," *Cinema Scope* 32 [Fall 2007]: 24).

79.  Liebman, "Why Kluge?," 12. "Pedagogical institutions": Kluge's phrase in Philipp Ekardt, "Returns of the Archaic, Reserves for the Future: A Conversation with Alexander Kluge," *October* 138 (Fall 2011): 126.

80.  Christopher Pavsek, *The Utopia of Film: Cinema and Its Futures in Godard, Kluge, and Tahimik* (New York: Columbia University Press, 2013), 152.

81.  Pavsek, 154. Kluge published his first essay in 1964 (160).

82.  Philipp Ekardt, "Returns of the Archaic, Reserves for the Future: A Conversation with Alexander Kluge," *October* 138 (Fall 2011): 126.

83.  Pavsek, "The Stubborn Utopian," 23, 24.

84.  Screenshots from television tape of an event on July 5, 1961, reproduced in Hillings, *Zero: Countdown to Tomorrow*, 53.

## 6. Adjustment and Its Discontents

1.  Sari Dienes, interview with Robert Berlind, *Art Journal* 53, no. 1 (Spring 1994): 38.

2.  Jackson Mac Low, email message to the author, September 30, 1999.

3.  William Seitz, *The Art of Assemblage* (New York: MoMA/Doubleday, 1961), 79.

4.  The phrase is that of Jasper Johns, a close friend and supporter of Sari Dienes's assemblage style. Quoted in Edward M. Plunkett, "Send Letters, Postcards, Drawings, and Objects . . . ," *Art Journal* 36, no. 3 (Spring 1977): 234.

5.  Unpublished transcription of interviews with Sari Dienes, made available by Barbara Pollitt and the Sari Dienes Foundation. This comment appears at 30:30 into the video recording of the interviews.

6.  Jasper Johns, quoted in Robert Genter, *Late Modernism: Art, Culture, and Politics in Cold War America* (Philadelphia: University of Pennsylvania Press, 2010), 198.

7. On Dienes and Johns, see Edward M. Plunkett, "Send Letters, Postcards, Drawings, and Objects . . .," 234; and Kirk Varnedoe, ed., *Jasper Johns: A Retrospective* (New York: MOMA/ Abrams), 1996; unpublished transcription of filmed interview with Sari Dienes in 1993 titled *Garbage Art*, made available by Barbara Pollitt and the Sari Dienes Foundation, comments at 12:10 in the film.

8. Transcript of the film *Hats, Bottles, and Bones: A Portrait of Sari Dienes* (1977), by Martha Edelheit, made available by Barbara Pollitt and the Sari Dienes Foundation.

9. Kaira M. Cabañas, "Yves Klein's Performative Realism," *Grey Room* 31 (Spring 2008): 7–31. Seitz: press release for "The Art of Assemblage," September 29, 1961, Museum of Modern Art, typescript, 3. www.moma.org/documents/moma_press-release_326252 .pdf.

10. Jackson Mac Low, email to the author, September 30, 1999.

11. "30 ARRESTS MAR H-DRILL," "31 Pacifists Defying Drill Arrested in City Park," "31 Flouting Test Seized by Police," "Millions Take Cover Here as Sirens Wail," *New York World-Telegram* 122, no. 239 (June 15, 1955): 1.

12. Letter from Jackson Mac Low to Henry Rago, August 7, 1955, Poetry Magazine Papers 1954–61, box 22, folder 4, Regenstein Library, University of Chicago.

13. "I've been a serious pacifist most of my life, & since about '45, I've also identified myself as an anarchist." Quoted by Jerome Rothenberg in the preface to Jackson Mac Low, *Representative Works, 1938–1985* (New York: Roof, 1986), viii.

14. Jackson Mac Low, "The Poetics of Chance and the Politics of Simultaneous Spontaneity, or the Sacred Heart of Jesus," in *Talking Poetics from Naropa Institute*, vol. 2, ed. Anne Waldman and Marilyn Webb (Boulder: Shambala, 1978), 171–94. See also Rothenberg, preface to *Representative Works*, viii.

15. Letter from Jackson Mac Low to Henry Rago, August 1, 1961, Poetry Magazine Papers 1954–61, box 22, folder 4, Regenstein Library, University of Chicago.

16. Jackson Mac Low, email message to the author, September 30, 1999.

17. Rothenberg, preface to *Representative Works*, ix.

18. Jackson Mac Low, *Stanzas for Iris Lezak* (Barton: Something Else, 1971), 399.

19. "Text of Stevenson Speech at Dinner Here Condemning Nixon on World Affairs," *New York Times*, October 19, 1960, 30.

20. Mac Low, *Stanzas for Iris Lezak*, 359.

21. Mac Low, 259–60.

22. Dan Wakefield, "Good-by New York: New York Prepares for Annihilation," *Esquire*, August 1960, 79.

23. Wakefield, 80, 82.

24. Mac Low, *Stanzas for Iris Lezak*, 264, 265.

25. Quoted by Wakefield in "Good-By New York," 79.

26. Transcript of discussion at *PhillyTalks* #2, November 5, 1997, Kelly Writers House, curated by Louis Cabri and recorded and edited by Aaron Levy. Audio recordings and PDF of the transcript are here: www.writing.upenn.edu/pennsound/x/phillytalks/Philly-Talks-Episode02.php.

27. One of Forrestal's policy advisors during his time as secretary of defense, John H. Ohly, was connected with RAND. Townsend Hoopes and Douglas Brinkley, *Driven Partner: The Life and Times of James Forrestal* (New York: Knopf, 1992), 359.

28. *PhillyTalks* #2 transcript.

29. Hoopes and Brinkley, *Driven Partner*, 3.

30. *PhillyTalks* #2 transcript.

31. Louis Cabri, "'Rebus Effort Remove Government': Jackson Mac Low, *Why?/Resistance, Anarcho-Pacifism*," *Crayon* 1 (1997): 113.

32. Jackson Mac Low, *Doings* (New York: Granary, 2005), 30.

33. The performance on July 16, 1961, was described in a letter from Jackson Mac Low to Henry Rago, August 1, 1961, Poetry Magazine Papers 1954–61, box 22, folder 4 (Regenstein Library, University of Chicago).

34. Jackson Mac Low, "A Piece for Sari Dienes" (3:55, MP3), voices, percussion instruments: Jackson Mac Low and Anne Tardos, 1990. http://writing.upenn.edu/pennsound/x/Mac -Low-Doings.php. See Jackson Mac Low, *Doings: Assorted Performance Pieces, 1955–2002* (New York: Granary, 2005), 13, 30.

35. Edwin Black, *IBM and the Holocaust: The Strategic Alliance Between Nazi Germany and America's Most Powerful Corporation* (New York: Crown, 2001), 8.

36. Black, 8–9, 97, 98. "Only IBM could make and sell the unique punch cards for its machines. . . . IBM derived as much as a third of its profit from card sales. . . . Germany was completely dependent on IBM NY for its punch cards" (98).

37. Black, 7, 8–9, 12, 43, 47, 91, 97–98, 132, 134, and passim.

38. Mac Low, *Doings*, 30.

39. Joan Arbeiter, "Chance and Change in the Art of Sari Dienes," *Woman's Art Journal* 7, no. 2 (Autumn 1986-Winter 1987), 28. Martha Edelheit, email to the author, February 16, 2020. In an interview, Sari Dienes described her wartime exile: "I was planning on coming on a visit, and stay for two months. And everybody said, 'well war was going to break out, but war never breaks out in Europe before the spring. You can go to America and stay there for a couple months and come back.' But they were wrong! Because I came to America, and I arrived here the day war broke out between England and Germany, in 1939, 2nd of September. And I never went back. . . . I make a very good American citizen, all that background of being Irish and Polish, and Hungarian, and Swiss, and southern German, and a little Serbian blood." Unpublished transcription of a compilation of five interviews with Sari Dienes, made available by Barbara Pollitt and the Sari Dienes Foundation.

40. Enclosed with letter from Mac Low to Rago, August 7, 1955, Poetry Magazine Papers 1954–61, box 22, folder 4 (Regenstein Library, University of Chicago).

41. Letter from Rago to Mac Low, August 17, 1955, Poetry Magazine Papers, 1954–61, box 22, folder 4 (Regenstein, Chicago).

42. Letter from Mac Low to Rago, April 4, 1960, Poetry Magazine Papers 1954–61, box 22, folder 4. On *Poetry*'s design and font choices: www.poetryfoundation.org/article/244922.

43. Letter from Mac Low to Rago, August 1, 1961, Poetry Magazine Papers 1954–61, box 22, folder 4 (Regenstein Library, University of Chicago).

44. Judith Malina, "Remembering Jackson Mac Low," *PAJ: A Journal of Performance and Art* 27, no. 2 (May 2005): 76–78.

45. John Tytell, *The Living Theater: Art, Exile, and Outrage* (New York: Grove, 1995), 9.

46. John Fuegi, *Brecht and Company: Sex, Politics, and the Making of the Modern Drama* (New York: Grove, 2002), 115.

47. Claude Hill, *Bertolt Brecht* (Boston: Twayne, 1975), 49.

48. Tytell, *The Living Theater*, 167.

49. Germaine Bree, "'New' Poetry and Poets in France in the United States," *Wisconsin Studies in Contemporary Literature* 2, no. 2 (Spring-Summer 1961): 6, 7.

50. Alain Bosquet, introduction to *Trente-Cinq Jeunes Poètes Américains*, trans. Maxime McKenna (Paris: Gallimard, 1960), 12–13, 15–16, 9–10, 26, 22, 19.

51. Bree, "'New' Poetry and Poets," 7, 8, emphasis added.

52. While the Situationist International had formed in 1957, the poetic avant-garde elements of the group, promoting situationist tactics such as détournement, began to split off from the political theory side of the movement at the Fourth SI Conference in London in 1960. The break would become permanent in 1962.

53. Bosquet, *Trente-Cinq Jeunes Poètes Américains*, 176.

54. "Prize Poet," *Life*, May 19, 1947, 91–92.

55. Letter from Carroll to Creeley, February 22, 1960 (Creeley Papers, Stanford University Special Collections, Paul Carroll folders, folder 4 [letters from 1954–60]).

56. Letter from O'Hara to Ashbery, July 14, 1960, Houghton Library ms. AM6, Harvard University.

57. John Ashbery, *Collected Poems, 1956–1987* (New York: Library of America, 2008), 97, 99.

58. David L. Sweet, "Plastic Language: John Ashbery's 'Europe,'" *Word and Image* 18, no. 3 (2012): 154.

59. Letter from Frank O'Hara to John Ashbery, July 14, 1960, Houghton Library ms. AM6, Harvard University.

60. Sweet, "Plastic Language," 160, 159, 154.

61. Anna Balakian, *Surrealism: The Road to the Absolute* (Chicago: University of Chicago Press, 1959; third edition, 1986), 7, 49.

62. Daniel Bell, *The End of Ideology: On the Exhaustion of Political Ideas in the Fifties* (Glencoe, IL: Free Press, 1960), 57, 92, 197, 288.

63. Hillberg's book is a detailed history of the political, legal, and especially financial mechanisms whereby the holocaust was perpetrated. His research again and again demonstrated the radical efficiency of the industrial project of genocide, and even, at times, its economic intentionality. Hillberg, *The Destruction of the European Jews* (Chicago: Quadrangle, 1961).

64. Taylor Stoehr, *Here Now Next: Paul Goodman and the Origins of Gestalt Therapy* (San Francisco: Jossey-Bass, 1994), 250.

65. Goodman makes a number of references to articles published in 1959 and even 1960—which could only have been rushed in at press time—and like Bell in *The End of Ideology* clearly intends for readers to believe his description to be contemporary.

66. Casey Nelson Blake, jacket blurb for a new edition of *Growing Up Absurd*, published by New York Review of Books Classics, 2012, www.nybooks.com/books/imprints/classics/growing-up-absurd-1/.

67. Goodman, *Growing Up Absurd: Problems of Youth in the Organized Society* (New York: New York Review Books, 2012), 102–3; originally published by Random House in 1960.

68. Jaap van der Bent, "Beating Them to It?: The Vienna Group and the Beat Generation," in *The Transnational Beat Generation*, ed. Nancy M. Grace and Jennie Skerl (New York: Palgrave Macmillan, 2012), 177.

69. Goodman, *Growing Up Absurd*, 112–13.

70. The quoted phrase is an accurate summary of Lipton's praise of Kerouac and of Beat writing generally, although it belongs to Gene Baro in a review for *The Nation* that commended Lipton's book but was expressing doubts about Kerouac's capacity to "discover" through "mistakes." Gene Baro, "Beatniks Now and Then," *Nation*, September 5, 1959, 117.

71. Quoted in John Arthur Maynard, *Venice West: The Beat Generation in Southern California* (New Brunswick, NJ: Rutgers University Press), 199 100.

72. Casey Nelson Blake, foreword to Goodman, *Growing Up Absurd*, ix, x.

73. Lawrence Lipton, *The Holy Barbarians* (New York: Julian Messner, 1959), 265.

74. Goodman, *Growing Up Absurd*, 170–72, emphasis added.

75. "I'm obsessed by Time Magazine. / I read it every week. / . . . It occurs to me that I am America. / I am talking to myself again." Allen Ginsberg, "America," in *Collected Poems: 1947–1980* (New York: Harper and Row, 1984), 147.

76. *Beatitude Anthology* (San Francisco: City Lights, 1960), 7, 20, 28, 46, 37, 22.

77. Goodman, *Growing Up Absurd*, 172.

78. Email from Mac Low to the author, November 10, 1998. Mac Low frequently cited Goodman's ideas about anarchism as an influence. Goodman participated in sessions of the *Why?* (later *Resistance*) discussion groups (email from Jackson Mac Low to the POETICS listserv, now stored at the Electronic Poetry Center [EPC], University of Pennsylvania: http://writing.upenn.edu/epc/authors/maclow/pound.html). The Jackson Mac Low Papers (Special Collections and Archives, University of California at San Diego) include a folder of correspondence and another folder of Goodman programs and writings. Judith Malina's first encounter with Mac Low was when he performed as Marcus Aurelius in Goodman's play *Faustina* (Judith Malina, "Remembering Jackson Mac Low," *PAJ: A Journal of Performance and Art*, 27, no. 2 [May 2005]: 76–78).

79. Blake, foreword to Goodman, *Growing Up Absurd*, ix. "To call Goodman one of the great cultural conservatives of the twentieth century will strike many as preposterous."

80. Quoted in Kingsley Widmer, *Paul Goodman* (Boston: Twayne, 1980), 59.

81. Daniel Bell, quoted in Martin Gardner, *The Whys of a Philosophical Scrivener* (New York: William Morrow, 1983), 427.

82. Bell, *End of Ideology*, 305–8, 393.

83. Bell, 301, emphasis added.

84. Bell, 307. Bruno Bettelheim, "Behavior in Extreme Situations," *Politics*, August 1944, 199–209. This was an excerpt; the full essay, as "Individual and Mass Behavior in Extreme Situations," was published in the *Journal of Abnormal and Social Psychology* 38, no. 4 (1943): 412–52.

85. Bettelheim, "Individual and Mass Behavior in Extreme Situations," 435, 444–45.

86. Terrence Des Pres, *The Survivor: An Anatomy of Life in the Death Camps* (New York: Oxford University Press, 1976), 56, 69, 71; see also 67.

87. Bell, *End of Ideology*, 301.

88. Jack Gould, "TV: Ghetto Tragedy," *New York Times*, May 19, 1960, 75, emphasis added.

89. Gordon Sander, *Serling: The Rise and Twilight of Television's Last Angry Man* (New York: Dutton, 1992), 143.

90. Anne Serling, *As I Knew Him: My Dad, Rod Serling* (New York: Citadel, 2013), 97.

91. Richard F. Shepard, "4 Dramas Listed by 'Play of the Week,'" *New York Times*, January 15, 1960, 57.

92. Serling was one of the most active members of the Hollywood chapter of Citizens for a Sane Nuclear Policy (its later acronym: SANE), starting in 1955 (Sander, *Serling*, 155). Anticommunists claimed that SANE was a communist front and the organization was redbaited during Serling's involvement (Robert Kleidman, *Organizing for Peace: Neutrality, the Test Ban, and the Freeze* [Syracuse: Syracuse University Press, 1993], 104, 106, 110–11, 131). See Christopher Vials, *Haunted by Hitler: Liberals, the Left, and the Fight Against Fascism in the United* States (Amherst: University of Massachusetts Press, 2014), 149.

93. Vials, *Haunted by Hitler*, 148–55. "Trauma-informed antifascism": 152; merging of anti-Semitism and racism: 152, 154.

94. This is Gordon F. Sander's point of view about Serling's maturation as a writer, in *Serling*, 96–97.

95. Peter Biskind, *Seeing Is Believing: How Hollywood Taught Us to Stop Worrying and Love the Fifties* (New York: Pantheon, 1983), 73.

96.   Serling, *As I Knew Him*, 102.
97.   Harry Brown was a serious choice to write the seemingly superficial flick. He was mainly a poet, his most significant book of verse having been about the aesthetic after-effects of the radical 1930s, titled *The End of a Decade* (1941). He was an acquaintance of Wallace Stevens, a comrade of Stevens's bisexual communist Depression-era publisher, and also a close friend of Robert Lowell, maintaining "a bit of a finger in the Harvard pie." He had come close to going to Spain in violation of U.S. neutrality laws to fight for the Abraham Lincoln Brigade against the Francoist insurrection. Brown's novel *A Walk in the Sun*, published in 1944, was a variation on *The Red Badge of Courage* set at the landing of an American platoon on an Italian beach—all utterly fog of war, following the naturalist-impressionist Stephen Crane original. Surely this was a specific source for the misty background of Anzio assigned to Danny Ocean's group of eleven fellow paratroopers. Brown had been inducted into the U.S. Army in 1941 and in 1945 cowrote *The True Glory*, a left-populist film documenting the collapse of Nazism as witnessed through multiple first-person narrative voices—including scenes of the liberation of Belsen and Buchenwald, and "told," so the promotional tagline ran, "by the guys who won it," in simultaneous subjective testimonies conveyed by "front-line actuality footage." Danny Ocean's colleagues in Brown's screenplay, fifteen years later, bespeak eleven such "guys who won it" and has about it more of the *True Glory* ethos of the liberal-left Office of War Information/Hollywood alliance—the 1945 film won the Academy Award for Best Documentary Feature—than critics of the Rat Pack vehicle took time to notice. Sources: Letter from Wallace Stevens to J. Ronald Lane Latimer, December 9, 1936 (Latimer Papers, Regenstein Library, University of Chicago). "Harry Brown, 69, a Screenwriter," *New York Times*, November 4, 1986, 2, 5. On friendship with Lowell: letter from Harry Brown to George Marion O'Donnell, May 9, [1937] (George Marion O'Donnell Papers, Washington University Libraries, St. Louis). "Harvard pie": letter from Harry Brown to O'Donnell, August 24, 1936 (O'Donnell Papers, Washington University). Stevens's publisher was J. Ronald Lane Latimer, whose real name was James Leippert. On Spain: letter from Harry Brown to O'Donnell, April 12, 1937 (O'Donnell Papers, Washington University). Harry Brown, *A Walk in the Sun* (New York: Knopf, 1944). Comparison with *Red Badge of Courage*: Ben Ray Redman, "The Cumulative Power of Harry Brown," *Saturday Review of Literature*, July 1, 1944, 11. Eric A. Gordon, *Mark the Music: The Life and Work of Marc Blitzstein* (New York: St. Martin's, 1989), 252. James Chapman, "'The Yanks of Shown to Such Advantage': Anglo-American Rivalry in the Production of 'The True Glory' (1945)," *Historical Journal of Film, Radio and Television* 16, no. 4 (1996): 533–54; Frank Krome, "The True Glory and the Failure of Anglo-American Film Propaganda in the Second World War," *Journal of Contemporary History* 33, no. 1 (1998): 21–34.
98.   Bosley Crowther, "The Screen: 'Ocean's 11,'" *New York Times*, August 11, 1960, 19.
99.   Leo Sullivan, "'The Clan' Pulls a Slick Sick One," *Washington Post*, August 13, 1960, D8.
100.  J. G., "Ocean's 11," *Monthly Film Bulletin* 27, no. 312 (1960): 139.
101.  Carl Castro, Sara Kintzle, and Anthony Hassan, "The Combat Veteran Paradox: Paradoxes and Dilemmas Encountered with Reintegrating Combat Veterans and the Agencies That Support Them," *Traumatology* 21, no. 4 (2015): 299–310. See Kathryn Bassam, "Combat Trauma," in *Trauma: Contemporary Directions in Trauma Theory, Research, and Practice*, 2nd ed., ed. Shoshana Ringel and Jerome R. Brandell (New York: Columbia University Press, 2020), 287.
102.  William Breuer, *Agony at Anzio: The Allies' Most Controversial Operation of World War II* (London: Hale, 1985).

## 7. Disaster Defies Utterance

1.  *A Canticle for Leibowitz* was published by J. B. Lippincott and Co. in 1960 but bore a 1959 copyright.
2.  David Hapgood and David Richardson, *Monte Cassino* (New York: Congdon and Weed/ St. Martin's, 1984), 237.
3.  Jane Scrivener, pseud., *Inside Rome with the Germans* (New York: Macmillan, 1945), 48, 65, 115, 188.
4.  Chad Oliver, quoted in William H. Roberson and Robert L. Buttenfield, *Walter M. Miller, Jr.: A Bio-Bibliography* (Westport, CT: Greenwood, 1992), 7.
5.  David Streitfeld, "Book Report," *Washington Post Book World*, October 9, 1997, 15.
6.  Walter M. Miller, Jr., *A Canticle for Leibowitz* (New York: HarperCollins, 2006), 22.
7.  Walker Percy, "Walker Percy on Walter M. Miller, Jr.'s A Canticle for Leibowitz," in *Rediscoveries: Informal Essays in Which Well-Known Novelists Rediscover Neglected Works of Fiction by One of Their Favorite Authors*, ed. David Madden (New York: Crown, 1971), 263.
8.  Martin Levin, "Incubator of the New Civilization," *New York Times Book Review*, March 27, 1960, 43.
9.  Miller, *A Canticle for Leibowitz*, 17, 21, 20, 21.
10. Percy, "Walker Percy on Walter M. Miller," 266, 267, 263, emphasis added.
11. See Russell Hillier, "SF Intertextuality: Hebrew Runes Among the Ruins in *A Canticle for Leibowitz*," *Science Fiction Studies* 31, no. 1 (March 2004): 169.
12. Miller, *A Canticle for Leibowitz*, 5.
13. Percy, "Walker Percy on William M. Miller," 265.
14. See Anne Quinney, "Excess and Identity: The Franco-Romanian Ionesco Combats Rhinoceritis," *South Central Review* 24, no. 3 (2007): 36–52; and William S. Haney, II, "Eugène Ionesco's *Rhinoceros*: Defiance vs. Conformism," *Interactions* 17, no. 1 (2008): 85.
15. Eugène Ionesco, *Rhinoceros* (New York: Grove/Evergreen Original, 1960), 68.
16. Ionesco, 13.
17. Rod Serling, *The Twilight Zone: Complete Stories* (New York: TB, 1986), 145. A copy of the original March 4, 1960, broadcast is here: http://www.hulu.com/watch/440892.
18. Serling, "The Odyssey of Flight 33," in *The Twilight Zone: Complete Stories*, 258.
19. Aharon Appelfeld, "Three," in *In the Wilderness* (Jerusalem: Achshav, 196[3?]), 10.
20. Paul Celan, *The Meridian: Final Version—Drafts—Materials*, ed. Bernhard Böschenstein and Heino Schmull, trans. Pierre Joris (Stanford, CA: Stanford University Press, 2011), 113.
21. Paul Celan, *Memory Rose Into Threshold Speech: The Collected Earlier Poetry*, trans. Pierre Joris (New York: Farrar, Straus and Giroux, 2020), 77.
22. John Cage, *Silence* (Middletown, CT: Wesleyan University Press, 1961), 109, 126.
23. Serling, "Odyssey," 263.
24. Serling, 269.
25. Serling, 258.
26. Serling, 261.
27. Appelfeld, *The Story of a Life* (1983; New York: Schocken, 2004), 102–3.
28. Maurice Blanchot, *The Writing of the Disaster*, trans. Ann Smock (Lincoln: University of Nebraska Press), 60.
29. Serling, "Odyssey," 261.
30. Blanchot, *The Writing of the Disaster*, 60.
31. "Text of Eisenhower's Address to the U.N. Assembly," *New York Times*, December 9, 1953, 2, 5.

32.  Val Peterson, "They Said It Would Never Happen," *New York Times Book Review*, January 17, 1954, 4.

33.  Cage, *Silence*, 106, 98.

34.  George Steiner, "On Difficulty," in *On Difficulty, and Other Essays* (London: Oxford University Press, 1978), 18.

35.  I am grateful to Stuart Kaufer for help with the translation from Fyodor's Russian.

36.  Appelfeld, *The Story of a Life*, 104.

37.  Peter Brunette, *Roberto Rossellini* (New York: Oxford University Press, 1987), 219.

38.  John Gillett, "Cannes 1960," *Sight and Sound* 29, no. 3 (July 1960): 121.

39.  Brunette, *Roberto Rossellini*, 219, 218.

40.  Scrivener, *Inside Rome with the Germans*, 8.

41.  Tag Gallagher, *The Adventures of Roberto Rossellini* (New York: Da Capo, 1998), 525. Quoted and translated from Rossellini, "Il neorealismo è morto," 1960.

42.  Andrew Sarris, quoted by Gallagher, *Adventures of Roberto Rossellini*, 525.

43.  Brunette, *Roberto Rossellini*, 223. See also Geoffrey Nowell-Smith, *Making Waves, Revised and Expanded: New Cinemas of the 1960s*, 103ff.

44.  Lawrence Langer, *Holocaust Testimonies: The Ruins of Memory* (New Haven, CT: Yale University Press, 1991), 3 and passim.

45.  Andrew Sarris, "Rossellini Rediscovered," *Film Culture* 32 (Spring 1964): 62.

46.  See Noah Shenker, *Reframing Holocaust Testimony* (Bloomington: Indiana University Press, 2015), 130–31; Langer, *Holocaust Testimonies*, 83, 92, 137.

47.  Brunette, *Roberto Rossellini*, 223.

48.  Primo Levi, *Survival in Auschwitz* (New York: Simon and Schuster/Touchstone, 1996), 60.

49.  Levi, 9, emphasis added.

50.  Alfred Werner, "Amid Suffering, the Divine Spark," *Saturday Review* 43 (January 1960): 23.

51.  Alfred Werner, unpublished typescript autobiography, Alfred Werner Papers, box 1, folder 3, Leo Baeck Institute, Center for Jewish History, New York (Collection AR 7158/MF 1100).

52.  Carole Angier, *The Double Bond: Primo Levi, a Biography* (New York: Farrar, Straus and Giroux, 2002), 509.

53.  Max Henry Fisher, "Life in Hell," *Times Literary Supplement*, April 15, 1960, 239.

54.  Terrence Des Pres, *The Survivor: An Anatomy of Life in the Death Camps* (New York: Oxford University Press, 1976), 46–47, 82–83.

55.  It should be noted, at the same time, that Hebrew was the only language he learned to *write*.

56.  Appelfeld, *The Story of a Life*, 103, 104, 72, 69, 72.

57.  Appelfeld, 85, 103, 107.

58.  Yigal Schwartz, *Aharon Appelfeld: From Individual Lament to Tribal Eternity*, trans. Jeffrey M. Green (Hanover, NH: Brandeis University Press, 2001), 10–11, 146n23. "The Dovecote of Childhood" is quoted on 9 and is Green's translation.

59.  Thomas Thornton, "Aharon Appelfeld," *Bomb*, Summer 1998, 28.

60.  Thornton, 28.

61.  Appelfeld, *The Story of a Life*, 112.

62.  Paul Celan, "The Meridian," in *Collected Prose*, trans. Rosemarie Waldrop (New York: Routledge, 2003), 40.

63.  Efraim Sicher, *The Holocaust Novel* (New York: Routledge, 2005), 17.

64.  Appelfeld, *The Story of a Life*, 111.

65.  Naomi B. Sokoloff, "Aharon Appelfeld," in *Holocaust Novelists*, ed. Efraim Sicher; *Dictionary of Literary Biography*, vol. 299 (Detroit: Gale, 2004), 20.

66.  Appelfeld, *The Story of a Life*, 111.

67. Blanchot, *The Writing of the Disaster*, 33, 29.

68. Appelfeld, *The Story of a Life*, 116.

69. Aharon Appelfeld, "The Café That I Go To," *Haaretz*, October 2, 2007: www.haaretz.com /weekend/week-s-end/the-cafe-that-i-go-to-1.230401.

70. English quotations from "Smoke" are from an unpublished translation of the story by Ariel Resnikoff and Rivka Weinstock, to whom I am also grateful for their insights into the unusual diction, idiom, and use of Yiddish, German, and other non-Hebrew words. I am also grateful to Nili Gold for her consultation and patient guidance.

71. Sokoloff, "Aharon Appelfeld," 20.

72. Interview with Aharon Appelfeld and the author, Kelly Writers House, October 27, 2011.

73. Aharon Appelfeld, *Ashan* (Jerusalem: Achshav, 1962).

74. Sicher, *The Holocaust Novel*, 18.

75. Appelfeld, *The Story of a Life*, 62–63.

76. Louis Zukofsky, *"A"* (New York: New Directions, 2011), 282.

## 8. Thaw Poetics

1. Levi, *The Reawakening*, trans. Stuart Woolf (New York: Collier, 1993), 91.

2. Levi, 55.

3. Vida Johnson, "Ballad of a Soldier," *The Criterion Collection*, www.criterion.com/current /posts/201-ballad-of-a-soldier.

4. Laura Olson, *The Early Years of the Folk Revival Movement in Contemporary Russian Culture, 1960s–1980s* (Washington, DC: National Council for Eurasian and East European Research, 2000), iii.

5. Olson, 3–4. Kathleen F. Parthe, *Russian Village Prose: The Radiant Past* (Princeton: Princeton University Press, 1992), 3.

6. Robert Cantwell, *When We Were Good: The Folk Revival* (Cambridge, MA: Harvard University Press, 1996), 296.

7. Joseph Hickerman, "Alan Lomax's 'Southern Journey': A Review-Essay," *Ethnomusicology* 9, no. 3 (September 1965): 319, 317.

8. Matthew Barton, "Collecting America's Music," *American History* 32, no. 4 (September-October 1997): 8.

9. Ronald D. Cohen, introduction to *Alan Lomax: Selected Writings, 1934–1997* (New York: Routledge, 2003), 237.

10. Cohen, 190, 239.

11. Susan Montgomery, "The Folk Furor," *Mademoiselle*, December 1960, 97.

12. Frances Monson quoted in Montgomery, 117.

13. Montgomery, 117.

14. Albert B. Lord, *The Singer of Tales* (Cambridge, MA: Harvard University Press, 1960), preface by Harry Levin, n.p.

15. Lord, n.p., 101.

16. Lord, *Singer of Tales*, Levin preface, n.p.

17. Jerome Rothenberg, email to the author, February 20, 2020. "Archaic techniques of ecstasy": Rothenberg was also influenced by Mircea Eliade's *Shamanism: Archaic Techniques of Ecstasy* (1951); the subtitle of Eliade's book led Rothenberg to the titular phrase "Technicians of the Sacred."

18. Jonathan Mayhew, *Apocryphal Lorca: Translation, Parody, Kitsch* (Chicago: University of Chicago Press, 2009), 85.

19. Email from Rothenberg to the author, February 20, 2020.

20. *The Poetry of Kabbalah*, ed. and trans. Peter Cole (New Haven: Yale University Press, 2012), xxii. Williams used the phrase in his introduction to *The Wedge* (1944). Williams wrote that "a poem is a small (or large) machine made of words." He stressed a poem's composition and movement rather than its content: "There is no poetry of distinction without formal invention, for it is in the intimate form that works of art achieve their exact meaning, in which they most resemble the machine, to give language its highest dignity, its illumination in the environment to which it is native." Williams, *Selected Essays of William Carlos Williams* (New York: New Directions, 1969), 256.

21. Quoted in Preston Whaley, *Blows Like a Horn: Beat Writing, Jazz, Style, and Markets in the Transformation of Culture* (Cambridge, MA: Harvard University Press, 2004), 71.

22. Email from Jerome Rothenberg to the author, February 20, 2020. A teacher gave him a copy of Rolfe Humphries's translations of Lorca.

23. William Carlos Williams, "Federico Garcia Lorca," *Kenyon Review* 1, no. 2 (Spring 1939): 148–58. Williams wrote about his planned essay on Lorca on December 29, 1937: Paul Mariani, *William Carlos Williams: A New World Naked* (New York: McGraw-Hill, 1981), 409. See Julio Marzán, *The Spanish American Roots of William Carlos Williams* (Austin: University of Texas Press, 1994), 137–38.

24. I owe this list to Jonathan Mayhew in *Apocryphal Lorca: Translation, Poetry, Kitsch* (Chicago: University of Chicago Press, 2009), xi and passim. See Baraka's statement on poetics in *The New American Poetry* (1960), "How You Sound??," where he lists Lorca as one of his "greatest influence[s]": Donald Allen, ed., *The New American Poetry, 1945–1960* (Berkeley: University of California Press, 1960), 424.

25. Federico García Lorca, "Theory and Play of *The Duende*," in *Deep Song and Other Prose*, ed. Christopher Maurer (New York: New Directions, 1980), 43.

26. Frank Alkyer, Ed Enright, Jason Koransky, eds., *The Miles Davis Reader* (New York: Hal Leonard, 2007), 213–15; Hua Hsu, "Nathaniel Mackey's Long Song," *New Yorker*, April 12, 2021, 24.

27. Louis Zukofsky, "Peri poietikes," *Nation*, November 7, 1959, 336. From Denise Levertov's review of *"A" 1–12*: "Zukofsky's way is by the ear."

28. Larryetta M. Schall, "The Ballad as Vehicle for Social Protest," *Studies in Popular Culture* 1, no. 1 (Winter 1977): 26–35; Myles Horton and Bill Moyers, "The Adventures of a Radical Hillbilly: An Interview with Myles Horton," *Appalachian Journal* 9, no. 4 (Summer 1982): 248–85. "This history of this song," writes Schall, "illustrates the relationship of the ballad to oral tradition and to the media which ordinarily popularizes a fixed version" (29).

29. See R. N. Currey, *Poets of the 1939–1945 War* (London: Longmans, 1960).

30. Libretto, *The Sound of Music*, music by Richard Rodgers, lyrics by Oscar Hammerstein II, book by Howard Lindsay and Russel Crouse ([New York:] Rodgers and Hammerstein Theatre Library, 1960), 8.

31. Gershom Scholem, *Kabbalah* (New York: Penguin, 1978), 3.

32. Louis Zukofsky, *Anew: Complete Shorter Poetry* (New York: New Directions, 2011), 163. The recording, given to the Library of Congress, is dated November 3, 1960. It is archived at PennSound: http://writing.upenn.edu/pennsound/x/Zukofsky.php.

33. Lord, *The Singer of Tales*, Levin preface, n.p., emphasis added.

34. Lewis Porter, "John Coltrane: The Atlantic Years," in *The John Coltrane Companion*, ed. Carl Woideck (New York: Schirmer, 1998), 177, 184, emphasis added. See Carl Clements, "John Coltrane and the Integration of Indian Concepts in Jazz Improvisation," *Jazz Research Journal* 2, no. 2 (2008), 155–75. "The discipline of composing in real time": Lewis Porter's summary of the definition of improvisation relevant to Coltrane in 1959–60 (*John Coltrane: His Life and Music* [Ann Arbor: University of Michigan Press, 1998], 165).

35. Levi, *The Reawakening*, 90–91.

36. Lorca, "Theory and Play of *the Duende*," 43, 53, 47.

37. Lorca, 46, emphasis added.

38. Levi, *The Reawakening*, 91–92.

39. Carole Angier, *The Double Bond: Primo Levi, a Biography* (New York: Farrar, Straus and Giroux, 2002), 471.

40. Levi, *The Reawakening*, 54–55.

41. Levi, 129.

42. Eleanory Gilburd, *To See Paris and Die: The Soviet Lives of Western Culture* (Cambridge, MA: Harvard University Press, 2018), 175.

43. Julia Levin, "Ballad of a Soldier," *Senses of Cinema: Cinémathèque Annotations on Film* 23 (December 2002), http://sensesofcinema.com/2002/cteq/ballad_soldier/.

44. Bosley Crowther, "Screen: Poignant 'Ballad of a Soldier' in Russia / Wartime Drama Opens at the Murray Hill / Film Is in Soviet Trend Toward Humaneness," *New York Times*, December 27, 1960, 22.

45. Levin, "Ballad of a Soldier," n.p.

46. Johnson, "Ballad of a Soldier."

47. Crowther, "Poignant 'Ballad,'" 22.

48. Lord, *The Singer of Tales*, 100, 94.

49. Warren Motte, *Oulipo: A Primer of Potential Literature* (Lincoln: University of Nebraska Press, 1986), 12, 4. "As old or almost as old": Motte quotes Jacques Roubaud.

50. Italo Calvino, "Cybernetics and Ghosts," in Motte, *Oulipo*, 5–6.

51. Lord, *The Singer of Tales*, 94.

52. Ian Thomson, *Primo Levi: A Life* (New York: Metropolitan, 2004), 301.

53. Roubaud quoted by Motte, *Oulipo*, 12.

54. Quoted in "RN Currey," *Guardian*, December 6, 2001, 22–24, at 23: www.theguardian.com /news/2001/dec/06/guardianobituaries.books.

55. See Janet Kaufman, "'But Not the Study': Writing as a Jew," in *How Shall We Tell Each Other of the Poet?: The Life and Writing of Muriel Rukeyser*, ed. Janet Kaufman and Anne F. Herzog (New York: St. Martin's, 1999), 56.

56. Muriel Rukeyser, *Collected Poems* (New York: McGraw Hill, 1978), 477.

57. Footnote in Rukeyser, *Collected Poems*, 473.

58. Muriel Rukeyser, "The Education of a Poet," in *The Writer on Her Work*, ed. Janet Sternburg (New York: Norton, 1980), 1:226.

59. Quoted in Kaufman, "'But Not the Study,'" 13. This footnote appeared in *American Judaism*, April 1961, 13.

60. Alan Filreis, *Counter-Revolution of the Word: The Conservative Attack on Modern Poetry, 1945–1960* (Chapel Hill: University of North Carolina Press, 2008), 146–47.

61. Rukeyser, "The Way Out," in *Collected Poems*, 455, emphasis added.

62. Catherine Gander, *Muriel Rukeyser and Documentary: The Poetics of Connection* (Edinburgh: Edinburgh University Press, 2013), 40–41.

63. Theodor W. Adorno, "Cultural Criticism and Society," in *Prisms*, trans. Samuel Weber and Sherry Weber (Cambridge, MA: MIT Press, 1981), 34.

64. Muriel Rukeyser, *The Life of Poetry* (New York: Morrow, 1949), 207.

65. Ranen Omer, "'Palestine Was a Halting Place, One of Many': Diasporism in the Poetry of Charles Reznikoff," *MELUS* 25, no. 1 (Spring 2000): 176.

66. Omer, 175.

67. Charlotte Mandel, "Rukeyser's Rabbi Akiba Inheritance," *Muriel Rukeyser, A Living Archive*: http://murielrukeyser.emuenglish.org/2015/05/03/charlotte-mandel-muriel-rukeysers-rabbi-akiba-inheritance/.

68. Rukeyser, *Collected Poems*, 460.

69. Charles Reznikoff, *The Complete Poems of Charles Reznikoff: Poems, 1937–1975*, ed. Seamus Cooney (Santa Rosa, CA: Black Sparrow, 1996), 2:76, 66.

70. Rukeyser, *The Life of Poetry*, 175.

71. Omer, "Diasporism in the Poetry of Charles Reznikoff," 174.

72. John Wheelwright, untitled review, *Partisan Review*, March 1938, 54–56.

73. See Wheelwright's review of *U.S. 1* in *Partisan Review* 4, no. 4 (March 1938): 54–56. He quotes her much-quoted programmatic phrase and offers the view that Rukeyser's reuse of documents is "rewriting [that] does not click" (55).

74. John ("Jack") Wheelwright, a politically radical poet a generation older than Rukeyser, affiliated with the *Partisan Review* by 1938. When reviewing Rukeyser's *U.S. 1* that year he offered both political and aesthetic criticisms of her that are now well understood to follow the anti-Stalinist stance of that journal. "Her socialism belongs to the inexperienced school—pre-war." Of her *Theory of Flight*: "Process of flight is not an accurate equivalent to process of emancipation. The overtones of flight imply escapism" (54).

75. Kenneth Burke, introduction to Charles Reznikoff, *Testimony* (New York: Objectivist, 1934), xiv.

76. William Carlos Williams, *The Collected Poems*, vol. 1, *1909–1939*, ed. A. Walton Litz and Christopher MacGowan (New York: New Directions, 1986), 1:384.

77. Reznikoff, *The Complete Poems*, 2:79.

78. Rachel Blau DuPlessis, ed., *The Selected Letters of George Oppen* (Durham, NC: Duke University Press, 1990), 39.

79. Quoted in DuPlessis, *Selected Letters of George Oppen*, 377n6.

80. Letter from Niedecker to Reznikoff, November 23, 1959, Mandeville Special Collections, University of California San Diego 9:4:1; quoted by Robert Franciosi, "Reading Reznikoff: Zukofsky, Oppen, and Niedecker," in *The Objectivist Nexus: Essays in Cultural Poetics*, ed. Rachel Blau DuPlessis and Peter Quartermain (Tuscaloosa: University of Alabama Press, 1999), 394. Stephen Fredman, *A Menorah for Athena: Charles Reznikoff and the Jewish Dilemmas of Objectivist Poetry* (Chicago: University of Chicago Press, 2001), 177n14.

81. Milton Hindus, "'. . . and Ask for a Poem,'" *New Leader* 44, no. 3 (January 16, 1961): 26.

82. Ranen Omer-Sherman, *Diaspora and Zionism in Jewish American Literature: Lazarus, Syrkin, Reznikoff, and Roth* (Hanover, NH: Brandeis University Press, University Press of New England, 2002), 130.

83. Quoted by Fredman, *A Menorah for Athena*, 75n15.

84. Omer-Sherman, *Diaspora and Zionism*, 130.

85. Sylvia Rothchild in her essay "From a Distance and Up Close: Charles Reznikoff and the Holocaust," in *Charles Reznikoff: Man and Poet*, ed. Milton Hindus (Orono, ME: National

Poetry Foundation, 1984), offers statistics on books of holocaust witnessing she received as a book reviewer in 1982 alone (295).

86. Rothchild, 293–94.
87. Rothchild, 295.
88. Reznikoff, *The Complete Poems*, 2:75.
89. Ranen Omer-Sherman, "'Palestine Was a Halting Place, One of Many': Diasporism in the Poetry of Charles Reznikoff," *MELUS* 25, no. 1 (Spring 2000): 174.
90. Fredman, *A Menorah for Athena*, 75.
91. Reznikoff, *Collected Poems*, 2:74.
92. Reznikoff, 2:71.
93. Reznikoff, 2:70–72.
94. Omer-Sherman, *Diaspora and Zionism*, 175.
95. A. R. Ammons, "Three Poets," *Poetry*, April 1960, 52.
96. Hindus, ". . . and Ask for a Poem," 26.
97. Franciosi, "Reading Reznikoff," 265.
98. DuPlessis, *Selected Letters of George Oppen*, 37, 39.
99. Levi, *The Reawakening*, 92.
100. Lord, *The Singer of Tales*, 97.

## 9. Abomunism

1. Mark Scroggins, "'There Are Less Jews Left in the World': Louis Zukofsky's Holocaust Poetry," *Shofar* 21, no. 1 (Fall 2002): 72.
2. Scroggins, 69–72.
3. Louis Zukofsky, *"A"* (New York: New Directions, 2011), 119.
4. Scroggins, "'There Are Less Jews Left in the World,'" 71.
5. Zukofsky, *"A,"* 205–6.
6. Zukofsky, 205.
7. I am quoting the general overview on Zukofsky provided by the Poetry Foundation website: www.poetryfoundation.org/bio/louis-zukofsky.
8. Denise Levertov, "A Necessary Poetry," *Poetry* 97, no. 2 (November 1960): 102.
9. Rachel Blau DuPlessis, ed., *The Selected Letters of George Oppen* (Durham, NC: Duke University Press, 1990), 37.
10. Barry Ahearn, *Zukofsky's "A": An Introduction* (Berkeley: University of California Press, 1983), 134.
11. Louis Zukofsky, "Poetry, / for My Son When He Can Read," in *Prepositions +: The Collected Critical Essays*, ed. Mark Scroggins (Middletown, CT: Wesleyan University Press, 2000), 3. First published in *Cronos* 2, no. 4 (March 1948): 22–30.
12. Zukofsky, *"A,"* 267.
13. Zukofsky, 273, 268.
14. Zukofsky, 283.
15. Zukofsky, 293.
16. Ahearn, *Zukofsky's "A,"* 131.
17. Zukofsky, *"A,"* 282.
18. Zukofsky, 272.
19. Zukofsky, 263, 264.
20. Zukofsky, 262, 281.

21. Stephen Fredman, *American Poetry as Transactional Art* (Tuscaloosa: University of Alabama Press, 2020). See especially 30–45.

22. Jerome Rothenberg, email message to the author, February 27, 2015, emphasis added.

23. Duncan, *The Opening of the Field* (New York: Grove, 1960), 7.

24. Peter Quartermain, *Disjunctive Poetics: From Gertrude Stein and Louis Zukofsky to Susan Howe* (New York: Cambridge University Press, 1992), 104. Quartermain is of course referring to Joyce's *Finnegan's Wake*. "Arcades-like": Walter Benjamin, unfinished collection of writings, 1927–40.

25. Zukofsky, *Bottom: On Shakespeare* (Middletown, CT: Wesleyan University Press, 2002), 171.

26. Zukofsky, 155, 39.

27. James Rother, "An Occluded Splendor," *Contemporary Poetry Review*, n.d., http://cprw.com/Rother/Zukofsky.htm.

28. Craig Dworkin, *Dictionary Poetics: Toward a Radical Lexicography* (New York: Fordham University Press, 2020), 73.

29. Gershom Scholem, *Kabbalah: A Definitive History of the Evolution, Ideas, Leading Figures and Extraordinary Influence of Jewish Mysticism* (New York: Penguin, 1978), 25.

30. *Poetry* 97, no. 3 (December 1960): 142.

31. Perelman, introduction to Zukofsky, *Bottom: On Shakespeare*, xiii.

32. Scholem, *Kabbalah*, 213.

33. This overview is indebted to Mark Scroggins's comments on *Bottom* in his biography of Zukofsky, 301ff.

34. Zukofsky, *Bottom: On Shakespeare*, 104, 67–69, 185, 156, 351.

35. Zukofsky, 155, 97, 348.

36. Zukofsky, xi.

37. Paul Celan, *The Meridian: Final Version—Drafts—Materials*, ed. Bernhard Böschenstein and Heino Schmull, trans. Pierre Joris (Stanford, CA: Stanford University Press, 2011), 163, 170.

38. Zukofsky, *"A,"* 290.

39. Zukofsky, 291–92.

40. Celan, *The Meridian: Final Version—Drafts—Materials*, 144.

41. Baldwin, "Fifth Avenue, Uptown," in *Nobody Knows My Name* (New York: Dell, 1963), 58.

42. Zukofsky, *"A,"* 281.

43. Zukofsky, 263.

44. T. S. Eliot, "Hamlet and His Problems," in *The Sacred Wood: Essays on Poetry and Criticism* (London: Methuen, 1920), 92. On the ubiquity of Eliot's idea in 1950s New Criticism, see, e.g., John Paul Russo, "The Tranquilized Poem: The Crisis of New Criticism in the 1950s," *Texas Studies in Literature and Language* 30 (1988): 198–227.

45. Oppen, *Collected Poems*, ed. Michael Davidson (New York: New Directions, 2002), 53.

46. Barbara Guest, *Collected Poems* (Middleton, CT: Wesleyan University Press, 2008), 30.

47. Kaufman, "Jail Poems," in *Beatitude Anthology* (San Francisco: City Lights, 1960), 5, 53.

48. Eigner, *The Collected Poems of Larry Eigner*, ed. Curtis Faville and Robert Grenier (Stanford, CA: Stanford University Press, 2010), 2:371.

49. Louis Zukofsky, "Poetry, / for My Son When He Can Read," in *Prepositions +: The Collected Critical Essays*, ed. Mark Scroggins (Middletown, CT: Wesleyan University Press, 2000), 8.

50. Levertov, "A Necessary Poetry," 102.

51. Amiri Baraka, *The System of Dante's Hell* (Brooklyn, NY: Akashic, 1965), 92.

52. The dating of these poems is owing to the scholarship of Rachel Blau DuPlessis. One cannot be precise, although on one draft of "Blood from a Stone" Oppen marked it "1949," which

is clearly a slip (as Oppen was not writing poems in that year) and meant "1959." "Virtually all dates [for Oppen poems of this period] are inferential," notes DuPlessis (email to the author, April 2, 2015).

53. DuPlessis, email to the author, April 2, 2015.

54. James Smethurst, "'Remembering When Indians Were Red': Bob Kaufman, the Popular Front, and the Black Arts Movement," *Callaloo* 25, no. 1 (Winter 2002): 146–64.

55. Bob Kaufman, *Abomunist Manifesto* (San Francisco: City Lights, 1959), n.p. The poems quoted from are, respectively, "Notes Dis- and Re- Garding Abomunism," "Abomunist Manifesto," and "Abomunist Election Manifesto."

56. Will Alexander, praise for Kaufman's *Collected Poems*, ed. Neeli Cherkovski, Raymond Foye, and Tate Swindell (San Francisco: City Lights, 2019); quoted in www.citylights.com /book/?GCOI=87286100255020.

57. In the *San Francisco Chronicle*, Caen used the term in print for the first time on April 2, 1958. Jesse Hamlin, "How Herb Caen Named a Generation," November 26, 1995, *SFGATE*, www.sfgate.com/entertainment/article/HOW-HERB-CAEN-NAMED-A-GENERATION -3018725.php. That the term referred to Kaufman has not been confirmed.

58. Norman Mailer, "Hipster and Beatnik, a Footnote to 'The White Negro,'" in *Advertisements for Myself* (New York: Putnam's, 1959), 372.

59. Maria Damon, "Introduction," *Callaloo* 25, no. 1 (Winter 2002): 108.

60. Damon, 108.

61. Quoted by Lewis Porter, *John Coltrane: His Life and Music* (Ann Arbor: University of Michigan Press, 1998), 158.

62. Coltrane famously used the phrase in "Coltrane on Coltrane" (published in 1960), borrowing the term (and citing it) from Ira Gitler. See Porter, *John Coltrane*, 133.

63. Smethurst, "'Remembering When Indians Were Red,'" 151.

64. A comment made by Creeley to Burton Hatlen, quoted in Craig Arnold, "In Good Company: Robert Creeley, Feeling for the Edge," *Austin Chronicle*, November 12, 1999. www .austinchronicle.com/books/1999-11-12/74587/.

65. Pages from Kaufman's FBI file, gathered by Billy Woodberry and his research team for the documentary *And When I Die, I Won't Stay Dead* (2015), are shown in the film. I quote from the page on view at 01:02:00.

66. Kaufman, "Jail Poems," 54.

67. Smethurst, "'Remembering When Indians Were Red,'" 147.

68. Wallace Stevens, *Collected Poetry and Prose* (New York: Library of America, 1997), 52–53.

69. Charlotte Delbo, *Auschwitz and After*, trans. Rosette C. Lamont, 2nd ed. (New Haven: Yale University Press, 1995), 237.

70. Eigner, *Collected Poems*, 2:370.

71. *The Sound of Music*, libretto, music by Richard Rodgers, lyrics by Oscar Hammerstein, II, book by Howard Lindsay and Russel Crouse ([New York:] Rodgers and Hammerstein Theatre Library, 1960), 8.

72. Kaufman, "Jail Poems," 53.

73. Letter from Cid Corman to Robert Creeley, March 21, 1961 (Robert Creeley Papers, Stanford University Special Collections, Series 1, Box 26 [M0662, correspondence 1950–1990]). Quoted Courtesy of the Department of Special Collections, Stanford University Libraries, and the literary estate of Cid Corman.

74. John Palattella, "The Marvel of the Obvious," *Nation*, March 25, 2002, 31.

75. DuPlessis, *Selected Letters of George Oppen*, 37.

76. Zukofsky, "A," 266–67.

77.    "An Interview with James E. Young," with Adi Gordon and Amos Goldberg, May 24, 1998, Shoah Resource Center, Yad Vashem, Jerusalem, Israel. The transcript is available at yad-vashem.org, www.yadvashem.org/odot_pdf/Microsoft%20Word%20-%203852.pdf.

78.    James E. Young, The Texture of Memory: Holocaust Memorials and Meaning (New Haven, CT: Yale University Press, 1993), see esp. 3–15.

## 10. Favorite Things

1.    Letter from Elizabeth Bishop to Robert Lowell, July 27, [1960], Series I, 62–264, item 175, Robert Lowell Papers, Houghton Library, Harvard University.

2.    "Lazy and anecdotal": Joseph Bennett, "Two Americans, a Brahmin and the Bourgeoisie," Hudson Review 12 (Autumn 1959): 435; "thrown together:" Richard Eberhart, "A Poet's People," New York Times Book Review, May 3, 1959, 4; "almost flippant" and "off-hand": Philip Larkin, "Collected Poems," Manchester Guardian Weekly, May 21, 1959, 10. "Loose" and "loosened" are terms used variously by Lowell himself and taken up by many contemporary reviews, and then adopted as a standard term in later overviews of the Life Studies turn. See, e.g., Ian Hamilton, Robert Lowell: A Biography (New York: Random House, 1982), 263; and Lawrence Kramer, "Freud and the Skunks: Genre and Language in Life Studies," in Robert Lowell: Essays on the Poetry, ed. Steven Axelrod and Helen Deese (Cambridge: Cambridge University Press, 1986), 80.

3.    Hamilton, Robert Lowell, 177.

4.    Robert Lowell, address at the National Book Awards, March 23, 1960 (Robert Lowell Papers, Houghton Library, Harvard).

5.    Letter from William Meredith to Robert Lowell, March 28, 1960 (Robert Lowell Papers, Houghton Library, Harvard University, Series I, folder 845). This would become part three of The Old Glory (1964).

6.    Drafts of "For the Union Dead," Robert Lowell Papers, MS Am 1905, Box 16 (2300), Houghton Library, Harvard University.

7.    Letter from Bishop to Lowell, May 19, 1960, Lowell Papers, Houghton Library (Series I, 62–264, folder 173).

8.    Marjorie Perloff, The Vienna Paradox (New York: New Directions, 2004), 209.

9.    Daniel G. Hoffman, "Arrivals and Rebirths," Sewanee Review 68, no. 1 (Winter 1960): 118.

10.    Perloff, The Vienna Paradox, xiv.

11.    Elizabeth Bishop, jacket text, Life Studies (quoted in Samuel French Morse, "Mostly Modern," College English 21, no. 6 [March 1960]: 358).

12.    Marjorie Perloff, Edge of Irony: Modernism in the Shadow of the Habsburg Empire (Chicago: University of Chicago Press, 2016), 126, 149–50, 184n6.

13.    Paul Celan, Selected Poems and Prose, ed. and trans. John Felstiner (New York: Norton, 2001), 14.

14.    Email from Marjorie Perloff to the author, February 17, 2020. See Daniel Morris, " 'Yes and No, Not Either/Or': Aesthetics, Identity, and Marjorie Perloff's Vienna Paradox," in Radical Poetics and Secular Jewish Culture, ed. Stephen Paul Miller and Daniel Morris (Tuscaloosa: University of Alabama Press, 2010), 277.

15.    Perloff, The Vienna Paradox, 58, 71, emphasis added.

16.    Marjorie Perloff, Unoriginal Genius: Poetry by Other Means in the New Century (Chicago: University of Chicago Press, 2010), 31.

17.    Perloff, The Vienna Paradox, 33, emphasis added.

18.	Perloff, 34, 68–69, 70.

19.	Beth B. Cohen, *Child Survivors of the Holocaust: The Youngest Remnant and the American Experience* (New Brunswick, NJ: Rutgers University Press, 2018).

20.	ruth weiss, *Gallery of Women*, quoted in Preston Whaley, *Blows Like a Horn: Beat Writing, Jazz, Style, and Markets in the Transformation of U.S. Culture* (Cambridge, MA: Harvard University Press, 2004), 64.

21.	Cohen, *Child Survivors*, 134–35.

22.	Perloff, *The Vienna Paradox*, 65.

23.	Perloff, 66, 117.

24.	Perloff, xv.

25.	Perloff, xv, 7, 220.

26.	Perloff wrote about this poem in "Poetry 1956: A Step Away from Them," for *Contemporary Literature* in 1973; republished in *Poetry On and Off the Page: Essays for Emergent Occasions* (Evanston, IL: Northwestern University Press, 1998), 83–115.

27.	Marjorie Perloff, *Infrathin: An Experiment in Micropoetics* (Chicago: University of Chicago Press, 2021), 189. Perloff is quoting Dan Gunn's introduction to *The Letters of Samuel Beckett, 1941–1956*, ed. Dan Gunn (Cambridge: Cambridge University Press, 2012), 2: xv–xvi.

28.	Marjorie Perloff, *Radical Artifice: Writing Poetry in the Age of Media* (Chicago: University of Chicago Press, 1991), 162–70.

29.	Perloff, *Infrathin*, 36.

30.	Marjorie Perloff, "Poetry Chronicle: 1970–71," *Contemporary Literature* 14, no. 1 (Winter 1973): 97. See Brian Reed, "Becoming Marjorie Perloff," in *Marjorie Perloff: A Celebration*, ed. Al Filreis and J. Gordon Faylor, *Jacket2*, November 8, 2012: https://jacket2.org/article/becoming-marjorie-perloff.

31.	Perloff, *The Vienna Paradox*, 21.

32.	Quoted in Perloff, 23–24.

33.	Quoted in Perloff, 24.

34.	Julie V. Iovine, "For Austria: A Tribute and Protest," *New York Times*, March 7, 2002, section F, 1.

35.	Perloff, *Vienna Paradox*, 169.

36.	Perloff, 26.

37.	Nancy M. Grace, "ruth weiss's Desert Journal: A Modern-Beat-Pomo Performance," in *Reconstructing the Beats*, ed. Jennie Skerl (New York: Palgrave MacMillan, 2004), 71n1.

38.	Perloff, *The Vienna Paradox*, 136, 137.

39.	Perloff, 178, 177.

40.	Marjorie Perloff, *Frank O'Hara: Poet Among Painters* (New York: George Braziller, 1977); Marjorie Perloff, "Revolving in Crystal: The Supreme Fiction and the Impasse of Modernist Lyric," in *Wallace Stevens: The Poetics of Modernism*, ed. Albert Gelpi (Cambridge: Cambridge University Press, 1985), 41–64.

41.	Marjorie Perloff, "The Return of Robert Lowell," *Parnassus* 27, nos. 1 and 2 (2003): 76.

42.	Perloff, 76; she is quoting Lowell's "Memories of West Street and Lepke" from *Life Studies* (1959).

43.	Perloff, 79, 89.

44.	Perloff, 90, 84, emphasis added.

45.	Perloff, 90–91.

46.	Perloff, 80. She is quoting "The Mount of the Hudson."

47.	Perloff, *Unoriginal Genius*, 123–45.

48.   Elaine Scarry, *The Body in Pain: The Making and Unmaking of the World* (New York: Oxford University Press, 1985), 133.

49.   Perloff, *The Vienna Paradox*, 229.

50.   Perloff, 233.

51.   James E. Young, *The Texture of Memory: Holocaust Memorials and Meaning* (New Haven, CT: Yale University Press, 1993), 5.

52.   Perloff, *Vienna Paradox*, 114–115.

53.   Shoshana Felman, "Education and Crisis, or the Vicissitudes of Teaching," in *Testimony: Crises of Witnessing and Literature, Psychoanalysis, and History*, ed. Shoshana Felman and Dori Laub (New York: Routlege, 1992), 25. Celan's Bremen speech: John Felstiner, note to "Translating Celan's Last Poem," *American Poetry Review*, July/August 1982, 23.

54.   Perloff, *The Vienna Paradox*, 117–18.

55.   See William L. Shirer, *The Rise and Fall of the Third Reich: A History of Nazi Germany* (New York: Simon and Schuster, 1960), 349–53; and Robert Keyserlingk, *Austria in World War II: An Anglo-American Dilemma* (Kingston, Ontario: McGill-Queen's University Press, 1968), 38ff.

56.   Katrin Maria Kohl and Ritchie Robertson, *A History of Austrian Literature, 1918–2000* (Rochester, NY: Camden House, 2006), 7.

57.   "Reich 'Flight Tax' Extended to Austria," *Jewish Telegraphic Agency* 4, no. 15 (April 18, 1938): 1.

58.   Perloff, *Vienna Paradox*, 53.

59.   Kohl and Robertson, *History of Austrian Literature*, 7.

60.   Dieter Nohlen and Philip Stöver, *Elections in Europe: A Data Handbook* (Baden-Baden, Germany: Namos, 2010), 176. The vote was accurate as a count of ballots, but, to say the least, "it took a brave Austrian to vote No." "Voters feared that their failure to cast an affirmative ballot might be found out" (Shirer, *Rise and Fall of the Third Reich*, 350).

61.   Maria Augusta Trapp, *The Story of the Trapp Family Singers* (Philadelphia: Lippincott, 1949), 114–15.

62.   Hanna Yablonka, *The State of Israel vs. Adolf Eichmann*, trans. Ora Cummings and David Herman (New York: Schocken, 2004), 22.

63.   Anton Pelinka, "The Second Republic's Reconstruction of History," in *Austrian Historical Memory and National Identity* (New Brunswick, NJ: Transaction, 1997), 95–103.

64.   Heidemarie Uhl, "From Victim Myth to Coresponsibility Thesis," in *The Politics of Memory in Postwar Europe* (Durham, NC: Duke University Press, 2006), 40–72.

65.   Karina Korostelina, *History Education in the Formation of Social Identity* (New York: Palgrave Macmillan, 2013), 141.

66.   B. J. C. McKercher, "Anschluss: The Chamberlain Government and the First Test of Appeasement, February-March 1938," *International History Review* 39, no. 2 (2017): 274–94, 290n13.

67.   See Gordon Martel, "The Revisionist as Moralist: A. J. P. Taylor and the Lessons of European History," in *The Origins of the Second World War Reconsidered*, ed. Gordon Martel (New York: Routledge, 1986), 1–12.

68.   See David Art, *The Politics of the Nazi Past in Germany and Austria* (Cambridge: Cambridge University Press, 2006).

69.   A. J. P. Taylor, *The Origins of the Second World War* (New York: Simon and Schuster, 1961), 172, emphasis added. See Paul Kennedy and Talbot Imlay, "Appeasement," in Martel, *The Origins of the Second World War Reconsidered*, 117–18.

70.   Korostelina, *History Education*, 139.

71. LeRoi Jones, *Home: Social Essays* (New York: William Morrow, 1966), 21. "Shaken": Amiri Baraka, *The Autobiography of LeRoi Jones* (Chicago: Lawrence Hill, 1984), 246. "Revelation": Kimberly W. Benston, "Amiri Baraka: An Interview," *boundary 2* 6, no. 2 (1978): 105.

72. Albert Camus, letter to Roland Barthes, January 11, 1955, in *Lyrical and Critical Essays*, ed. Philip Thody, trans. Ellen Conroy Kennedy (New York: Knopf Doubleday, 2012), 340.

73. "Political Science 1104, Miss Arendt, Final Examination," June 6, 1955, The Hannah Arendt Papers, Manuscript Division, Library of Congress, item #024163.

74. Perloff, *The Vienna Paradox*, 207.

75. Julian Woolford, *Rogers and Hammerstein's "The Sound of Music"* (New York: Routledge, 2020), 51.

76. Howard Lindsay, Russel Crouse, Richard Rodgers, Oscar Hammerstein, II, *The Sound of Music* ([New York]: Rodgers and Hammerstein Theatre Library, 1960), 78. Hereafter cited as *The Sound of Music* libretto.

77. Julia Antopol Hirsch, *The Sound of Music: The Making of America's Favorite Movie* (Chicago: Chicago Review Press, 1993), 23.

78. Quoted by Hirsch, 13.

79. Bosley Crowther, "'The Sound of Music' Opens at Rivoli," *New York Times*, March 3, 1965, BR1. (This was actually Crowther's reprise review at the time of the release of the movie version.)

80. Hirsch, *The Sound of Music*, 5.

81. Brooks Atkinson, "The Theatre: 'The Sound of Music,'" *New York Times*, November 17, 1959, 40.

82. Woolford, *Rodgers and Hammerstein's "The Sound of Music,"* author's jacket statement, n.p.

83. Quoted in McKercher, "Anschluss," 283.

84. *The Sound of Music* libretto, 32.

85. See Woolford, *The Sound of Music*, 28–36.

86. Woolford, 4.

87. *The Sound of Music* libretto, 51.

88. *The Sound of Music* libretto, 86.

89. Woolford, *The Sound of Music*, 54.

90. *The Sound of Music* libretto, 67.

91. *The Sound of Music* libretto, 8, 17.

92. *The Sound of Music* libretto, 14.

93. Ingeborg Bachmann, "Das schreibende Ich," in *Werke*, vol. 4, ed. Christine Koschel, Inge von Weidenbaum, and Clemens Münster (Munich: Piper, 1993), 218–19, 237. Translation by Selena Dyer.

94. Shirer, *Rise and Fall of the Third Reich*, 350. Innitzer eventually became a critic of the Nazis. See Radomir Luža, "Nazi Control of the Austrian Catholic Church, 1939–1941," *Catholic Historical Review* 63, no. 4 (October 1977): 537–72.

95. "Hitler Enters Austria in Triumphal Parade," *New York Times*, March 13, 1938, 31.

96. Quoted in Hugh Fordin, *Getting to Know Him: Oscar Hammerstein II* (New York: Ungar, 1986), 349.

97. *The Sound of Music* libretto, 14.

98. *The Sound of Music* libretto, 74–75.

99. *The Sound of Music* libretto, 75–76.

100. Fordin, *Getting to Know Him*, 142, 143, 211, 284, 312–13, 335.

101. Woolford, *The Sound of Music*, 5.

102. Craig Zadan, *Sondheim & Co.* (New York: Harper and Row, 1974), 4, emphasis added.

103. Ludovic Hunter-Tilney, "Lunch with the FT: Stephen Sondheim: 'I Once Made Cole Porter Gasp,'" *Financial Times*, October 16, 2010, 3.

104. Draft lyric of "Face Life," unpublished, quoted in Fordin, *Getting to Know Him*, 350.

105. J. C. Thomas, *Chasin' the Trane: The Music and Mystique of John Coltrane* (Garden City, NY: Doubleday, 1975), 131.

106. John Coltrane in collaboration with Don DeMichael, "Coltrane on Coltrane," republished in *Coltrane on Coltrane: The John Coltrane Interviews*, ed. Chris DeVito (Chicago: Chicago Review Press, 2010), 70. The collaboration took place in August 1960.

107. Hentoff, "*Giant Steps* Liner Notes," in DeVito, *Coltrane on Coltrane*, 51. "Fury" is Hentoff's word; "more presentable" is Coltrane's phrase.

108. Hentoff, "*Giant Steps* Liner Notes," 52.

109. Carl-Erik Lindgren, "Interview with John Coltrane," March 22, 1960, republished in DeVito, *Coltrane on Coltrane*, 59.

110. Hentoff, "*Giant Steps* Liner Notes," 56.

111. Ekkehard Jost, *Free Jazz* (1974; Boston: De Capo, 1994), 19. "What prompted the introduction of modal playing at the end of the Fifties cannot be said for sure," Jost writes, yet his chapter on Coltrane's modal playing (17–34) sets the date at 1960 with Coltrane's new quartet and its summer and especially October sessions. See Darius Brubeck, "1959: The Beginning of Beyond," in *The Cambridge Companion to Jazz*, ed. Merywn Cook and David Horn (Cambridge: Cambridge University Press, 2002), 177–201.

112. Quoted in Robin Washington et al., *My Favorite Things at 60*, radio documentary (PRX, 2010).

113. Jost, *Free Jazz*, 19.

114. See Jost, 20–33.

115. Baraka, *Autobiography*, 259–60.

116. Meta DuEwa Jones, *The Music Is Music: Jazz Poetry from the Harlem Renaissance to Spoken Word* (Urbana: University of Illinois Press, 2013), 85–89. Jones describes moving from multiphonics to multiphonemics ("scripting jazz sounds") on 101–4 and passim. Nathaniel Mackey, "Song of the Andoumboulou: 142," *The Nation*, August 12, 2014, 42.

117. Lewis Porter, *John Coltrane, His Life and Music* (Ann Arbor: University of Michigan Press, 1999), 182.

118. Felman and Laub, *Testimony*, 2.

119. Porter, *John Coltrane*, 182.

120. The title of a song on Coltrane's *Blue Train* (1958). Through the work of Art Lange, Nathaniel Mackey (in *Moment's Notice: Jazz in Poetry and Prose* [Minneapolis: Coffee House Press, 1993]), and others, the phrase has come to refer to the aspect of anticipation in improvisation. See Mackey's *Splay Anthem* (New York: New Directions, 2006).

121. Porter, *John Coltrane*, 183.

122. *The Sound of Music* libretto, 28.

123. Ingrid Monson, *Saying Something: Jazz Improvisation and Interaction* (Chicago: University of Chicago Press, 1996), 116. Her astute, detailed reading of the song appears on 106–21.

124. Ingrid Monson, from interview in Washington et al., *My Favorite Things at 60*. See also Monson, "Doubleness and Jazz Improvisation: Irony, Parody, and Ethnomusicology," *Critical Inquiry* 20, no. 2 (Winter 1994): 283–313.

125. Porter, *John Coltrane*, 182. In the biography Porter did not mention Monson by name, but he did in "John Coltrane: The Atlantic Years" (CD liner notes), published in *The Heavyweight Champion: The Complete Atlantic Recordings*, Rhine/Atlantic R2 71984, 1995.

126. Quoted by Ben Ratliff, *Coltrane: The Story of a Sound* (New York: Farrar, Straus and Giroux, 2007), 59.

127. Postif quoted in Porter, *John Coltrane*, 184.

128. Monson, *Saying Something*, 117.

129. Reinhold Wagnleitner, *Coca-Colanization and the Cold War: The Cultural Mission of the United States in Austria After the Second World War* (Chapel Hill: University of North Carolina Press, 1994), 207. Jaap van der Bent, "Beating Them to It?: The Vienna Group and the Beat Generation," in *The Transnational Beat Generation*, ed. Nancy M. Grace and Jennie Skerl (New York: Palgrave Macmillan, 2012), 170.

130. Michael Kater, *Different Drummers: Jazz in the Culture of Nazi Germany* (New York: Oxford University Press, 1992).

131. Ben Ratliff, *Coltrane, the Story of a Sound* (New York: Farrar, Straus and Giroux, 2007), 60.

132. John Tynan, *Down Beat*, April 14, 1960, 42.

133. John Tynan, "Take Five," *Down Beat* 28 (November 23, 1961), 40. "Sequential development": Iain Anderson, *This Is Our Music: Free Jazz, the Sixties, and American Culture* (Philadelphia: University of Pennsylvania Press, 2007), 73.

134. "Ambivalence" was Fontana's term. See Luca Massimo Barbero, "Lucio Fontana: Venice / New York," in *Lucio Fontana Venezia/New York* (New York: Guggenheim Foundation, 2006), 21.

135. Fontana wrote: "My art too is all based on . . . the philosophy of nothing, which is not a destructive nothing but a creative nothing. . . . And the slash, and the holes, the first holes, were not the destruction of the painting . . . it was a dimension beyond the painting, the freedom to conceive art through any means, through any form." Quoted in *Lucio Fontana*, exhibition catalogue, Palazzo delle Esposizioni (Rome, 1998), 246.

136. Quoted by Porter, *John Coltrane*, 158.

137. Lindgren, "Interview with John Coltrane," 55.

138. DeVito, *Coltrane on Coltrane*, 71. The republishing of the article includes some material from an early draft quoted from C. O. Simpkins's *Coltrane: A Biography*.

139. Michael Bruce McDonald, "Traning the Nineties, or the Present Relevance of John Coltrane's Music of Theophany and Negation," *African American Review* 29, no. 2 (1995): 276.

140. McDonald, 275.

141. Jerome Rothenberg, ed., *New Young German Poets* (San Francisco: City Lights, 1959), [3].

# Index

CPSIA information can be obtained
at www.ICGtesting.com
Printed in the USA
JSHW031721171221
21327JS00003B/5